Fifty-Two Years in the Cockpit

VOLUME TWO

Best Wishes

Jacko Jackson

by
Sqn Ldr KR (Jacko) Jackson
M.B.E., A.F.C., R.A.F. (Ret)

First Published in Great Britain in 2006 by Tucann Books
Text © Sqn Ldr KR Jackson
All rights reserved
Design © TUCANN*design&print*

No part of this publication may be reproduced or transmitted in any way or by any means, including electronic storage and retrieval, without prior permission of the publisher.

ISBN Nº 1 873257 70 8

Produced by: TUCANN*design&print*, 19 High Street, Heighington Lincoln LN4 1RG
Tel & Fax: 01522 790009
www.tucann.co.uk

DEDICATION

I wish to dedicate both volumes of my autobiography "52 Years in the Cockpit" to my dear wife Betty, the former Betty Elliott of Northumberland. Her support, help and encouragement during the past 57 years of our marriage enabled me to achieve so many of my ambitions. God bless Her.

CONTENTS

Chapter One: The Hastings, Colerne and Christmas Island 9
Chapter Two: The Transport World 38
Chapter Three: On detachment with the UN in the Congo 55
Chapter Four: Instructing Again with No.242 OCU 67
Chapter Five: Wing Examiner-RAF Changi and Singapore 95
Chapter Six: Flying the Belfast on No 53 Squadron 163
Chapter Seven: Return to the Hastings 203
Chapter Eight: The Cod War, the BBMF and the end of the Hastings 226
Chapter Nine: Hiatus 277
Chapter Ten: OC BBMF and back on Display 292
Chapter Eleven: RAF Finale 302
Chapter Twelve: CFI, Sherburn in Elmet Flying Club 313
Chapter Thirteen: Afterlife 327
Epilogue 329

FOREWORD
by Sir Christopher Coville, Air Marshal (Retired)

The first time I really met Jacko Jackson was in the early 1980s. I was a young Wing Commander with Lightning and Phantom credentials, but ambition and promotion had taken their toll and I was on a ground job at the NATO Headquarters in Brussels. To keep me sane, I used to spend the summer months flying Air Cadets at Coningsby, where I could also pinch the occasional Phantom flight from old friends. Jacko was what Winston Churchill would have called 'A Wuthering Heights of a man': awesome reputation, legendary record as an aviator, by then with quite a severe demeanour. He was a Squadron Leader, OC the Battle of Britain Memorial Flight, in charge of Cadet flying. But it didn't stop him picking up this slack Wing Commander who, living in Woodhall Spa in holiday mode with his wife, had a habit of being late for take-off. I arrived on my second morning to find emblazoned in the Authorisation Sheets for my sortie, the time 0900 hrs underlined several times in black ink! I tried not to cross him again!

Some might believe that Jacko missed the best part of the RAF's flying history, arriving on his first operational unit, No 152 Squadron, at the tail-end of the War. But the fascinating pages of these two volumes tell a story that is full of adventure, packed with excitement and, surprisingly to those who were not involved in air operations of the time, with not a little tragedy. It is hard to believe that some 300 aircrew were dying each year, even in the absence of hostilities, but such was life for post-War aircrew, as the World came to terms with the Iron Curtain which split East and West.

The Cold War, with its conflicts in Korea and Suez, and of

course Vietnam for the USAF, was a period of astonishing change and development in aviation. The propeller-driven aircraft of WW2 gave way to jets, and timescales were shrunk from days to hours. In the face of an enemy with fearsome nuclear and conventional capabilities, the West embarked on a long period of equipment modernisation, which went from Canberras and Hunters dropping dumb bombs and firing 30 mm cannon, to Tornados and F15s deploying staggering firepower with Precision-Guided Munitions and lethal Air-to-Air Missiles. What it took a Squadron of Lancasters to achieve in 1945 can now be replicated by a single fighter-bomber, and with guaranteed accuracy and lethality.

Jacko Jackson's 'Fifty-Two Years in the Cockpit' is more than just a story of one man's journey through this period of military aviation; it is the history of the RAF and indeed of military flying over five decades. Told in a typically understated way, Jacko lays out a life from boy to man devoted to professionalism in the air. From Halton Brat to senior officer, the essential Jacko shines through: witty, determined, passionate about his job and just occasionally disdainful of senior officers' judgement! As one who held similar beliefs in the past, and as a fellow kid from Merseyside, I forgive him this minor insubordination! Who could fail to agree his point once they have read the story of the Air Marshal who mistakenly took the Khamseen to be a local tribal custom rather than the savagely hot wind of the region!

Although Jacko would be the first to admit that many shared his experiences, he would have to concede that few had enjoyed the range of flying, postings and relationships that he experienced over a fascinating career. The journey starts at Halton, one of Trenchard's pillars of excellence as he built the future RAF. As War slowly and painfully drew to a close, he was one of many aircrew who learned their skills in the Commonwealth Air Training Programme. For him, Rhodesia and Poona must have been enthralling locations, and his subsequent tours in Singapore and Japan were rich in experiences and enlivened by some fascinating people, whom Jack describes so admirably and with typical humour. Any of us who have suffered the lash of a Flying Instructor's tongue can associate with Sergeant Bunny Austin, who characterises the RAF qualities of demanding perfection whist rewarding incompetence with scathing sarcasm! As all who have enjoyed a full career in the services can testify, it is the people we met and the places where we served which make life so rewarding. Jacko's story of being sent to where he thought was close to home with a posting to 'Accrington', only to find that it was in fact Acclington in the far North East of England, rang a familiar chord with me. I was told, or so I thought, that as a young officer I was being posted to Houston in Texas, with obvious aspirations for the Space programme, only to be told that it was in fact Ouston in Northumberland!

But it is the stories of flying that really catch the imagination in these compelling volumes. Jacko has a wonderful way of capturing the joy, the fear, the exhilaration and the passion of flying. Honestly, with a pilot's precision, but in a way that unravels the mysteries of aviation to anyone, he recounts the amazing history of his life in the RAF. It was with amazement that I read of his time at the Central Flying School, where he flew no less than eight different aircraft types; with envy that I followed his time flying the Mosquito, which he and many others still believe to have been the finest military aircraft of its generation; and with damp palms that I shared his many episodes when he came close to his Maker: the vertical dive in Egypt and his control problems in a Spitfire come to mind, but there are so many occasions when only his consummate skill brought him and his aeroplanes home safely.

His long and distinguished spell as a Transport pilot will probably stand out to many as the high point of his career. At a time when Great Britain still had an Empire, the epic journeys and key operational roles that he and others undertook provided the essential lifeblood for a range of operations worldwide. But I confess, that when I think of the man, I will always remember the Jacko Jackson of the Battle of Britain Memorial Flight; the Captain of the only flying Lancaster in the World, as indeed it then was; the Jacko who could make that beautiful aircraft even more wonderful to behold as he put her through her paces over so many airfields and towns across the length and breadth of the country. It was in this role that Jacko moved on from celebrated aviator to become a legendary and revered figure, whose reputation and example lives on in the souls of young aircrew today.

Finally, these books are his own tribute: to the people with whom he served, and especially to those who lost their lives; to the many fascinating aircraft that he had the joy to fly; and not least to his closest crewman, his wife Betty, who was always there alongside him, and whose support throughout their marriage gave him the firm foundation that we all need to build happy and successful careers.

Jacko Jackson's story is one of an ordinary boy who strove to achieve a dream; it is a story of a man who though not extraordinary by nature became so through sheer determination and hard work. It is an inspiration and example to all young people today, who should draw from these pages the simple truth that Jacko's life and career underlines: you can reach the stars.

CHAPTER 1
The Hastings, Colerne and Christmas Island

After completing a highly satisfactory course my posting turned out to be to No 36 Squadron, one of three based at Colerne. I was also told that I would probably return to Dishforth as an instructor after a couple of years or so to instruct. In the event, it was two years to the day! No. 36 Squadron had been one of the ill fated torpedo bomber operators, still flying Wildebeest bi-planes out of Singapore when the Japanese attacked in December of 1941. They, along with No 100 Sqdn, were virtually wiped out and ceased to exist for some months in 1942. The other two squadrons at Colerne, No 24 and No 114, had markedly differing views on life. No 24 was steeped in RAF transport history, such as it was at that time, having been continuously employed on those duties since 1920 in one form or another and, during WWII, carried many VIPs and even VVIPs. It may be something of a record that No 24 served every single day of WWII on one station only, RAF Hendon. In 1947 it was renamed No 24 (Commonwealth) Squadron and, invariably, a member of the Squadron staff would be a senior commonwealth Air Force member. During my time it was the ever popular Australian Sqdn Ldr Dave Hutchins. I've never found out the truth of the story that was doing the rounds in the Far East that, supposedly, during the Vietnam war, an Australian by the name of Hutchins was making a disciplinary charge against a Corporal at the end of which the officer went through the usual ritual of asking the accused if he would accept his punishment or go for a court martial. On this occasion, the Corporal said he would accept the officer's punishment whereupon the officer rose to his feet and thumped him between the eyes! Can anybody invent stories like that? Quite possibly.

For obvious reasons, No 24 and their members were very proud of their Squadron and it's origins. On the other hand, and this might be a lesson in man management, so too were No 114, but for very different reasons. After disbanding and reforming on a number of occasions, it became the last Hastings Squadron to be formed, just before I arrived at Colerne in 1959. Obviously, when a Squadron is raised from scratch it's members will invariably be posted in from other Squadrons already flying that type whenever possible. This case was no exception, but with a slight difference in that the COs of the Squadrons due to provide crews were told in no uncertain terms that this was not to be an excuse for off loading misfits, malcontents or any others that their CO did not see eye to eye with. Perhaps they should not have been read the riot act because the outcome was predictable; no Squadron Commander likes being told what to do. However, it was like putting a lot of old lags together, with the result that they become elitist and decide to show the rest of the world just what they could do. The esprit de corps was quite remarkable and never better exemplified than that coming Christmas when everybody was wondering who would draw the short straw for sending two crews to Christmas Island in the Pacific, for the normal three month detachment, which would overlap all of the festive season. At the next Wing conference, which was due to discuss that topic, COs of No 24 and 36 Squadrons got quite a shock when the commander of No 114 said he had already got two volunteer crews for that task!

The building up of hours to qualify for passenger carrying status, Cat "C", had it's benefits and at least one of the trips was a leisurely jaunt around the Med. taking in Cyprus, Malta and Gibraltar. The landing at Gibraltar killed two birds with one stone as we had the Squadron training officer aboard to point out the ins and outs of the various staging stations as well as overseeing the actual flying. In the case of Gibraltar, it was one of two aerodromes that no RAF transport captain was allowed to land at for the first time without having a supervising captain on board. The other was Hong Kong, which was very tricky from the mainland approach, but simplicity itself from the sea. After qualifying for Gibraltar I would no longer need another check out when I started carrying passengers. Gibraltar was similar to Hong Kong in one respect in that the approach to one end of the single runway was much easier to cope with than the other, although both were from over the sea. The problem there was that when approaching from the east, the runway only started from a point virtually under the rock and even a slight wind, if it happened to be a Southerly, caused quite a bit of turbulence and, of course, a hefty wind, even if within the crosswind limits of the type being flown, took a lot of physical effort and fine judgement. From the opposite end, the runway had been extended into Algeciras Bay and caused no extra problems as regards turbulence because aircraft would normally be well and truly down before reaching the turbulent area. The real problem from that end for first timers was the perceived width of the runway as seen from the cockpit. In England, for instance, a strip of concrete, or Tarmac, would be laid across a green field and pilots would become used to the standard width, However, when a runway had been built out into the sea, extra width was required for safety reasons and that was what caused the problem. Whether or not a pilot was highly skilled or otherwise he would tend to hold off too high on a wide runway and on narrow ones touch down before round out with a possible bounce or two. A similar illusion can occur at Malta where a standard width runway looks wider than it actually is because most of that island is bare rock and the runway surface, under certain conditions of light, looks very wide indeed. Runways that slant upwards or downwards markedly also give false impressions to pilots with similar results. The return from Gibraltar to Colerne, via Lyneham, of course, for inbound customs clearance was carried out with an overflight of mainland Spain. The Spanish government allowed the RAF this concession until the late sixties when they were upset, yet again, about the British presence in Gibraltar, although they themselves held, and still do, the enclave of Ceuta in Morocco, just across the water from Gibraltar. The early part of the flight was interesting in one respect from an aviation point of view, and that was the extremely poor, for a high ranking western European country, communications network that then existed. For long periods we were out of contact on VHF, the voice radio, which indicated that relay stations had not yet been introduced which, of course, downgraded the safety margins for all transmitting aircraft, civil and military alike. Perhaps the sea route to the west of Portugal would have been a better bet, although much longer.

Another cargo trip that was a good hour builder for me, was particularly interesting, but seemed to be so important that a very experienced Captain came along to supervise the crew. This trip was to take a certain load to the atomic testing grounds at Maralinga in South Australia. The route was via Malta, El Adem, Aden, Karachi, Ceylon, Singapore, Darwin and after unloading at Maralinga, onto Adelaide before returning over the same sectors, except that Maralinga was overflown northbound. It had been after Maralinga south bound and shortly after reaching cruising altitude, that the loadmaster asked me if I'd like to come and see what he had found in one of the rear toilets. What on earth could it be, I pondered, surely not cigarettes that should have been confiscated in Karachi? As I made my way to the rear a desert snake, a baby kangaroo or Wallaby appeared in my thoughts. Although we had been on the ground for only an hour or so, the AQM had discovered that the ladies loo was jam packed from floor to ceiling with tinned food. It was well known that Maralinga was by that time in steep decline and we assumed that stuffing aircraft with surplus food might have been an easy option for somebody or other. However, it was well received and double rations was the order of the day for the rest of the trip. One extra officer was aboard throughout, and he was forever using a thermometer and stated that was the main reason for his presence, or was it? He surprised us all by staying all night on board during the night stop in Karachi, saying he'd need to make sure the temperature stayed within limits. If it had been ok in Aden, surely it would be all right in Karachi but, then again, Karachi was our only stop that was not RAF or RAAF manned. This UK-Australia return flight was physically tiring and, in that context, although Transport Command fixed a maximum limit of 115 hours flying in any 28 day period, they had been forced to make an exception for that route, pushing the limit up to 125. When one considers that the average annual rate for instructors and fighter pilots in those days was around the 200 mark, 125 in eighteen days was quite something. At one time civilian contractors had been employed on the Maralinga task but on routes of their own making, which included flying one sector from Cyprus to the Gulf over Northern Turkey and Iran. For whatever reason, and I suppose it was obvious, the Russians had installed a radio beacon just inside their border with Turkey that operated on the same frequency as a Turkish one in that area which was a recognised one for stopping aircraft straying into Russian airspace.

All RAF transport aircraft, rightly or wrongly, have been fitted with backward facing seats since some long forgotten accident indicated that was the best bet for passengers in the event of a crash landing, and even the Hastings was not old enough to have escaped that diktat. These seats could be fitted, or removed, within minutes and it was not uncommon to set off on a route trip with forty five fitted, yet return to base with no seats, but plenty of freight. The number of seats available at each staging post seemed to even itself out over a period of time, and, with the paperwork that would be involved in keeping track of each one, it was decided to class them as "C" class stores. In the RAF that meant expendable, just like nuts and bolts, etc. Who would wish to steal a seat that could only be fixed into a special recess in a floor anyway? The system worked remarkably well for a good number of years until a sudden shortage set in. Captains of aircraft and air quartermasters were asked if they could recall any particular station that might be involved in "the mystery of the missing Hastings passenger seats". None could, so Command HQ decided to send an equipment officer down the route to see if he could come up with a solution. The officer was having no luck at all until fate took a hand. He was, like myself, something of a football fanatic and at a station in the canal zone of Egypt, having carried out his check without a result, he heard two airmen discussing the chances of their first eleven against another Canal zone team that evening, and decided to go along to see what a match on hard packed sand was like. On first seeing the ground, he was very impressed to note that a viewing embankment had been built alongside one touchline, and even more so to see spectator seats in use. Yes, the mystery of the missing seats had been solved, but with those seats having been set in concrete, recovery was impossible. By a remarkable coincidence, the F/Sgt responsible for the misappropriation had returned to the UK on a medical discharge a few weeks prior to the discovery- lucky old him, or did he even exist?

There was always one route station when something or other out of the ordinary was likely to take place for no reason in particular and for me it was Karachi. All night stoppers in that city will well remember the name of the hotel that was invariably used for both crews and passengers. It's name of Minwallahs was almost a music hall joke in Transport Command and could easily outdo "Fawlty Towers" on occasions, only they were deadly serious. One little trick that became well known was that the hotel would remove fuses from air coolers in each room when the temperature dropped to what, to them, was cool but to the English, equated to a hot summers day. The solution was simple, we took fuses with us on that route or, if we forgot, made one out of numerous silver strips of paper from cigarette packets.

Before my very first trip to that city since joining Transport Command the wisecracks of that world, and every Squadron had at least two, had warned me that forbearance was needed in large amounts when submitting a flight plan before departure from Karachi, because most of the staff that dealt with them had been well indoctrinated by British civil servants before independence. I was told that each plan would be gone over with a fine tooth comb and a lot of knit picking might well take place before it was accepted. Another tip was that one must not get upset if you were kept waiting like a lemon in front of the Officer's desk, it was all part of the ritual. Another part of it was that, after acceptance, the officer would gently tap his hand bell and his assistant, seated all of three feet away, would arise from his own desk and solemnly take it from his chief and proceed to a department in the next room for it's transmission. Even when I got to the head of the queue, an aircraft captain who turned out to be an American flying for Pan Am, suddenly lost his cool and came charging up to the desk shouting, "say bud, how much darn longer you gonna keep us waiting? I'm in one hell of a hurry". Needless to say, all hell was let loose, with the hand bell being really thumped at about 100 times per minute. The sound was horrendous, and I had visions of the bell top coming adrift and the poor chap's hand being impaled on its vertical support. After giving up on the bell, the official yelled at the American to "get back in line immediately, cannot you see that I'm just about to deal with one of Her Majesty's Royal Britannic Air Force Captains"? The American slunk off back to his place like a whipped dog. My flight plan got the most cursory once over imaginable, before the bell was gently rung and I was on my way with the thought that the Raj lived on, and God bless America of course.

Another ritual at Karachi outbound was a British one in that it was an RAF Group Captain who invariably came striding across the Tarmac, about thirty minutes before departure time, even when we had been parked the furthest distance from the terminal, which was more often than not the case. After a few pleasantries, he always asked which base in the UK we operated from, but standing in front of a Hastings aircraft, he must have known the answer was bound to be RAF Colerne, but no sooner had we answered "RAF Colerne, Sir" then he snapped out, "Jolly old Colun, what"? Before striding off into the distance. Colun was how the locals of Bath pronounced Colerne and, no doubt, he was just letting us know that he had been there at some time or other. For our part, we wondered what the Air Attache would be doing to occupy the rest of his working day.

I should have started out on a three month detachment to Christmas Island during the first week of 1960 but heavy snowfalls, particularly so in the Cotswolds that year, put everything back by 10 days, but we eventually got away from Lyneham after yet another horrible night in the transit camp at Cliffe Pypard when steam actually rose from our beds after we had obtained some hot water bottles. The media often refer to places in the Far East as "Halfway round the world" but in our case that was more than true, because we were to go east about and eventually cross the date line in mid Pacific before reaching our destination. Another feature, which almost marked the end of an era, was that we would be night stopping, and not crew slipping, at each staging post and also keeping our twenty or so RAF passengers with us throughout. Similar to the Imperial Airways mode of operations with their Short "C" Class flying boats and HP 42s from the thirties onwards. That all changed with the introduction of Comets, Britannia's and VC10s into service, when crew slipping became the norm. The take off from Colerne was rather emotional because a 3 month separation can seem a very long time on day one, but for the passengers that would be a full year, although most of them were unmarried and for many of them it was just the beginning of a great adventure, with a fair percentage never having left the UK before. The take off from Colerne was on the usual Western runway which called for a turn downwind to head towards Lyneham and, as arranged with Betty beforehand, I managed to overfly our rented house in Colerne village and, even caught sight of her waving a white towel like mad in the back garden despite the snow covered backdrop.

When flying long haul, on west or east sectors, aircrew and passengers alike will have noticed that night falls suddenly when eastbound and takes a long time coming westbound, and the same for daybreak is true of course. From an operating point of view, this means more daylight hours, and less night ones, in any one day westbound, and the reverse outbound. With our routing being forever eastwards, with one or two sectors being in excess of ten flying hours, some night flying was unavoidable which was no big deal except for the fact that the Hastings was not fitted with weather avoidance radar, which would have been particularly useful in dodging one or two of the tropical storms which we actually hit during the night hours. The return journey, three months later, was completely free of night flying which was more to our liking.

Between El Adem and Aden the usual refuelling stop was necessary at Khartoum, and I was able to fulfil a promise that I had made to one of the best known locals, to the RAF that is, employed on the staging post there. Apparently, he had been employed since before WWII on refuelling duties for the RAF, and his hobby was collecting, and wearing on his overalls, the Squadron badges of aircraft he had worked on. One day his No 36 Squadron badge, a flying torpedo, had come adrift and gone missing. On my last passage through there I had promised a replacement and, in those days, an Englishman's word was his bond, even if he was only an RAF pilot. He sported about twenty badges in total, but seemed particularly proud of his flying torpedo after I gave him his replacement, it taking pride of place in the pecking order. I always got a special welcome on landing there from then on, which puzzled some members of my crew when they were passing through for the first time.

The arrival and departure from Karachi was completely uneventful for a change, helped out by our squadron commander, Wing Commander Bill Green, who was flying out to Christmas Island with us and then returning with the crew that we were replacing. He was well aware that the air attache would, no doubt, turn up before departure and he took him under his wing when he duly arrived, while the rest of us got on with our job of pre-flighting the aircraft. The usual day off in Singapore had been increased to two for no obvious reason which was a most welcome break for the crew, and probably more so for our passengers, who had endured five days of ear bashing from the continuous roar of our four Hercules engines, but they still had four more to go! The arrival at Darwin was interesting enough when, for the first time, I felt the full force of a thunderstorm without actually being in one. It was on final approach to land when everything seemed to be going according to plan at first until no matter how much power I took off, the aircraft had not only stopped descending but was actually climbing. There was nothing for it but to hold off until the storm, which was about two miles away, had moved on.

It was rumoured that Darwin was a so called "bad boys posting" for the Australian Air Force and by the antics that I saw going on in their bar that evening I could well believe it! The bar itself was definitely different in that it was on a platform supported by a number of very thick poles. This arrangement, I was told, was to lessen the chances of snakes making their way in. I was also reliably informed that anywhere under the structure at ground level could be used as a gents urinal. The first time I went to use it that evening, one of the Aussie "Bad boys" was already there using it for other purposes- with a female, of course.

Our next stop was another RAAF station by the name of Amberley, near Brisbane and another shock awaited me. We had accommodation on base, and although I have always been an early riser since my Halton days, I was awoken much earlier than normal, just after dawn in fact, by the beating of drums and the blowing of bugles. Peeking through my drawn curtains I noticed that my allotted room was within yards of the station parade ground and it was being put to full use that early morn. We were certainly lucky to get any breakfast that day before flying our next leg to Nandi in Fiji, because the Officers' Mess catering department was just about to shut up shop as we presented ourselves. I was stupid enough to ask if that was due to the early station parade and was it being held as a practice for something important that was due in the near future? Of course not, bluey, we have a working parade every day except Sundays, don't you lot do the same in England then?" was the rather blunt answer. In fact I couldn't remember the last time I'd been on a parade ground apart from annual AOC's inspections and, even then, a band was most unlikely to be in attendance. The early morning start, however, made sense in the semi tropics when combined with a 10 o'clock finish, which was standard for the RAF in the Middle East and other areas during the "Hot season".

The flight to Fiji was one of our shorter legs and we even managed it in daylight hours. With no military presence on the island, we were accommodated in a hotel on the airfield itself which took out the usual hassle of transportation. One extra passenger picked up there turned out to be the RC priest on Christmas Island who had managed a spot of leave away from it all. Although a Methodist, I got on particularly well with him to the extent that when he finally left Christmas Island I was invited to his farewell party, although some members of his flock were passed over. In fact, I was approached by two other officers who asked outright how come I, a non Catholic, had been invited to it and they had not? One of the questions in life to which there is no answer except a shrug of the shoulders.

For the 25th January 1960, my log book records that I flew for over eighteen hours on that day between Australia and our destination of Christmas Island. As the old saying goes, there are lies, damned lies and statistics, and my log book must come under the latter. That one day had lasted 48 hours because we had crossed the international dateline after leaving Fiji which meant we had two Thursdays, or whatever, to live through. It was one of the most difficult tasks I was ever presented with as a transport captain trying to explain to 20 airmen, many out of England for the first time, that we would have two Thursdays that week. For some strange reason, no one seemed to mind on the reverse of that leg, returning to the UK, when we missed a day completely. Perhaps they thought that they would be back in the UK a day early! From a personal point of view, working eleven hours to the west of the Greenwich Meridian had one big advantage in that I was very happy that over breakfast on Saturday mornings I was able to receive that afternoon's English football results that had already been played. In Singapore, one had to wait until just after midnight for them.

Our eventual arrival on Christmas Island was well after nightfall, but a rather large crowd was, nevertheless, assembled to greet our arrival, which I was to find out later was the norm for all such inbound flights from the UK. Like all other English schoolboys, I knew that Christmas Island had acquired its name from Captain Cook who had chanced upon it on the Christmas Eve of 1777, just before the end of his final voyage, being killed a few weeks later by the Hawaiian natives. Other than that I had little knowledge of the central Pacific. Luckily, a booklet entitled "A short history of Christmas Island", by Cpl T Kelly RAF, was published between 1958 and 1959, during his time on the island, which gave many interesting facts about our base for the next three months. The writer had been helped in his research by the then District Commissioner, another RAF Corporal, a Lieutenant in the British Army and a serving Lt Cmdr in the Royal Navy- quite a combination. Some of the interesting snippets confirmed that Christmas, the biggest coral island in the world, measuring 35 miles west to east and 17 miles north to south, was only rich in two natural products: Guarno, which is a white powder high in Phosphate, used for fertilizers- the product of hundreds of years of bird droppings; The second was Copra oil from coconuts, harvested by imported labour from the then Gilbert and Ellice Islands, now called the Kiribati Republic. Their term of duty, with families, was four long years. The mystery of why on that Coral atoll place names such as Port London, Paris and Poland had been given was also revealed. All three revolved around a renegade French priest by the name of Father Rougier. The father had first arrived on the island in 1912 from Fanning Island, for a recce to ascertain it's potential as a Copra growing station. His report resulted in the buying of the lease from Lever Brothers by the London firm of Central Pacific Coconut Plantations Ltd, who then made Father Rougier their manager. On one land spur at the entrance to the one large lagoon, a village for his labour force of Fijians and Tahitians was built and named Port London. From there, he constructed his own house and called it Paris. The name Poland he gave to a jetty, just to the south of his home, because his imported mistress came from that country. The Father died in 1921, but it was certainly not due to heat exhaustion, because the temperature rarely rose much above 90°F!

The two major forms of animal life on the island consisted of lizards and land crabs, and it was a bit of a ritual that, sooner or later, Hastings aircrew would capture a crab and put the still alive creature in the bed of their aircraft Captain during the late night hours, when he was still in the Mess bar. It came as quite a shock after a few beers! Idle hands and all that sort of stuff. The atoll was also the home of twenty varieties of sea birds and one, in particular, I will always remember. It was the Frigate bird, well known also as the "Man o' War bird", perhaps because it was rather large, with the characteristic of snatching food from other birds when in flight. Despite warnings, our crew, on one of the many free days during our stay, decided to take the jeep allocated to the Hastings flight and visit a known breeding area of that bird which nested in a desolate area of the atoll, and that was really saying something- a massive swamp in fact. We soon found the ground based nests all right, but what a reaction we received, as predicted before we set out. It consisted of steep diving attacks from the Frigates, which came within inches of our heads with their beaks open as if to bite. We beat a hasty retreat, comparing the attacks to what it must have been like to have been on the receiving end of German Stuka dive bombers in WWII. I seem to remember that Sir David Attenborough met a similar fate when he visited the same area during the making of one of his natural history films.

One other warning that we did heed was that swimming, even in the water between the mainland and the reefs, about 100 yards out, was just not on because sharks of up to 20 feet long used that stretch for a spot of feeding on other fish and, no doubt, humans as well if the chance ever arose. In lieu of swimming, we did try beach line fishing and our navigator, Flt Lt Bob Hughes, managed to catch a baby shark one day. After a few days rest following our arrival, it was time to start the job in hand which was, basically, running a ferry shuttle service between the island and Honolulu, 1200 miles away- exactly the same distance as the Lyneham to Malta run, which meant six hours flying time, plus or minus ten minutes at the most. Our loads outbound consisted of passengers of all three services who, having completed their one year stint were due to catch a civil airliner in Hawaii en route to dear old blighty (which made us very popular indeed) plus mail for the UK. On the return we also carried fresh fruit and veg, in addition to inbound mail and passengers, about to start their year of solitary! The only thing that made us really popular on the return leg was the mail. I must say that it seemed a little strange sitting in the Mess bar, having a beer or two after landing, awaiting the sorting and delivery of the UK mail, which took about two hours, knowing that the letters that we would eventually read had been on our own aircraft during the last leg of the very long haul from England. Even in peacetime, it was not unknown for some of the young airmen to receive "Dear John" letters, so it was not always glad tidings that we brought. I suppose it was just another case of sod's law that my very first approach to land in Hawaii was the only one I was to make there which included cloud penetration to a lowish level before touchdown. We had been given many alterations to heading, called radar vectors, and descents to various altitudes which we assumed, wrongly, would continue until we had broken cloud and could see the runway for a visual landing. However, with some known highish ground in our 12 o'clock position, the so called controller suddenly called, continue with your low frequency approach" and also gave us a change of radio frequency to contact the tower on. I had never heard the term "low frequency approach" before and felt that I had been left in limbo. Luckily our Squadron Commander had stayed on in Christmas Island, awaiting for a return flight to England via another of his Hastings, and had decided to have a last look at Honolulu before his already known posting. Obviously he was up front and quickly called "they mean NDB (non directional beacon) so you need a quick right turn". The international term was indeed NDB, and why that controller was not using it beggared belief. Small things like that have caused many accidents in aviation and, no doubt, in many other forms of transportation as well. After landing we had to be processed by American customs officers on each and every occasion although only inbound from a Robinson Crusoe Island. Invariably, in our case, there was always the same grossly overweight officer on duty on our arrival who, without so much as a smile, always asked each one of us in turn if we were "carrying any narcotics, pornographic pictures or material or any other proscribed paraphernalia. I would have given my proverbial right arm to have taken him on a trip to our Island Kingdom to show him the futility of his questions. Our crew thought we might be pushing our luck somewhat if we asked him what he had in mind as regards paraphernalia!

 The Hastings aircraft always aroused considerable interest amongst the American military, some of whom had never seen such a large tail wheeled aircraft before. Over the RAF's Christmas Island years it became affectionately known as "The Gooney Bird" (an Albatross bird, common to Pacific Islands) to those actually based at Wheelus Air Force base. The Americans, unlike the RAF, did not name airfields after locations they used famous names from their past. On one occasion, when I and the rest of the crew were standing around awaiting our passengers, an

American top-sergeant arrived on the scene, and after a good prowl around without speaking, eventually came up to me and said "say bud, did you build it yourself"? before marching off cackling like an old hen. On another occasion, our prime navigational device named "Loran", and first produced in the USA at the height of WWII, had played up a bit on our inbound leg so our navigator had requested the assistance of a US Air Force specialist to see if he could help in any way. He duly arrived, complete with a natty little tool kit and was shown up front. He seemed very impressed with the very spacious crew working area but eventually asked, "Where is your Loran that I'm supposed to have a look at"? When Bob Hughes pointed at the black box that had replaced the normal Gee box (a British navigational aid no longer in use) he exclaimed, "That's Loran? As sure as hell the Smithsonian would like to get their hands on that, it must be one of the very first made". However, he did make a fix and it served us well for the rest of our time in the Pacific. Loran was a fantastic device for its day, and was so accurate that during all of our north or south bound runs we never failed to sight the Hastings that was flying on the reverse run on such days, which meant that apart from three hours or so there was always a Hastings on Honolulu to fly emergency medical supplies and/or specialists to our island should it be necessary.

It was on the 13th February, 1960 that I became involved in my only successful search and rescue (SAR) mission. Luckily for the ship's crew concerned, members of a Japanese cadet training vessel, belonging to their fishing fleet and called the "Toyama Maru", although not on a Honolulu flight that day, I was with the rest of the crew, down at the airfield, some miles away from our quarters, giving monthly flying training to our co-pilot. It was just after landing and completing two hours of touch and go's that a signal was received from the USA Coast Guard station in Hawaii, stating that an SOS had been received from a ship in a reported position, some 400 miles from Christmas Island. It took about 30 minutes to turn our aircraft around which included, needless to say, the topping up of fuel to full tanks, and then we were away. We reached the reported position after the estimated two hours of flying, only to find it completely void of shipping, so the usual square search was set up and about one hour later we spotted the vessel listing badly. There was nothing we could do to help except keep it under observation and relay her now known position. After another hour an American Coast Guard aircraft called us on the voice distress radio channel and asked us to transmit continuously on our long range radio (HF) on a certain frequency, and they would home in on us. It worked perfectly, and the American aircraft came into sight, 30 minutes later. Unbeknown to us, it carried ships pumping gear which it duly parachuted to the ship when we were safely off the scene a few minutes later. We actually saw the ship again, tied up safely in Honolulu about ten days later during a bus ride to down town Hawaii. The Americans duly sent a letter of commendation to No 36 Squadron back in England, and also reported that the Japanese crew had decided to abandon ship, just before our arrival, but then thought better of it knowing that help was at hand.

The only other form of flying taking place from the island was the daily spraying of the plantation areas with insecticide from an Auster light aircraft, to help keep the mosquito population under control. It was well known that in the past transport captains had been allowed to take part in that activity, until one pilot slightly damaged the aircraft that is, when the kybosh was put on it. I would have loved to have taken part, the most relaxing forms of flying being, in my opinion, piloting small aircraft at low level. At RAF Shawbury, there had been on strength a Master Pilot Clayton, a very popular NCO, who eventually found himself on Christmas Island for a full tour of spraying from the Auster, becoming very well known in the RAF from then on as "Flit " Clayton. I was to meet "Flit" again in Singapore in the mid sixties, when we both found ourselves serving at RAF Changi. However, he was to die at a very early age, and I have often wondered if one year of toxic spraying had anything to do with his premature demise.

Apart from being away from Betty, I found life pleasant enough, no doubt because we would only be away from home for three months and spending a fair amount of it on Hawaii with it's Wakiki beach, etc, but it must have been hellish for married personnel having to endure a full year on the atoll without even leaving it. It certainly told on all of them in varying degrees with minor irritations becoming big problems, and one or two petty jealousies springing up. One big upset took place at about our own mid tour point when it became known that a civil British trooping aircraft, a Bristol Britannia, was due to make a night stop on the island: the first for over a year. Everybody wanted to be in on the crew hosting act, particularly of the stewardesses of course. Many harsh words were exchanged among the long serving inmates, although the event passed off wonderfully well. The civil crew excelled to a man, and a woman, of course, being happy to chat up and be chatted up by all, although those of us from the RAF Transport Command in the bar that night recognised one or two signs indicating that after a long flight, with another one due the next day, a spot of sleep was what most of them longed for, particularly so with only 14 hours ground time being the norm in those days.

One relic from the heyday of civil charters to the mid-Pacific was the discarded engine of a Tudor aircraft abandoned behind our flight office on the airfield. Perhaps it is still there, if anybody really needs one! One cultural shock that awaited me on my first arrival on the island was that, as detachment commander of the Hastings fleet, I was allocated a jeep for my personal use, but a recently introduced RAF diktat required me to take a full driving test before using it. I recorded previously that in England, having been issued with a licence during WWII, I had never been required to take a test. Now here I was, twenty years on, needing one to drive on what was virtually a desert, with only about twenty miles of road, no traffic lights, stop signs, give way signs, roundabouts and with a total vehicle population of only 100 or so. Even if a jeep had been written off, the Americans had left about 200 behind at the end of WWII: which is something of a story in itself. At the height of the Pacific war, they had 10,000 military personnel based on the island, it being one of the most important aircraft staging posts on the route to Fiji and all other points in the South West Pacific. At wars end, the British told the Americans that a levy would be placed on all pieces of equipment left there so they took the easy option. However, I think the Americans must have tired of dumping aircraft, etc into the Pacific, and built a mound, still there in our day, to cover the last two hundred jeeps. They also buried scientific equipment to the value of one million dollars, probably $50m in today's money, on the airfield in a location which is only recorded in a top secret file in Washington. This prompted, in 1949, an American lawyer to arrive by aircraft, which also carried his gaudily painted jeep, to claim the island in the name of the American government. He was immediately arrested by the British resident Commissioner and fined his jeep, and then allowed to depart in the way he had arrived.

Although the RAF had only been on the island for just over three years at the time of my arrival, folklore already abounded in such a close knit community, and at least one story was often related which I knew to be perfectly true, having heard it first hand from the officer concerned. I'm sure that the late Flt Lt Bob H--- would not have minded my retelling it, because his sense of humour, a little like my own, was well off centre. The incident concerned the Duke of Edinburgh who, on the Royal Yacht Britannia, was on a round the world cruise which was to take, with all the official visits, about six long months. One event for the Duke, and all others aboard the Royal Yacht on one leg of that journey was that longed for mail from England would be dropped by parachute from a Hastings as it passed within range of Christmas Island. In the event, it would have turned out far better if HRH had decided to visit the atoll because the drop went pear shaped, resulting in a signal of complaint from the RN Commander. Apparently, Bob received a right dressing down from the Group Captain on Christmas Island and was not even given the chance to give his reasonable explanation for the mishap. On the day of Bob's departure for England, some two weeks later, he left a strongly worded letter about his treatment, which he gave to an airman working in Air Traffic Control with instructions that he was to take it personally to the Group Captain when Bob's aircraft had been airborne for four hours, but not before. Four hours flying was, of course, the point of no return on his first leg home. Airmail to the UK took about five days on average, whereas Bob's westbound flight, more than halfway round the world, took ten and, therefore, Bob's letter had really hit the fan even before he had landed back in the UK. The first words of greeting for Bob, after landing at RAF Lyneham, came from a movements officer who started by saying "I don't know what it is all about, but I've received instructions to tell you that a staff car will be waiting to take you to see the C in C at Upavon, first thing tomorrow morning". The movements officer might not have known the reason, but Bob certainly did! After he had arrived at Upavon the following morning and been ushered into the C in C's office, the old gag of the chap behind the desk continuing to read a document, while the interviewee was left standing at attention, was played to the full. During the long silence, Bob couldn't help but notice that the document in question was a copy of the Air Force list. The C in C eventually broke the silence by saying "I see, H---, that you have a lot of seniority as a Flight Lieutenant, but no academic qualifications. I suppose you are one of the uneducated officers that we took on during the war"? "I suppose so, Sir", was all Bob could think of saying to the pompous ass, even if he was an Air Chief Marshal. It might be as well at this stage to record that up until the 1950s, officers in the general duties branch, that is commissioned pilots, navigators and other aircrew were not allowed to add academic qualifications after their names in the list, although all other officers in the RAF could. The irony of it all was that Bob was at a university on a BSc course in the late 1930s, but gave it up at the start of the war to join the RAF, becoming a bomber pilot on Wellingtons and completing a full tour of ops alongside Flt Lt Nettleton, who was later awarded the VC. At wars end, Bob returned to his university and duly gained his BSc, before re-joining the RAF. After that very strange rule was rescinded, Bob, up until then that is, had never bothered to ask for his BSc to be added to his name, probably thinking his DFC was enough credit for anybody. We all know what happens when a small pebble is dropped into a pool, and it certainly did in Bob's case, because within weeks of the latest air force list being published, with Bob's BSc now recorded, he received a phone call from a senior officer, who was well known to him saying, "I've just been trawling through the latest list, Bob, and I never knew until now that you had a BSc, you are just the type that we have been on the look out for. We need officers with your background to man these new ground to ground Thor missiles that we are getting from the Americans". Bob's plea to remain on flying duties fell on deaf ears, and he was soon to be on his way, but not before another of Bob's waspish remarks was doing the rounds.

His wife was holding a ladies coffee morning on a day when Bob was suddenly given an urgent task that would keep him flying until late that night, so he thought he had better nip back to his quarter for a quick bite of food before setting off. He had, of course, to meet the ladies and during his brief stay his wife was asked by one of the guests about the rumoured engagement of their daughter, and was it by any chance to one of the young officers on the squadron. "Oh no, of course not", Bob's wife replied, "He is well up in the gas board you know", to which Bob quickly added, "he reads the meters actually". The fact of the matter was that the young chap was "Well up the ladder" for his age, having joined management straight from university. Every wife present, including my own wife Betty, feared for Bob's life later that night, but we all thought it very funny, all the same. Another of Bob's, sometimes improbable stories, was that he would always associate the Royal Yacht Britannia with the date of birth of the present Duke of York and not his mail drop, because he was born, more or less, nine months after the ships eventual arrival back in the UK. The story sounded so improbable that I've never got around to working that one out. Yet again, it could just be true!

On Christmas Island we had many free days from flying without a great deal to do, only enlivened with the odd visitation, and on being informed one day that an aircraft was due in from Canton Island we all made off to the airfield to greet a visiting transport from the Royal New Zealand Air Force which would be spending a night on the island en-route to

Hawaii, for some reason or other. It was quite a shock to see the British built Bristol Freighter for the first time. It looked so ungainly with it's high wing configuration, ugly looking fuselage and fixed undercarriage but a very dependable beast all the same according to British motorists who flew in them with their cars on Channel crossings. If the dear old Hastings was called a "Gooney Bird" by the Americans on Hawaii, what name would they accord to this aircraft the following day, was uppermost in our minds after it's arrival. We eventually found out on our next trip up north, because we heard a lot of talk about a "Bristol Freightener" that had made a recent visit to Hawaii. There was a permanent RAF presence in that one Squadron Leader and two Flight Lieutenants were based there on that island to look after our interests and the steady flow of passengers to and from England. Being accompanied tours, with wives and children, they completed a full term of three years or so and had served there during the atom tests of 1957 to 1959. One little story that they told was that well before each test was due, known members of the Russian diplomatic presence on Hawaii, would stand just outside the wire fencing near the Hastings parking area, to take note of the passengers disembarking from aircraft because it had become known that the three WVS ladies on Christmas Island had always been evacuated from there prior to each test! Perhaps Russian subs would close in at that point to get a better view, or even try and get samples, who knows?

    We had a very good working relationship with that small RAF group, especially because not all of our passengers were just bums on seats. One or two returning to the UK had received some particularly bad news, and needed looking after during the flight, others returning under the cloak of medical reasons covered, of course, many things. Some with broken bones suffered as a result of accidents on the island, including one Hastings co-pilot who was paralyzed from the neck downwards, and others with what is nowadays called alcohol abuse but, until recently, was called professional boozers or drunks, and the last group (but thankfully small) who had found life out there just too much for them and had flipped, or "gone off their trolleys". They, of course, had a medical escort which allowed loadmasters to get on with their jobs. Each crew would, sooner or later, have a VIP aboard and in my case I was particularly lucky in that ours was the Bishop to the Forces and Bishop of Maidstone, Geoffrey Betts. He was an absolute charmer and with six hours of perfect weather on the flight into Christmas Island, there was plenty of time for all our crew to have a chat with him. To jump ahead a few years, I found it very ironic that I was to fly with him again, but on that occasion we never even met. It was on the short hop of Singapore to Borneo, again in a Hastings, when he was still carrying out his stint of visiting as many of the British Forces overseas as possible. However, on this occasion we had to dodge around thunderstorms soon after take off up to the descent into Kuching, which meant I never even unstrapped my safety harness, let alone leave my seat. By the time we left the aircraft, he was being whisked away in a VIP car. It would have been nice to have had another chat with the Bishop, but it was not to be. There was no such rush to be away after our landing on Christmas Island with a very large crowd gathered on the Tarmac to meet him and wish him well. All the top brass of course, turned out in force, plus the padres of all denominations and their respective church go-ers.

We often hear of close knit communities nowadays, particularly since the miners' strike of the early eighties, but RAF Christmas Island must rank top of the list in peacetime for that dubious accolade. Many have tried to equate it with life on Gan in the Indian Ocean in that context, but there was no real comparison. For those on Gan, life was hectic in the extreme with aircraft coming and going day and night. In addition to being on the RAF trunk route between the UK and Singapore, the permanent presence of an air/sea rescue aircraft in the form of an Avro Shackleton on detachment from Singapore added up to a 24 hour station, just like the RAF master diversion airfields in the UK. With shift work being the norm for many, there was little time for those there to hang around the bar in the evenings feeling sorry for themselves. Another big bonus for those on Gan, compared with Christmas Island, was that if anything untoward happened to any of their families back in the UK, they could be sent home within hours instead of days. Unlike Gan, those on Christmas Island in the early 1960s often wondered what life was all about at times, with the last British atom bomb test having taken place in late 1958 and another one seeming less and less likely as the months rolled by during their one year stint. It must be pointed out, however, that the British government allowed the Americans to conduct some tests on the island before the final British military withdrawal in 1964.

It was not all doom and gloom of course, and we "visitors", short stay Hastings crews, met some interesting people during our three month detachments. In one group that I became friendly with there was a Fijian Army Officer, who would certainly not have looked out of place in the British Brigade of Guards, who was in charge of troops from his country manning Port London, plus a British Army officer who often said that aged 48 he had a maximum of four years to live, because no male member of his family, going back over the last hundred years, had passed the age of 52. Being a regular reader of Telegraph obituary columns, even in those days, I noted that he kept the family tradition going. Yet other members of the group included the R C Father, the civilian Fire Officer- who must have taken a liking for overseas service because he turned up in Singapore five years later for a voluntary tour there and the civilian in charge of NAAF on the island who always had a tale of woe to tell. It seemed that airmen due for a return to the UK, would, quite naturally, decide to take a duty free bottle of some exotic drink or other for their girlfriend, if they still had one that is, back in England. The only snag was that when one airman had decided what the "In" drink was at that time, there would be a mad rush by others to buy the same, and that brand would be sold out in the mad panic that ensued. The manager would then have to order another 10,000 bottles or so to satisfy demand, but due to the fact that it was sometimes up to six months before the next supply ship was due, the "in" drink had often changed by that time, the panic would then be on for something else. 10,000 bottles of whatever that had just arrived would be unlikely to find a market.

The final member of the gang was the civilian meteorologist who set our crew a real puzzle about his own highly technical world, but managed to solve it for himself before our lesser brains could come to terms with it. I have already mentioned that we always saw on Honolulu flights, the Hastings flying in the opposite direction, such was the accuracy of the Loran navigational device. However, the Met officer, always anxious to compare his predictions of wind speed and direction with those that our navigators actually found on the route, noticed that those from the aircraft northbound recorded higher speeds than the aircraft southbound on the same day in the areas near Christmas Island. All in the flying world will well know that navigation is based on the triangle of velocities, comprising the required track, the wind speed and direction in degrees true and, finally, the true course to steer which will, of course, vary according to the wind speed and direction. After the Navigator has worked out the true heading to steer he will then have to increase or decrease that figure by a number called magnetic variation. That figure is the difference between the North Pole and the Magnetic Pole. The Magnetic Pole moves from year to year, which increases or decreases the variation depending on world locations. When using Loran, the navigator would give a slight left or right turn to maintain track from his estimated heading, and after noting the eventual constant heading that keeps the aircraft steady on track, work out the wind. The Met officer concluded, quite rightly, that the magnetic variation marked on our charts for the area within a few hundred yards around Christmas Island was incorrect. Could it just be possible that the magnetic field had been upset by the atom bombs? Unlikely, or perhaps impossible, but it was rather strange.

If most people felt a little sorry for themselves out there, one officer that everyone else felt particularly sorry for was the base commander, Air Commodore Fitzpatrick who, living in separate accommodation with staff, a few hundred yards along the shoreline from our Mess, was unlikely to have anybody to speak to after his evening dinner had been served. This was exacerbated, of course, at weekends, when there was no office work to attend to, and it was really brought home to our crew when we went hand line fishing one Sunday afternoon and strayed a little too close to his chalet. He came out like a flash and we all thought it was to tell us to clear off. It was nothing of the sort, he just wanted a good old chinwag which covered our service backgrounds and a little of his own. It turned out that living on a coral island was not completely foreign to him, because he had spent a fair chunk of WWII on them when flying anti-submarine patrols over the Indian Ocean. He certainly gave me food for thought that night in the bar when I recalled his observation about my having been employed as a jet instructor until mid '59 and now in the first two months of '60 being a Hastings Captain in the mid Pacific, "Quite a change" to use the Air Commodore's words. He did have some company during our time on the island when we received a visitation from Air Vice Marshal Jameson, a distinguished South African fighter pilot of WWII, who was now our ultimate commander, based in the Air Ministry. He was absolutely charming to all and sundry during his inspection of the various installations, a real breath of fresh air.

One final memory of Christmas Island was that one evening, not long before we left, our crew had been invited to the native labourers camp, where they were holding a sing song. It was held in what was virtually a massive straw covered hut without sides. They grouped themselves with their families, 50/50 at the two ends of the edifice and started singing one group at a time at first and then all together. We could not understand the words of course, but it left an impression on all of us on that hot, humid night in dead calm conditions. It became very emotional when they all started swaying in unison and appeared to go into a trance. For our crew that was a nice finale and our insight into another world was nearly over- for the time being anyway.

A few days later, we made our last journey to the airfield for a westbound departure to the UK. The trans flight for the return showed three alterations compared with our outbound routine. We would be landing on Canton Island before Fiji, then an extra leg had been inserted in Australia when we would be deviating to Edinburgh Field, near Adelaide after Brisbane, instead of going direct to Darwin and, lastly, and interestingly, a landing on Gan for our first time instead of Ceylon. We had a massive turn out to see us off, but it had absolutely nothing to do with our crew, as such, but revolved around the reason for our landing on Canton Island before Fiji. Two of our passengers were the District Commissioner, and his lady, of the Gilbert and Ellice Islands who had been on an extended visit to see that all was well with the labour force from their empire. Needless to say, the Air Commodore was there to pay his respects to the D C on his departure, which induced many lesser mortals in the pecking order to follow suit. With two WVS ladies having left Christmas Island shortly before the departure of the DC's wife, it also marked the end of any European female presence on this ultimate outpost of Empire. One nice touch was that one Army Officer, who was head of the Royal Engineers on the Island, came down specially to bid farewell to our crew in particular and I felt quite certain he would have turned up anyway, even if the top brass hadn't. He was one of the few who did not get too involved in the Mess life, but if anybody wanted a new bit of road laying, or a building touching up, all they had to do was sit next to him at breakfast time and the wheels would start turning by the end of that day.

The flight to Canton was uneventful, but without any prior briefing, not even from our DC passenger, who probably thought we would know anyway, we soon found out during our one hour on the ground that Canton was not just another bit of the Empire and all that. In fact, it was under the joint rule of America and the UK and, even to this day, I have never found out which sector the aerodrome lay in. We certainly had to deal with officials from both countries in the arrival and departure processes. We bid our own farewell to the DC, and his charming lady, who would be taking an onward flight to the Gilbert and Ellice Capital. They were an obviously devoted couple, and I suppose they needed to be to spend so much time together in such places as small islands in the mid Pacific. Naturally, we did not expect to hear of them again but we certainly did, just a couple of hours after landing on Fiji.

It was a very relaxed crew who came down to the airport hotel bar that evening after a quick bath and change, not least of all because it was the first time in nearly three months when the officers and NCO aircrew could enjoy each other's company and, of course, we had completed our first leg of the long flight home. It was a custom for crews leaving Christmas Island for the UK to have a full round of drinks bought by the Captain at their first stopover. I duly presented myself at the bar and asked the New Zealand bartender- New Zealanders seemed to run the entire airfield- if we could have "six pints of beer, please", to which he replied, and I think he must have picked up some bad habits from Australians, "we don't sell pints here, bluey, only effing big jugs", to which I was forced to reply, "in that case six effing big jugs, bluey, if you please". If looks could kill! Obviously, what he meant was that I should accept six empty glasses and one effing big jug of beer.

It was a good night all right, except that our D C passenger reared up again by way of a very urgent signal. It was a very excited operations officer who interrupted our evenings merriment. The duty officer freely interpreted the signal that he had received from a British diplomat, to the effect that the RAF Hastings aircraft now on the ground at Fiji must be searched immediately for a missing piece of luggage that should have been off loaded at Canton. For a few seconds, I thought like the duty officer obviously did, that it might be luggage containing confidential information, but then dismissed the idea with the thought that nothing remained secret for very long on Christmas Island! The Loadmaster, who never over indulged, volunteered to carry out the search. He seemed to be away rather a long time and I began to wonder if I should show willing and go and join him when he suddenly appeared with a big smile on his face. "It looks like you found it then"? I proffered, "How come we missed it then"? "Well it was in the gents toilet, thats why we missed it, Sir", he protested. "A suitcase in a toilet? How come, you can hardly swing a cat in one?", was all I could think of saying. "Oh, it was only a small one and I think it belonged to the wife anyway. It contained lipstick, face powder and all that sort of thing", was his reply. The Loadmaster got a little flustered when I asked the obvious question of why was Mrs D C using the gents and not the ladies. "Well, Sir, remember that trip we did together to Maralinga last October, and we found the ladies toilet full of tinned food? Well it's happened again, but there is even more of it this time. I should have told you before Canton, but you always seemed to be busy when I came up front". I put his mind at rest on that one by saying, "no doubt we can work our way through them during our long haul back". Well, what was so important about a small piece of hand held luggage only containing lipstick and powder then? We all mused. Surely, even on a small Pacific Island that sort of tackle could be replaced without urgent signals flashing around. The Loadmaster then started to splutter a bit, and eventually managed to say that there was also a device in the bag which might not be replaceable in these parts. "A device", I exclaimed, "what do you mean by a device". "Well a female device, Sir. You know what I mean, don't you Sir, I think they don't want to start a family just yet". "Well", I said, "I think we ought to make very sure that it arrives on the Gilbert's safely, and that nobody else gets a look inside the case". "I've thought about that one already, Sir, and I've bound it with a lot of that thick masking tape that we always carry with us. I've also addressed it for the personal attention of the District Commissioner and added Diplomatic Mail". "Very diplomatic", was the wry remark of our crew wag. The extra rations found on our aircraft, however, played a small part in a very sad story that did not surface for another six months or so.

It was when giving my Daily Telegraph a quick look see over breakfast one morning that I caught sight of a report about an RAF officer being court martialled at RAF Upavon, Transport Command's HQ. I could hardly believe it when I read that the alleged offence against the Catering Officer concerned was that a large amount of provisions on Christmas Island, under his direct control, could not be accounted for on a snap audit check. A chat around the crewroom later that morning concluded that as regards in flight rations out there, we had never lived better, and all crews had had a similar experience to our own on final departure from that Island- enough vitals for a 100 day sea voyage, let alone a ten day flight. All of us who had known the catering officer concerned, could only recall a fairly straight laced chap who would be the least likely type of person to try and profit from any type of underhand skulduggery and, in any event, just who could think of a way to dispose of rations for gain on a coral island whose only inhabitants, apart from the small native labour force and their families, lived in one of the three service messes? Apart from being over generous with in flight rations, which would only have been a drop in the ocean, left the only logical conclusion, especially to those who had spent any time at all on that island, and that was that a massive book keeping error had been made and a court martial was far from appropriate in this particular case.

To go back to my log book, once again, it would appear to any casual reader that our crew had been given a day off in Fiji after completing just one day of our journey home, but it was not the case. The international date line had struck again and we had missed out on a Friday, or whatever day it was. A day off was the last thing that we would have wanted anyway, but there would, eventually, be an enforced one in Singapore after completing the maximum of five full days of route flying allowed by Transport Command, amounting to about 45 hours of airborne time in all. Looking at any map of Australia, it is plain that flying from Brisbane to Darwin via Adelaide was not a particularly good idea unless, of course, important passengers, or load, was awaiting transportation. With this very much in mind, we set off on day three for the overland leg to Edinburgh Field. On landing nobody seemed to know about anything that needed to be humped to Darwin in any particular hurry but, as they say in the theatrical world, all was revealed the next morning when the Movements Officer announced that we would, in fact, be onloading two extra passengers for Darwin. These PAX, as they are known in the trade, appeared to be little more than school boys. During the flight, however, the Loadmaster had established that they were in fact the sons of the RAAF Group Captain commanding Darwin. Talk about wheels within wheels, I never did hear what the RAAF might have told the RAF to induce our diversion, but it had certainly worked. However, ours is not to reason why.

During this particular flight, when nearing Alice Springs, Bob Hughes- our superb navigator- found time to relate a rather odd story about that place. Apparently, the Australians had located a eureka beacon there during the latter war years which gave the distance in nautical miles from it's location to any aircraft fitted with a receiving device. However, with the end of WWII, it soon disappeared from the aeronautical charts as the number of aircraft fitted with it diminished to almost zero, apart from the dear old Hastings and just one or two other types that did not normally operate in that country. However, in the early 1950s, when the Hastings started a regular run to Maralinga, a long serving Transport Command navigator came across an old wartime chart and noted the frequency of the Alice beacon. On his next trip to Australia he thought he would give it a try and even he was amazed that it gave a perfect signal. The jungle drums really started beating in the navigational world, but one day the beacon went off the air completely. Representations to both the RAAF and the Australian civil aviation authorities brought the same response, both denied any knowledge of a Eureka beacon ever having been sited at Alice Springs. A rum do indeed, it probably only needed a new fuse, or a switch re-setting to set it off again on some high spot in that outpost of the Outback.

Another rum do awaited us on arrival in Darwin, relating to our two one stage only passengers. As usual, all passengers had been taken away by coach for processing by the time me and the rest of the crew had left the aircraft. As the Flight Operations section was close by, we made our way there on foot to prepare for the next day's flight to Singapore. It must have been a Saturday or Sunday because the RAAF area seemed to be almost deserted, except that in the navigation room there sat a chap in civilian clothes at the far end, who seemed to be taking more than a passing interest in our crew. Bob Hughes eventually managed to whisper, "I recognise that chap now, he was on an exchange posting with No. 24 Squadron a few years ago, and I've heard since he had become a Group Captain". Why on earth did he not make himself known to us remains a mystery, at the end of the day we had done him a favour. Our own crew bus arrived shortly afterwards and we never saw him or his sons again. I had always got on particularly well with Australians in England, but that was just one of some incidents which seemed to suggest that when en mass in their own country the English were just "Pommie Bastards" at the end of the day.

The flight from Darwin to Changi was completely uneventful with the Inter Tropical Front, also known as the Inter Tropical Convergence Zone, now to the south of us. The rest day in Singapore was most welcome and, apart from a bit of shopping, we also managed some swimming at the Officers' Club without the fear of being taken by sharks. It was also nice to have some of the families to speak to after our recent monastic life. Quite a few asked how we had managed to get such a deep sun tan because they had never managed one such as ours even though they had been out there for some years. One chap came up with the answer to that one, he said you could even see the difference in that respect between people serving in Kuala Lumpur, for instance, and those based in Singapore. It was all to do with industrial air pollution, it couldn't be seen but it was there over the island even in those days.

We had been looking forward to our next leg to RAF Gan to compare it with our recent life in the Pacific. It was to be a rather long day because even though we thought a direct flight was possible with a Hastings, our lords and master at Upavon had inserted a re-fuelling stop at the RAAF base at Butterworth, on the Malayan mainland, just opposite Penang Island. After the briefest of stops there we set off again to have our first look at Gan, but this time without the aid of the Loran Navigation system which did not cover the Indian Ocean. Gan, of course, had it's own NDB beacon, but what if it suddenly went off the air due to a power cut or for technical reasons? Bob and myself, having noted from the charts that Gan was the very last in a chain of Islands running North to South, decided to build in a deliberate track error of about 30 miles to the North and after visual contact with the chain follow it South until reaching Gan. In the event we picked up Gan's NDB at very long range and homed in on it. We received quite a reception after landing because we were one of the first aircraft, other than those based in the Far East Air Force, to use their facilities to the extent that we had to fill in a very detailed proforma before departure the next day. Gan was so different to Christmas Island, it was so small that the runway took up the maximum width of the Island. It also had separate transit accommodation for both crews and passengers, although we did receive an invite that evening to visit the permanent Staff Mess which, in the event, proved to be most useful. The inmates seemed just as keen to learn something about our ex-coral Island as we were to gain information on their's. One chap at the bar turned out to be an Operations Officer and when Bob and I mentioned that we couldn't understand why the next day we would be off to Karachi and then Aden when Aden was not all that much further from Gan than Karachi. He made a sudden departure and within the hour was back with the good news that Upavon had agreed to cut out Karachi from our itinerary. However, Upavon also pointed out that we would not be back in the UK a day early because the diplomatic clearance now required for flights over the Sudan could not be brought forward.

Another officer I met that night, was a Medical Officer, I found that out when I mentioned that one of the passengers we had picked up in Singapore, a Group Captain, was probably the most senior RAF officer on the island that particular night. "I suppose he's a staff officer from FEAF's HQ" he opined. "No", I said, "a medic from El Adem, in fact, who was out there on a spot of leave". My new found friend was off like a bunny to the Transit Mess saying, "so am I, we probably know each other and I'll go and bring him over for a drink." I well remember the Group Captain being in the medical world because when we did eventually arrive at El Adem for our last night of our three month stint, he suddenly appeared in their Transit Mess with one of his Princess Mary's

Nursing Sisters in tow, known to all as PM's. She was probably bored to tears having to chat us up under the eyes of her boss, but it never showed at all and the chat at least kept the drinking under control.

The leg from Gan to Aden was one of the longest that I ever flew without seeing any land, apart from a brief glimpse of the Horn of Africa. We had not particularly looked forward to a day off in Aden, but at least it gave me a chance to have another look around the Crater district after last seeing it fourteen years previously when en-route from Japan to the UK on a troopship.

The last two days of our homeward flight to the UK became direct flights without re-fuelling stops at either Khartoum, or Malta, because we had no freight aboard and very few passengers. Our landing in the UK was at RAF Lyneham for the usual Customs clearance. The RAF Movements Officer who greeted us looked rather young and probably new to the job. He seemed a little tongue tied when he said he had an urgent message for me. It was to the effect that my wife had rung to say I was to be told that we no longer lived where I thought we lived, because we had moved. He said he couldn't quite understand it all, neither could I, but he had a telephone number to ring. It turned out that Betty had decided to move out of our two up and two down accommodation, which was next to a pub in Colerne village, because she had found a lovely flat in Bathford, a village just outside Bath itself. She had rung because, as usual, if in crew duty time we would bring the aircraft back to Colerne but, if not, it would be left at Lyneham for another crew to collect later. We had suffered a slight technical problem at El Adem, which had delayed our departure from there to such an extent that put us well outside the limits. When Betty eventually arrived at Lyneham by car I was in for another shock, not only had we moved house but she had also acquired a brand new car, a Ford Zephyr, to replace our old Consul. When one marries a girl from the North East of England one soon gets used to their knack of taking unilateral action under certain circumstances and, thankfully, they almost invariably turn out to be the correct choice. The Squadron had informed us by a phone call to Lyneham that we had all been given four weeks leave, starting that day, but a later call told us that the entire crew was to report back the very next morning for a photo call in connection with the rescue of the Japanese fishing crew. They had failed to mention what dress was required so it was a mixture of those in best blue and others in battle dress that assembled the next morning. The Bath evening paper duly gave a write up with photograph in their next edition, but I wished they hadn't because up to that point I had yet to meet our new landlord in Bathford who lived next door to our flat.

Jacko plus crew who saved a Japanese from sinking during their three month detatchment to Christmas Island. Photo taken on the return to the UK. Captain - Jacko, Co-pilot - F/O J Frans, ENG - M.E. McEwan, SIG - Sgt R Smith, ALM - Sgt M Allan, Station NAV - F/Lt R Inness, Crew NAV - F/Lt RG Hughes

The introductions took place the very next morning when the immaculately dressed gentleman, clearly from an upper strata of society, looked me straight in the eye and said as he shook my hand, "You should have let the bastards drown". He had obviously read the previous night's paper. It turned out that, having been a rubber planter in Malaya before the war he had become a guest of the Japanese for four long years after they had entered the war. I never heard him swear ever again, and we got on famously after he learnt that I had been in on the liberation of Malaya and the occupation of Japan. Things got even better when I mentioned having actually attended the war crimes trial in Tokyo.

CHAPTER 2
The Transport World

With a full month away from the RAF, Betty and I saw more of each other than ever before since our marriage 11 years ago, and there could be no better place to be than Spring time in the Cotswolds. Although some of the local cynics said that people came to Bath to "take the waters" in the hope of curing their rheumatics, while others who came to live there from other places would certainly catch the disease, if they had not already done so, as it was so wet and damp on the western tip of the Cotswolds, we did not stay long enough to find out if that was true, but we both loved the place at that time. They say you should never go back, but Betty and I, thirty years on, paid a visit there and booked into a hotel that would not have been out of place in New York, but seemed completely out of place on the banks of the River Avon. With hindsight, we should have opted for the "Landsdown Grove", high up on the hill overlooking Bath.

However, we certainly made full use of that hotel for social reasons during our two year tour at Colerne, along with many other RAF types. In fact, one of our young co-pilots by the name of Chris Harwood, who later became a Wing Commander in the air traffic world, actually married a particularly good looking, and highly popular, lady receptionist from that hotel. The wedding reception was held in the Officers' Mess at Colerne and was a truly grand occasion for all Squadron members who had managed to dodge route flying for that special day. One particular lady guest from the same hotel was also highly regarded by us all and often manned the bar there. She always had an answer ready when a drink was offered, and it was always the same one, "I'll just take sixpence if you don't mind because I never drink on duty". Sixpence is only about two to three pence in today's money but, even in those days, still well short of the gin and tonic price that some barmaids took in such high class hotels. The foregoing is only well remembered because towards the end of festivities on that wedding day, an RAF steward approached our group and asked if we could point out Miss-----, because her taxi had arrived. I said, "I know the lady and will pass on the message". I told her that any one of us could have taken her back to her hotel in due course, and she shouldn't have gone to the expense of ordering a taxi. "Oh, there's a little more to it than that, Jacko, after collecting my luggage it will take me on to London airport, I'm off on a Mediterranean holiday". I was lost for words for a moment, but then managed to say, "a taxi to London airport and an overseas holiday, that's going to cost a real bomb". "Not really", she replied with a very sweet smile, "remember all those sixpences I took off you and your friends, that will cover it nicely". The concept of anybody taking a taxi to London airport, plus a foreign holiday, was certainly not the norm in those days, unlike today of course. I've not named that dear lady, who came from a well to do family, because she met a very sad end. We all felt very happy for her when she became engaged to a European Count but, after being jilted, she took the drastic step of jumping into the Thames from a London bridge. I still cannot come to terms with the fact that she should even have thought of any such action; she seemed so full of life and would, no doubt, have met Mr Right one day. How sad and what a waste.

Yet another RAF type wedding that would have been a very grand affair, due to it's location, if nothing else, was to have taken place in Bath Abbey but was, like some airlines are fond of saying, slightly delayed. It certainly hit the headlines of national newspapers when the bridegroom failed to turn up. Rumour control was full of what went on, or didn't, the previous evening during the stag night. The wedding did eventually take place later, but I very much doubt that it was in the Abbey.

A constant reminder of that hotel long after I had left the area, was the reading of a steady flow of missives sent to a national newspaper by their very own retired colonel, who sat at the end of the lounge bar all night and every night. When they suddenly stopped I feared the worst and, yes, he had taken off for the pearly gates. I never met anybody who could say for certain how long he had taken up permanent residence in the "Landsdown Grove", it was so far in the distant past.

Although we spent most of our time on short and long range route flying, the reason for our existence, in theory at least, was the dropping of paratroopers and their supporting equipment. Some of the equipment was released from our aircraft without a parachute attached and called

"Free fall", whereas the loads with a parachute went rattling down the fuselage on rollers before exiting through the open port door. Whatever the load, human or otherwise, a lowish flying speed was a critical factor and to this end 15° of flap was required to increase lift and drag, the latter so that more throttle was required which gave more flexibility on throttle movement so as to maintain a precise speed for the drop. We also flew sorties for the basic training of soldiers hoping to join the Parachute Regiment, and with the main dropping zone being at Weston-on-the-Green, to the North of Oxford, it was only logical that the main ground training should be in that area and RAF Abingdon was the chosen site. It would have been extremely wasteful in time and money to have taken our squadron aircraft over from Colerne to Abingdon each day for those drops and to that end a small detachment of aircraft was set up to meet the requirements and crews from the three Colerne Squadrons took it in turns to spend a week there. For freight dropping, the old grass airfield at Watchfield, just across the road from Shriveringham, was the chosen location. Watchfield sometimes gets a mention in RAF history as being one of the first WWII airfields dedicated to the training of Air Traffic controllers. The week or so at Abingdon was quite a welcome break for most, and usually some untoward incident took place which stuck in the mind. One of my own was a call from the Jumpmaster that one trooper had failed to go. Most of us up front just gave each other a quick glance as we all thought the same. That was, poor chap- all that training and now he had opted out at the first fence. After landing I was quickly out of my seat to see how he would be dealt with. The first thing I noted on entering the cabin was a soldier cowering in the front corner wondering, no doubt, what his fate would be. It being none of my business, I strode straight on, but managed to say to the jump master and his assistant, "pity about that, ducking out on his first one". "It's certainly not his first one, he's up from the Regiment at Aldershot for a few refresher jumps, must have done over 500 in his time. It does happen sometimes, but not all that often." I never did find out the outcome, but I understood that the Army moved people sideways to other units on those rare occasions.

   My interest in Flight Safety was still riding high and that, combined with having trained at Halton as an airframe fitter, led to a chain of thought that nagged at me at that time. To start with, all service men and women will always remember their service number, come what may, and for ex-Brats it indicates the year and entry of joining which makes it even more precious. In my case it started with 577 and at Abingdon it was the number of a Hastings aircraft which was permanently based there. It was also the aircraft that I seemed to fly in on my numerous detachments to that station. I will now digress and refer back to my two years as a Fitter Airframes before becoming a pilot. During that time, I worked on Wellingtons at both RAF Sealand and Pershore and came across, for the first time, a system that made an interconnect between selecting flaps down and the trim change required. It must have been a big change of trim that was required because the design team had seen fit to insert a cable that automatically changed the elevator trim on flap selection. Could this flying around with the elevator well out of it's normal position place excessive pressure on the elevator torque tubes and their securing points was a thought, only alleviated, up to a point, by thinking that aircraft only used flaps normally for a short period during and after take off, and for a slightly longer time when positioning for landing. I guesstimate for only about 3% of the total flight time on transport type aircraft. Here at Abingdon, with the Hastings being fitted with a similar interconnect, and with two dropping zones of Weston and Watchfield only ten minutes flying time away, it was more likely to be about 90% because when an aircraft had arrived over the DZ for it's drops, it might well spend up to an hour or more going around and around for numerous drops with the 15° of flap selected. A very sobering thought was that a Hastings had already suffered an elevator failure, with fatal results, out at Seleter, in Singapore and that had resulted in modifications to the elevator securing points. That, of course, should have been the ultimate fix, and the chances of it ever happening again seemed remote to most operators. However, five years later, when I was the Hastings Wing Pilot at Changi, and also the Station Flight Safety Officer, word came through that a Hastings aircraft had crashed at RAF Abingdon, killing more than 40 people aboard. Even to this day the highest number of people killed in any one RAF aircraft, and that until further notice all Hastings aircraft were grounded. When our OC Ops, Wing Commander Graham Ibbotson, and long time Hastings pilot, first came around with the news I said, "I don't suppose it was 577 by any chance"? The WingCo said the signal did not give the aircraft number, but he could make some enquiries, and then asked, "why did you say 577". "Oh, nothing really, Sir, it just happens to be my first three and I well remember flying one with that number at Abingdon some years ago, but surely it couldn't still be there?" The Wing Commander re-appeared about an hour later and said, "Yes, Jacko, it was TG 577" and then came a pregnant pause, as if some response was required, but I thought better keep my trap shut for the time being, no use stirring things up with any remote possibilities of any conceptions of mine being true.

One other standard role for the Hastings at that time was taking part in "Exercise Mayflights" every three months or so. This was the redeployment of the V bombers to Stations well away from their normal bases. The V bombers were, of course, the delivery system for our nuclear deterrent, right up to the very late sixties when the Royal Navy took over with their Polaris nuclear submarines. The call out for Hastings crews to transport V force ground crew and equipment could happen at any time of the day and any day of the week. About two hours became the average notice from the Operations Centre at Colerne receiving the alert, and our first aircraft becoming airborne. Obviously, some people had to have prior warning of an impending exercise, particularly so because some non-operational airfields were involved who would not normally have been open for out of hours flying and certainly not at weekends. Almost needless to say, one or two cock ups occurred, and sometimes the Hastings fleet would be called out too late or too early. I well remember landing at one bomber base and being told by some bomber crews that the first they knew something was up was when they saw two of our Hastings joining the circuit to land. They themselves had not been called out until 30 minutes after our arrival!

Transport flying of any type, normally comes in short sharp bursts, leaving one or two days of having absolutely nothing to do. That can be even more tiring than flying regularly under certain conditions, but help was at hand in the summer of 1960. The RAF had suddenly found themselves flush with Chipmunk aircraft after the introduction of all through jet training and the replacement of the Chipmunk with Jet Provosts. A number of Air Experience Flights had then been formed to give flights to Air Training Corps Cadets at various airfields around the country. However, at summer camp time, when virtually every RAF flying station in the UK ran one, it made a lot of sense to disperse Chipmunks far and wide and call for volunteer pilots, some part timers from the AEFs and others from normal RAF duties, to fly these cadets during their annual camp. When it was first found out that RAF Colerne was, for the first time, expected to provide some pilots for that duty, I was the only pilot on the three squadrons to admit to having flown on that type- at least until it was established that it was for flying at Colerne and not a posting back to Flying Training Command, then a few more surfaced. I suppose it was the old adage of never volunteer for anything until you know what is really involved.

For a few short weeks I was living in an ideal world, flying Hastings as and when required, and spending all other duty time flying Chipmunks. It could not last, however, and another Singapore return really cut into that summer at the height of the Chipmunk season. This last trip out to the Far East with a Hastings just about marked the end of such flights on a regular basis, because the Bristol Britannia, introduced into the RAF in 1959, was really making it's mark, which meant that all Hastings Squadrons, three in the UK, one in Cyprus at Nicosia and the final one in Singapore, could now concentrate on tactical work and leave most of the strategic work to the big boys; Britannias and Comets and, from 1966 onwards, VC 10s. When I was handed the transflight for that flight, one or two things immediately leapt out at me. The first I was quite pleased about, it being an extra sector which involved a night stop in Nairobi, last visited as a passenger towards the end of WWII, but two other points I just could not understand. Having landed on Gan from Singapore and then flown direct to Aden after our stint on Christmas Island I thought that the days of night stopping in Karachi and Ceylon had gone forever, but here it was, the same old routing rearing up again. Perhaps it was just a case of showing the flag at those two places with the RAF now mostly using Gan. Then again, perhaps an Ops officer at Upavon had got so used to Hastings having flown that route that he had just written it up as he had always done over the years after getting over the shock of inserting a night stop in Nairobi between El Adem and Aden.

I doubt if any long range trip such as this one will ever go smoothly, and there is usually one incident or another that will be remembered years later. In this case it was our landing in Nairobi, at the pre-war RAF base at Eastleigh, that I met a situation that was almost unbelievable. I had better start by saying that our main load, and only reason for being routed that way, consisted of ground crew of No 208 Squadron, then based there, who had been in the UK during the change over of aircraft from Venom FB4s to Hunter FGA9s at RAF Stadishall. The Technical Officer in charge of that party I had last met at Lichfield when he had been the F/Sgt NCO I/C the Servicing Flight on Wellingtons, so we had plenty to chat about during the night stops in Malta and at El Adem. It had been a long day with just over 12 hours of flying time, plus a re-fuelling stop at Khartoum, and a night landing on an airfield that I had never used before as a pilot. The Air Quartermaster, still known as such in 1960 until they eventually gained well earned recognition by being awarded a flying brevet and a change of title to Air Loadmaster later that year, had, as usual, opened the back entrance door and supervised the placing of passenger steps wheeled up to it. Up front, the navigator was still reading out the after landing checks, to which a response was required from either myself, the co-pilot, flight engineer or air signaller when the locally based Air Movements Officer appeared on the flight deck demanding to know why we had seen fit to land there on a Whit Monday, and outside normal working hours to boot. We told him in no uncertain terms to stop interrupting crew procedures and vacate the flight deck immediately, and we would see him later. I added, and it seemed to puzzle him somewhat, that no doubt if he concentrated on processing the passengers aboard he might notice that they, at least, would show some pleasure in landing on this airfield after two months away from their families, even if it was a Whit Monday. We did not see him immediately after leaving the aircraft, but he did surface again later and said that until our flight plan from Khartoum was received, he had been given to understand that our arrival would be the next day and he would need to see our documents to check that we had not speeded things up by not night stopping at Khartoum. I told him that our transflight was now locked up in the aircraft and he would either have to wait until the next morning or go and dig out the Station copy which would be identical to ours. I added, for good measure, that anybody who thought they could over fly the Sudan at any old time without diplomatic clearance wasn't quite with it. This did not help one little bit, of course, but we had all had enough for one day and all we wanted now was a few cold beers. I was particularly pleased to find out after discrete inquiries that he was not a run of the mill Movements Officer, normally male and female officers taken from the equipment branch because they were always most helpful to crews and passengers alike, and nothing was too much trouble for them. This chap, in fact, turned out to have been rear crew during WWII and was now out of the flying world forever so perhaps he had a bit of a chip on his shoulder. Ironically, within two months I was back at Nairobi with many other aircraft and crews for a three month detachment, and unlike transitting crews, lived in the Mess and even though our paths often crossed he did not seem to recognise me and, for my part, I was more than happy not to know him.

    The accommodation for our night in Kenya was what might be called a cross between a shooting lodge and a normal type hotel, which was located a few miles outside of Nairobi. Although there was no air conditioning in the very spacious rooms, all of the many windows had a cross wired arrangement covering them so that no one could enter when the window was open. However, the English hotel manager briefed us that we should always place wallets, watches and any other valuable items under our pillows before going to sleep for the night, because some of the natives had been known to arrive at his hotel during the dead of the night for a spot of fishing. Fishing certainly seemed to be an odd term for it, but he went on to say that they did indeed arrive with a rod, line and hook, but no sinker and, having put the rod through the wire mesh, attempt to hook a jacket, trousers or whatever and, if successful, reel the catch in and then bring the rod back towards the window frame so that they could get their hands through the mesh to ransack the pockets!

The flight up to Aden was, apart from a short spell just before landing there, entirely over land, and that was the second day running that we had something to look at other than the ocean blue: most unusual in those days of worldwide travel for RAF transporters, or truckies as the rest of the RAF chose to call us.

The next three legs after Aden were something of a well worn path for me by this time. However, an engine fault developed on the first of those legs to Karachi and stayed with us all the way to Singapore. It was always after going into the cruise around 10,000' that there would be a God almighty backfire from one particular engine. This occurred on average at about every 20 minutes or so and no sooner did you begin to think that, whatever it was, it had cured itself than there would be another bang. We, of course, recorded this defect in our Technical log, the Form 700, after landing at both Karachi and in Ceylon with an entry at both places reading something like "Ground run carried out and no defect found". We had picked up one indulgence passenger in Aden who was a nursing sister based there who was rather keen to meet up with her boyfriend, now based in Singapore. She had certainly picked the wrong time to travel because, on one leg with a completely weather free sky, I had decided to take my lunch sitting in one of the empty passenger seats which happened to be directly behind her's. During that half hour or so, we had two of the ear shattering bangs when that poor lady shot about a foot in the air.

After landing in Singapore we, as a crew, decided that we could not carry on back to the UK without a technical fix because it could, eventually, lead to a complete engine failure. However, the ground engineers at Changi could not reproduce the symptoms, even though they had run the engine continuously for over half an hour. Although the next day was, in theory, a rest day, I was down at the dispersal area asking the engineers if they could think of anything else that could be done to ensure a trouble free flight home. By a remarkable piece of good luck, an interested civilian bystander eventually said although he was the Rolls Royce rep for the area, he was also familiar with the Bristol Hercules radial engine. In those days, of course, Rolls Royce specialised in "in line" engines which had to be liquid cooled and Bristols on "radial" engines which relied on airflow for that purpose. Both had many pros and cons, but it turned out to be one of the cons of the radial set up that caused our particular problem. Having said that, I had never experienced that particular defect, either before or since, and had never met anyone else who had. In fact, the RAF engineers in Singapore and the UK had never come across it before either, but here was a civilian engineer who got it right first time. He had immediately latched onto the fact that it only happened at altitude, and said all you needed was a complete set of new plugs for that engine, and that somebody must have forgotten to change them, as required, on the last 300 hr inspection. Both the ground crew and myself must have looked mystified because he gave us a mini brief on the subject. The fault was "Cylinder head tracking" which only occurred when at, or above, 10,000' combined with dirty and/or defective plugs. Apparently, the electrical impulse to the plugs, which normally induced the spark for petrol combustion, took a short cut up the outside of the radial cyclinders to earth without causing a spark. The engineers set too to insert brand new plugs on the offending engine, but I said I would still do an air test to make sure. The rep said, "If you wish, but you'll be wasting your time". Not only did we go flying for a full hour around the island at 10,000' but we also took him with us. He didn't exactly say "I told you so" after the successful test, but he might just as well have. He certainly had a self satisfied look on his face, and who could blame him. With having the aircraft put right on our rest day, we were back on schedule and arrived in the UK dead on time, thanks to an unknown civilian gentleman in Singapore.

 Like all other transport crews of that generation who happened to be inbound to Lyneham on a Saturday afternoon for Customs clearance, we got our signaller to tune his long range radio into the BBC to check out the football results of games played that day, just in case the chief Customs Officer was on duty. His name was Don Piercy, and known throughout the transport world more for the fact that he was a director of Swindon

Town FC than anything else. A win for Swindon that day would produce a big smile and, almost a wave through, a draw was not too bad, but a lost game, particularly if played at home, meant that the Customs check could take rather a long time!

After our more than generous leave, given after all such trips, it was back to para drops, etc. One innovation, for me at least, was formation night drops. Keeping station at night was one thing, but flying it at the low speeds required by the paratroopers for their drop was quite something in such a relatively large aircraft as the Hastings.

It seemed no time at all before I was off on another three month detachment, The difference this time was that the required number of aircraft, with plenty of flying hours left before their next second line inspection, were already out in Nairobi and it was more of a crew change rather than anything else. The upshot of this was that crews flew out as passengers in a Bristol Britannia from Lyneham and by the same means on their return. Our briefing on day one was that we would not get much flying in, and our primary role was as a stand by force to evacuate Europeans from the eastern part of the Belgian Congo if the situation there got worse than it already was at that time, which was shortly after the Congo had gained independence. Later revelations indicate that our mixed force of Beverleys and Hastings was, in fact, the dropping force for a proposed attack on Southern Rhodesia after Mr Smith had upset British Prime Minister Harold Wilson by declaring independence. Having gained my wings in that country and knowing of Mr Smith's reputation as a Spitfire pilot in the Western Desert, I was particularly pleased when the stand down of our force was called after about six weeks.

However, life on stand by was not as bad as we had expected. For starters, there was a Chipmunk aircraft based there that nobody seemed to want to fly, so I jumped at the chance of converting a few of our co-pilots to type. Not many pilots get the opportunity of flying one make of light aircraft in the UK at sea level one week and flying the same type in the tropics at 6,000' the next. Both the take off run and landing distance was noticeably longer and the general handling sluggish, to say the least, at that altitude and temperature. I also managed some dual in a Twin Pioneer of No 21 Squadron, which was a real eye opener as regards slow flying in a twin piston aircraft. I also made my first ever flight in a Sycamore helicopter around a local game reserve which was most impressive to say the least.

Twin Pioneer

We also managed some Hastings flying as well, the most popular being day returns to Mombassa to take full loads of Army personnel for, literally, a days swimming at the seaside. While the Army swam, RAF crews took cover in a top class hotel on Mombassa's lovely beach, partaking of soft drinks for the five hours or so of down time, and meeting many interesting people to boot. The runway at RAF Eastleigh, as opposed to the new post war civil airport close by, was most unusual in that it was a natural surface, being made of rolled Marum, a red coloured soil found in those parts, which could stand no end of wear and tear. Even on detachment, Transport Command insisted on some practice flying called Monthly Continuation flying, which gave us some scope for having a good look around the surrounding area at various altitudes, and it was on one of my low level sorties that I chanced upon a herd of my favourite animals- the African Elephant. After flashing over them I said to my co-pilot, "starting timing now and call me every 15 seconds, I'm starting a rate one turn to port and we will run in after 1 minute and 30 seconds and then, with a bit of luck, we might pick them up again". A rate one turn in aviation can be achieved by reference to the old turn and slip indicator which results in passing through 3° every second and, therefore, achieving a full circle in two minutes. Having already passed our target before starting the turn, I was aiming to come in from 90° abeam our original track, which would be achieved by levelling off at the 90 seconds point. Before stopping the turn the co-pilot said in a rather caustic voice, "I don't think you'll have much trouble in finding them again, Captain, look at your 10 o'clock. A quick glance in that direction revealed what appeared to be a Tornado, or twister as the Americans would have it; A massive dust cloud was rising from the stampeding herd. Needless to say, we pulled away, not wishing to cause any more distress to those lovely creatures. Another aerial flight for nature lovers, was the short flight north to the Lake at Nanyuki to see the thousands upon thousands of Flamingoes. After one such "Training" flight I was somewhat surprised to see a Canberra aircraft parked at the end of our majestic line of four engined transports. At first I thought that it was a little off the beaten track for an RAF Canberra, but then noticed that it was in Rhodesian markings. All the RAF establishments in East Africa obviously thought that our presence was all to do with the Congo, but Mr Smith and his government must have known otherwise. A number of snapshots of our aircraft were taken by the Canberra crew just before their departure.

Life in the Mess at Eastleigh was pleasant enough, not least of all because it had been built on almost identical lines to those of the RAF in the 1930s expansion scheme. One nice touch was that the main ground floor corridor ran exactly East and West, and with Nairobi being almost on the equator, one could see the sun rise at one corridor end in the morning, and set at the other end in the early evening. With many crews from different squadrons living in the Mess at that time, life could get a little hectic, which was enhanced by the low cost of spirits. Only threepence for a gin, which went up to fourpence if a tonic was added and that was in the old money! One other No 36 Squadron Captain on the detachment was Ken Sneller who, being a batchelor, was always ready and willing to jump at any overseas detachments on offer and long range route trips as well. He was also the Captain of the RAF's last Lancaster, I was destined to take over that post from him fifteen years on when he finally retired from active flying. His regular signaller, Flt Lt Syd Evans, was also a batchelor who had been born and bred in Kenya, so the pair of them revelled in the life as lived in darkest Africa. Ken had spent so much of his time overseas since joining No 36 Squadron that one night, after having had more than just a few drinks, lost touch with reality and managed to completely bamboozle a visiting Wing Commander sent out from Transport Command HQ to rain check our detachment in general.

The Wing Commander was in the bar that night, and doing the rounds to chat up as many visiting crews as possible. He eventually approached our group and asked Ken if he was on No 36 Squadron, or one of the others. Ken said, "I don't think I've ever heard of 36 Squadron, except that they might just have been in North Africa with us during the war, but I'm not sure about that". The Wing Commander went away muttering to himself just as Syd gave Ken a mighty nudge and said, "we are on 36 Squadron, have you forgotten"? For anyone who came across the terrible twins I can report that Ken is in happy retirement in Kent, but poor old Syd met his end as he might have wished. It was after leaving the RAF that he obtained a position with the United Nations Organisation and was sitting on a bar stool, where else, in Cambodia when the building was attacked by rebels. One rifle shot into the bar ricocheted off a wall and then struck poor old Syd. At least he died with a glass in his hand.

Our Mess bar was open house to many white settlers who seemed to enjoy our company just as much as we enjoyed theirs, and we had some good laughs together. One rather superior looking lady announced one night that she would "shortly be returning to England by BOAC" in a rather strained voice, to which a white farmer, who looked the type that might not have ever left Kenya in his life quipped "It might be quicker if you went by B O A T" in an equally strained voice.

One gentleman from the diplomatic corps was also a frequent visitor and he regaled us all one night with a story about his first tour in Kenya just after the war. Apparently his boss had received orders from the Foreign Office in London that a senior figure in the newly elected Labour Government in Britain would shortly be visiting Africa, and he wished to meet as many native chiefs as possible during his stay in Kenya. So orders went out that all chiefs living within 100 miles of Nairobi were to assemble in a field outside the city on a certain day for an address by a big white chief from London. Our raconteur went on to say that he had been left with the overseeing of the visit and had a dais positioned in a field just off the dirt track that passed through it. All seemed to be going well on the arrival of the official party, with over 50 native chiefs sitting patiently in their best warlike dress, complete with spears and shields. The minister got off to a slow start when he stated that as they would probably all know, (most probably didn't), that a Labour Government was now in power and there would be many changes. This brought a few calls of "Umbala", but not many. He then went on to state that at some time in the future they would have roads and running water, and their wives would no longer have to collect it from the rivers which induced many more "Umbalas" and the brandishing of spears. The visitor was now really getting into his stride and with each and every extravagant promise, the number of "Umbalas" grew in strength. The Minister's final promise was that a Labour Government would no longer tolerate them having to live in mud huts, and limit their normal four or five wives to just one in future. This really set the scene alight, with all the native chiefs on their feet performing a war dance with spears and shields held aloft, chanting Umbala, Umbala continuously. The Minister turned to the British High Commissioner with a big smile on his face and said, "I think that went down rather well, don't you? I'd just like to go down and shake a few hands". To which the High Commissioner replied, "If you really must Minister, but be rather careful where you tread, the field is covered in Elephant Umbala".

In the diplomat's more serious moments he talked about the predictable, as far as the local farmers were concerned, disaster that followed the first post war Government's decision to introduce the growing of ground nuts in East Africa. On the up side, he recalled that one predicted disaster for Kenya proved to be the complete opposite in the event. It was after receiving information that an American film company intended making a full length film in Kenya, which would result in the pumping of four million pounds into the local economy, that government officials got really worried about it's aftermath. The upshot in Kenya after the filming was, according to our diplomat friend, akin to the dropping of a pebble in a pond. Everything took off in a big way and, not least, by a massive surge in tourists eager to experience first hand what they had seen at the theatre in many parts of the world. The Mau Mau troubles of the 1950s put a damper on that activity, but by our time in 1960, hotels, safari parks and lodges had sprung up all over the place and Kenya was a very contented country once again.

It was early October when the plug was pulled on our East African detachment, and with more Hastings crews than aircraft out there, it was of more than passing interest to see which crews would be nominated as operators for the return flights to the UK, and which crews would draw the short straw and be passengers for the two day slog. Luck may have played a part in our crew being selected for flying but, then again, our Detachments Commander was Squadron Leader P O McCann who I had first met at RAF Lichfield and with whom I had always got on particularly well. My log book records that in the 36 hours elapsed time between taking off from Nairobi to landing back at RAF Colerne, we had flown the Eastleigh/El Adem leg with a re-fuelling stop in Khartoum in just over 12 hours airbourne time. Day two consisted of a direct flight from El Adem to RAF Lyneham for Customs clearance, followed by a 10 minute flip home to Colerne, taking up just over 9 hours in total. So, it was a tired crew, and passengers for that matter, who eventually arrived back for normal Squadron duties. Unlike Christmas Island, it had, at the end of the day, been something of a jolly, although we were given the usual three weeks to recover. It was to be early November before I started flying in earnest again and also the month that all aircrew in the RAF had to record their flying hours for the proceeding 12 months. Having been given more than the usual 42 days of leave as a result of two long detachments, and not having flown a great deal in East Africa I was more than surprised to find that I had still accumulated over 700 hours of flying time. In the flying training world, it would have taken over three years to total that number but, then again, flying instructors and student pilots did not fly around on auto-pilot for most of the time like us truckies.

In the RAF the best place to find out what was really going on at a station was, more often than not, via members of the Sergeants' Mess. I had noted that everybody mucked in together whereas officers tended to be just a little cliquey according to which branch they belonged to. The exception was on overseas Stations when larger numbers lived in, and even those that lived out preferred to use the Mess Bar. Some officers even referred to NCOs as the Freemasons of the Royal Air Force! One of our No 36 Squadron NCO flight engineers usually had a tale or two to impart, but before going into one particular tale of his I'd better explain that at RAF Colerne, which had been built pre-WWII with the normal short grass landing area, during the heady days of WWII, when the military could do whatever they wished without all the business of planning permission, an enlarged Tarmac runway had been laid right up to the limitation imposed by a public road which ran across it's western end. The road itself was perched on the edge of an escarpment before the steep drop down into Bath. Although traffic lights had been installed and showed red whenever an aircraft was on finals to land on that particular runway, in case the unlikely event of an aircraft overrunning the runway occurred and a collision with a passing car or truck ensued. Some local drivers tended to ignore the lights, particularly at night when they thought no one would notice. To that end, a sentry box was placed near the lights and manned during the night hours by an airman when flying was in progress to try and deter those reckless actions. Less than two hundred yards from the sentry box stood a very old mansion house which had in the dim and distant past been converted into what was called, in those days, a reform school. This one was one of the very few in England to cater for naughty teenage girls. The flight engineer started his story by saying that he had been in his Mess Bar the previous night and had heard the newly posted in Station Warrant Officer (SWO) who was in charge of discipline and rostering of picket and guard duties, saying that in all his years in the Service it was the very first time that he had got volunteers for guard duty, and on most other stations airmen had every excuse under the sun for not being rostered for them. "I suppose they all want to man the traffic lights on the airfield boundary", replied the NCO who he was talking to. "Yes, that's right", said the new SWO, "but it's still a bit of a mystery". "You obviously haven't heard about the girls remand home yet then"? "No, I've not, what on earth has that got to do with it"? snorted the SWO. "Absolutely everything, it must be about two months ago by now since an airman on that duty complained that at about midnight on his stint he had been set upon by about five or six girls from the school and sexually molested" was the startling reply. Another old stager in the bar that night chipped in with "well, at least he lived to tell the tale, not like my time in Mesopotamia before the war when we all had to carry "Goolie Chits" when we went flying. Worth about £500 to the Arabs if you forced landed in the desert and they caught you". "And what if you hadn't got this here Goolie Chit with you?" Enquired a very young, fresh faced NCO. "No chit, no goolies, the Arab wives loved nothing better than attending to that", concluded the very true story.

From the middle of November 1960 I collected two Aden return trips in quick succession which amounted to about 80 hours flying in no time at all. Both started with the usual one night stay in Clyffe Pypard and then it was two days out and two on the return with night stops at El Adem and refuelling at Khartoum in both cases. I cannot recall anything special, or urgent for that matter, about either, except that on the second we became probably the most unwanted crew on the route. Our transflight called for a late New Year's Eve landing in Aden with an early departure on the big day itself, plus a late landing at El Adem that evening. Movements staff at both Aden and El Adem had thought our itinerary was stupid. All we could think of saying was that we thought so too.

The El Adem legs, via Khartoum could have been somewhat boring due to the desolation of the area in general, but we had one or two distractions having to avoid Egyptian territory like the plague, we had to head due south out of El Adem for rather a long way, which took us over the Kufra Oasis, after which we made a slight turn left to try and pick up the south western corner of Egypt which was identifiable by two giant towers of rock which rose out of the otherwise flat desert for no apparent reason. Those two pieces of rock were known to all transporters as the witch's tits. After landing at Khartoum, and meeting our mate, the Arab refueller, it was then due East to pass over Asmara airfield in Eritrea before meandering down the Red Sea. The passing of Asmara airfield was nearly always interesting because the controllers almost invariably allowed us to maintain our cruising altitude of around 10,000', which meant that the airfield was only a few hundred feet below us as we swept over it. The passage down the Red Sea became very interesting as we approached a virtual bottleneck at it's Southern end with ships of all shapes and sizes abounding.

Although life on the squadron seemed as hectic as ever, our flying hours dropped dramatically during 1961 with our area of operations being confined to mainland Europe and the Mediterranean, except for emergencies such as the 1960 Kuwait Crisis and the UNO's involvement in the former Belgian Congo. Mass parachute exercises really came to the fore, and the biggest post war drop by British forces was held in Cyprus during that year. Many of us had a member of parliament on board to observe it and I was particularly lucky in having a young Conservative who kept well out of the way at the critical stage of dropping. Other crews reported less favorably on their presence! It is usually on big events like these that a bit of a cock up occurs and it certainly did that day. The routine for the drop is to call "Red On", at which point a red light will shine near the exit door and indicates to jumpers and their dispatchers that it is time to prepare to jump. This is later followed by the call "Green On" at which point the dispatcher will gently give the first para in line a push and the rest will follow. We had good radio contact with the dropping zone so why they also thought it necessary to fire a green Vary pistol remains a mystery. However, for one of our crews it was very unfortunate that the co-pilot saw fit to call "there goes the green" when he sighted the Vary. The rest was predictable, the despatcher gave the first trooper in line a push, without looking up at his indicator lights, and all the rest followed- 10 miles short of the zone.

CHAPTER 3
On detachment with the UN in the Congo

In August of 1961 I was to set off on the last of my three long detachments during my time on No 36 Squadron. It was to be a fateful one, but I shall start at the beginning. The troubles in the Belgian Congo since independence had steadily worsened to such an extent that UNO Forces eventually became involved with troops from many African countries and also a fairly large force from India. The main problem area revolved around the fact that the mineral rich Katanga province had declared independence from the newly elected Government in Leopoldville, leading to a civil war between the two, but without any clear cut front line. Forces from both factions roamed far and wide and skirmishes between the two sides took place without warning in many places. In addition to the Indian element, the British Commonwealth was mainly represented by troops from Ghana and Nigeria. With both of these two African countries having asked the British government for air support for initial deployment and re-supply, RAF detachments had been set up at both Lagos and Accra.

At the time I thought that I was lucky to have been delegated for the Ghanaian detachment for it's better weather if nothing else. With total rainfall at only 27" per annum it was less than half of that in Lagos, which was only two hundred miles to the East, and also less than in the UK for that matter. The flight out was by a replacement Hastings aircraft which we flew via Idris in Libya for a night stop, and then onto Kano for fuel before Lagos for another night stop before the one hour hop to our destination of Accra. The first night stop in Idris was of interest because at least half of our No 36 Squadron, with their aircraft, were also pitched up there. They were part of a force which had been on standby for a number of days as a result of intelligence reports concerning Kuwait. When the call for all Hastings crews to attend a mass briefing went out, we felt duty bound to go along just in case our own plans had been altered. That was not to be, but I sensed a bit of unease all round when it was announced that the Gulf bound aircraft would be taking off the next night and over fly one Arab state in complete radio silence because there had not been time to obtain diplomatic clearance. Most of us concurred later that the truth of the matter was probably that no diplomatic clearance had even been asked for because it would not have been given, but what if one of our aircraft had been forced to land in that country for technical reasons? It hardly bore thinking about.

Life in Accra could not have been better when not actually flying into the Congo. Our Mess was on the outskirts of Accra and although it was part and parcel of the Ghanaian Army since Ghana had obtained independence in 1957, virtually all living in members were ex-British Army Officers or on secondment from it. They all made us very welcome indeed. Motor transport was abundant and always on hand, not only to ferry crews to and from the airport but also to take them to a marvellous swimming beach whenever required. However, I didn't have time to savour the delights of that beach immediately, because the very next day after our arrival I was off to the Congo with another crew to pick up tips on the intricacies of operating into a country at war with itself. The first landing was always at the capital, then called Leopoldsville and without fail the Air Attache, or one of his staff, would be on hand not only to welcome us but also to give a briefing on the latest situation. It seemed rather strange that on that look see trip that the destination after the capital was to be Luluabourg with night stop accommodation in an Indian Army run Mess, with protocol very evident, whereas all my future trips with my own crew terminated at Albertville on the shores of Lake Tanganyika. Albertville was technically in Katanga, but it changed hands frequently between rebel and government forces. With Albertville being a daylight only airfield, we always night stopped there and used the same hotel, in fact it may have been the only one.

It was run by an aged Belgian couple, both appeared to be over 80, who always made a tremendous fuss of us every time that we arrived. Their main story, however, was always along similar lines and that was; it was a pity we had not been here a few days ago when a battle had raged along the lake side road in front of their hotel, we would have enjoyed it! Would we really.

Two memories linger of operating out of Albertsville and the first was that one morning when we presented ourselves at the wooden shack that was the Operations Room where flight plans had to be submitted before departing, it was found to be securely locked without a soul in sight. Did the airfield staff know something that we didn't? Another battle was imminent perhaps? We did not hang around long enough to find out and nailed our flight plan to the door and departed without even radio contact. A good job the punctilious route checkers of Transport Command never ventured into this extreme limit of their remit.

The second incident occurred when a senior RAF officer, possibly having heard of the primitiveness of the airfield, joined our crew on a fact finding mission to the Congo. Just before our time of departure he said he would like to inspect the runway surface which was of Tarmac, not the normal concrete for such high temperature places. When he asked if he could walk along it's entire length he was told that our eventual departure would almost certainly be the first and last aircraft movement of that day, so he could help himself. I was alongside the senior officer as we set off with my co-pilot and commissioned Flight Engineer bringing up the rear about 20 yards astern. Every now and again the Senior Officer would stop, bend down and press his thumb into the far from solid Tarmac and then give me a knowing look as if to say, should Hastings aircraft really be operating off this surface? This became all too much for Paddy, my engineer, who said in a very loud voice to the co-pilot "I wonder if it will take spin today"? The very senior officer's face turned bright red and I thought his eyes would pop out but, to his credit, he didn't say a word.

In the early days of the Congo troubles one RAF crew ran into a spot of bother when the Belgic speaking natives had translated "Royal Air Force Transport Command, painted on all Command aircraft, into "Commando Force of the Air Royal" and sprayed machine gun bullets above the crew and aircraft after a landing in one rebel held part of that country. From that time onwards we all had to wear UNO's distinctive light blue beret to try and indicate our true purpose.

On every other flight in the Congo we would night stop in the capital, inbound or outbound. The airfield itself was under American control and they had turned one massive hangar into accommodation for transmitting crews and sectioned it off into three areas. Tier bunks in the sleeping part, messing in another and ablutions in the third. It worked rather well and we got to know one or two American mercenary pilots who used the facilities. They were flying up to 1500 Hours per year in aid of the Government and that being about 500 more than allowed by the American FAA they knew full well that their licences would be withdrawn when they eventually arrived home. All said, they would be so rich by that time it would not really matter. When the next African war started, having a licence might not be a requirement if they did run short of pilots! One of these renegade pilots proudly showed me around his aircraft one day, which was a latest state of the art American plane, bought and paid for by the Congo Government. It was a real eye opener, and left the English piston engine manufacturers way behind as far as modern technology was concerned. Gauges indicated the performances of each and every cylinder. If only we had one on that last Singapore trip was uppermost in my mind.

The utter boredom of a night on the airfield about 15 to 20 miles out of the city was relieved one evening when my crew and another from the Lagos detachment received an invitation to drinks at the home of the Air Attache. The invitation had been relayed by one of the Wing Commander's staff who often greeted us on arrival. This chap was always polite, most helpful and immaculately dressed. It transpired that the Commissioned Flight Engineer on the Lagos crew was in the habit of calling him "Sir" thinking he might be a Squadron Leader, or even well up the ladder in the civil service. After the drinks had flowed freely one member of the other crew asked the Air Attache just what was the status of the chap who had met us on arrival that afternoon. "Oh", said Wing Commander Cogan, "he's one of us, an RAF Sergeant clerk in fact, loves working out here and going out to the airfield to meet you lot two or three times a week". Smirks all round from the Lagos crew who, luckily, were on their last flight into the Congo before returning to the UK. In effect, the meeting of the Flight Lieutenant who called a Sergeant "Sir", and the Sergeant who looked like a senior officer when in very smart mufti in the tropics, was never to take place again. In case anybody should wonder why, after forty years, I can remember the name of the Wing Commander Air Attache, I will just point out that shortly after returning to the UK I was to become an instructor at the Hastings conversion unit, and one of my very first students was an ex Air Attache who, when it transpired that I had spent some time with the UNO force in West Africa, had immediately said "I'll bet you came across Cogan of the Congo then"? When I said, "do you mean Wing Commander Cogan by any chance"?, he replied, "That will be him, he brought the house down at an Air Attache's conference in London a few months ago when he got up to introduce himself and started by saying, "I'm Cogan of the Congo". It sounded a bit like "Dr Livingstone, I presume" from Stanley in the Congo in 1871.

About two weeks before our departure from the UK, I had been summoned to what was the then Air Ministry and told that during our stay in Accra we would probably come across a Russian Transport Aircraft that operated from there, and if I could possibly get aboard it they would be interested in finding out if it carried a certain piece of equipment. I will not, go into exact details, but I knew exactly what to look for if I got a chance. Eventually the Hastings I was about to fly, dear old WG 334, the plane I had already flown for over 300 hours during our Christmas Island detachment, was parked right next to the Russian aircraft in question. I thought it might look less obvious as to what I was up to if our entire crew went aboard the Russian aircraft, so we walked over, all together, at my suggestion. The Russian ground crew were obviously preparing the aircraft for take off and two of them started waving one flat hand up and down quite rapidly, which we all took to mean "clear off". After coming to an abrupt halt my mind suddenly went back fifteen years to my time in Japan and I recalled that in that country if the palm of the hand is pointing downwards such waving means "please do come forward", so I said a quick "it's ok, we can go ahead". In the event they seemed to be pleased to show us around their aircraft, although not a word was understood between either group. I spotted what I was looking for, so I was quite pleased with myself, although not allowed to show it, or talk about it even to my crew.

The trip down to the Congo that day was to be my second from last and although my Loadmaster, Colin Friend, was absolutely super throughout the detachment under far from ideal conditions, he really excelled on the leg between Albertville and Leopoldville inbound. It was only after we had settled down into the cruise that he came up front and said that according to his manifest we had personnel from twelve different countries among the forty passengers, and with none being from Commonwealth Countries he doubted if they had understood a word of his emergency procedure briefing. Life was like that at that time, we never did have any specific orders as to who we could, or couldn't, take on board as passengers during internal flights in the Congo and a blue beret had to serve that purpose.

Our social life in Accra revolved around beach runs in the afternoons and drinks parties on the Mess patio in the evenings, when many ex-pats joined us, very much in line with life in Nairobi. One addition this time round was a bevy of ladies who worked for the British High Commission who always arrived en-masse and departed in the same fashion. Many seemed homesick and loved nothing better than to talk about the UK and ask us about the situation back home. Occasionally, one of the male Diplomats would also pitch up and, almost needless to say, one night cracked one of their jokes. This one was to the effect that shortly after independence, he had been asked to go along to their new Law Courts and see how they now administered justice. His escort proudly pointed out that the judge and others wore wigs, as in England, and that, unlike the District Commissioner days, there was a prosecutor and defending lawyer. The diplomat said he had been particularly impressed until a topless young native girl rushed through the middle of the court so, turning to his escort had asked, "what on earth was that all about?" "Oh", he replied, "we have often read in our newspapers that during old Bailey trials in London a titter often runs around the court and we've copied it just like the wigs and gowns".

Other visitors to the mess in the evenings were often RAF officers on secondment to the newly formed Ghana Air Force on accompanied tours. The senior officer in charge of the Accra element was Wing Commander Grundy-White, a distinguished ex-bomber pilot of WWII. He often asked my co-pilot and myself if we fancied a flight with him in one of his aircraft. On one such occasion it coincided with a sudden drop in Congo flights, possibly because the West African UNO force was now fully in place, so we both took up the Wing Commander's offer. The trip was up country in a DH Otter and, although only a single engined piston aircraft, it could carry several passengers in addition to the two pilots up front. The intended flight was to be to Tamale with an intermediate stop at Kintampo. The Wing Commander had always indicated that I would be up front with him if we ever managed to get time off for the flight, but on that day a Ghanaian General, who had recently been informed that he was to be the new Commander in Chief of all UNO forces in the Congo shortly, had decided he also would join the flight and indicated that he would like to occupy the co-pilot's position. The Wing Co had, obviously, agreed but told me I would get the chance to be up front on the second leg. I later found this to be very strange indeed when one of the other passengers turned out to be an Air Commodore Whittle who was the RAF Commander of the Ghanaian Air Force. He was, incidentally, also the ex Station Commander of RAF Scampton at the time of the Dams raid of 1943. Two other passengers, thank God, were RAF parachute jumping instructors, but more of that shortly. I never found out, even later, why the aircraft was to land at Kintampo before Tamale, it being very much an out of the way primitive strip and the omens for our departure were not particularly good, even before we had landed. All pilots know that for most aircraft types the landing run can be achieved in a shorter distance than the take off provided that a lower than normal approach speed is used. Being down the back I never saw the strip from the air, but the fact that about five go-arounds took place before the eventual landing did not bode well for our departure.

On the ground we were taken to the residence of an Englishman and his lady for refreshments. It was built on the palatial lines of "Up Country" living by English families in Africa of those times. He might well have been the District Commissioner for that area, being obviously well known to the Air Commodore and Wing Commander. I can still recall that he had a double barrelled name which was well known in the UK pre-war. It was during the genteel coffee drinking and small talk session that the Wing Commander caught my eye and managed to impart the news that the General wished to be up front for the arrival in Tamale, so I'd have to wait until our return flight from there to Accra for my go at the controls. I will point out at this stage that it is not possible to gain access to the cockpit from the passenger cabin in the DH Otter, otherwise we might have changed places in flight for a short spell.

Wing Commander Grundy-White did all the right things for the start of a short take off run using the last inch of ground and running up to full power before releasing the brakes. The aircraft really leapt forward but shortly after lift off the stall warning started to blare out and we realised that we were in dead trouble. The aircraft duly hit high trees and crashed to the ground. A fire broke out from the engine area and swept back to the passenger cabin. I was furthest forward in that area, along with my co-pilot John Sully. My first thought after unstrapping my safety harness was "well, thank God we are still alive", but worse was to follow. As John and I made our way to the rear exit door a cry went up from the two RAF parachute instructors, "the bloody door is jammed shut", or words to that effect. Eventually the two heroes decided to jump at the door with both feet in unison and worked the oracle. They shot off around the wing tip and then extricated the General and the Wing Commander from the burning cockpit. My co-pilot escaped scot free, but I sported minor burning and a few cuts and bruises. The Air Commodore had sustained damage to an ankle but managed, by leaning on the shoulder of my co-pilot, to make it to a safe distance from the burning wreckage. We assumed, at first, that the two up front must have died on impact but it was serious burns which led to the death of both. The General within two days, but Wing Commander Grundy-White the predicted 21 days later, back in the burns unit of the RAF Hospital at RAF Halton. I say "the predicted 21 days" because a doctor member of the Army Mess in Accra, knowing the degree of burns suffered, mentioned that figure. The English newspapers sent out to West Africa mentioned that the General had taken over control of the UNO Forces in the Congo some little time after his demise, which indicated a lack of communication somewhere along the line.

After the crash there was a remarkable piece of co-operation between two very different nations. A Russian MIG 4 (hound) military helicopter soon arrived to take all survivors, excepting the General and Wing Commander, to the full blown airfield of Kumasi, which was about halfway back to Accra, where a Ghanaian Air Force four engined DH Heron took us the rest of the way. Before boarding the helicopter, a medic attending to the Wing Commander came out of the makeshift hospital and said the Wing Commander wished to speak to me. He asked if John Sully and I were all right and seemed to buck up a bit when I said "fine, and all the other passengers are too". A very nice touch from the dying Wing Commander Grundy-White.

On arrival back at our barrack home I went along to the camp medical centre for treatment. The local native orderly applied some green gunge to the finger wounds before the usual bandages. The gunge, whatever it was, worked wonders but the bandages seemed a little slack, even on day one which led, later that night, to a slight mishap. It was the usual night for the visitation by the High Commission ladies and, on the patio, during drinks, I made an arm waving gesture to emphasize some point or other which led to one bandage taking off into space. It didn't actually land in anyone's drink but the sight of the wound on the now unbandaged finger caused shrieks from some of the girls.

My last flight into the Congo was a little unusual in that after a night stop at Leopoldville outbound we had a complete day off in Albertville after day two, and managed to see quite a bit of that lakeside town. Another unusual event was that we had two Accra based Hastings night stopping on the same evening in Leopoldville. The co-pilot of the other crew was Flt Lt Bob Beckley, who I had first met when he was one of the SEG students changing over to piloting after re-joining the RAF. I was just coming out of a shower when he was entering and he did the original double take when he saw how badly bruised I still was in the stomach area after the accident. He asked if a doctor had seen me and I had to admit that none had. Bob was married to an ex RAF PM (Nursing Sister) so perhaps he had become ultra cautious in such matters. After our final landing back in Accra, the usual efficient transport service was in operation and during the ride back to camp from the airfield one of our crew happened to say that he "wondered how the Lagos crews were getting on", which sent the Ghanaian driver into overdrive, and he said, "Master wants me to drive you to Lagos, fine, but I'll need to top up with petrol first". He seemed very disappointed when we said not today, thank you, maybe some other time. When one considers that to get from Accra to Lagos you would have to traverse two other Countries in the process was a little mind blowing, even if it was only two hundred miles away.

In every strata of life there is always one person who is accident prone and likely to put their foot in it sooner or later, and we certainly had one in darkest Africa. He was one of our Hastings Captains who thought the world came to an end at Calais. I have already mentioned that virtually every living in officer was from the UK, although that was about to change towards the end of our detachment. Captain X, on return from, no doubt, a rather tiring Congo flight, entered the Mess hell bent on some form of refreshment and seeing an obvious looking local in the dining area and assuming him to be a civilian waiter went up and, after pointing from an outstretched arm, said "you get master tea, hot, plenty quick or me report you". The rather stunned gentleman, one of Ghana's first returned Army graduate officers from Sandhurst replied, "I'm terribly sorry, old boy, but I don't quite understand".

Captain X had obviously not learned a thing from a previous faux pas down in the Congo. On that occasion, he had gone up to another African Officer from a Commonwealth Country whom he had seen smoking near his aircraft and started with plenty of deep breathing and exhaling and finished his performance by pointing skywards. That Officer, in perfectly modulated English, had retorted "I understand that perhaps it is a little too close to your aircraft, Captain, to be smoking a cigarette because it might cause an explosion in the event of a petrol leakage".

The night before our departure for the UK the Detachment Commander, Sqdn Ldr Wells, who I had first met at RAF Ternhill when he had been Station Adjutant there ten years previously, confided that neither our crew, or aircraft, would be replaced because the now obvious over manning for the Congo operations had been deliberately kept going during the last month or so because the Foreign Office had received intelligence reports that trouble was brewing in the British Cameroons and a rapid airlift of British nationals out of that territory might be required at short notice. It seemed the panic was now over and we were on our way. With an empty aircraft, except for the personal effects of the now late W C Grundy-White, and the odd bit of local furniture, such as elephant tables and chairs, that all crews tend to collect over the years, rear ballast weights were not fitted as they should have been. This led to two basic facts. Firstly, we could take off with full tanks which meant a non-stop flight could be made but, secondly, that after arrival at Idris there would be little petrol left and the landing would need some careful handling with no rear ballast aboard. The Hastings, having manual controls, required a fair bit of two handed muscle at the best of times. After take off, all further engine power control settings were left to the flight engineer, as directed by the pilot, and that included the slow cut just before touchdown. The slow cut always resulted in a sharp nose drop which, under normal load conditions, could be contained by a hard pull back on the control column by the pilot. However, with little petrol and no ballast it was going to be a little tricky with the trim wheel already reaching it's limits after joining the Idris circuit at reduced speed and power. I therefore called the flight engineer to say that I would be flying it onto the runway and not calling for the slow cut until the main wheels had made contact. I also told the co-pilot to follow me through on the controls on finals and add some pull on the stick during each power reduction called for on finals to land. Thank goodness I did, because it was a real handful, but the technique worked. We had plenty of trade the next day on the flight to Lyneham so that was the first and last time that I was faced with a lack of rear weight problem.

However, my ground time in Idris did not pass without incident. Having lost my service No 1 hat in the crashed Otter, I was reduced to wearing the UNO blue beret in lieu, and I soon realised that not many RAF personnel, least of all the Standard Warrant Officer (SWO) had ever seen one before. Wherever I went on that Station that afternoon and the next morning, our paths always seemed to cross and although he gave very respectful salutes he always glared at the blue beret in apparent disbelief. It gave the word stalking a completely new meaning. The Mess members in Accra had got used to my missing eyebrows, burnt off in the aircraft fire, but for those in Idris, meeting me for the first time gave me quizzical looks. They might just as well have had balloon captions above their heads which read, I wonder if he was born without eyebrows.

I had not wished to upset my wife, Betty, with news about the Ghana accident by letter but I had overlooked the obvious, another wife had received the information via her husband and in the middle of a coffee morning had said to Betty "I'm glad Jacko was not seriously hurt in the accident". The best laid plans and all that had hit the fan!

With my two years on No 36 Squadron now up a posting back to instructing came through during the normal stand down after a detachment so I had made my last flight with No 36 Squadron. It is a rarity in life to remember just exactly where and when one first met a particular person who you remained friends with over a good number of years, and rarer still to recall the initial conversation with that person. However, a first meeting with Paul Jenner has always stuck in my memory. It was whilst loading my car at the back of the Officers' Mess at RAF Colerne after that final landing with No 36 Squadron, that I heard a voice from my rear say "Can I help you with your loading, Sir"? My first thought was "Good God, surely not an airman on the Mess staff offering help"? No, it was a very young officer. My first words to Paul were, "I'm just like you, not a Sir". From that point on we got on famously and our paths crossed frequently over his shortish RAF career, but we have remained in contact to this day. He was the son of a one time RAF Wing Commander and had just graduated from the RAF College at Cranwell where, no doubt, he was used to calling all RAF officers Sir. On my next but one tour, which was in Singapore, I had the privilege of giving the bride away at his wedding to a SAFFA sister by the name of Mo, a lovely lady. After deciding to transfer to civilian flying he had acquired a post with a Maltese airline but that firm went into liquidation before he even went out to Malta. Unfortunately, not before he had dispatched all his worldly goods by sea which were stranded on a quay in Valetta harbour. His next activity was flying Russian MIG fighters in Biafra in support of their uprising against Nigeria. His final and long lasting post was with Cathay Pacific in Hong Kong, working his way up to senior Captain status before final retirement to live in France.

It had just become known that the Transport Command operational conversion unit was to be moved from Dishforth to Thorney Island at the years end of 1961, so I would be living in Mess again for a few months at Dishforth. However, with the navigational school at Thorney Island already having moved on there were plenty of empty married quarters available and Betty duly took advantage of the situation and became installed there before our arrival. The run down at Dishforth was very sad indeed, it had been a happy Station during it's transport days but it was somewhat off the beaten track for that type of flying. I had plenty of time to frequent some of my old haunts of both my Leeming days and my first taste of Dishforth two years previously. One new one that I picked up was via a members invitation to the Boroughbridge Conservative club, where I met the one and only Freddie Trueman, just before he set off on another winter tour. He seemed quite pleased when I made mention of his RAF football career at Hemswell. A welcome change of topic from cricket, no doubt; from his point of view anyway.

CHAPTER 4
Instructing again with No. 242 OCU

Life at Thorney Island was to be very pleasant indeed, apart from the first couple of months of 1962 when our flying programme was constantly interrupted by the weather. Snow being the big problem, laying for more days at a time than any of the locals could recall for many years past. It was concluded that in no way could we ever catch up on the back log of student training, even when the conditions eventually improved, and so it was decided that during the next break in the weather we would all depart for warmer climes. It was to be Nicosia, and what an eye opener that turned out to be.

Like all other transport crews of that era, I had transited through there many times, but only on one night stands, which was a case of here today and gone tomorrow. There never was any time left during 14 hour ground time schedules to even leave one's accommodation to explore the local area and mingle with the resident population. Now, here in Nicosia, on an RAF camp with plenty of our ex-students based there who were more than willing to take us around the island to see the sights, life was to be idyllic for six long weeks. It turned out to be true that one can ski up in the Trudos mountains and swim in the sea on the same day in Cyprus, although I never fancied the former. Stan Breckon, another SEG transferee during my Tern Hill days, was our main transport provider and his favourite place for a day out was the harbour town of Kyrenia which suited us fine except for one hectic, hair raising return run. Apparently there was an unofficial timed speed record from Kyrenia to the Nicosia Officers' Mess, based on the honour system, and Stan was the current best time holder. It had been a long hot day in Kyrenia, which had taken in the harbour haunts and the nearest establishment to an English pub in Cyprus, in fact a drinking den around which the novel "Bitter Lemon" is based. When Stan suddenly announced that he would try and break his own speed record on the return run we should have feared the worst. The uphill climb into the mountain range after leaving the coast was not too bad, but after the start of going downhill towards Nicosia it became faster and faster. It was a great relief to arrive back safely, even though it wasn't another record. In those six weeks we had achieved our objective of clearing the backlog and our students would now pass out on time.

Back in England we soon settled into a normal routine but it only lasted until our first session of serious night flying. Noise complaints became so numerous that drastic action was called for and, luckily, the answer was obvious, all transport crews towards the end of their course had to carry out a route trainer, normally to the Mediterranean area, to be shown the end product of transport flying. That is moving freight and or bodies from Point A to Point B, so why not make it to an airfield where the night training could be carried out without disturbing the natives, and in that context El Adem and Idris, both in Libya, could not have been better placed. It would also drum up trade for those two airfields and thereby enhance morale. The noise complaints were understandable because until our arrival at Thorney Island it had been a Navigational Training School using the twin engined Varsity aircraft which spent most of their time well away from the area on long cross country flights and suddenly it had become a Pilot Training establishment, using three different types of four engined aircraft, all needing a fair amount of night circuits and bumps with each aircraft producing twice the amount of noise. The three types being the Hastings, Beverley, and Argosy. I was Duty Officer one night during the initial complaints season when a very irate gentleman rang up and said "As a retired Lieutenant Commander he could not understand why we did not carry out our touch and gos on the sea in the English Channel on lighted buoys". I gave him the good news about it's impending demise at Thorney Island, but mentally thought he was barking mad. On later reflection I felt that if he was about eighty years old, as he sounded, he could have been born up to twenty years before man had flown!

One part of the syllabus for young co-pilots was training them up to first solo on type, which I found very difficult to come to terms with for the Hastings tail wheeled aircraft. This was for various differing reasons. Firstly, these pilots had nearly all trained to Wings standard on the Jet Provosts and then the Vampire or Varsity, all three aircraft with tricycle type undercarriages. The Hastings Aircraft was quite difficult to handle at the best of times, and often referred to as the greatest leveller of them all, so was it right or proper to let them solo with so little previous experience, and none at all on tail wheeled aircraft? It seemed a pointless exercise and yes, we did have a number of accidents but, luckily, none fatal. To be fair to those young co-pilots suddenly becoming Captains of a four engined aircraft with a five man crew and making their first solo on a tail wheeled aircraft, it must be pointed out that they were not alone as regards accidents, and two instructors were Captains of Hastings aircraft that suffered major accidents during my time on No 242 OCU at Thorney Island. One, when on a roller landing a student pilot lost control, despite his instructors best efforts to correct a violent swing, and the aircraft left the runway and impacted into a ground servicing hut. Although the crew survived without a scratch, unfortunately a ground radio Sergeant Technician was killed. The second accident occurred just outside our hangar accommodation when a similar loss of control resulted in the Hastings cartwheeling before coming to rest just in front of the Control Tower, again without any crew members being seriously hurt, but for those of us who happened to be looking out of the crew room window at the time, it was the nearest we had ever been to an accident without actually being involved. Without any knowledge of the inquiry's findings, I think that a rich mixture cut on one of the four engines was the most likely cause in both of the two cases. Like accelerators on cars, aircraft throttles induce extra petrol into the engine cylinders on opening up for extra power, and if applied too quickly an inverse situation occurs in that too much petrol for normal combustion takes place and an engine cut results. It seems that might have been the cause of the Blenheim accident of some years ago when it was badly damaged on a touch and go after eighteen years of restoration work. One report indicated that although the Captain had amassed over 10,000 flying hours, virtually all had been on turbine powered aircraft. Jet engines do not suffer from such cuts, they are just slow to spool up at the best of times.

One very serious accident did eventually occur but that was to a massive Blackburn Beverley, the largest aircraft that the RAF operated at that time, with a wing span of 162'. This one impacted with the sea in Chichester harbour during it's final approach to land but, luckily, all crew members survived except the navigator and flight engineer. Obviously their bodies had to be recovered, if possible, so as to be given a decent funeral. The project was not without it's problems because the survivors thought the missing two had vacated the aircraft and must have died by drowning. But where would be the best place to look for the two missing crew members with the usual two tides a day? A local fisherman was consulted and he opined that they would eventually be washed ashore in x number of days and within two points on the island. He added that if and when that occurred only medics, or other people with strong stomachs should be involved in the recovery because the crabs would have been at work. He was proved right. Local knowledge won out again.

    I was to spend three happy years instructing on Hastings Aircraft at ideally placed Thorney Island, so close to the famous seaside resorts of the Channel coast and Portsmouth steeped in Naval history. However, what made it a particularly happy period in my RAF career was the diversity of background and friendliness of the other instructors on the flight. My own particular instructor when I had first joined the transport force at Dishforth, Flt Lt Jim Collyer, was now the highly respected Flight Commander, others who I will always remember included "Chalky" White, a bomber baron who had completed tours in the Middle East and the UK during WWII, John Horrocks a Burma DFC, Jimmy McVie a Battle of Britain pilot, one of two Flt Lts holding that distinction who were flying Hastings aircraft at the time- rarities to say the least, "Taff" John DFM, who I had served with previously on the ANS at RAF Lichfield, "Paddy" Irish DFC from Wales, had been one of the very first Spitfire pilots to shoot down a FW 190, Roy Greggs, a Canadian who had opted for life in England after the war, Jimmy Glover newly arrived from the post of British Embassy pilot in Washington where he had travelled far and wide in his DH Heron, Bill Youd known to all as Yogi Bear, a Parachute Regiment trooper in his time plus Les Sands, Douggie Butler and John Mathieson also Flt Lt. Ken Owen a Flight Engineer who served with coastal command in WWII. Three very long serving transport captains. Quite a collection by any standards. Sad to relate, Flight commander Jim Collyer, after leaving the RAF in the mid 1960s, took up an appointment with a civil airline flying 707s and became the first voice recorded on a black box, just seconds before an accident. That fatal crash in Africa was the result of a rear end failure. This tour also gave me my first insight into the back door trading that sometimes went on in the transport world.

    No doubt civil servants in the Air Ministry would automatically assume that all flying taking place on training Stations would be confined to the production of aircrew and, therefore, serving a very useful purpose with no monitoring required. Life is never like that of course, and we got a steady flow of special trips which would otherwise have been turned down flat at Command level as not being important enough to warrant the use of front line squadron aircraft and crews. One beauty of these trips was that the minimum ground time of 14 hours was not the norm, and we often stayed for two or three nights at some very pleasurable locations. Most of these "one off" trips left memories for one reason or another. One of my first was ferrying CFS ground crew and their equipment to Karup in Denmark in support of Little Rissington's jet formation aerobatic team, "The Pelicans". The first leg called for a night stop at Gutersloh, and that was the first big difference from my time on No 36 Squadron when I had made many return trips to Germany but never night stopped. It was during the evening in the Mess bar that I learnt that the Germans do have a sense of humour after all. I had better explain that pre-war the Luftwaffe did not go in for the Officers' Mess style of living, the only exception being Gatow airfield in Berlin, equivalent to the RAF's Cranwell. That changed slightly when Hermann Goering ordered a hunting lodge to be built on Gutersloh, complete with a tall tower where he used to regale young officers with tales of his daring do, flying over the trenches in WWI. He tended to over cook his use of the German saying which went "I hope the roof falls in if I'm telling lies". This became all too much for the young officers who made a false beam in the tower, just above the spot that the Field Marshal stood during his harangues. The rest is history, needless to say, Goering finishing up with a sore head after his first "If I'm telling a lie...", when the rope holding the beam in place was released.

 The air display involving this CFS team went off particularly well, however I couldn't help but notice that the Danish spectators looked a little more staid than even their near neighbours in Germany. Perhaps I was a little disappointed that on first hearing of the trip I had mixed up Karup with Castrop, the latter being close to the city of Copenhagen, whereas our Karup was in the middle of nowhere. On the return journey to Little Rissington we had to clear UK customs at RAF Manston, but the wind was so strong across their only concrete runway that my one and only grass runway landing in a Hastings took place. I had previously used the hard packed Marum runway in Nairobi of course, but this was something different, although it turned out to be a non event. The CFS jets with nose wheels and, therefore, higher cross wind limits had already landed so there was a little pressure on me to do so too. A superb letter of thanks for our efforts duly arrived from Rissington and was deeply appreciated.

 Other trips of this nature came thick and fast with my first landing in Berlin being one of them. It was a Friday to Monday job so we had two full free days to see the sights. With Gatow being off the beaten track for RAF flights, the Movements staff seemed very pleased with our appearance and really gave us regal treatment. The Hastings was also something of a star turn, being well remembered by the locals as having played such a vital role in the Berlin blockade of 1948/49. One of the Movements staff took us to one of his favourite haunts in downtown Berlin on the Friday night which went under the name of "The Telefunkan Club". On entry it soon became apparent why it went under such a name. It was waiter service only at tables slightly elevated on three sides of a dance floor. Each table had it's own telephone and also what looked like a mini lamp stand, only in this case internal lighting shone outwards on four sides, illuminating the table tele number. The idea was that if you wished to dance with someone on another table, all you had to do was give their table a ring. Once you had given your own table number and sorted out which lady/ gent you had in mind, they would give you a quick glance and either give a nod or put the phone down rather quickly. The only person to try it out that night was our "Yogi Bear", Bill Youd, who was co-Captain for the trip. He had no luck at all after ringing several tables. Was it because he was English, sounded a little drunk or a bit of both perhaps? We never found out, or cared for that matter. It had been a great night out with service transport provided. Another treat awaited us on Saturday when we took to the water on the Harvel Lake. Not many people realise that RAF flying boats, in the form of Short Sunderlands, played quite a part in the re-supply of Berlin during the blockade of that city by the Russians, using the Lake for alighting and taking off. For some reason or another the rather large flying boat tender had been left intact after the ending of the flying boat operations and became a leisure activities item for general RAF use. We took along several crates of German beers, which have always seemed to be much stronger than their English counterparts, to imbibe on that perfect day for messing about on boats. The beer began to tell and Yogi Bear was soon at the helm, shouting many nautical oddities, such as "Hard a starboard" and "Full steam ahead". We managed to get the craft back safely after, no doubt, spoiling the day for the many Germans also out on the Lake that afternoon. With the session continuing back in the Mess bar that evening, not everyone was on top form the following day. It was during the recovery period that Sunday morn when a well meaning WVS lady approached our gang and asked if any of us wished to join her group that was touring East Berlin later, we would be more than welcome to join in. One of our crew was obviously interested, and asked what was the time of departure. Luckily, she had her back to Yogi when she said "12 noon", because he leapt to his feet and, pointing to the bar, started going through the visual motions of drinking from a pint pot. Some of the crew did go along and see at first hand just how bad conditions were past "Checkpoint Charlie", under Communist rule. It became one of my regrets in life that I had not gone along too, but my time did eventually arrive over ten years later, after I had delivered the third from last Hastings ever to fly to Gatow to become a gate guardian and later a museum piece when Gatow ceased to be an RAF Station.

Another regret in my flying life also concerned Berlin. It was all to do with keeping the Berlin air corridor open to traffic and to that end a few RAF pilots carried out three month stints of flying British civil airliners in and out of that city at regular intervals using Viscounts and, later, BAe 111s. My number never came up.

Yet another jolly came my way when the United Services Rugby team were due to play their French counterparts in a top class Paris stadium, and had been on the lookout for suitable transportation. I doubt if they thought a Hastings aircraft suitable but our location on the south coast was ideal for gathering of tri-service personnel with the venue being just across the Channel. No other instructor seemed interested in going along as co-Captain so I needed to recruit a course pilot for the trip. With my French only being basic in the extreme I asked the first few student pilots I came across the same question without divulging my reasons. "How good is your French"? I went through quite a few until I chanced upon Flying Officer Mike Beal, who answered rather proudly, "Quite good, in fact, one of my better subjects at school". He was signed up straight away and given details of the trip which did not seem to surprise him at all, perhaps he had got wind of it on the grapevine? Because of the nature of the trip we would be using the Paris Military airfield of Villacoublay, sadly in the news after Princess Diana's death in 1997, when her body was flown out of that base to RAF Northolt, the British equivalent of Villacoublay. It was quite busy at the French base that Friday afternoon and everything went tickety boo with a civilian coach awaiting to take us all to a city centre hotel. We went along to the match and although my game is football I gathered that we had a fine team, with plenty of potential, even though national service was by then in the dustbin of history, for the British anyway. Later I wished that I had kept a copy of the passenger manifest because, no doubt, many of those players would go on to make their mark on the game in later years and it would have been nice to follow their progress.

All good things come to an end and I was reflecting on a lovely Sunday morning, as the coach took us back to the airfield, how smoothly things had gone, certainly better than expected, and we had not even used Mike Beal's mastery of the French language. Suddenly, all that was to change because on our arrival at the gates of Villacoublay airfield the coach had to park on the opposite side of the public road because the vast iron gates were firmly locked with a Military Policeman standing guard. He showed a passing interest in our arrival and made no attempt at letting us through, so I turned to Mike and said, "Now's your chance to use your excellent French". Mike did not seem too happy as he left the coach and approached the guard. There followed a lot of arm waving from both the guard and Mike until the guard suddenly pulled out his pistol from it's holster and pointed it straight at Mike. Mike put his hands up in the air and backed slowly away. This was becoming more and more like a good western by the second. The guard waved his pistol around indicating that he wanted Mike further away still from the gate until he finally made off through a much smaller gate towards his guardroom. Mike came across the road and into our coach looking like a whipped dog, and even worse when I quipped "So much for your French, Mike". The guard, with one other helper, eventually came out of the guardroom and ever so slowly opened the gates before giving us a half hearted wave through.

Not all of these trips were beer and skittle runs and the one day trips could be quite tiring. One such was an early morning run down to Orange in the south of France and, after many hours of hanging around doing nothing, a very late arrival back at base. I have always thought that it was the time doing nothing in aviation that increased the fatigue factor rather than the actual flying on short haul days. One UK only trip covering a full weekend was most enjoyable and productive. It revolved around getting a Squadron's aerobatic team from Leconfield to the Biggin Hill Battle of Britain Air Display day and included over 12 sectors with a double run between Leconfield and Waterbeach, both before and after the display day. It was the first major Air Display day I had attended which turned out to be a portent of things to come. It was a tired but happy crew that landed back at Thorney Island late on a Sunday night to be greeted by the news that TV cameras had lingered on our slow taxying both before and after the air show. Was the dear old Hastings beginning to become an oddity in the jet age? Perhaps viewers at our Command HQ at Upavon might even have asked themselves who had authorised the trip. Two other trips to one particular destination was a little nostalgic to say the least. They were to Ronaldsway in the Isle of Man, and that was the place in the mid 1930s that I had first landed as an air passenger. It was also the airfield that I had first taken to the skies from in a four engined aircraft later the same day. Both trips, one out of Stansted and the other from RAF Northolt, were to convey young female would be officers to that island to attend a training course on the old wartime airfield of Jurby. It seemed crazy that in the mid 1960s the RAF should have seen fit to relocate one of their Officer Cadet Training Units (OCTU) to an island in the middle of the Irish Sea, although it did survive for ten years and it certainly put the knockers on weekend leave for personnel serving there if nothing else. At the Stansted pick up point on my first run, I got the distinct impression that the Flt Lt WRAF in charge of the 30 or so young ladies might have been a little difficult to please at the best of times but it proved to be a completely wrong impression. Flt Lt Jeannie Oakes appeared in Singapore during my first tour after Thorney Island, and became an instant friend of both Betty and myself, a friendship which has lasted to this day.

The training of pilots on Hastings was, of course, the reason for our existence, and not traipsing around the skies on jollies, although I might have given that impression. Looking through my log book confirms that the away from it all trips took up only a small percentage of my flying time and over 90% was spent on the primary task of producing Hastings Captains and co-pilots. These ranged from eager young Pilot Officer co-pilots who had just been awarded their wings, through to Squadron Leaders and Wing Commanders about to take up appointments as Flight and Squadron commanders in the Transport world although, strange to say many without previous Transport flying experience. No doubt the situation existed in other commands also. The RAF, at two points, promoted the most promising officers each year, and then had the problem of finding suitable appointments for those moving to an executive flying post. I suppose the system worked well when virtually all bombers and fighters were single engined bi-planes up until the mid 1930s. We also had one or two older officers who had previously peaked as regards further promotion and the adage of "you cannot teach an old dog new tricks" took on a whole new meaning because some of those old dogs had not performed any tricks at all, in the flying sphere that is, for many, many years.

One Wing Commander who had been on quite a few Air Attache tours had not flown for over 16 years, and that had been on Spitfires during WWII! However, he seemed to have mastered the Hastings until coming into the final furlong with only a couple of fences to go. One of them was the final solo cross country detail, lasting for about five hours. With our proximity to the main runway, instructors and students alike, during ground time periods, often stood by the windows of the crewroom drinking coffee and watching the world go by. It was when the Wing Commander started his take off run that the can of worms was opened and a big shout went up when his Hastings was seen to swing violently to port and head towards the little copse surrounding the Officers' Mess and adjacent to the married quarters. Surely he would cut his power, we all thought, but no, he carried on and just missed the top of the Mess by feet. Having survived that, we assumed that he would call it a day and land immediately. Once again, it was not to be, with the Hastings continuing it's climb and disappearing into the distance. The take off itself had been delayed for one reason or another and, being a Friday afternoon, a drift towards the Mess bar for happy hour had set in. Another reason for a lessening of interest was that the estimated time of arrival of the Hastings back at base was after 6 pm. A few staff remained to form a welcome home party, or was it an inquisition by a few senior officers? All in the bar that night debated the wisdom of the planned flight continuing and reflected that until Monday morning we would be none the wiser, as the Wing Commander Captain always made off to the big city every weekend. In the event, we never saw him again. A letter written to the Station Commander, and received on the Monday morning, informed him that the Wing Commander had submitted his resignation from the Service. It was the nearest thing one could ever equate to falling on one's sword, or committing Hari Kari for that matter.

During my time on the OCU, I was to become the instructor to two Group Captains, and feared the worst on each occasion, it being a little difficult to point out errors to persons of such high rank on the intercom with all other crew members listening. I adopted the procedure of one to one de-briefings after landing, except in exceptional circumstances. It seemed to work out just as well as the usual yak, yak on other flights. One of the Group Captains was to take over RAF Colerne at noon on a certain day and asked (told) me to arrange a landing there at one minute past twelve on that particular day. He also said that he would prefer it (demanded) if it was kept secret so that he could get a feel for the station after his unusual arrival. I certainly told no one about it, but after calling up Colerne tower with about ten minutes to go before landing, I was bombarded with questions after requesting permission to join the circuit. Some of the questions with answers (in brackets) went along the following lines: Reason for the trip? (training). Would I be just doing a touch and go? (No a full stop). Would I need fuel? (No). Could you make it a touch and go in that case (no). Why not? No reply was given to that one, I just called down wind to land. I think someone in the Ops world at Thorney Island must have let the cat out of the bag after I had, for obvious reasons, indicated my intentions to land away at Colerne to their department just before take off. I don't think any harm was done to the new Station Commander's plans in the event, because he seemed quite pleased when he taxied in under the directions of two immaculately dressed marshallers in their white overalls using newly painted red bats. Another touch that pleased him was that the three Wing Commanders, in their No 1 uniforms, stood at the salute as we came to a slow halt.

From the time that a veto had been put on the use of Thorney Island for course night training, the Hastings fleet had been very lucky in always being allocated to Idris, in Libya, for our sessions which came up every three months. One big bonus from training in North Africa, particularly in the summer months, was that we had more night hours to play with than in the UK, and a full nights work could be accomplished well before midnight. The social life was also a little hectic and we often received invites to the permanent Officers' Mess to go over to their establishment and help out with their entertaining. This almost invariably meant chatting up young English ladies, who far outnumbered the bachelor RAF living in members by a large margin. These ladies came in two distinct groups. The first were the usual bevy of school teachers, sometimes jokingly referred to as Toolscreechers, who had thrown in their lot with the British military and found living in downtown Tripoli a little inhibiting to the extent that a night out with the RAF, 20 miles into the desert, was a good form of relaxation. The second group who, on average, seemed just a little more street wise, to use modern parlance, all worked for one oil company or another and became known, affectionately, as the "oily girls". Like their male counterparts, hundreds of miles out in the desert, they made quite a buck or two. To see some of the desert chaps living it up in Tripoli during their weeks leave was quite something. One or two had to sign IOUs with their favourite taxi driver at the airport before departing for their desert outpost yet again. Mention of Americans reminds me that they had an air base on the coast near Tripoli with the usual PX, a kind of mini department store, which held open house to the British military. I made only one visit, courtesy of a car ride there by an Idris movements officer, and suffered one of my very few cultural shocks during overseas service.

Chatting to an American couple in the store who had latched onto us after hearing our British accents, it transpired that although nearing the end of their tour, and due to return to the "Good old USA", neither of them had ever left the base, not even to Tripoli, a few miles to the West, saying that life on the base was just fine with everything that they could possibly need being on hand. I had already noted that US dollar bills was the norm in every other USA overseas Station. They might just as well have been on Mars and not on one of the ancient coastlines of the civilised world. There are always exceptions, of course, and one typical American who had ventured along the coast road towards Benghazi was getting a little worried about the state of his petrol supply when he spotted an Arab on his camel and, after pulling up alongside, said "Say, bud. You speak English, by any chance? I'm looking for a gas station hereabouts, any ideas"? The reply was, "Well, actually, I do old boy because I am English, I think you'll find one of sorts 10 miles on up the road". With that the camel rider, who was in fact an RAF officer from Idris who had gone native, rode slowly off into the setting sun, but not before as related by him in the bar later, noticing that the American's jaw had fallen open so far that his cigar fell out and hearing him mutter "God damn Limeys, trust them to get dressed up like that pretending to be Arabs".

RAF Idris was also very useful for daylight training details in addition to night flying, and any back log due to the unpredictable English weather was soon made up out there and even the odd 'one off' flight sometimes cropped up from nowhere. One of those which I well remember was the dropping of free fall parachutists from 12,000'. After they had all gone I thought that I would try out one of the Vampire flame out tricks, when safe landings could be made from up to 20 or 30 miles away, depending on altitude, with a closed throttle. Obviously, I would need some power on a four engined piston so I selected -6" of boosts, which was the usual setting just before the final slow cut for a normal landing. It worked out amazingly well, even if I say so myself. I positioned for the downwind leg at twice the normal height and by selecting undercarriage down and flap settings at various non-standard points the eventual slow cut was called at the correct speed and distance from the threshold. I received one or two ironic cheers from other crew members over the intercom and that was that.

I have already mentioned that the transit flying between the UK and North Africa was put to good use for student route training and to that end we occasionally built in an extra leg to cater for larger than normal course numbers by flying via Gibraltar with a night stop there before, or after, our Idris detachment. It was during one evening in Gib that one of our student Captains nearly went spare. It was the very highly respected John Slater, who served with No 617 (Dambuster) Squadron during WWII and, after becoming a pilot under the SEG scheme at RAF Syerston, had seen action again. A Canberra bomber pilot during the Suez campaign of 1956, he barely talked about his past, and was so highly regarded by the service that he was about to be promoted and put in charge of the prestigious Far East Air Force's Communication Squadron. What had really upset him was the fact that we had all been ordered out of the Officers' Mess bar, even before we had a drink, because a new ruling required all transit crews, to use a side mini bar and not the main one which was now for the exclusive use of permanent officers. He really simmered for the rest of the evening, talking about first and second class officers not being on in his book. When the crew transport arrived the next morning I thought that perhaps it was something that would have been forgotten about, but I have always been glad that it hadn't. I noted that John was missing but soon found him writing away in the Mess suggestions book which is, sooner or later, read by all Officers from the station commander downwards. It was very strong stuff indeed, and the word "apartheid" got more than one mention in the general gist of what on earth is the Royal Air Force coming to? It was some time before I re-visited Gibraltar, but the rule about who could, or couldn't, use the main bar had been rescinded and our welcome by resident officers could not have been better. One story still doing the rounds on that occasion was about one of the Hastings fleet's better known pilot who went under the names of "Dad Owen". It was during the time that the frontier with Spain was still open to all when he led a party of new boys to the Spanish town of La Linea. In no time at all they were approached by a Spanish male who said, "you all wanna see man fighta da bull"? To which "Dad" retorted in no uncertain terms, "In the Royal Air Force we fighta da bull all day and everyday", which seemed to baffle the local gent.

The social life at Thorney Island lacked nothing and in addition to the instructor pilots, we very often had Jeff Bashford from the Navigator world and also Ken Owen, the senior Flight Engineer, to join our runs ashore. The Bosham country club would always open up their bar for us for late afternoon sessions on the few days that we managed to complete our flying details early. Another favourite watering hole was the "Ship Inn" on the waters edge of Chichester Harbour, with it's magnificent views. However, the only place to be come midday on Saturdays was the "Crown Hotel", in the then smallish village of Emsworth, which attracted many regulars, not only from the RAF but also quite a few senior retired naval officers who seemed more than happy to mix with serving officers, even if they were from the RAF and, therefore, land crabs.

The landlord, who was somewhat older than his wife, was a happy go lucky type who fitted in well with the RAF. In fact he underlined the old saying that there is usually a grain of truth in most claims in that he boasted of having been in the former Royal Flying Corps before the RAF had been invented. It turned out that he had started his military career with the RFC on the very last day of it's existence before the RAF was formed on 1st April 1918. Another claim of his was that he had once played cricket for Middlesex. A local MCC member on his next visit to Lords established that he had indeed played for then but only in the second eleven. Ah well, it was all good clean fun! Not so funny was that the much younger wife of the landlord was a winter sports enthusiast and one winter managed to break one of her legs skiing in Switzerland. After being flown home in a special plane, she was laid up in bed for a number of weeks, the break being pretty serious. When I was ushered into her top of the hotel bedroom to pay my respects I was eventually proffered a pen and she asked me if I would like to add a few words to those already there on the leg plaster. Under the sole of her foot, and therefore out of her sight, to say that some of the best wishes written were both lewd and crude would be an understatement. After restraining myself to a get well soon message I said, "I suppose it's only our little gang who have seen them"?, to which she replied, "Oh no, I've shown them to my girlfriends as well". "And what did they say?", I countered. "One or two laughed and some giggled and said, 'your RAF friends no doubt', but none of them would tell me what has been written". Just as well, I mused, and let's hope the plaster is taken away by the medics after it comes off, which it was.

It was in the Crown saloon bar one Saturday morning that I was told not to be fatuous by our Station Commander, and lightening struck again during my very next tour in Singapore when I received the very same directive. In this first case, I had better start by saying, it was almost routine that a certain lady would appear and, after a couple of drinks sit on a side bench, buy a bottle of gin and then disappear. She never wore make up and invariably dressed in slacks with a duffle coat with baggy pockets into which the gin bottle fitted nicely. She had short straight hair which should complete the picture, but I must add that she seemed very pleased when one or other of us went over for a chat. It soon became known that she was the unmarried sister of an Air Chief Marshal who was, in fact, our C in C at that time. Her surname, which I will not mention, plus her address of Hayling Island, confirmed her identity. It was during my chat with her, one Saturday, when we all got a shock to our systems. In walked our Group Captain Station Commander, one of three I served under at Thorney, who said to all the others at the bar that he had heard quite a bit about what went on in "The Crown" on Saturday mornings and thought he would call in while his wife went shopping. I thought that I had better return to the bar counter, due to his arrival and mix with the rest. It did not take long before he came alongside and said, "Jacko, who is that lady you have just been consorting with, who I happen to know is not your wife"? "Oh, she's the C in C's sister, Sir", I said in a possibly off hand way, which is my want at times. However, it was not long, unsurprisingly, before the Station Commander, asked if I would care to make an introduction!

Other social occasions that have stuck in my mind over the years include one that got off to a rather shaky start. It was a special invite from no less a person than Black Rod himself, Marshal Sir Brian Horrocks, regarded by many as the finest British Army Commander of the twentieth century, who had proposed to our Station that he would like to host a conducted tour of the Houses of Parliament to a dozen or so officers and their ladies. It was something that I had always wanted to do, and could there have ever been a better way of doing it than being a guest of Black Rod? The bad start occurred after our party had assembled in that holy of holies, and Sir Brian had asked, "Which one of you gents is the Meteorology officer then"? Deadly silence followed, so Sir Brian quickly said "My main reason for inviting you was to show my sincere gratitude to the Met office at Thorney who, over the years, have provided such a first class service to me and my yachting friends each weekend before we set sail from Chichester harbour". I think that was the first that the RAF contingent, including the CO, had ever heard of this arrangement. The rest of the day was enjoyed by all with one of Sir Brian's observations, after leaving the stranger's gallery, rather telling. He said that now we had just seen MPs shouting insults at each other, we would go and see the 'Other Place", where it sometimes took up to a week before one peer suddenly realised that he had been insulted by another member! The remarks by some Lordships being so subtle for the most part.

That was unlike a remark made by our C in C's wife after HM the Queen had paid Thorney Island a visit. It was after one of our retreats from Idris, and yet another night flying detachment, that we were all met by the Station Commander to brief us on the impending visit that would take place later that week. It was on the grass outside our crew room that the CO briefed us, and we must have looked a motley crew after our seven hour flights, with some officers still in khaki drill and all of us in need of a bath. The bottom line was what he had already told all the other station Officers; best blue for all on the big day; hair cuts, ties properly knotted and SD hats tucked under the left arm when not being worn, which I happened to be doing as he spoke so I became an instant role model for a few seconds as he pointed me out. I thought one point the CO made was rather strange, which was that he had been informed from on high that the Buckingham Palace protocol department had noted the proposed itinerary and that afternoon tea was on the Officers' Mess lawn at the conclusion of the visit, and no one need take offence if Her Majesty did not partake of any proffered sandwiches because she did not eat a great deal at that time of day. By a remarkable chance, Betty and I, with one of her nieces who had been staying with us at the time, had been allocated seats on a row directly behind Her Majesty and couldn't help but notice that HM seemed to thoroughly enjoy the sandwiches. It was quite a night in the mess bar after what seemed to have been a faultless visit, but it did not last.

Our Station Commander was particularly proud of the bar because it had been restructured to his modish outlook on life. I must admit that it was probably the only Officers' Mess bar in the RAF that now had numerous false wooden beams under the original ceiling of the service area which protruded out above the bar stools. He made the fatal error of asking the wife of the C in C, who had obviously been on hand with her husband throughout the royal visit, if she would care to have a quick look at his bar before departing the station. The look on her face as she surveyed the scene was quite a picture and when she said "I suppose it might look all right after you take the scaffolding down" in a rather haughty voice. It stretched our self control to the limits. It must be pointed out that any wife of an Air Chief Marshal in the early 1960s, was more than likely to have married in the 1930s, which was before any Officers Mess bar ever existed, and ladies could only use one special room in the entire building on social visits. That room, known as the "Ladies room", still lives on, but is rarely used for it's original purpose nowadays.

On the flying side a welcome return to the Hastings fold was the ever popular "Bob" H---- of Christmas Island/ Royal Yacht fame. The officer who had been shipped off to the Thor missile programme on account of his BSc was back and his ground tour had lasted for three years before the concept was ditched in favour of the V bombers. The cost to the British taxpayer does not bear thinking about. The refresher training of Bob on Hastings was obviously -from his first trip- going to be a formality, but a respectable minimum number of flying hours would still have to be flown before his return to squadron service. That was the reason why we collected an hour building air experience flight at the request of the Royal Navy. We assumed that our passengers might well be hairy old Matelots, recently returned from waters deep and blue who would like to see their ship from the air. Our actual passengers certainly wanted to see Pompey from the air but they were, in fact, twenty or so young Wrens with an Officer Wren in charge.

Our local flying was a little restricted, particularly on sightseeing flights such as this, because of the RN gunnery school at Whale Island which had to be avoided like the plague. In fact on No 242 OCU's arrival from Dishforth, the RAF had put in a rather tentative inquiry about the possibility of moving it to some more remote location in the interests of safety. The junior service, not for the first time, got a right blast from the old sea dogs at Portsmouth along the lines of "didn't the boys in light blue realise that Nelson had trained there, and it would only be moved over their dead bodies". However, it was live bodies that caused a slight hickup on our flight. Bob was in the Captain's seat with myself in the Co-pilot's, which was the normal situation on instructional details, and we had already briefed our Air Loadmaster that when safely airborne he could bring the passengers, two at a time, up front so that they could see the crew in action and also have a better view by standing on a step between our two seats. All seemed to be going well except that Bob, looking across at me and, therefore, getting a side view of each Wren in turn, who was invariably bending forward to get a better view, commentated over the intercom on their attributes, for want of a better word. It was not long before our Loadmaster came running up front and, pulling one side of my helmet from my left ear shouted "Is everything all right Captain, I've given my helmet to the Wren officer so she can listen in, but she's gone red in the face and her eyes are bulging". My microphone was switched off so I shouted "Tell her it's her turn next and get her up here quick and hang on to your helmet for the rest of the flight when you get it back". The Wren officer duly arrived up front and looked to have recovered her composure, but declined Bob's wave onto the step. We both got quizzical looks and the balloon caption this time read, "I wonder which one of you two dirty old men talked about my girls like that"? After landing, they all gladly accepted coffee, without rum, in our crew room and the young girls obviously made for our co-pilots while our Squadron Commander, thankfully, hosted the Wren officer.

It was also at Thorney Island that our Hastings Engineer Officer, Paddy King, also fell foul of one member of the female race. His staff, having failed to cure a mag drop on one Hastings engine had admitted defeat and turned the job over to Paddy himself. His constant running of that engine behind the Ops Wing HQs block soon gave rise to complaints about engine noise, plus some snide remarks from interested aviators. It all became too much for Paddy, so he had the aircraft towed across the airfield to a point just behind some married quarters to continue his test runs there. It was after another failed run that he took a breather by leaning on the back garden fence of one quarter which, quite by chance, was occupied by one of our instructors. It was John Horrocks, who had married a young WAAF during the war when she had served as an engine mechanic and had, in fact, worked on Hercules engines. John's wife saw her main chance and walked down her path and said "By the way, Paddy, have you thought about changing the Mags"? He completely flipped, and his language could not possibly be repeated. Paddy flipped again some months later when one of us asked, "By the way, Paddy, had you thought about changing those Mags"?

I was to get a full week away from instructing after the OCU had been called upon to provide one Hastings aircraft and crew to take part in a mass support drop on Salisbury plain. This event turned out to be of some importance and would be watched by military VIPs from many countries and, to that end, more than one dummy run was called for. In fact it was to last for 10 days of practice runs before exercise "Saucy Sue" actually took place, but it was only on the dress rehearsal day that I was to take off, for the first time ever, with an underslung load of panniers- 24 in all, and what a shock it was with virtually all of Abingdon's 2,000' of runway being used before lift off. Formation keeping was also a problem with the throttles needing to be well forward with little left for station keeping. I never came across any written information about what to expect when carrying an external load in the pilot's notes for the Hastings, or anywhere else for that matter. I came across a flight engineer in later years who had been involved in the Suez war and had carried an underslung Army jeep on one drop out of Cyprus. The high power settings required, and the low speed attained in that configuration, led to the overheating of all four engines, but the shutting down of each engine in turn for short periods, which did not reduce the aircraft speed by all that much, saved the day. It was a great pity that the Hastings was built with a tail wheel, at the Army's insistence, just so that it could carry an underslung jeep in the first place. The Americans never fell for that one and back door ramps for loading and unloading or air dropping became the order of the day which was not possible on tail wheel aircraft, of course.

Early on in my time at Thorney I had been appointed to be the Hastings representative on the Station Flight Safety Committee, and told that I would need to attend the next safety course in London. I told my lords and masters that I had already been on the course in 1953, but the response to that was with it now being nearly ten years on I'd better do it again to bring myself up to date. That was just as well because things had changed somewhat over the years.

It was a greatly improved course and also, in a larger building which was just off Russell Square. Even the name of the organisation had changed from the old "Accident Prevention" to "Flight Safety". Many of the new concepts one could easily come to terms with, such as basic awareness, which is so vital to the safe operation of aircraft. Although a reasonable level of education had always been a pre-requisite for acceptance for RAF pilot training, it did not follow that such people would always be 'with it', either on the ground or in the air. During the course we had all been asked if there was anybody in the room who had come across a fellow aircrew member who was always the last to know about new concepts in handling technique, orders or even impending social events, every single hand went up. Statistics indicated that many such people had been involved in some unnecessary accidents and incidents.

Another factor highlighted was that although piloting all aircraft was only by physical manipulation, it was more of an art form rather than pure manual labour, and did not necessarily equate with high intellect. I think that the last point had been proved beyond doubt in the Battle of Britain. If you think too long about anything it might be too late when flying. Even before this last Flight Safety course I had two bees in my bonnet. The first was that although in civil aviation there was a thing called RVR which stood for Runway Visual Range, a distance measured in feet at ground level along the runway in use from it's threshold which, after falling below a certain figure, called for the closure of the airfield, or at least that particular runway, to all traffic. The RAF had not followed suit, perhaps because of the post war idiocy of the "flying to the limits" theory and also the "all weather flying" concept which had caused so many accidents and loss of life. Low visibilities on, and just above, ground level often indicated the onset of night fogs which tended to be low in depth with good visibility remaining on top of the thin layers and there lay the problem. A pilot might have picked up the runway lights on a straight in approach to land at up to 10 or 20 miles, but on the last few hundred feet flown into dazzling fog or mist as a result of reflections from his landing lights. Having suffered minor forms of this phenomenon myself over the years I had, after a more severe case at Thorney Island, verbally asked our Wing Commander Flying if it was time that RVR was introduced in the service. He had replied that he, personally, did not think it was necessary. I might just add that the Wing Commander in question had on a previous tour been an aircraft Captain on the Queen's Flight. I let the matter rest there but, six years later, after returning to the UK from Singapore and joining No 53 Squadron flying Belfast freighters, returned to the attack again.

On one particular night after a long route leg I was pleasantly surprised to find perfect weather over Southern England with almost unlimited visibility and elected for a straight in approach to land. Everything was going fine with the runway lights having been picked up with several miles to go, but in the last two hundred feet we had suddenly entered a thick fog bank and declared a go around. The wind had already been given as light and variable so a request to land from the opposite end was granted and achieved safely. The lack of warning from the tower was in no way the fault of the controllers because it was not apparent to them from their position when the insidious drift in of the fog to one end of the active runway only had first started. However, the automatic distance measuring devices, which are part and parcel of the minimum RVR concept would have alerted them to the problem if they had been fitted. This time I did not bother with any verbal observations but wrote a letter direct to the Flight Safety Headquarters in London. I received a very prompt reply thanking me for my observations but also stating that the matter was already under active consideration. Their letter, which I have retained to this day, was signed by a Wing Commander Ferguson in 1969. In 1983, when I finally retired from the RAF, RVR had still not been introduced.

The other bee in my bonnet had already been vetoed by the Chief of the CFS Examining Wing at Little Rissington. I had noted over the years that the RAF seemed to be suffering a large number of accidents and fatalities on twin and four engined aircraft during asymmetric flying in the approach to land and overshooting phases of flight. Some of these had been in real emergencies, but many others occurred during practice sessions when one engine had been deliberately shut down. It was only after my transfer from service to civilian flying in 1983 that I found out that deliberate shut downs were forbidden by the CAA on British registered civil aircraft below 3,000' AGL and 5,000' AGL by the FAA in the USA. However, the RAF continued the practise, shutting engines down completely although the CAA had come up with a very simple procedure which could simulate that situation exactly. The RAF also taught the concept that all visual circuits on asymmetric power should be flown as normal, that is to say the same height, shape and size. My theory was that there was not enough time left to make adjustments to height and or speed between completing the final turn onto finals and the decision height for a landing or go around. I proposed that all vertical circuits on asymmetric power, for real or practice, should be started at a higher height at the start of the downwind leg and on a bigger pattern which would give a higher completion of final turn height and therefore more time on finals to adjust speed and/or height. I also propounded that, if available, a pilot should request a Radar Approach (PAR) or ILS (Instrument Landing System) when he would be able to see (ILS) or be given (PAR) indications of height above or below the ideal 3° approach path and then he could concentrate on maintaining the correct speed. On that occasion I had put it all into writing and submitted it to the RAF's monthly flight safety magazine which was titled "Air Clues". It met with the Editor's full approval but, in the same magazine a month later, the CO of the CFS Exam Wing wrote to say it was just not on. All other transport pilots that I met thought my concept was a step forward and they would certainly carry it out if in anger but, in the meantime, they would still have to preach the laid down system of normal visual circuits come what may.

No 36 Squadron had, just three months before I joined them, suffered a tragic accident which might well have been prevented if my idea of higher and bigger circuits on asymmetric power had been carried out. It was tragic in more ways than one because the crew, returning from a Christmas Island detachment, had not seen their families for three long months and their final goodbyes before departing the UK also turned out to be their last. All five operating crew up front lost their lives after taking off from Khartoum on the penultimate leg of their way home. Luckily, the Loadmaster, who was plugged in to the intercom down in the rear, and all his twenty odd passengers, survived. The loadmaster had heard all the crew calls on his headset and could, therefore, give a full re-call of all that happened. Before going into detail, it must be pointed out that Khartoum was one of many hot and high airfields in Africa which, compared with the low and temperate UK ones, caused problems on two fronts. High temperatures and height will both increase the true speed of the aircraft compared with the indicated one and, on the nothing for nothing principle, require more power from the engines to sustain any given flight conditions. The loadmaster was able to report that after take off from Khartoum No 2 engine had failed and duly feathered. The Captain had then, quite rightly, jettisoned excess fuel, and positioned for a circuit and landing. Towards the end of the finals turn, juddering was felt, probably the onset of a stall, due to the Captain trying to arrest a high rate of descent, built up in the descending turn, but which the Captain took to be a failure of No 1 engine and duly feathered that one too, not having time to confirm the failure with the flight engineer. From that point on, being on only two engines and, with the undercarriage down and partial flap, a crash became a certainty. If only he had been higher; he could have turned a powered approach into a glide approach on finals and all might have survived although the old adage of "It's better to go off the end of a landing runway at 10 miles an hour than it is to crash into the undershoot area" may have pertained.

    Most of what I have written about asymmetric flying and it's danger is now just history in the jet age. Jet engines are far more reliable, powerful and, for the obvious reason of not having propellers to drive, positioned closer inboard, which lessens the impact of asymmetric flight. However, the biggest bonus of all in the context of asymmetric flight and training is that virtually all military and civil passenger carrying aircraft now have ground simulators in which practice emergency situations can be carried out until the cows come home. One of the very few RAF aircraft which is still in service with more than one engine and without a flight simulator, is the dear old Canberra. A book called "Lost to Service" by Colin Cummings, details the losses of RAF aircraft between 1959 and 1996. Of the 1100 or so write offs recorded, 84 Canberras are listed. In that rather high total, six were lost during asymmetric flight but only one after a real engine failure with the other five during practice asymmetric situations.

One other aerial adventure that I really enjoyed during my time on the OCU was by way of an RAF pilot who I had first met during his school days. He was the son of a Newark garage owner by the name of Hawkins, who I had made friends with during my first commissioned tour at RAF Syerston in 1951.

English Electric Canberra

He had a nice little story to tell with an aviation connection. It went back to pre-WWII days when the late Douglas Bader was a Cranwell cadet and also a keen motor cyclist who Mr Hawkins senior had helped out one night after an accident. For many years after the war, Douglas Bader would still pop into his garage whenever he was in the area and renew his thanks. A nice touch from such a distinguished fighter ace. The school boy son soon became a Canberra pilot after joining the RAF and, after a posting to RAF Tangmere on calibration duties, which was just a few miles from Thorney, he made contact with me with an offer of a trip in a Canberra. He brought it over to Thorney, which raised a few eyebrows on the day of the flight. The Canbera turned out to be a delightful aircraft to fly which made it a most memorable day.

In the crewroom on non-flying days somebody or other usually had a story to tell, true or otherwise, and one that I had first heard when a student at Dishforth was again trotted out by just about the oldest Pilot Instructor on staff. It was to the effect that although his marriage was childless, he and his wife had tried desperately hard to produce an offspring and had resorted to the military medical world for help. On reporting to the regional medical centre, a doctor, after a cursory examination, had produced a bottle and asked him to go to the gents and produce a specimen. Much later he returned and said he had failed. The doctor was then supposed to have said "Go back to the waiting room for the time being". Not long after that, a strapping blonde Army nurse entered and said "Would you kindly follow me, sir". End of story, which was followed by some embarrassed looks from the younger students, looks of disbelief from the older ones and the rolling of eyes from those that had heard it all before.

Another story that was definitely true, because it had been overheard by an earwigger, concerned our very Welsh "Taff" John, who had been instructing a young co-pilot and during a fast walk back from dispersal after the trip was asked by the poor lad, trying hard to keep up the pace, "How did I do, sir, how did I do"? Taff in his best sing song voice, had replied "How do you spell atrocious, boyho, is it one t or two ts". I got a bit of egg on my face in the Crown Hotel the next Saturday after relating the incident to a civilian friend of mine when he said, with a blank look on his face, "Well, how do you spell atrocious"? You cannot win them all.

My final night flying detachment was to Nicosia because Idris was to be host to a major bomber exercise for part of our required time. Not a great deal had changed except the Station Commander was now Group Captain "Micky" Martin of Dambuster fame. Stan Breckon was now back in England but we still had plenty of offers of transportation from some of our ex-students but, in any event, with the primary task on this occasion being night training, we were not likely to be going very far. It often seemed that, in the RAF at least, young rips often would end up on one particular squadron, and the resident Hastings Squadron, No 70, had their fair share. Andy Band, John Hope and Mike Sawbridge certainly formed quite a trio in that department, all Hastings co-pilots at that time. They had become known as "The band of Hope and Sawbridge". Although the Eoka troubles had faded in Cyprus, a curfew of 'after midnight' still prevailed in downtown Nicosia, and one of the happy band had transgressed in that he had been questioned by the RAF police outside a nightclub after the witching hour. After a report of the incident arrived, one of the trio eventually found himself stood to attention in front of "Micky" Martin. The usual proceedings started by the Station Commander saying "I have a report in front of me which states that you were seen coming out of a night club after midnight. What have you to say to that"? "That is not true, sir", replied the accused. The exchange was repeated twice more before the CO, in exasperation, barked, "Are we going to have to suffer the extreme embarrassment of having the Corporal who wrote the report brought here to swear on oath that he actually saw you, an officer, leaving a nightclub after midnight"? "No need for that, sir, I said I was not leaving that club, I was, in fact, still trying to get in", was the last piece of evidence given, but Micky Martin, being the man he was, said, "I was thinking of giving you one weeks orderly, officer, you've now got a month". Once again, being in lowish latitudes, our night flying was often over by about nine o'clock and then it was off to the Mess bar for a nightcap or two. Since our last visit, a new game had been invented by the young living in members which consisted of throwing beer cans, after the contents had been consumed of course, into the cooling fans above the bar. To start with I ducked and weaved whenever one was thrown until a chap I was talking to at the time said there was no need, nobody had been hit with a can so far. A minute later, another officer in the group was, in fact, clobbered and suffered a cut head. It was the R C Father who was not best pleased with life. Two others in the group were Flt Lt John Aiken and his charming wife who, sadly, was to be widowed within a year when John was the Captain of Hastings TG 577 which suffered an elevator failure when on a parachute drop out of Abingdon, with a total loss of life of 41.

Our departure from Nicosia to the UK was not without incident. All the student captains needed a night cross country to complete the course, and we could get two for the price of one by night stopping in Malta on the way back. The Squadron Commander, having come under the spell of Libya and having already ascertained that the major exercise at Idris was now over, decided to route his own aircraft back via that station instead of Malta. We were due to take off at 30 minute intervals with the boss going first with our crew in second place. It was normal on all courses to train mostly Pilots and Navigators because Flight Engineers and Air Signallers tended to stay put once they had joined a Squadron as not many RAF aircraft types now needed them. It was for that reason that on that trip I had a staff Flight Engineer and Air Signaller. After arriving at the aircraft from the flight planning room I was met by a very worried looking flight engineer who reported that we had a major problem. Mechanical, flashed through my mind, but he went on to say "I think the Air Signaller is the worse for drink". If only I had used that term when the duty Medical Officer arrived on the scene instead of "I think one member of my crew is drunk". I got the same answer that I had received from an MO 25 years previously at RAF Halton after stating that I was "suffering from a cold".

It was to the effect that patients gave symptoms and doctor's diagnosed the disease. On this occasion I said "OK doctor, but I don't think he'll be able to give you symptoms, or anything else, because he's slumped over his desk, but he does smell like a brewery? After a quick check, the MO said "I will certainly need to talk to your CO about this, where is he"? Just then there was a mighty roar as the CO's Hastings passed over our heads with it's navigation lights twinkling in the night sky en-route to Idris. The Flight Engineer shouted, "He's up there, sir, just setting course". The MO, unfamiliar with our operations, then said "When will he be landing back"? "He won't, sir, he's off to Idris and will soon be out of radio range". Luckily, one other Hastings due to depart that night was carrying an extra ciggy so we were soon on our way, as soon as the MO and his 'patient', had departed to the sick quarters in fact.

One last thought on RAF Nicosia concerned the three batchelor officers who were occupying an old civilian house, which was now within the confines of the camp. After repeated complaints by Ken Sneller, and his old mate Syd Evans of East Africa fame, plus Tony Weigh, who was to become a distinguished Britannia Captain later, about the food in the Officers' Mess, the catering officer, in desperation, said one night in the bar "I think the best thing that I can do is to get my staff to deliver weekly rations for three officers to your billet and let you get on with the cooking yourselves, and see how that works out". I don't know if his staff got their sums right, but it worked out just fine. More food than they knew what to do with, and one of that trio being an excellent cook it became the 'in place' to be invited to. I have often wondered exactly how long that system lasted.

Back in the UK, I was lucky enough to be given a one off trip of some importance. It was to pick up a group of senior Transport Command Officers at RAF Lyneham and fly them up to the Avro works at Woodford to discuss the progress of work on the RAF's new Avro Andover transport aircraft. This turned out to be one of the few such flights that went like clockwork, even if I say it myself. Another bonus was that a Sqdn Ldr Morris, who I had met on a few previous occasions, was a member of the party. He was the officer at Upavon who held our destiny, in terms of future postings, in his hands. During a coffee break at Woodford he said "I expect Tommy Glover has told you all about his time as the Embassy Pilot in Washington?" I concurred and said he certainly seemed to enjoy it. He then went on to say Tommy's replacement would be tour-ex in a few months time and was I interested in taking on that job. You bet I was, and it seemed for the next couple of months or so that Betty and I would be on our way to the USA. It was on a social visit to Thorney Island at the invitation of Tommy Glover that Sqdn Ldr Morris broke the news that my Washington posting was off and, instead, I would be going out to Singapore to take up the Wing Pilot post. He did let me into a little secret and that was the Embassy Pilot would, in future, also have to act as an ADC to the air attache and, therefore, be a bachelor, youngish, blue eyed, blond, slender and 6' tall! I only qualified for the last attribute. He also let slip that whoever took on that position might not be there for a full tour in any case. The Heron Aircraft was in fact withdrawn within a year, so it was just as well that I was eastbound again.

We were given about two months notice of our departure to Singapore, during which time I managed to impress the Transport Command examining unit enough to be awarded an "A" category certificate, much to my surprise, I must admit. Just as Betty and I had made all our arrangements for our departure for Singapore, including the selling of our much loved Zephyr car, HQ in the Far Eastern Air Force wished it to be confirmed that Flt Lt Jackson had completed a "Flight Safety Course" as the Hastings Wing pilot position carried with it the secondary duty of Station Flight Safety Officer. It was with relief that I reported that I had completed two in fact. A couple of days later HQ FEAR asked for dates of these two courses. With one having been completed within the last three years I thought that would be it. However, a signal soon arrived stating that three years was too far in the past, and I was to attend another, and my posting was to be delayed by two weeks to accommodate the requirement. With one week left before the course, and no car, I was in a state of limbo having signed off with my last students. However, a ferry flight to deliver one of our aircraft to No 70 Squadron, in Nicosia, was offered and gladly taken. To ensure a rapid passenger return to the UK via a RAF Britannia flight, it was essential to land in Nicosia soon after morning open hours, so an eleven pm take off time was planned. With it being the one and only movement that night, I had to field no end of questions as to why I could not go much earlier, or even the next morning, but time was of the essence to meet the deadline for the Flight safety Course. The flight out went off quite well but is best remembered as my last on No 242 OCU and for the fact that I was back at Thorney Island, after a return landing at RAF Lyneham within 36 hours.

My third, and last, Flight Safety Course turned out to be by far the best with many new innovations having been introduced. Two stick in my mind to this day, with the first being a visit to an operational RAF station to look at things from the outside, so to speak. That visit got off to an unusual start when, dressed in No. one uniform, a rare sight in post war London, I was walking down a platform at Kings Cross station to board a train for Huntingdon and then on by service transport to RAF Wyton when passengers who had just arrived on an incoming train thronged the gangways, but in the distance I spotted two six foot something policemen walking a yard or so apart towards me. It flashed through my mind that it was most likely that they were escorting some villain or other and that, whoever it was, would be handcuffed to one or other of his escorts. The villain in question turned out to be about half the size of the coppers and far from being cuffed, he managed to take his pipe out of his mouth and give a steady stare at my uniform with a questioning look. It was in fact, the Prime Minister of the day, Harold Wilson.

The visit itself went off very well indeed and only one aspect of it left a big question mark in my mind. Having many friends in civil aviation, I knew full well that secondary radar, which could identify any one particular aircraft that was suitably equipped, had well and truly arrived. However, it was not as yet in use in any RAF control tower. The Senior Air Traffic Controller told me that there was just not enough numbers to go around for the RAF to be included in the UK area of operations. The numbering system for secondary radar consisted of setting four digit numbers which could be dialled from zero to seven so any number between 0000 and 7777 could be used. Even allowing for the fact that the first two numbers indicated a ground station, it still left plenty of scope to include some RAF airfields. This has proved to be true since those early days.

CHAPTER 5
Wing Examiner- RAF Changi, Singapore

At long last, Betty and I were off to Singapore, passengers on a "British Eagle" trooping flight aboard a Britannia aircraft. It was a long tiring flight lasting about 29 hours, that included two refuelling stops at Istanbul and Bombay. With three abreast, rearward facing seats we wondered who would occupy the third seat. It turned out to be the teenage son of an Army Officer who was somewhat disabled. He spoke only twice during the trip, the first time being to demand the window seat which Betty was already sitting in at the direction of a Stewardess. This suited Betty just fine because she had recently damaged her back trying to push a car that was blocking our garage door at Thorney Island. That the car belonged to an RAF Medical Officer who lived next door was a bit ironic! However, sitting next to the centre isle did allow her to stretch her legs and make unnecessary walks to the loo quite often without disturbing the young lad and myself.

The first leg, which we just managed in daylight was quite delightful and mainly over land, unlike RAF Transport Command Mediterranean flights, which took the sea route after Southern France for eastbound flights. After take off from Istanbul we got the usual "This is your Captain speaking" spiel. On this leg it was a Captain Jones, to be precise. I can well imagine readers wondering how come I can recall it was a Captain Jones thirty odd years later. Well, it was all to do with the teenage lad occupying one of our three seats and it is a little story I have often repeated over the years. That lad had not uttered a single word during the ten plus hours between Turkey and India. The landing at Bombay was horrific, the worst that I have ever experienced, and I felt sure that the undercarriage would collapse. There were plenty of shrieks from the other passengers, but all the young lad did was look up at the cabin roof where the "This is your Captain speaking..." messages came from and shouted "Captain Bloody Jones, uhh!" I told Betty after disembarking that we might well be stuck in Bombay for the night while the undercarriage was inspected however the flight continued on time. I certainly kept my fingers crossed during our landing in Singapore. A nice touch about our Singapore arrival was that the officer I was to succeed in the post of Hastings Wing Pilot, Flt Lt Douggie Butler, who I had served with at both Dishforth and Thorney Island, was there to meet us and transport Betty and I to a hotel called the "Dragon Inn", situated on the east coast on top of one of the very few areas of high ground on the island and overlooking the sea.

During our three years at Thorney Island we had met many couples who had completed an accompanied tour in Singapore, so we knew pretty well what to expect about life out there for Europeans. One point that always got a mention was that a guard dog was essential if you lived in a married quarter, or a private house off base, and the saddest part of returning to the UK was leaving these loyal animals behind due to the difficulties of transportation, plus the prospect of six month quarantine for the few that were brought back. Many owners did pass on their animals to families taking over their accommodation but, alas, one of the most upsetting sights on the island was the odd half starved stray roaming the streets. I think it was that factor more than anything else that influenced our decision to spend our entire tour in the "Dragon Inn", along with one or two other childless couples. Some families did have their old faithfuls put down rather than wonder for the next few years about their fate. Long after returning to England I came across an RAF couple who after completing a tour in Germany had decided to have their cat put down out there rather than have it in quarantine for six months. When they approached a German vet with their request he replied, "Certainly, so long as one of you holds the cat down while I inject it". The cat was duly brought back to the UK and lived to a ripe old age.

If any recommendation for the Dragon Inn was needed, the fact that for one couple it was their second tour in Singapore and also their second in the hotel was proof enough. The wife in question had first arrived on the Island as an RAF nurse, a member of the Princess Mary's Nursing Service and known to all others in the RAF as the PMs, a fine dedicated part of the RAF medical world. This particular couple were full of stories about their first tour in the east, with some graphic details of life as lived by the locals. Although I myself had been based in Singapore for a few short months after the Japanese surrender I might just as well have lived in a monastery such was the confines of being based on an RAF station in the uncertain period of late 1945. We had seen most of the island, but almost invariably in groups of two or more with little contact with the local Malays or Chinese. One of this lady's best stories was that on seeing an aged gentleman sitting upright in a big wooden chair outside a shop and looking very pale, she had decided to check his pulse. A near riot immediately broke out with many of the onlookers going into orbit. It was explained later that it was a mark of respect by the Chinese to place a dead gentleman outside his last place of business before burial!

Living off base, Betty and I soon came to terms with other facets of the local way of life. The first was again to do with death. During the funeral march the coffin is preceded by local bands, the number indicating the status of the deceased. When the time came for a multi millionaire Chinese businessman, who lived in a vast mansion next to the Dragon, to go and meet his ancestors, it was a massive occasion with about seven bands leading the way. Many of the tunes played that day were not unfamiliar to western ears, and I well remember "Marching to Georgia" and "Polly Wolly Doodle" being played with gusto. One vast difference to our way of life was that due to the Chinese view that 13 is a lucky number, their dinner parties invariably included 13 dishes on the menu. I can recall that at one such event I was beginning to wilt a little at about the halfway stage when another massive dish of something or other was placed in front of me and I was foolish enough to ask what it consisted of "Oh, it is one of our real delicacies" was the hostess's reply, "it's monkey brains". Coming from the north of England I'd heard about sheep's brains being something of a treat for the menfolk, but monkey's! One taboo during dinner is not to accept a tit bit offered by the hostess via her well used chop sticks. It indicated that you were greatly favoured. Just as well it was not from the host, often crossed my mind on such occasions. Another taboo that I learnt about the hard way was that a finger must never be pointed at another person, intentionally or otherwise. In my case, it was completely unintentional when a locally employed Chinese worker came into our office one morning to carry out electrical repairs and it was when trying to point to an offending light switch that my finger happened to sweep across his standing position. He went spare, and I've not got the slightest doubt that my parentage was questioned in his rapid fire harangue.

Having been employed continuously since the end of WWII on what I considered to be duties of productive nature, that is to say flying for a purpose- be it the training of other pilots, navigators, air traffic controllers, towing targets for ground and air to air gun firing plus one front line Transport tour I was less than happy to be passing judgement on others in my new capacity of Wing Pilot which, in the main, was testing the ability of other pilots. There are, of course, many occasions when people do not give of their best when under scrutiny, and driving and flying tests must be near the top of the list in that department. The other side of the coin is that the odd person in any walk of life can give the impression that their knowledge and know how is far in excess of what it actually is. One indisputable fact, however, is that ability will normally go hand in hand with experience and in the piloting world that will be total flying hours in general and hours on type of aircraft in particular. The testing of qualified pilots on type comes under three distinct headings. Instrument flying, general handling and route checks, which had a lot to do with crew co-ordination, particularly with the Navigator and Flight Engineer.

Unlike the UK, the route flying in the Far East was somewhat restricted with the Indonesian confrontation with Malaya ruling out virtually all flying to the south of Singapore which left only three main trunk routes; these being to Borneo to support the Army, to Hong Kong- a Station that did not have a fixed wing transport force-, plus the very occasional flight to the staging post of Gan in the middle of the Indian Ocean. The RAF, quite rightly, did not allow flights into Hong Kong by any pilot until he had been checked out by another pilot who was experienced with that rather difficult airfield. It was, therefore, that my first flight out of Singapore on this new posting was to that destination under supervision, and it was quite an eye opener. The approach to Hong Kong's one runway from the sea was a bit of a non-event but from the landward end it could be quite tricky. The start of that approach was fairly straight forward, starting from the sea again, and homing in on a beacon located on Green Island, but from then on in it was all go, heading towards a rock face called the Chequered Board which, literally, had chequered paint work emblazoned on it's rock face. One had then to hold one's nerve and give a fierce right handed turn of 90° on to the runway heading at the last minute. The pulling required on the control column was probably more than that required for today's jumbo jets. If the wind was behaving itself things would go smoothly from then on in, except that one was flying just above roof top height for the last half mile or so. This has passed into aviation history with the opening of the new airport. The Chinese government would not allow any British Military aircraft to divert into their territory, which meant that in the event of adverse weather, or runway blockage, RAF aircraft would have to make the long haul back to the Philippines should any such situation arise. To cater for that possible contingency, extra fuel was called for. If the extra fuel had been loaded in Singapore the number of passengers and/or freight would have been downgraded out of sight, so a refuelling stop at Saigon north bound was built in to the schedule. The Vietnam war was in full swing by 1964 so we never lingered and about 30 minute turn rounds became the norm. The general briefing was to the effect that we should arrive overhead Saigon at, or above, 7,000' and spiral down to be out of range of ground rifle and machine gun fire. After take off a rapid climb to above 7,000' was the order of the day for the same reason. Towards the end of my time in Singapore, the war was not going at all well for the Americans and with all Vietnamese, like the Chinese, looking alike to untrained Western eyes, they could discard their uniforms and turn up virtually anywhere, and often well behind the supposed front line. On one occasion I had to forget the 7,000' overhead rule due to weather and take a radar approach to land. I was passing 1,500', which equates to 5 miles to run, when the laconic voice of the American controller advised me to ignore the B57s ground strafing below me, "they are just dealing with a few Viet Cong". The B57 was the British Canberra bomber built under licence in the USA. Quite an accolade for our aircraft industry.

Apart from two months that the Hastings fleet was grounded after the Abingdon disaster, I must have averaged over two trips per month into Hong Kong via Saigon, and there was never a stop when we did not fail to see body bags being loaded onto American transport aircraft bound for the USA. It being their policy to have, whenever possible, all their war dead buried in the States. A very sad sight indeed, which so upset Betty on the two trips that she made to Hong Kong via Saigon.

One big surprise of our working life at RAF Changi was that a pre-war tradition of working until mid day on Saturdays, to make up for Wednesday afternoon sports, was still in force. Anybody who played sports other than golf and swimming in the tropics needed their heads examined. Luckily, it was phased out about six months after our arrival, but how on earth it had lasted for years after it was long gone in the UK beggared belief. After it was finally abolished in FEAF having both Saturdays and Sundays off duty when not on route was a real boost to families and serving personnel alike.

With the Borneo campaign in full swing I took an early opportunity to take a few days off from testing and go on a detachment to Kuching to make a few air drops of supplies in anger. The British had become one of the few nations to win a jungle war when they defeated the Chinese communist uprising in Malaya during the late forties and fifties. They had learnt the hard way that the key to success was to build strong points at key strategic locations and resupply them by air drops if required. In Borneo, of course, the enemy was operating from it's own territory, but the concept learnt in Malaya was even more effective because the only way of advance, such was the density of the rain forest, was along river beds and the building of makeshift forts on stilts near the border on each river proved to be highly effective.

The supply drops were by way of small parachutes with many distinctive colours indicating the type of load such as ammo, medical, food and even alcohol. Immediately after a drop the fort would radio back to the Army HQs in Kuching to indicate the success, or otherwise, of the drop. Reporting, for example, that it was a red or blue parachute that had drifted off into the jungle and was not retrievable without undue risk. The colour for ammo or food would call for immediate action but it eventually dawned on the powers that be that it was the parachute with a colour indicating alcohol that more often than not went missing! After a great deal of thought by the Army they came up with the obvious answer. The packers would change the colour scheme at random intervals. The number of supposedly non-recoverable chutes dropped dramatically!

On one of our sorties during my short stay in Kuching we caught sight of an Indonesian Mustang fighter patrolling our area just on the other side of the frontier. This was a fairly familiar sight and for that very reason, all dropping flights had an escort of either a Javelin or Hunter fighter on detachment from RAF Tengah. Although this escort always deterred the Indonesian Air Force, it did not stop their Army from taking pot shots at supply dropping aircraft, with two Hastings aircraft being hit. In one incident a bullet lodged in the Flight Engineer's throttle quadrant just as he was making a power adjustment. The second incident had a lighter side to what could have so easily been a fatality. Quite a few navigators took a breather when they had successfully directed their aircraft to the dropping zone and went down to the back of the aircraft to watch the dispatchers at work as the aircraft went around and around on numerous dropping runs over the drop zone. It was just at the point of picking up his coffee while siting on the sideways facing bench seats that a bullet fired from just over the border entered the aircraft and took away his coffee carton. What a near miss that was. However, when I met him back in England, after the terms of who could, or could not, claim the general service medal for the confrontation period had been promulgated, he seemed very angry about missing out on the medal by one day's service in Borneo.

The British government had become so fed up of incursions by Indonesian troops from over their border in Borneo that they gave permission for British troops to reciprocate, but within strict limits as regards distance. It was after an incident of yet another firing on one of our aircraft from across the frontier that a Gurkha patrol was sent out later that evening and returned at dawn with one of the troop carrying a sack over his shoulder from which he removed two severed heads. He announced "two of those who shot at our dropping aircraft yesterday".

Anybody who had worked alongside the Gurkhas for any length of time became accustomed to their way of life and held them in the highest esteem. However, for those not in the know, there were one or two pitfalls, not least of all as regards their personal weapons. It so happened that a newly arrived Hastings Captain in Singapore found himself flying a full load of Gurkha troops to Borneo and after reaching the top of the climb took a wander down to the rear toilets. Having noted a rifle impeding his progress down the centre aisle, instead of waking the soldier who it belonged to, he made the error of trying to pick it up to reposition it. Next minute the Captain was flat on his back looking up at an angry Gurkha who now held his Kukri far too close to his throat for comfort.

One pleasing aspect of my short stay in Kuching was finding that one seat at the end of the Officers' Mess bar was occupied each evening by the one and only Ginger Lacey, who preferred the name James, last seen in Japan twenty years previously, and now downgraded to Flt Lt and in the Air Traffic Control world. It has always irritated me a little that so few of the WWII heroes moved up the promotion ladder with the exception of fighter ace Johnnie Johnson (AVM) and Dambuster Micky Martin who made Group Captain. Was it a version of "Tommy this and Tommy that, when the bugle sounds?"

The social life could not have been better with the Officers' Mess bar and the Officers' Club, jutting out into Changi Creek, just one mile apart. The very spacious bar in the Mess had three sides to it and usually all Hastings crews, which came from No 48 Squadron and FECS (Far East Communications Squadron) took up position on the verandah side, Argosy crews of No 215 Squadron opposite to them and the long stretch between those two by Shackleton crews of no 205 Squadron. The Shackleton crews needed the long stretch of the bar, not only because of the size of each crew, but also during the confrontation period, detachments came out from the UK with their own aircraft and all lived in Mess during their three month stay. The New Zealanders, of No 41 Sqdn Bristol Freighters, plus the few pilots from the Meteor towing flight seemed more than happy to mix wherever and whenever with all and sundry. This also applied to the Medics, Equippers, Educators and Admin wallahs which made for a very happy mix, unlike some messes in the UK where a rather parochial outlook on life pertained at times. Above and beyond those already mentioned, we had three nursing sisters belonging to SSAFFA (Sailors, Soldiers and Air Force Families Association) who lived in quarters along with the WRAF officers plus numerous lady school teachers who had a free run of the Mess, although all lived in private houses off base.

Betty and I made particular friends of the three nurses and happily all three met men of their dreams during their tours. Morag married the very likeable Fred Barnes, an engineering officer, Gretta a young Shackleton pilot known to all as Yogi and the third, Mo, married the officer who had offered to carry my bags when I had first met him behind the Mess at RAF Colerne on my arrival back from Ghana. It was Paul Jenner, who had nearly made a mess of things by not popping the question before Mo had finished her tour and returned to the UK. When the penny finally dropped, a few days after her departure, he made a frantic phone call one Saturday morning but completely forgot the time difference and although he got a 'yes', he also got an earful about waking people up in the middle of the night. In due course I had the privilege of giving the bride away at RAF Changi followed by a never to be forgotten party.

One true story about Paul Jenner and his tour in Singapore concerned his massive American car which he had acquired on arrival. Outside the Temple Hill Mess was a side by side parking area which stretched along its full frontage with the usual kerb type restraining ridge which was essential in that particular area because the ground fell away fairly steeply beyond it towards the female officers sleeping accommodation. To cater for the two monsoon periods each year in particular, ample drainage was essential, so gaps in the kerb had been deliberately left along its length. Paul had not noticed that the front of his car was parked exactly in front of one such gap as he made his usual fast entry into the bar one Sunday lunchtime. Some time later he decided to motor down to the officers club for a few more but was startled to find that his car had gone missing. Seeing a native cleaner using his twig like device in front of the Mess, he asked him if he had seen anyone near his car to which he got the strange reply of "It's run away master". "Run away", queried Paul, "Who's run away with it?" "Run away all by itself master". This was just too much for Paul, but he meekly followed the sweeper who led him towards the edge of the dip and with a slight smirk on his face pointed down the gully at Paul's car now lodged firmly against the ladies quarters. I heard the story being retold many years later with the usual bit added on. It now finished with, when Paul was checking his car for damage a lady Officer, still in her shreddies, popped out of her room and said "You are not supposed to park here, you know".

There were two WRAF officers that we also made particular friends with. Jeannie Oaks, a full time career admin officer who later retired to her native Derby and married a wartime RAF aircrew member who had carried out bomber operations from India in his time. We still meet them at annual Aircrew Association dinners and it is always pleasant to talk about one tour that will always stick in anyone's mind who was lucky enough to serve in Singapore post war. The other lady Officer was Ann Reeve, an education officer and daughter of a retired RAF Wing Commander engineer. She also met her future husband at Changi. He was Mike Speed, serving on No 205 sqdn on Shackletons as a Navigator, who went on to make his mark in the RAF, always being just one step behind his elder brother, also a navigator. I think it finished with Mike a Group Captain and his brother Air Commodore.

The final romance that always comes to mind when thinking about Singapore concerned a very popular officer from the Equipment Branch, who was on an Air Movements tour at the Air Terminal, so we saw a lot of Mike Brown, both on and off duty: being one of the regular bar attenders. Mike's career had started with the Hong Kong Police soon after leaving a top public school. Some of his stories about vice raids we did not altogether believe at the time, but in this more liberated age most have now been recorded in print. After joining the RAF, Mike-who enjoyed the nickname of "Bad News Brown"- had first become an RAF Regiment Officer, gaining his parachute wings in the process. He met his match just as Betty and I were leaving the Far East when a new "Malcolm Club" lady arrived in the Mess and swept "Bad News" off his feet. Yvonne was also a world traveller, having worked in Canada, the West Indies and also the Gulf before Changi. An ideal match if ever there was one. Both full of fun and vigour, and a couple we always look forward to meeting all these years on.

For one reason or another, both No 48 Squadron and FECS sometimes ran out of Pilots for their allocated tasks and quite often Paddy Irish, now the other Hastings Wing Pilot and myself would be asked if we would care to fill a gap. We both accepted with alacrity at any time. Life would have been quite dreadful if we had spent two and a half years just watching other pilots perform. I must say that it was not only the bread and butter day returns to Labuan and Kuching that came our way, they also offered one or two to Hong Kong and Bangkok. The latter was a much sought after trip, it being just far enough from Singapore to warrant a night stop. We always stayed in the same hotel, The Crown, in which RAF crews always seemed particularly welcome. The city itself fully lived up to expectations and there was only one local custom that no one could ever get used to; that was that the ever smiling barmaids thought there was nothing amiss in cleaning out their nostrils with their fingers whilst still smiling sweetly at customers. I suppose the tourist authorities will have sorted that one out by now. It never did put us completely off our beer, so I suppose it could be put down as a minor irritation if you can pardon the pun. For some strange reason Bangkok's airport was a 30 minute drive from the city although from the air the vast flatlands in that area suggested that it could have been built much closer. However, the drive itself was always entertaining enough, passing many bullock carts en-route with all drivers appearing to be fast asleep. Perhaps the bullocks knew the route better than their keepers! One treat for train buffs like myself was seeing ancient steam trains puffing along on the rails alongside the road. One thing that might have sent present day conservationists into orbit was that instead of using very scarce coal they used teak!

One aspect of arriving and departing the international airport was the shear efficiency of the RAF's appointed ground handling agent. He was a local Thai who operated from a small room in the terminal building who listened in to the Airport's operating radio frequency and never missed a trick. Fuel, catering, transportation to the city and back was always spot on and considering that he was also the agent for one or two international airlines also that was quite an achievement. The RAF in Singapore needed about eight people per shift to get the same results, and even then, things did not always go according to plan. I well remember having to intervene one day when a French Air Force crew had been awaiting transport outside our operations block for over an hour in the midday sun. All the RAF staff on duty were behind their desks in air conditioned accommodation without the whit to go outside to see off their downtown departure. After calling MT and giving them a blast I stood talking to the crew until the arrival of their crew coach. After profuse apologies on my part, their high ranking chief just gave a massive gallic shrug of the shoulders and shook my hand with a knowing look. I took it that such cock ups were not completely unknown in the French Air Force either.

I have often wondered if one day in Thailand I had become a Queen's Messenger or not. Our destination on that occasion was a rare trip to Chiang Mai in the extreme north of the country and on arrival at Bangkok from Singapore our man there stated that he had received a message from the British Embassy to the effect that a male member of their staff would be at the airport the next morning to see us off. It left us all wondering what on earth it could be all about, but he duly arrived as planned and turned out to be a British gent with a Military background who was now chief of security at the Embassy. After a great deal of palaver about proof of identity, he gave me a parcel which he said must never leave my sight until handing it to the Chief British Consul agent in Chiang Mai, who he named, and no one else under any circumstance. He went on to say I would be regarded as a Queen's Messenger if challenged. After our arrival in that town a British agent was certainly there to meet us but not the named person. He was full of apologies and said that their chief had gone up country on urgent business but if our crew transport, a couple of taxis in fact, could follow him to the diplomatic residence, members of staff would vouch for his credentials. It all seemed fairly straight forward enough and duly took place.

That evening on the balcony of my hotel bedroom, which happened to be facing north, I had a most magnificent view of the Burmese mountains on my left, which swept round into the country of Laos, enclosing land which later earned the title of "The Golden Triangle" that then supplied a large proportion of the illegal drugs coming into general use. One thing that bugged me that evening as I took in the spectacular scene was "Where on earth was 'up country", that the diplomat had taken off to in this part of the world? Our maps indicated that the railway terminated at Chiang Mai and the road network at the one and only settlement to the north, just short of the massive mountain range beyond. Otherwise, however, it was the most relaxing place that I ever night stopped at in my transport flying days.

When not actually flying I was kept busy on the ground in my capacity of Station Flight Safety Officer, and with seven different types of aircraft based there; Argosy, Andover, Bristol freighter, Hastings, Meteor, Valetta and Shackleton, plus regular scheduled flights of Comets and Britannias of Transport Command's strategic fleet meant It might well have been even more hectic. Other frequent visitors included aircraft from Royal Navy Aircraft Carriers when their ships were not out on patrol. The only problem arising out of their visitations was that they invariably landed their aircraft as if on a carrier, which was on the same spot each time with the usual thud. That of course, did not do our runway any good at all, often calling for urgent repairs causing disruption to the flying programmes. About every few weeks or so we also hosted a big four engined American built freighter aircraft operated by "Ace Freighters" out of Coventry. On one occasion their style of operating nearly caused the die-hards of Transport Command to go into fits of apoplexy. It had always been taught from the early days of the Command that if an engine was lost in flight, a diversion to the nearest airfield with a runway long enough to take that type was to be made. On the occasion that caused rather more than the proverbial "raised eyebrows", an "Ace Freighter" aircraft was seen after its take off from Changi on its return to the UK to be streaming smoke from it's No 4 engine, followed by a shutdown of that engine. Having witnessed the incident myself from the Ops balcony I, with others, thought we would hang around to see what the Captain made of his asymmetric approach and landing. When the aircraft started to disappear into the distance I made for the nearest phone to contact the tower to find out just what was going on. The SATCO himself told me that they were on full alert with all fire engines at the ready, but the Captain had reported that he intended to continue back to the UK, just using No 4 engine for takeoffs and initial climbs. It was certainly a talking point in the Flight Safety world for many a day.

One chore that I was not averse to was the writing of light hearted articles for FEAF's Flight Safety magazine. Being a fairly regular visitor to the Officers' Mess bar, I often picked up snippets of information about unreported incidents, or non standard operating procedures, sometimes freely given after tongues had been loosened by the demon drink, on other occasions by careless talk. Whichever, I thought that if it might only lead to greater flight safety awareness it should be put into print in a casual sort of way, with no mention of names or units. I think it must have struck home at times because in the following issues I sometimes got a good telling off and twice it was not from the unit I had in mind, which gave food for thought indeed.

I have already recorded that at Thorney island I was once pulled up for being facetious and that lightning would strike again, the second time on this tour at Changi. I had better start by saying that in addition to two Wing Pilots for Hastings, we also had on strength of Ops Wing another two for the Argosy fleet. One of these was an officer by the name of Sqdn Ldr Simon Dalton-Morris, who was a most likeable and well respected officer who I got on with particularly well, although he was somewhat reserved by RAF aircrew standards. He confided to me one day that his wife, an absolute charmer by any standards, was the daughter of a serving Air Marshal, but neither wanted to bandy that around for obvious reasons. Simon had managed to acquire a married quarter but it was on the Toh estate, which was definitely at the lowest end of the pecking order and normally reserved for Flt Lts and below. Wives of some senior officers tended to look down their noses at the mere mention of it. Simon, like Paddy Irish and myself, operated from office accommodation at the back of the Ops block up on the first floor, and it must have been the only non-air conditioned area in the entire flying wing so unless we were actually writing reports or answering the telephone we tended to conduct oral business out on the verandah to try and catch any wind that might be blowing. It was when talking to Sqdn Ldr Amos, my immediate boss, that our Ops Wing Commander, Graham Ibbotson, came walking round the corner looking very much as if he had something on his mind. He was obviously only addressing Sqdn Ldr Amos when he started by saying, "HQ FEAF have been on the phone and asked if we knew anything about a proposed unofficial visit by the AOC of Aden Command, an Air Marshal Sir David Lee, and, if so, what type of accommodation had we in mind". The Wing Co and Sqdn Ldr soon ruled out the Officers' Mess as unthinkable for an officer of such high rank, but what other options were there occupied their thoughts for the next couple of minutes until I said "Toh estate?" It was the only time that I heard Wing Co Ibbotson sound a little ratty when he replied "This is no time to be facetious, Jacko, this is a serious matter", to which I replied "Sorry sir, I didn't mean to be, I understood he was staying with his daughter". That really opened the flood gates. An Air Marshals daughter living on Toh estate! Who was she married to? How come nobody knew about it? Which Squadron was he on? To which I replied, "Your Wing, Sir, in fact". "Good God, who to?" I just nodded to the Argosy Wing pilots office and said "Simon". Luckily, Simon was away on a route check but Sqdn Ldr "Crash" Amos asked me as the W/C stalked off, "It wasn't one of your little jokes by any chance Jacko?" To which I sheepishly replied, "Not this time, I'm afraid".

Our Sqdn Ldr "Crash" Amos, later Group Captain before dumping the

RAF, had always been known to all as "Crash". At one time his dear wife, who also liked a little verbal fun, had been asked by one nosey parker wife, "Why was her husband called crash?" The dear lady seized her main chance and said, "Well! He's crashed a Hunter, a Javelin, a Provost and I seem to remember a Canberra". The face of the nosey parker got longer and longer. I only recall that incident because, as usual, there was a story behind it. 'Crash' was of Germanic descent and somewhere along the line, probably during WWI, when it was common practice, the family had anglicised their name from Kraus-Amos to plain Amos.

Air Marshal Sir David Lee's visit to Singapore passed off particularly well and in addition to seeing his daughter he was probably undertaking a little research into the RAF's involvement in the Far East because after a final retirement from the service in 1972, with the rank of Air Chief Marshal, he wrote a book called "Eastward", a history of the Royal Air Force in the Far East 1945-72. I found it particularly interesting because it turned out that Sir David had commanded a P47 Thunderbolt wing in Java immediately after the Japanese surrender in 1945, which was at the same time that I was on the Spitfire Wing at RAF Tengah. I last saw Sir David in the RAF's Historical Department in the late 1970s when I was trying to track down details of the BBMF's aircraft. During a very pleasant chat between two officers of such vastly differing ranks he mentioned his forthcoming book which I then looked forward to reading with great expectations, which it lived up to.

We had been in Singapore for less than a year when news of the RAF's worst peacetime disaster came through. That was the second failure of Hastings elevators and my parochial thought was 'Would the aircraft now be phased out altogether?" However, it was soon confirmed that a fix would be implemented in due course. "Due course" could have meant anything, and I didn't look forward to hanging around with no flying at all for an unknown length of time. However, the powers that be decided that I should keep my hand in with flying the Valettas of the Far Eastern Communication Flight, which certainly broadened my horizons in the context of route flying, landing at such places as Jesselton and Tawau in Borneo, both of which were off the beaten track as far as Hastings operations were concerned. Another bonus was that whereas Borneo was just an away day normally, FECF, being in the VIP trade often called for night stops for obvious reasons. It was only because of that factor that I was able to savour the relative luxury of the Officers' Mess on Labuan Island which had at one time been the Shell HQ for Borneo. The same trip also took in Tawau which was definitely in the front line as far as the confrontation with Indonesia was concerned. It was on Borneo's north east coast and on the northern shoreline of an inlet, with Indonesia on it's south bank. An eyeball to eyeball situation.

Long after the Hastings fleet was back in operation I was sometimes asked if I wanted a Valetta trip when two pilots were required aboard for VIP work. Whenever possible I gladly accepted, and well remember one such flight which involved a very mixed bag of MPs out from the UK. It soon became apparent which party each individual belonged to, with the Conservatives all wearing jackets and ties regardless of temperature, and the Labour members without either and wearing braces to boot. After the final landing back at Changi, the MPs, except one, gathered to give thanks to our crew. The odd one out stood a few yards away with his thumbs stuck under his braces and shouted, "Come on you lot, can't you see the lads want to get shut". I seemed to recall that "Get shut" meant cease work in those days.

Vickers Valetta

Fifty-Two Years in the Cockpit - Volume Two

Armstrong Whitworth Argosy

Hawker Siddeley Andover

During the Hastings grounding I was also given flights in Argosy aircraft and a VIP Andover. After about two months of work by civilians sent out by Handley Page, the first Hastings was just about ready for its Air Test and Wing Commander Ibbotson said he would be the co-pilot for the flight. Having had long talks with the contractors and seeing their work at first hand, I was not unduly worried about the flight test and also, at the back of my mind, I had convinced myself that the fate of Hastings TG 577 at Abingdon had a lot more to do with it spending hours on end with a quarter flap setting than anything else. The Air Test actually took place on a Sunday morning when the airfield was fairly quiet, but only after a slight hiccup when W C Ibbotson said he thought we should try a take off run up to just before lift off speed and carry out an abort. I was forced to point out that that tactic would almost certainly burn out the pneumatic brake bags and we would finish up in the overshoot area. The Wing Co, to his credit, readily went along with a full take off which went without a hitch. I think my wife was rather worried and she said, after dropping me off at Ops, she would continue to the Club and if I cared to carry out a pass over there at the end of the flight, she would pick me up again and then we could have a drink together in the Mess. What I had not foreseen was that being a Sunday, and all other Hastings firmly on the ground, a large percentage of the crews would be having a family day out at the club and my wife reported later a mighty roar went up as we swept over the pool. She was not quite sure who shouted the loudest; the wives thinking that at long last they would soon be getting their husbands from under their feet, or the husbands themselves, seeing the light at the end of the tunnel. Whichever, the party in the Mess rapidly grew in numbers and continued for longer than it should have.

The Hastings began to come off the repair line at an ever increasing speed so it became quite hectic checking out crews and aircraft. One aircraft, however, was destined to be the very last Hastings in the Far East to be brought back on line. It was one of only three such aircraft built for VIP work only, and it had been on one such trip to Australia when the grounding occurred. The OC Ops ruled that I should be the Captain on the Air Test at Sydney and in charge of the return flight, although all FECS aircrew were now fully back in harness. I thought it would cause a little friction but that was not the case. Bill Corkerton, one of their Captains, came along and also got his fair share of the flying.

It had been decided that we would transit to Sydney by a Qantas airlines 707 out of Paya Leber at about midnight. Obviously, we arrived in good time for the flight and I got chatting to the Australian Qantas Operations Director, and asked about details of the flight. He said that it might be a direct flight to Sydney or there could be a refuelling stop at Darwin, depending on what type of engines were fitted: American or Rolls Royce, and we would not know which until the aircraft arrived. I couldn't help but say "Rolls Royce and we go direct or American and we will need to land at Darwin for fuel, correct?" "Afraid not, bluey, the American engines use far less fuel than Rolls Royce" was his answer. I could hardly believe it, but it was quite true and fitted in with my view that Americans usually catch up, and then overtake, in Engineering. The Aussie manager did lead us up the garden path a bit with a typical Australian joke. He started by saying that if the chief air stewardess on our flight was the same one who had passed through Singapore, London bound, the previous week, we should not be surprised if she was still red in the face. That sounded very interesting, and we pressed him for details. He soon got into his stride and said that on that trip the weather had been appalling, with the aircraft passing through a couple of thunderstorms before a very turbulent approach to Singapore International. During the taxi into dispersal, the Captain held forth to his co-pilot in very colourful language, even by Australian standards, and the final part of his tirade finished with, "...after that little lot, all I need now is a very cold can of lager and a very hot woman". Unbeknown to the two pilots up front, the "This is your Captain speaking" switch had been accidentally knocked on in the severe turbulence and all passengers had heard every word. The Chief Air Stewardess, fearing even worse indiscretions, rushed up the aisle towards the cockpit, but when passing the proverbial little old lady on the way heard the shout of "I think you've forgotten the very cold can of lager, miss". Our 707 was fitted with Rolls Royce engines so we did land at Darwin on what was a very pleasant flight, with an extremely high class cabin crew service. However, I did receive a slight shock after landing when an Australian porter ask if he could carry my bags. A year in the tropics can seem a very long time and during that period I had not seen a white man carry anything in the way of luggage!

    The RAAF took care of us during our three day stay and billeted us at their "Bankstown" base which was on a rail line some little distance from the city. We went into Sydney each day and it so reminded me of a similar ride in to Durban from Clairwood transit camp after my first arrival in South Africa. The distance, type of carriage and surrounding countryside were incredibly alike. Two highlights of our visits to town included living it up a bit in an area known as Kings Cross and a ferry trip across the harbour which must be one of the finest sights in the world. The only trouble we found was getting the name of the international airport right. If we mentioned Mascot, invariably we would be corrected by a reply of "Kingsford-Smith"?, or if we called it Kingsford-Smith it invariably elicited the response of "Do you mean Mascot"? It's name had been changed from one to the other somewhere along the line.

We wasted no time on the Air Test which lasted about twenty minutes in all and then it was a last fling in the bars of Kings Cross before the start of the long flog back to Singapore the next day. I say long flog because RAF aircraft were banned from over flying Indonesia, which necessitated a routing of Sydney-Perth-Cocos Island and then a flight around the northern tip of Sumatra before turning south east down the Malacca straights. Each leg was of about nine hours duration and one disappointment was that the military airfield of Pearce was too far out of Perth to make a visit to that city feasible after a long hot day flying across the entire breadth of Australia. I was looking forward to comparing Cocos Islands to Christmas Island but it was like chalk and cheese. It was much smaller, but had one or two relics of the RAF presence during WWII, when it was used by RAF Liberators and, in the last stages of the conflict, by No 136 Spitfire Squadron. It had reached another peak when a mini exodus of British immigrants to Australia set in during the late 1940s, and the piston powered passenger aircraft of that time could not fly the Ceylon-Australia route with a worthwhile payload thus necessitating the revamping of this remote island's facilities to not only cater for fuel uplifts but also the possibility of housing passengers should technical delays occur. This was brought home to us when we asked about our accommodation for the night and we were told to take our pick, they had about 250 vacant rooms, all ready and waiting. It must have been late evening when we made our final landing of that recovery flight and also a Sunday because it was the one and only landing that Air Traffic had to deal with according to the tower staff we met later in the bar.

One little postscript to the Valetta trip carrying visiting MPs around the Far East that I had been involved in surfaced during my first week back at work. In the MPs report they had mentioned one of the better features of life at Changi for aircrew and ground crew alike. It concerned a 24 hour cafe that an enterprising Chinese group had set up in the aircraft dispersal area. It was immensely popular with all, the food being plentiful, well cooked and cheap, and much preferred by those on shift work to the trail back to their respective messes or quarters. In fact, the Officers' Mess stopped catering for locally based crews departing or arriving for most of the night hours, which must have resulted in quite a saving in food and overtime wages. However, the MPs raised the question of whether the caterers were paying for the electricity used and was any rental being charged? No doubt the official reply was polite, and probably evasive, but at the coal face all ranks from the top downwards thought the questions too ludicrous for words.

With the ending of Saturday morning work, a new dimension had been added to the social life out there. Betty who never did come to terms with the hot, humid climate of the tropics, loved to go shopping, and with myself now being free on Saturdays, unless away on route, I often found myself in the super shopping areas of the city, such as Orchard Road, by about 9 am with nothing to do except trail around Robinsons or CK Tangs trying hard to look interested in the goods on offer. Invariably, Betty would say, sooner or later, "Why don't you go off and have a drink, and I'll see you in the lounge bar of the Singapore Hotel later"? Needless to say, that was certainly opening the flood gates, all bars in the city opened at about 6 am and closed at 2 am the next day and it was certainly a case of being spoilt for choice. On Orchard Rd alone there were several top class hotels plus two English type public houses. One was called the "Tanglin Inn", owned and run by a very down to earth Yorkshire lady while the other, which was opposite C K Tangs, went under different names glorifying in the title of "The Churchill Rooms" on the front and another name, which I have long forgotten, over the side entrance. What I've definitely not forgotten was that it boasted the best sales gimmick that I've ever come across which was the provision of an unlimited number of free curried puffs to all customers. It certainly beat hands down the supply of free pickled eggs which I once came across in Shropshire!

One Saturday morning I thought I'd better play safe and go straight to the Singapore's superb lounge bar and watch the world go by. In that particular case, it was the few people passing the bar entrance on their way to the very high class, and expensive, shopping arcade housed within the hotel confines. One European couple who had actually passed by suddenly turned back and gave me a knowing look with both looking at their watches. They were, in fact, both from Changi Mess and it was Morag, one of the SSAFFA sisters, with Fred Barnes an RAF Officer, whose marriage proposal the previous evening had been accepted, and had decided to buy an engagement ring early the next morning. Despite muttering during my congratulations that I was just killing time awaiting Betty's arrival, couldn't help but notice quick glances between the happy couple. A quick glance at my own watch after their departure, which read something less than 9 o'clock, led me to believe that I also would have concluded that anybody who was sitting on a bar stool with a pint pot in front of him at such an ungodly hour might well have been there all night.

Singapore late at night could also have it's moments and often started with a meal at the well known "Fosters Steak House" where the air conditioning kept the temperature so low that stoles had to be kept at the ready by the management for use by ladies dressed in flimsy tropical wear. A bit gimmicky, I thought, but at least the steaks were absolutely first class being flown in from Australia on a regular basis. There was, in fact, a real Mr Foster who had spent most of his life in Malaya, who also owned and managed a hotel by the name of the "Smoke House" high up in the Cameron Highlands, in which both Betty and I loved to spend leaves there later in our tour.

One part of Singapore which brought back memories of late 1945 to me, was a visit to the Cathay Cinema in the centre of the city which had changed little since the NAAFI operated it in what, by the mid-60s, seemed an eternity ago. It was not the cinema, as such, that gave me uneasy feelings whenever we went there, but the sight of the old YMCA building, just opposite, which during the Japanese occupation had been used by their Kampitit, a kind of German SS only worse, to interrogate POWs and local suspected resistance members. It was, for many, to be the end of the road on God's earth. In fact, right next to the "Dragon's Inn", in which we lived, was an old quarry which remained completely unoccupied in land hungry Singapore- they had even started reclaiming land from the sea on the east coast for building purposes. So one day I asked one aged hotel retainer why nobody had snapped it up to build a villa on such an ideal location. He seemed reluctant to reply at first, but eventually said it would never be built on as long as people remained alive who remembered the days of the Japanese occupation when many executions took place there. After a cinema visit it was often down to Bugie Street, of world notoriety, for a late night open air chinese meal and to watch the action. The action was, in the main, the promenading of local Chinese ladies of the night looking for trade. They all looked beautiful and immaculate in national dress but the snag was that they were not ladies, nor even female. In fact they were males busking for clients, who often attracted the attention of other unsuspecting males, such as visiting merchant seamen. One night in particular a Royal Navy seaman who thought he had got off with a local beauty was so drunk that it was most unlikely that he would ever realise his mistake until it was too late.

One other form of relaxation was a visit on Sundays to a place called "The Gap" up on slightly higher ground, just to the west of Singapore city, which had excellent views of the harbour and the Malacca straights across towards Sumatra. It was an official club for all British Military personnel on the island and a happy meeting place for the three main RAF bases, with such diverse rolls.

I mentioned previously that both Hastings units at Changi often came cap in hand to the Wing Staff when aircrew shortages hit them particularly hard and, on one occasion, a court martial involving FECS meant that many officers were called upon to give evidence for one side or the other, resulting in a severe shortage of pilots. An offer of a round trip to Hong Kong could not be resisted, particularly as it involved a full weekend stay there and knowing the predicament that they faced, I drove a hard bargain and requested a passenger seat be found for Betty. It was tongue in cheek but it worked. The outbound trip went more or less according to plan except for the fact that although crews were used to the sight of body bags being loaded onto USA military transports during the refuelling stop at Saigon. It tended to upset passengers and Betty was no exception. Although it was her second trip she still found it very unsettling, having lost relatives during WWII, including two Canadian aircrew cousins over Europe. Although the approach to Hong Kong was from over the sea and should, therefore, have been straightforward, the turbulence was more severe than I had previously encountered. Betty recalled later that the lady passenger next to her suddenly produced a bottle of water from her handbag and said "Would you like to hold with me my bottle of holy water to ensure a safe landing, it's from the River Jordan", to which Betty replied "I don't think I'll bother, my husbands the Captain". A bottle of holy water indeed, what on earth was it doing on an RAF aircraft inbound to Honkers? It turned out that the dear lady's husband was a Wing Commander Doctor who specialised in eye surgery and each year he took unpaid leave to perform such Ops in the Middle East. Betty really fell in love with Hong Kong and we managed to take in most of the sights, including the Star ferry to Hong Kong Island, followed by a trip to the peak on it's famous railway and an evening meal on a floating restaurant moored off Aberdeen Harbour. We paid in advance for photographs taken on the very small boat that took us the few hundred yards to the floating restaurant but assumed, wrongly, that we would never actually see them. However, during breakfast in our hotel the next morning, they were duly delivered. After a hectic round of shopping later, which included a visit to "Samtarnies" who could make a suit within 24 hours, and always gave you a bakers dozen if you ordered 12 shirts, it was on to the Peninsular hotel for morning coffee. In my book this hotel, with its magnificent setting overlooking the harbour, far exceeded it's more famous sister- "The Raffles" of Singapore fame. Many visiting aircrew living in Mess at Hong Kong, often took a taxi ride to the Peninsular just for breakfast, such was it's magnetic attraction. One piece of good news for Betty was that although the price of any particular item was remarkably similar to what one would pay in Singapore, the exchange rate was 16 HK Dollars to the pound against only 8 in Singapore.

Back in Singapore the steady plod of route checks and flying tests continued apace and on at least two of the Borneo away days we brought back a British soldier killed in action for burial in Singapore's Krangi War Cemetery, which already contained so many who had died fighting the Japanese or held by them in captivity. Such flights really subdued the crews concerned and not many words passed between them en route. I think the worst part was the sight of the escort party as we taxied into dispersal. We always scanned the UK papers, when they eventually arrived, to see if any mention had been made of casualties during the confrontation period but I never came across one. One snippet that also failed to get a mention in the UK, or even in the local Singapore press at the time, was that Indonesian transport planes had dropped some of their paratroopers into mainland Malaya. I have often wondered why such a decision was made. Needless to say, the enemy Paras achieved nothing and most people, even in those days, thought that the British and French drop on Suez had been the last throw of the dice for that form of attack.

One big bonus of living in the Dragon Inn was that we soon acquired the best, and topmost flat in the main accommodation block which included the sole use of the massive sun roof above it. It was during sundowner sessions there that we saw two remarkable sights. The first was when we were watching a passenger jet on it's long final approach to Paya Lebar Airport, which overflew some Indonesian Islands, not all that far away. I was absolutely shattered when I saw anti aircraft tracers shooting into the sky from one of those islands towards the airliner. Luckily, the gunners had obviously not learnt the art of deflection shooting and must have fixed their sights on the airliner and not the spot in the sky that it was most likely to be in by the time the tracers arrived. The second burst of fire was much closer to the jet, but it was well out of range by the time of the third burst. I rushed for the phone and rang the FEAF HQ at Temple Hill to impart news of the incident. The chap at the other end sounded as if he couldn't believe his ears, and who could blame him. If the airliner had been shot down it would have certainly led to something far bigger than confrontation. I received quite a number of return phone calls that night from an increasing level of rank asking me to go over the event again. I did learn during one of those conversations that it was a Qantas 707 which had been shot at and that a different approach pattern would be flown till further notice. The second sighting from our roof top perch was the Russian Sputnik with the first man in space aboard. It made a magnificent spectacle against the star studded night sky and left Betty and I in complete bewilderment that a man was actually up there in space.

One of the few Hastings flights inbound from the U.K. during our tour was particularly interesting in that it was from Farnborough which, in itself, aroused interest all round. The Captain of the aircraft was the late Peter Mancy, who I had previously served with on No 36 Squadron. He was still a bachelor at that time and lived life to the full, particularly so in the Officers' Mess bar in the evenings. One night in particular I have never forgotten and it concerned his partiality to Malt Whisky. Pete thought it was "not done" to refuse a drink from a fellow officer so if his glass happened to be nearly full he would ask the barman to pop one into a half pint beer glass which he would drink later. On that occasion, his half pint glass was getting quite full so he asked for the whisky to be transferred to a full pint glass. When the Chinese bar tender finally called time, the pint glass was near to overflowing so I said, "Well Pete, it looks as if I can't get you a final drink", to which he replied, "Oh, I don't know about that Jacko, give it a go". What stamina! Like a lot of hardened drinkers, he looked none the worse for wear the next day, when in fact, he was off on an important mission along with his boffin passengers. It was still early days for infra red work from aircraft, but they had come up with a device that, if successful, would be of immense value to the Army in their counter measures against Indonesian incursions across the frontier into Borneo. It was hoped to be able to pick up the locations of past camp fires in the jungle for up to 24 hours after they had been extinguished which would, of course, have led to predictions of enemy movements.

I never heard the results of those trials which, obviously, they kept very much to themselves. The end of confrontation came not all that long after the Farnborough visit, so I don't think that it was used in that particular conflict.

The work of being a Wing pilot was far from uniform and tended to come in sudden bursts followed by a few days of not having a lot to do, which led, of course, to being fobbed off with the odd admin job. These were sometimes quite interesting but mainly deadly dull. One of the better ones was being tasked with looking after an Australian crew who would be night stopping at RAF Changi en-route to the UK. When I asked what type of aircraft they would be arriving in I got quite a shock when the OC Ops said "Quite unique, in fact, an Avro Lancaster". Quite unique indeed for that day and age at least. Little did I realise what part that particular aircraft was to play in my future life. The Lancaster, NX611, a Mk VII, had been built in 1945, just too late to take part in WWII but it had been snapped up by the French Navy in 1952, along with 53 others, for maritime work in Morocco and, later New Caledonia. After the French could no longer find any more useful work for it the Australian Air Force took it on charge for a year or so before it was decided to ferry it back to the UK to join the flying display world.

The Lancaster looked absolutely splendid in its all white paintwork and the crew of eight or nine could not have been more varied in background, and all easy to get on with. Between them they sported 4 DFCs and one AFM and although the three pilots were in flying appointments, one suspected that the rest of the crew had not operated as aircrew for a long, long time. They seemed a trifle worried that their next stage was up to Calcutta and, due to the time of year, they would be flying through the inter-tropical front sooner or later. I proffered the suggestion that perhaps RAF Gan would be a better bet, however when they said they were not fitted with a non directional beacon and I quickly concurred that Calcutta was their only option. After the Lancasters' arrival in England it was taken around the display world and flown exclusively by Neil Williams, the best known name in that sector of British aviation at the time. However, that was only after extensive engineering work had been carried out to bring the aircraft up to the standards called for by the CAA. This took all of two years to complete and it was not long after that point that the RAF's last airworthy Lancaster PA474, later named "City of Lincoln" took to the air again and financially undercut the price of keeping NX611 airborne as a viable proposition in the display world.

So, after only 16 flights since its return to the UK, NX611 made it's final landing at Squires Gate Blackpool in 1970. It was to fly no more and, instead, formed the centre piece of an aviation museum at that location. That project, too, fell by the wayside and two years later it was purchased privately by Lord Lilford after it had failed to reach the reserved price at auction. The only reason that Lord Lilford had taken it on board was to ensure that it not only remained in England, but also that it could be found a good home. With the transfer of the famous "S" for Sugar Lancaster, the RAF Scampton gate guardian, to the RAF Museum at Hendon, the solution appeared obvious. It was after Lord Lilford had agreed to put NX611 on semi-permanent loan to the RAF at Scampton that I was to set eyes on it again after 8 years.

After my return to England in mid 1967 to fly the Short Belfast freighter I was, after flying it for 4 years, told that I was to become a simulator instructor on type, but finding out that a slot on one of the last units equipped with Hastings was up for grabs I jumped at the chance. It was on the Strike Command Bombing School at RAF Lindhome and apart from our primary task of giving airborne radar experience to V bomber and Phantom navigators, we undertook flights to here, there and everywhere on one off trips. So one day, after the unit's move to RAF Scampton, it came as no real surprise when I was told that I would be taking our station Commander, Group Captain Lockyer, and his OC Engineering Wing, Wg Cdr Maurice Gee, on an away day trip to Blackpool. All I thought about after take off was how nostalgic it was to be landing there again forty years after my first days flying which had included the Isle of Man and Blackpool. In the 1930s paved runways virtually did not exist, only vast green fields, and now as a pilot I was looking down on five runways and trying to make sure that I got the right one! Even after landing I still had not been told about the purpose of our visit and by the time our crew had disembarked the CO and his Chief Engineer were seen stalking off towards a shoddy looking Lancaster which was beginning to look it's age. The end result of our day trip to Blackpool was that the RAF took on the Lancaster on a ten year loan and undertook to restore it to a respectable condition and then display it as the Scampton Gate Guardian. After landing back at base, I was told by W C Gee that it would have to be brought over the Pennines by Queen Mary motor transporters, made famous during WWII as recovery vehicles for crashed aircraft, because it would never fly again without a tremendous amount of repair work. I'm not normally in the business of one-up-manship, but when he went on to say that he had first seen the Lanc many moons ago when he supervised its passage through Muharraq (Bahrein), I couldn't help but say "In that case I saw it before you did when I looked after the crew in Singapore". Childish, yes. NX611, after tarting up, duly took its place near the main gate. It certainly slowed the traffic on the A15 as motorists gave admiring glances, with many of the locals convinced that S for Sugar was back home. That was not to be the end of the story though, because its next move was after two Lincolnshire farmers, the Panton Brothers, who had lost a third brother on the infamous Nuremburg raid of 1944, wished to set up a living memorial to Christopher on the old East Kirkby airfield, near Boston, part of which they owned. Lord Lilford agreed to sell it for such a worthy cause so, once again, it was dismantled and set off to its new home on a fleet of Queen Marys. After prolonged, dedicated work by two ex-BBMF ground engineers, all four engines became usable again and so as an added attraction to a first class museum, taxi runs started on special occasions. Mike Chatterton, a BBMF Lancaster Captain was the first pilot to carry out a run, but as his commitments to the BBMF increased I was invited to join in and what a privilege I consider it to be at the ripe old age of 70 plus, and over 35 years since I first set eyes on NX611.

One of the deadly dull chores was next on the list, although its implications for Transport Squadrons in the Far East Air Force was all too obvious. FEAF HQ had tasked RAF Changi with finding the most suitable site on the Station for the building of a C130 Hercules simulator which, in effect, meant that the writing was on the wall for not only the Hastings fleet, but also the Argosy squadron based at Changi and the Beverley over at RAF Seletar too. The plans submitted were never used and I, for one, was far from being surprised. My surmise resulted from yet another one off job and that was to join a VIP Comet crew for a flight to Hong Kong and back. As RAF pilots could not fly into Gibraltar or Hong Kong for the first time without being under the supervision of a pilot well versed in operations into those two places, No 216 Squadron; the only RAF Squadron to operate Comets, had run out of pilots who had actually flown into Hong Kong. RAF Transport Command HQ at Upavon had insisted that the rule would still apply even if the extra pilot aboard had not even flown the type concerned. As the VIP turned out to be the Minister of Defence, Dennis Healy, the aircraft would be using Singapore's International Airport of Paya Lebar and not RAF Changi. There was to be a night stop in Jesselton in Borneo so that the minister could have more political talks before going on to Hong Kong. I virtually had a rear compartment of the Comet to myself, with the Minister and his military and civilian staff being well forward. Needless to say, I was well looked after by the Air Quartermasters and had frequent visits by an Army Colonel who gave the impression that he was glad to get away from the main party and talk to anyone about anything except politics, and who could blame him? I must say that having met many senior officers who passed through the Joint Services Staff College when Dennis Healy gave a lecture to each course during his tenure of office, all held him in the highest regard and often mentioned his down to earth common sense: Perhaps it was that rare quality in politicians that impressed them most. Although everybody aboard was discretion itself one could not help but pick up one or two vibes and not long after that particular visitation to the Far East, it was announced that a gradual withdrawal of all British forces east of Suez would start and be completed by 1972.

After a night in Jesselton I made my first venture to the flight deck about 30 minutes out from Hong Kong and after it was confirmed that the runway in use was from seaward the only help I could offer was that with the wind as reported, a spot of turbulence might be experienced as we passed high ground on our left at the three miles to go point. For me it was then down to the back for the landing, however I really came into my own on the ground. As the crew were accommodated in the Shamrock Hotel for two nights I was able to answer all the questions regarding where to go and what to see. However, we got precious little sleep on the second night, being awakened in the middle of the night with the news that a typhoon warning had been issued and it had been decided that the Comet and all crew and passengers should take off ASAP. It was already getting quite turbulent by take off time but the wind had swung through 180° and our departure pattern was over the sea, so this crew could now say they were Hong Kong qualified, although they had not flown what really mattered, and that was from the far from easy ride via the chequered board and the built up area of Kowloon.

I continued my own to-ing and fro-ing to Hong Kong on route checks and the odd trip as Captain whenever the two Hastings units ran out of crews for one reason or another, and on one such trip managed to get Betty aboard for her last trip there. This was quite legal in FEAF, if seats were available, although it was frowned upon in the UK for families to fly as passengers in aircraft operated by their husbands. She really made the most of it and took advantage of an extended stay returning by Beverley some days after my own departure, routing via Labuan in Borneo, which added interest to the journey. She also managed to bring back a redwood altar chest, a long low table and a set of coffee tables made to her own design, with Queen Ann legs, which the craftsman had never tackled before, so Betty had to make pencil drawings of them for his edification. They are all still in our possession and in good condition, unlike some furniture bought by people in Singapore. The reason for that was in Singapore the temperature and humidity remained constant throughout the year, so local wood never seasoned properly and the first cold spell back in England caused no end of problems.

After numerous trips up to Hong Kong I thought that I had seen all there was to see until one of the locally based officers living in Mess said that at weekends for a few hours, he took the Hong Kong to Canton train and alighted at the last stop in the New Territories, just before the Chinese border, and then took a stroll back down the goods yard of that Station to a purpose built copy of an English pub. It really was an oasis with food served in English style and a bar that would have graced any English country pub. The lady who ran it was out from the old country but we never discovered how she managed to wind up at the end of the line, so to speak. One other splendid day out I came upon quite by chance when overhearing some tourists saying that the best day of their Far Eastern tour had been their day trip across the Yellow river to the Portuguese enclave of Macoa by Hydrofoil. Still having the weekend ahead before returning to Singapore I made haste to the booking office where I was told in no uncertain terms that a visa was required before a ticket could be purchased. And so it was that I wound up at a small Portuguese office asking how one obtained a visa and although the chap behind the desk was most helpful he stated that it usually took ten days to process and was only valid for a particular departure date. It was during my walk to the exit door that the man suddenly shouted "You look as if you might be military, are you in one of the British Forces by any chance"? When I replied "Yes, the Royal Air Force" he said, "In that case you can go across today if you wish because Portugal is also in Nato and your identity card will do fine". A fascinating day followed with a very fast and smooth ride both ways, despite many turns to keep clear of other vessels and Chinese junks plying their trade. Unlike Hong Kong, which was forever growing, even during our two and a half year tour in the Far East, Macoa seemed to have become stuck in a time warp and one could easily visualise some of the buildings dating back to shortly after the Portuguese first arrived in the 1550s. One well remembered place, which was not a building of architectural interest, was a moored ship in the delightful little harbour. It looked as if it had never set sail for many a day and that was soon confirmed. In fact, it catered for the well known Chinese obsession with gambling. This was no plush casino, but a ship of many decks, all with one big square hole cut in the floor, except the bottom deck where the action took place. Each ascending deck had a minimum betting stake with the very top deck having a price of $1,000 or more. Being European, I had a free run of the ship but guards manned each deck and many chinese were directed to a deck that fitted their apparel. It seemed that it was not only the British who were class conscious. For a few decks up, punters would shout down the numbers required and lower their stakes in wicker baskets attached to ropes and received confirmation of their bets by the same route. Shouting was not on for the wealthy Chinese on the upper deck and they invariably brought along a flunky to cover that chore and the lowering of the bucket full of dollar bills.

Back in Singapore we got the usual amount of leave each year and Betty and I saw most of the Malayan peninsular during frequent visits, although it was rather surprising how many British military personnel and their families never left Singapore Island, seemingly quite content to sit around the swimming pools of various clubs. Our first venture was up the east coast to stay in a government guest house in Mersing, which was very much a way of life for pre-war planters in their heyday. During that stay we took a boat across to a small island which had featured in the film "South Pacific", and it was off that island that I learnt the hard way about the dangers of snorkelling in the tropics. It was my first and last effort finishing up with severe sunburn on my exposed back. I had been so captivated by the scene below the water that the time just flew by. We also took in the west coast right up to Penang island and even in the mid sixties one river could only be crossed by ferry boat, although it was not all that wide by our standards. On the way up we had a couple of nights in the "Panti Motel" near Port Dickson and right on the waters edge. It was so relaxing to walk along the shoreline in the evenings to watch the setting sun. However, the place we really fell for, and returned to many times, was the "Smokehouse Hotel" high up in the Cameron Highlands at about 8,000'. On the 2°C/ 1000' rule the temperature was down to below what one might expect in midsummer England. The all important humidity was also well down on that of Singapore which, led to a very restful location in magnificent scenery. This particular hotel was owned by the same Mr

Foster who ran the Fosters Steakhouse in Singapore and on two particular occasions gave rise to some laughter between Betty and myself after he had departed. On the first occasion, it was on the day of our departure and after approaching us in a rather diffident manner, and giving one or two polite coughs, said in a Jeeves type voice "I hope you will not be too surprised when you receive your account, but I most respectfully point out that the liquor item is far in excess of that for accommodation and meals added together"! The low daytime temperature for those parts of course, automatically led to quite cold evenings to the extent that there was always a log fire in the lounge each night. It was a two sided affair, but normally only the grate furthest from the lounge entrance was lit and was a favourite gathering place for guests after dinner. However, towards the end of another of our visits we were again approached by the one and only Mr Foster who began by saying "It seems that we are about to play host to some American GIs who are arriving from Vietnam on Rest and Recuperation leave so to preserve your privacy we will be lighting two fires tonight and they can use the other side. I'm sure you don't want to hear any horror stories about the war up there". Personally, I would have loved to have heard them, but the ways of the ex-colonial settlers still lived on.

One familiar sight during the rather torturous drives up and down the road from sea level to 8,000' was the sudden appearance from the roadside jungle of pygmies complete with hunting spears and precious little else, but they always seemed friendly enough. On the first sighting I thought that I must have missed out on something at school because up until then I had thought they only lived in darkest Africa.

With the end of confrontation with Indonesia in 1966, Transport operations were stepped down a gear or two which, in turn, led to two milestones. The first was the reintroduction in the Far East of long route trainers which in Royal Navy terms would have been called "Showing the flag" visits. These trips often broke new ground and when I was asked to submit an itinerary for the wing examiners to fly, my mind immediately thought of Japan and how nice it would be to see Iwakuni and or Mimo after 20 years. HQ FEAF thought Japan would be OK, but when they said we could only fly as far as the island of Okinawa, which was, and probably still is, a vast military base, I went a bit cold on the idea and said in that case perhaps a South West Pacific routing might be in order now that we could over fly Indonesia again. They came up with a dream itinerary which took in the Phillipines (Zambowanga), Papua New

Guinea (Port Moresby), New Caledonia, New Zealand (Auckland) and Australia (Sydney, Adelaide, Darwin).

Having taken an avid interest in meteorology since my introduction to transport flying at RAF Dishforth I had carried around a world atlas which also gave details of average rainfalls and temperatures for most of the prominent locations on earth and became quite fascinated at times by the large differences in that department between places quite close to each other in aeronautical terms. For example, when I was operating into the Congo from West Africa, the rainfall in Accra was only 27", which was less than the London average, while in Lagos, just 200 odd miles to the east, it was 72", more than double that figure. For the trip in hand I noted with interest that Port Moresby, on the southern side of the tropical island of NewGuinea, suffered only 40", not much more than in the UK, but less than half of Singapore's average of 95".

The aircraft allotted for this "swan" trip had just come off a major servicing which really put our flight engineer on his guard because aircraft sometimes return to service with defects that had not been noticed before such inspections. The American adage of "If it ain't broke, don't mend it" was even gaining ground in the rather conservative world of RAF Engineering. On our first landing in the Phillipines, at Zambowanga, some vibration was felt from the tail wheel structure during the landing run. The flight engineer, needless to say, gave that area a very critical inspection after shut down. He opined that no failure was likely in the short term, and with only two more landings due before reaching New Zealand, he recommended that the flight should continue until landing there, when their engineers could carry out whatever rectification and /or replacement work was required. One bonus in Zambowanga was that we had a downtown hotel for accommodation which gave us all an insight into the way of life on those islands. All my previous night stops in the Phillipines had been on American bases and if you've seen one you've seen them all, no matter what part of the world you are in.

The next day's leg of just over 10 hours flying time was to be the longest of the trip but the last hour or so was particularly interesting for anyone who, like myself, had taken more than a passing interest in the fortunes of the Japanese in their abortive attempt to take all of New Guinea during WWII. We had kept to a sea route until north east of Port Moresby before coasting in, not only for better weather reasons but also, flying a non-pressurised aircraft, we wished to remain around the 10,000' mark whenever possible and a direct track would have taken us close to Mt Wilhelm (15,400') and Mt Albert (13,100'). The landing at Port Moresby was pretty much like the previous one, some vibration from the tail wheel area but no worse than before so we looked all set to continue to New Zealand.

Port Moresby in those days was very much a one horse town as far as that concept goes in the tropics. There was certainly only one main street of any kind, but plenty of bars to sample and that proved to be of some interest in a way. Our senior WRAF Officer, Jeanie Oaks, had managed to bag a seat on the trip so that she could liase with lady counterparts in the RNZAF and the RAAF. Jeanie was no great drinker, but she was always game to join in social events and tagged along on our one night stay there, One Aussie who gave every impression of having been on the tonk all day soon took more than a passing interest in our little party, particularly so of our one lady member. He couldn't keep his eyes off Jeannie and no matter how often we changed bars he would sooner or later catch up with us. We learnt the next morning, just before take off, that he had been banging on her bedroom door for most of the night. Perhaps he had not seen an unattached white female for many a year!

Our next leg down to Noumea in New Caledonia was pleasant enough although the tail wheel assembly was never far away from our thoughts. We fell at the last fence so to speak in that although the landing was not much different to the two previous ones, the Flight Engineer was not at all happy about his post flight inspection this time round and pulled the plug saying that one more landing might lead to a complete tail wheel structure collapse. If one had to be delayed en-route, I could think of many worse places than that French run colony, as it then was. An idyllic setting by any standards and, like the Belgium run Congo, the races mixed on equal terms, how different from what I had experienced in the British parts of Southern Africa during WWII. Needless to say, signals flew thick and fast between us and our Headquarters in Singapore plus, of course, the New Zealand Air Force. It was the RNZAF who rode the white horse and within 24 hours one of their Canberra bombers arrived on the scene with all the spares required, an excellent effort indeed. It took two full days to fit the new tail wheel assembly and it would have been much longer if the French Naval Air Arm based there had not provided a great deal of help- so it was a tri national effort of the highest order.

The stay over also introduced me to the French sense of honour. I had always been an early riser since my Halton apprentice days and I also liked a lonesome breakfast whenever possible, which tied in nicely for most route days, and so it was that on the Sunday morning of our enforced, but very pleasant, stay on the island that on passing the bar enroute to the hotel restaurant, I was hailed by four Frenchmen, all of above retirement age, who more or less insisted that I join them for a drink. It was still only 7 am but it crossed my mind that when in Rome, etc, and probably politic too to just have a quick one or two and show the flag a bit. The first thing I noticed from my stool which, in the event, I was to occupy for ten hours or so, was the sight of four fishing rods propped up in a corner with all the accoutrements one associates with amateur fishermen. They seemed quite interested in the strange looking, to them at least, aircraft that they had seen on the airfield and many other subjects too, and only seemed a little reticent when I asked about their fishing boat and what type of fish they caught. I was thinking about sharks, which might upend them in the worst scenario, but all I got was a few smirks and sideways glances. Towards mid afternoon, I couldn't contain myself any longer and asked if they would be in trouble with their wives if they returned home with nothing to show for a full days fishing. This nearly brought the house down, and their laughter went on and on until one of them said with tears streaming down his face that if he did take some fish home his wife would probably die of a heart attack. This set them off again. It was certainly a day to remember, but I came in for a lot of ribbing from the rest of the crew the next day as they had all managed to avoid the bar that Sunday morning.

With our aircraft now fully air worthy it was almost a non-deviating track of nothing but sea for just over five hours to Whenuapai, near Auckland, which was virtually on the 180° east/west line of longitude. I say almost non-deviating, but we could not resist over flying the settlement of remote Norfolk Island, en route, just a few miles off track, and I think we really made the Islands' Air Traffic Control Officers' day.

It was non-stop chat from first contact until passing out of range to the south. New Zealand turned out to be very much as expected, a very laid back and ultra quiet way of life. However, one sight that will live with me forever was seeing from our accommodation a Squadron of Short Sunderland flying boats at anchor in a wonderful picturesque setting. It was after returning to Singapore and talking to a member of No 41 New Zealand Squadron that I discovered the CO of the flying boat Squadron was Sqdn Ldr Dywer, brother of one of my Swinderby students. Having been lucky enough to command the last military flying boat Squadron in the world. Sadly Sqdn Ldr Dwyer died of natural causes within the year.

The next day we flew two consecutive legs to make up for lost time, which made it a rather long and tiring flight in the middle of the Southern Hemisphere summer. The first was to be the RAAF base of Richmond near Sydney and then on to Edinburgh Field, Adelaide, which was very familiar to me from my Christmas Island and Maralinga days with No 36 Squadron. We did manage another day off there and took the train to the city centre and then up to the top of a very tall building overlooking the test cricket ground but, unluckily, no match of any importance was in progress.

The second last day of our trip was from the south coast of Australia to Darwin, which more or less followed the railway line as far as Alice Springs, a place that always aroused great interest among crew and passengers alike. The RAAF base at Darwin still seemed to be a bad boys posting and a final night's partying was enjoyed by all.

Two important letters awaited my arrival back at Changi which would shape my future in certain ways. One from "Ace Freighters", whose crews I had got to know quite well during their frequent stop overs in Singapore, stating that they understood I was due to leave the RAF in about a years time- which was quite true- and that they could probably take me on board if interested. The second letter was from the RAF's "Air Secretary's Department" stating that I could extend my service to the age of 55 if I wished to. This was all rather strange because up to that point aircrew usually had to write to them, not vice versa, so I gave it a day or so to ponder on things. On the one hand Ace Freighters was a definite flying appointment and on the other, too many of my contemporaries, many highly qualified pilots, had been shunted into ground appointments such as Air Traffic Control, Operations, Photographic Interpretation, etc, over the recent years, with no hope of flying again due to age. I took the plunge and wrote back to ask if they could give me some idea as to what I was likely to be employed on if I signed on the dotted line. Much to my amazement, they sent a reply saying I could look forward to a Captain's course on VC10s, Comets, Britannias or the Belfast. Luckily, I retained that letter as it saved the day for me eighteen months later.

With the end of Indonesian confrontation, one event that had been an annual affair before then, was reintroduced, and that was a liaison visit between the United States Air Force in the Phillipines and RAF Changi. After the arrival in a C130 they offered familiarisation flights and I was lucky enough to get 30 minutes worth of circuits and bumps, which I really enjoyed. The only time the USAF pilot took control was to demonstrate a power off landing from 1,500' which started just short of the threshold. I was more than surprised when he invited me to do the same for the last landing which, in the event, was achieved with plenty of runway to spare. The approach looked more like dive bombing in a Spitfire than that of a transport aircraft lumbering in.

One interesting event on the social scene occurred when Jerry Garforth, one of the two Argosy Wing pilots asked if I could make a point of being in the bar one particular night because an old mate of his was passing through Singapore on his way to settle in Australia and he was sure that he was an ex-brat like myself, and about my vintage. It was a long shot but no excuse was needed to go along and chat about dear old Halton and what had happened to whom and when. On the night in question, no introductions were needed, it was none other than Jack Scrine; same entry, same trade and even the same barrack room as myself at Halton. He also had transferred to aircrew during the war, training as a Navigator. With a Nav course being somewhat shorter than that of a pilot he had really finished up in the thick of things. It was a hair raising story that finally emerged as the drink flowed that evening. It transpired that Jack had been on Mosquitos operating over Burma against the Japanese and taken prisoner when his aircraft was shot down during a raid on Rangoon. After much ill treatment, he was finally tied to a tree and a group of Japanese Army men had, with fixed bayonets, carried out dummy thrusts towards him. It was obviously only a matter of time before it was carried out for real. However, at the last moment a senior Japanese officer arrived on the scene and Jack was untied taken back to his place of imprisonment. Perhaps this was one of the first signs by the Japanese that they had finally accepted that the war could not be won and that the losers would soon be held responsible for their actions. I could not help but notice that a couple of "earwiggers' at the bar could hardly believe what was being said; WWII was by then over twenty years in the past.

Another event of a completely different nature also included Betty. Each RAF station had what was called a runner whose job was to distribute, and collect, mail about twice a day from each section. Invariably this was a civilian and this practice also applied at overseas outposts. At RAF Changi we had one of our own in Operations Wing and he was a young Malay by the name of Abdul, no doubt because most Malays were practising Moslems. Abdul was super efficient at his job and also always willing to take on any other chore that we could think of. I had no idea that romance was in the air when I was invited to attend his wedding along with Betty. We gladly accepted, but I was a little surprised when it turned out that Betty and myself were the only two Europeans due to attend. Had we been specially selected? Although we had mixed freely with a couple of Chinese families this was our first real contact with the Malay race. It turned out to be a splendid occasion, although it got off to an uncertain start in that it was the custom to walk in procession from the village of the bridegroom to that of the bride, before the ceremony. With the sun blazing down on us we wondered just how faraway the bride's village would be. Luckily it was only about a mile away! Some years later, when I was passing through Singapore on one of my Belfast trips I was wandering aimlessly down Changi's main street on a rest day when Abdul appeared from nowhere and after throwing his bicycle to the ground, he greeted me like a long lost brother, although it was then four years since we had last met.

One "little" local difficulty, was to lead in the longer run to a most unfortunate loss of life when an RAF Beverley transport aircraft crashed. I had better start at the beginning and record that the RAF's medium range transport squadrons competed annually for the "Lord Trophy", which was named after the late Flt Lt Lord, VC, the only transport VC of WWII, who had gained his posthumous award for extreme bravery when Captain of a Dakota aircraft during the ill fated Arnhem battle of 1944. The general idea was that the competition for the trophy would take in a low level cross country with precision timing, followed by a drop of parachutists and/or cargo over a nominated drop zone with points being awarded in all departments to decided the winner. During the early 1960s, the event had been held at RAF El Adem in Eastern Libya, about 20 miles south of Tobruk, which was fairly convenient for most of the RAF transport world in Aden, Cyprus and the UK. However, for the Far Eastern squadrons based in Singapore, it meant transitting both India and Pakistan, which was not possible for the 1966 event due to one of the all too frequent disputes in the north of the Sub Continent. I must hold my hand up to suggesting that perhaps we should organise our own event that year and even proposed a name for it, "The B C Bennett Trophy"; Group Captain Bennett not only being our Station Commander at RAF Changi but also had a vast transport background. As is usual in such cases, I was told to get on with it, Paddy Irish and myself set to compiling rules, routes and all the rest of it. At Changi we had three full blown transport squadrons with No 48 flying Hastings, No 215 Argosy aircraft and No 41 RNZAF with Bristol Freighters who were very eager to join in. Paddy and I made a trip over to RAF Seletar to see if No 34 Beverley Squadron was interested in entering and found that they too were keen. It caused a great deal of interest in the RAF on the island and one or two bets were made about the eventual winners. The odds on the Bristol Freighters were rather long due to their limited speed range for coping with falling behind scheduled time on the Navigation route, but it goes without saying that the underdogs stole the show, coming in winners. Everybody thought it was a one off but it was not to be. After I had returned to the UK one more annual competition took place in Singapore and it was during a practice run that a Beverley of No 34 Squadron flew into high ground when still in cloud. The book "Lost to Service" by Colin Cummings gives graphic details of this aircraft loss and it's six crew members. The book records that 1100 aircraft were lost to RAF service between 1959 and 1996, about the same number in the five years 1954 to 1959, and- almost beyond belief- 1,000 in the first full year of peace after WWII.

One point of interest I noted on this Beverley accident report was that the Captain was a Sqdn Ldr. Although I have no knowledge of his flying background, it was the norm at that time, and I understand still is, that executive positions such as Flight Commanders and Squadron Commanders are filled on an ad hoc basis, many on promotion to senior officer status and very often from a ground tour. Some of these officers had no previous experience of their new role, be it fighter, transport or maritime. The only exception was Pilot Flying Training Stations when CFS insisted on refresher flying and/or re-categorisation. Referring back to Lost in Service", it is quite remarkable to read just how many senior officers came to grief, with quite a high percentage probably due to pilot error.

In the early sixties when RAF strength was still well over the 100,000 mark, despite the ending of National Service in the late 50s, Flying Instructors did not often meet their ex-students from pre-wings days, but I did meet one, around the swimming pool at the Officers' Club and it turned out to be a very sad occasion. It was Betty who first spotted Alex York, who had passed through Swinderby in our time, sitting all by himself and looking really down in the dumps, which was soon explained. He had been flying a Devon, based in Saigon for the use of the Embassy staff there when he had been struck down by the dreaded big "C" and was now on his way home to face an uncertain future. Indeed a very sad meeting to say the least.

It might seem strange to those serving in today's RAF that a Devon aircraft should be made available for use of Embassy staff in such a place as Vietnam, but that was not their only location. In fact, they were scattered far and wide; North and South America, Africa, the Middle East and even Austria. A luxury even in those far off days, one might conclude.

In the transport world, however, meeting your ex-student co-pilots, now newly qualified Captains, became a way of life which was hardly surprising when one considered that the Transport force was more than doubled in the 12 years from 1955 onwards, which led to rapid progress for those young officers, many making Captaincy before Flight Lieutenant rank even. Up until 1955 the RAF had relied almost entirely on Hastings and Valetta aircraft, then the floodgates opened with the introduction of Beverley, Comet, Britannia, Argosy and VC10 aircraft for the medium and long range tasks. Fairly often, the change in these new Captains' outlook on life was quite remarkable once the responsibilities began to sink in. Some of the "Jack the Lad" types became fairly sober figures. Another turning point was marriage, a big line in the sand in anyone's life. Among those I served with nearly all the marriages seemed to have been made in heaven and long lasting. One of them was John Hope, of the "Band of Hope and Glory" Cyprus notoriety, who on leaving the RAF was to make a rapid rise up the promotion ladder of Britannia Airways at Luton, finishing his time to retirement as a Senior Training Captain. Not only was John's marriage made in heaven but also on the flight deck of a Hastings en route from the UK to Gibraltar. One of the passengers was a young WRAF officer and, as such, she was accommodated along with the officers of the crew in the Mess at Gib. For a change, John, now a Captain, was to experience a jape played on himself by his own co-pilot. The young WRAF officer and John had long retired to their respective rooms for the night before the rest of the crew finally left the bar. It was still the custom at that time for Officers to leave shoes outside their bedrooms at night for cleaning by batmen early the next morning. The co-pilot, now well under the weather, thought it was a brilliant idea to remove the WRAF's shoes from outside her room and place them alongside John's and let anyone passing by draw their own conclusions! In the turmoil that followed the next day, John and Ann really got to know each other and the rest is history, as they say.

The end of our 2 $^1/_2$ year tour was in sight when it was announced that No 48 Squadron would lose their Hastings and temporarily disband until receiving C130 Hercules aircraft six months later. After the re-equipment took place No 48 Squadron's Hercules aircraft displaced the Beverley aircraft of No 34 Squadron at RAF Seletar and the Argosys of No 215 Squadron at Changi. However, the Argosy aircraft were flown to No 70 Squadron in Cyprus and another Hastings Squadron bit the dust. At a stroke, the Wing checking of Hastings aircrew flights had been reduced by over three quarters, with only three or four VIP crews of the Far East Communications Flight remaining. The upshot was that Paddy Irish, the other Hastings Wing pilot, who had longer to serve out there than myself, was posted onto a ground tour at FEAF HQ Fairy Point. With trade now being slack to say the least, I jumped at every chance to act as a Co-Captain on FECS VIP flights and one, a day return to Kuantan in a Valetta, an airfield I had never previously visited would, hopefully, confirm a rumour doing the rounds in the aviation world for some years.

It was to the effect that under the conditions of a dead calm sea and good downwards visibility, the outline of HMS Prince of Wales and HMS Repulse, both sunk by the Japanese on the 10th December 1941, due East of Kuantan, could be seen from the air. The FECS captain on the flight was a Polish pilot named Joe Kamecik, who seemed just as keen as myself to indulge in the search. We found nothing, but the rumour persisted.

It was also in my last six months in Singapore that good news for specialist aircrew, those pilots and navigators who had been told that there would be no promotion beyond the rank of Flight Lieutenant no matter how long they were prepared to serve, came through. It was announced that about ten officers would henceforth be promoted to Squadron Leader on each six monthly promotion list. A much needed boost for morale, although virtually all aircrew, by the very nature of their calling, gave of their best at all times.

One drawback of any overseas tour was that the transportation of excess luggage that could not be carried by air was sent both ways by sea and, in fact, called 'deep sea luggage'. With ships plying the Far East route now few and far between, and taking up to three or four weeks each way to Singapore, families could be left without items of everyday use for some considerable time. Another irritation was having to sell one's car in England before departure and, more often than not, at a loss when the buyer realised the urgency of the sale! Although Betty and I made a considerable loss outbound on a recently purchased Ford Zephyr, our luck was in at the end of our time in the East. As there was only two of us and Singapore Island so small, we plumped for a small 1200cc Ford Anglia which proved to be ideal and cost little. However, even by the

On arrival at Gaydon my mind returned to my time on No 6 ANS in the early 1950s when "Taff" John had converted me to Wellingtons in just over two hours and "Phil" Hudson to Ansons in under one hour. I thought that something similar would happen again, especially as I had been checked out on the Valetta, the tail wheel version of the Varsity, in Singapore. Nothing remains the same forever and I was soon on my way to the School of Refresher Flying for a "proper" conversion to the Varsity, as it was put, at RAF Manby in Lincolnshire. The refresher bit amused me somewhat having at that time been flying continuously for 25 years. However, it was an excellent course and with Manby also housing the School of Air Warfare we often mixed with quite senior officer students in the evenings. One very popular haunt was the "Splash", being next to a ford, just a couple of miles away.

The Varsity was a particularly easy aircraft to fly and land with its tricycle undercarriage and asymmetric flight was almost a non-event compared with wartime twin pistons. The course of 30 odd flying hours seemed excessive, although some of that was taken up on odd job flying taking in a night stop in Germany in my case. Another was flying the Commandant of the Air Warfare course up to RAF Leconfield on an official day visit with his WRAF officer ADC, when both stood behind Tilly Fisher, my instructor, and myself throughout both legs, even for takeoffs and landings. The day was not wasted because whilst at Leconfield we took to the skies over South Yorkshire for yet more dual instruction. The WRAF officer looked particularly smart with the extra embellishment worn by all ADCs, and was also vaguely familiar. It was after our final landing back at Manby and asking Tilly her name that the penny dropped. A year or so before, Wendy Barnett had appeared in the Mess at Changi on a visit to her parents who happened to be stationed there. Her career in the RAF thereafter was quite something.

A story doing the rounds of the junior officer staff on the Air Warfare establishment, but certainly not among the senior staff, was to the effect that after a visit by an American Air Force team they had heaped praise to high heaven about the course content, but finally put the boot in by saying "It was a great pity that the good old USA could not possibly afford such an equivalent in their Air Force".

Back at RAF Gaydon I soon settled into the old routine of flying U/T Navigators around the UK on four or five hour sorties. With Gaydon sitting right under "Amber One", the main routing to the North West, out of London, particular attention was required during departures and

Vickers Varsity

arrivals at base. Unlike the dear old Wellington, the Varsity had many of the new gadgets for safe navigation fitted, including "Decca" and a "NDB Homer". However, I could not understand why Gaydon did not have a ground radio transmitter for NDB homings. Still being interested in flight safety, I went into print on that point but was told that although the suggestion would be sent up the line, the chances of anything being done about it were very slim. Times had changed and not only was an NDB sited on the station within a few months, but later, when the two Navigation Schools of Gaydon and Stradishall amalgamated and moved to RAF Finningley, near Doncaster, they also relocated the NDB there. I was to use it frequently after leaving the RAF and starting my 12 years of civvy flying at Sherburn-in-Elmet.

The staff pilot situation on the ANS was much the same as at Lichfield, with a preponderance of NCOs, all very experienced indeed, being of WWII vintage. Nearly all had turned down a commission for one reason or another and seemed to be very happy indeed to be playing out time on a steady flying job to conclude their service careers. At the other extreme there were a few newly graduated pilots awaiting operational training courses. They came along on many flights to act as co-pilots, the right hand seat, however, was normally the preserve of the Air Signaller. I came across many of the young pilots later in life when most of them had jumped ship during the late sixties defence cuts. One exception was Jeff Bullen who eventually became the Station Commander at RAF Lyneham.

One lasting impression in my mind whenever I look back on my short stay at Gaydon concerned the one and only time I was clobbered to be the Station Duty Officer. The other ranks clubs in the services had always been called the NAAFI until about the mid sixties when some stations started to re-name them. At Gaydon the NAAFI became the "Cockpit Club". It turned out that the previous weekend a local hospital had been asked if any of the nurses on staff would like to attend an airman's dance. Some of the nurses had complained bitterly to their Matron afterwards about the ungentlemanly behaviour of some of our young lads. It was my misfortune that the only outside call I took during my duty time was from the irate Matron and what an ear bashing followed! I eventually fell into a well prepared trap when she said "And what is the name of your airman's club?" After I meekly replied "The Cockpit club" she shouted, "Yes, that's it, and its particularly well named if you ask me", before slamming her phone down and, no doubt, having a triumphant smirk on her face.

After about eight months of flogging around on these navigational trips I heard some interesting news from the transport world. The Belfast fix had proved successful and the build up of crews for No 53 Squadron, the only Squadron to fly all of the ten Belfasts built during the entire life of that type in RAF service, would soon commence for the re-start of training. When my name did not turn up, I made the usual inquiries and was told that I would be kept at Gaydon for at least one full tour and so it was that I produced the letter which I had retained, stating that if I signed on for further service I would be flying either Comets, VC10s, Britannias or Belfasts. It worked wonders, I was re-posted to Brize Norton within weeks and offered a married quarter in, for me at least, the aptly named Halton Drive. The course was to last six months with about 50/50 ground school and flying. The ground side was along the same lines as the Hastings at Dishforth with two extra bits thrown in. It was to be RAF Mountbatten at Plymouth for sea dinghy drill again and then RAF North Luffenham for aviation medicine tuition with the decompression chamber to contend with once more, followed by a full week at the Rolls Royce factory in Derby for the type engine course. For this last course we had hotel accommodation and being a football fanatic I soon spotted a Scottish international in the hotel bar, who played for Derby County at that time. I thought we would see less of him as the weekend approached but he still appeared from time to time and often gave us graphic accounts of behind the scenes activities at your average football club- most interesting indeed!

Our ground instructor got us off to a fine start on the first morning by asking the usual question, "Are you nicely settled in your seats"? After which there was the most shattering noise I have ever heard in so confined a space. It turned out to be the ignition spark from one of the two ignitors fitted to the Tyne engines. We all came out with our own favoured expletives. He went on to say that it was his little joke which he played on all courses passing through, although it had misfired on one notorious occasion., Rolls Royce encouraged group visits to their factory which included, of course, the joke played on us on day one. However, one visiting group arrived in the standard 32 Seletar coach, but this time they were all Vicars and you can probably guess the result after the big bang. 31 one of them took it in their stride, but the odd one shouted "F****** hell, what was that"? Our instructor went on to say that when the R R team gathered to wave their guests goodbye, they did not get the usual response. In fact, no acknowledgements whatsoever, only 31 Vicars looking straight ahead with noses held high and the 32nd slumped in a back seat looking down towards his feet.

The second extension to the average Transport Command course was time in a type simulator, all 50 hours of it, which some thought excessive but for myself I thoroughly enjoyed. It was a first class grounding for the real thing. One story told during that period of the course was that the simulator makers had to send their top boffins to Brize in the early days when the simulator was playing up a bit, they were so carried away that when the beast got out of control; pitching and rolling, and with plenty of vibration from the turbulence inducer, that they all fled to the exit door, completely forgetting that they were not in a real aeroplane. Ian Waller, another captain on the course and myself did manage to escape one afternoon when the first British Concorde was due to make it's first ever landing at RAF Fairford, having taken off from Filton. It was not one of Brian Trubshaw's better landings, but he did explain that his radio altimeter had failed on finals.

I had always considered myself very fortunate to have flown the vastly underrated Short Belfast aircraft, one of the best cargo aircraft of its day and I do not think it was ever fully appreciated by the British military establishment just what a fine aircraft they had at their disposal, although the Americans always marvelled at it's capabilities when given the load carrying details. Perhaps the best tribute to the Belfast was that after the RAF had disposed of it's fleet of ten aircraft they had, during the Falklands war, to go cap in hand to Heavy Lift, a UK civilian operator who had snapped up four or five of them, to lift special equipment to Ascension Island. Of all its special features the most important was the cargo hold headroom of 12' which, in effect, meant it could take on board certain items of equipment that would not fit into any other aircraft in the western world, other than the American C-5A. The basic weight of the Belfast was 125,000 lbs with a maximum take off weight of 251,000 lbs, which left plenty of scope for the mix of fuel (10,000 gallons max) and cargo, particularly the latter with a hold 80' long. The largest ever recorded load was, in fact, 77,853 lbs when Wing Commander Spottiswood, No 53 Squadrons OC at the time, took on board two Abbot self-propelled guns for a flight from Boscombe Down to Brize Norton.

Most pilots will tell you that no matter how long you have been flying, when you convert to another aircraft type there is always something in the aircraft that you have never come across before and that was certainly true for me in a big way in the Belfast. Although I had a very brief fling with a USAF C130 in Singapore, this was to be my first command of a turbo prop aircraft. Other novelties included water-meth injection for the Tyne engines, auto land facility which called for three ILS receivers, in flight re-fuelling capability, auxiliary power unit, Maxret braking, reverse thrust on the engines, a powered yaw damper, tyre pressure plugs that popped at high temperatures usually associated with unintentional harsh braking resulting from the failure of the Maxret system and, finally, but of most importance, the flying controls which, although of the manual control type, were almost unique in aviation in the Belfast. The pilot was not actually moving the ailerons, elevators and the rudder from the cockpit, only tabs fitted to those controls which only became active when the airflow generated during the take off run centralised all five sections of the flying controls. To stop these controls flapping in the wind before take off, they were held fully locked until entering the runway. At the point of release it was not uncommon, for instance, for the two ailerons to be both up or down. This often led to frantic radio calls from very observant Air Traffic Controllers, but later in the Belfast's life a call from the tower at Brize Norton was of a very different nature. It was to inform the aircraft Captain that one of his elevators was not only down with the other neutral, but actually hanging off. It seems strange, to say the least, that Bristol Britannias had, before that time, suffered similar elevator bracket failures and that Short Bros, on sub-contract, had not only assembled all of them at their Northern Ireland factory, but had also fitted modified brackets to cure the problem when it first arose on the Britannia. The upshot of that was with the entire RAF Britannia fleet now also based at Brize, the technical stores had enough of the modified elevator brackets to refit the Belfasts within days rather than months.

Unfortunately, that was not the only serious problem that had a connection with the co-production of Britannia and Belfast aircraft. The Britannia had also suffered from elevator tab control rod seizures due to icing in the rear fuselage area. However, the remedy was simple, the fitting of warm air fans near the offending brackets, but no one had seen fit to install them in the Belfast during production. It could have been an absolute disaster when the first problem of control icing occurred in a Belfast. The aircraft had taken off from the particularly well named Cold Lake in Canada in the midst of winter on a flight back to the UK with a scheduled re-fuelling stop at Gandar, Newfoundland. All was well until an increase in altitude was fed into the auto pilot which failed to respond. After two more attempts the auto pilot suddenly disengaged itself and the aircraft went into a violent climb. With a rapidly diminishing airspeed the co-pilot on watch at the time, Jock Manson, switched off the auto pilot and tried to fly the aircraft manually, but could not even move the control column/ tab control fore or aft. Just in time, he tried the trim wheel which more or less brought the aircraft back into level flight, just before stalling speed. With the temperature at Gander well below freezing, the fault would certainly not have cured itself before a landing there to pick up a slip crew due to fly the aircraft back to base. The prospect of trying to land the mighty Belfast on trim alone was unthinkable, so the flight was continued across the Atlantic with little fuel to spare, and it was only when passing 2,500' on the descent to Brize Norton that the controls became free again. An incident that could have had fatal results. The flight engineer on duty at the time was also well named, bearing the surname of Frost. The co-pilot, many years later, produced a book "United in effort" the story of No 53 Squadron, Royal Air Force 1916-76, published by Air Britain publications. It is by far the most in depth and readable Squadron history that I have so far come across having read many over the years.

Some of the high tech parts fitted to the Belfast I was never to use at all. Firstly, the auto land system, which had required the fitting of three ILS systems. Apparently it was only at the behest of the British government that the system had been called for in the first place. The idea was that the British army presence in Germany could be cut substantially if the German government could be convinced that reinforcements would be flown back to the continent regardless of weather in an emergency. One of the snags was that very few airfields anywhere in the world had the ground facilities for auto landings at that time, and certainly no military bases in Germany. Auto landings could only be carried out if the ILS beam, which was normally off-set from the runway heading was brought into line and also made pencil thin. Brize Norton, London Heathrow and the Ministry of Defence airfield at Bedford were the only UK aerodromes so fitted in the 1960s and so it was that one of the ten Belfasts built was sent to Bedford for trials. The trials went on forever, with over 800 successful landings being made there. One sure result soon surfaced in that the system was so accurate that the runway in the area that the Belfast always thumped on soon started to break up and the boffins had to set too and build in a random landing spread for the system. Long before the trials had finished the RAF had given up on the idea completely, and the head up display part was removed from the nine aircraft at Brize. The aircraft at Bedford, XR364, continued on its merry way, but after those trials it had to be returned to Short Bros for the drag alleviation modification to the rear fuselage. When it eventually arrived at Brize it was late 1971, over 5 years after No 53 Squadron had officially re-formed with Belfasts, and less than five years before the Squadron disbanded forever. After 364's arrival it was soon noticed that the head up display was still fitted and we all had a go at using it with mixed feelings. For myself, I did not regard it as being of much benefit and in any event it was soon removed by the engineers.

One other item that was new to me was the flight re-fuelling capability and that was one thing I would have liked to have had a go at, although it was not to be. It was another concept for the Belfast that had to be abandoned early on in its life. This was entirely due to the Tyne engines' very high oil consumption rate at times, which would have made flights of the envisaged 18 hours or so inadvisable. The Belfast, unlike the contemporary DC 6, did not carry oil contents gauges, nor the ability to pump in extra oil carried aboard in the case of low readings for any particular engine. The DC 6 was also way ahead of its time in that the Flight Engineer could keep a check on the temperatures of each individual cylinder on his piston engines. His after landing report often stated, check plugs on such and such a cylinder on No 3 engine or whatever. Although in flight re-fuelling was definitely not on, it had, in fact, been tested out by one or two crews in the early days before it had been abandoned. One of those pilots was Squadron Leader Bruce McDonald, who was in charge of the Belfast conversion courses. He told me it was quite difficult because in addition to trying to spear the fuelling drogue, when you throttled back on the Tyne engine the aircraft actually accelerated for a couple of seconds before decelerating. How anything can jerk forward after a power reduction has baffled me ever since, if true it must have had something to do with prop blade angle change. The water-meth injection system fitted to the Tyne engine was for use at hot and high airfields when all turbine engines suffered a fairly big power loss just when an increase was most needed because although indicated take off and landings speeds- and all others for that matter- remained the same the true airspeed went up considerably; 1.75% per 1,000' of altitude plus some more if the temperature was above ISA. ISA being the standard international standard atmosphere, which deems atmospheric air pressure to be 1013 millibars at sea level, reducing by 1 millibar per 30' of altitude and temperature to be +15° C at sea level, reducing by 1.92° C per 1,000', up to 36,000'. Although I went through the take off graphs religiously, like every other Captain, the occasions when I used the water meth injection system could be counted on one hand, mainly because the load carrying capability was mostly under used.

I expect some readers will wonder why I should mention such trivia, but there is a bottom line to it. During my two and a half years as the Station Flight Safety Officer at Changi I had to process all incident reports raised and there was never one recording a Rolls Royce dart engine failure, with a full squadron of Argosy aircraft based there, that was quite something. At Brize the average failure time for Tyne engines was about 400 hours, which was going towards the other extreme. At that time I put it down to the fact that the Tyne developed more than twice the power than that of the Dart. However, in later years, I met both French and German crews who both flew Trancells fitted with Tyne engines, but without water-meth injectors, and both stated that engine failures were almost unheard of in their fleets. One point made by the ground engineers at Brize Norton was that engines reconditioned by Rolls at one of their plants in Canada lasted longer on average before failure than those getting the same treatment at Derby, although that was pure hearsay. In a book entitled "Belfast" by Molly O'Loughlin-White, it is recorded that the RAF's Tyne engine changing team were called out to fly to various parts of the world on 150 occasions!

On the flying side of the Belfast conversion course I was very lucky indeed in coming under the wing of Sqdn Ldr Andy Wilson for my dual instruction. He had flown four engined aircraft for most of his time in the service, having completed a tour on Halifax bombers during WWII after which he first flew with No 53 Squadron operating Liberators in the transport world and had also completed a tour with them on Hastings before being selected for an exchange tour with the American air force flying Douglas C-133 Cargomasters. It was when flying with them that he acquired the nickname of the Big "A". With Andy standing over 6' tall and well built, it was hardly surprising. I was often asked, "How was the Big A getting on?", after landing at many USAF transport stations. The Big A hardly ever talked about the past, however one day he did mention that his worst night on bomber ops was when a night fighter shot a fair amount of both his elevators away and landing back in England had only been achieved with great difficulty and a bit of luck. By a remarkable coincidence, a few weeks later a photograph of the rear end of a Halifax that fitted the bill exactly appeared in a Flight magazine with a write up asking if anybody happened to know who the pilot might have been. The Big A duly confirmed that it was his aircraft all right.

Although I had approached the flying of the biggest aircraft the RAF then operated as a direct entry Captain with some apprehension, I was soon falling in love with the beast, no doubt due to the excellent tuition and finding it reasonably easy to fly. Stalling characteristics were a little unusual for a big four engined aircraft, however, in that it was difficult to achieve with guaranteed safety because it was well below take off speed when the effectiveness of the elevator control tabs to move the control column forward for recovery from the very high angle of attack (A of A) needed to fully stall the aircraft at about 22° was doubtful. Shorts decided to install a stick shaker and warning horn activated at about 15° A of A at which point normal recovery action was to be taken.

The course took a well worn path for the transport world: about 5 hours of dual before solo and then plenty of instrument flying including a vast number of let downs at various airfields, one of which was at Gaydon where I noticed a big turn out of interested spectators- I suspect they guessed who the pilot was! One massive departure from the Hastings OCU days was that instead of a Malta or Cyprus route trainer, ours was to be a round the world trip. The standard route was taken as far as

Singapore, which was Cyprus, Bahrain, and Gan. After a couple of days off in Singapore, it was then forever eastwards to Guam, Wake Island, Honolulu, San Francisco, Alberta, Newfoundland and finally the Atlantic crossing back to Brize. With two student crews aboard we took alternate legs throughout.

The flight deck of the Belfast was massive by any standards, wide enough for both the Captain and Co-pilot to take their seats from the fuselage side of the aircraft and deep enough to allow the non-operating pilots and navigators to stand and watch the approach and landings to any airfield that they had not previously visited. This proved to be excellent training; there was nothing to beat listening and watching another crew operating without being personally involved before doing it oneself.

During our two days off at Changi I visited my old haunts of the Officers' Club and the Changi Officers Mess on Temple Hill. Although it was by then two years since I had left Singapore, the Chinese barman, with an inscrutable face, said "Bar number 347, sir"? Yes, it was my old bar number although it took a few moments for the penny to drop.

I was the trainee Captain for the Changi to Guam leg and the Navigator's calculation of an 11 hour flight called for plenty of fuel. At Changi we had picked up our first useful load, a Meteor aircraft fuselage to be returned to the UK. All seemed to be going according to plan until nearing our cruising altitude when the aircraft pressurisation and cooling system failed. One of the few annoying features about the Belfast was that when that system tripped, as in our case, the resetting could be achieved in a few minutes, but this could only be done from outside the aircraft up in one of the wings. Surely it should have had an auto-reset built in which could be operated by the Flight Engineer? The upshot was that we had to return to land at Changi, but only after dumping thousands of gallons of fuel into the ocean to get down to landing weight. That took up 45 minutes of flying time, plus the ground fix time and then the eventual flight of 10 hours and 40 minutes. It had been the longest day by far when we eventually arrived on Guam. It appeared to be a lovely island and our hotel, like many others, catered mainly for Japanese honeymooners. I couldn't help but wonder if any of them realised that the two B29s that had atom bombed their country had taken off from there? Perhaps that was the last thing on their minds under the circumstances! Our own treat the following morning was to see both a U2 take off and landing. Which was particularly interesting because two jeeps raced alongside the aircraft after landing in close formation in the hope, we supposed, to re attach the wing tip type wheels to the U2 after it finally stopped to avoid any damage.

The next leg was from the sublime to the ridiculous, after the luxury of Guam to the very basic attractions of Wake Island. It was a very small island which just seemed to serve as a re-fuelling outpost and very little else. The sleeping accommodation of bunk type beds hardly measured up to troopship standards let along anything else. It was on Wake the next morning that a ground crew chief- travelling with us and responsible for carrying out inspections and minor repairs- said to me, "Never mind, the day after tomorrow we will be in San Francisco and it will be the 4th of July, so we should have a good time". I was forced to say that it would be 'tonight' when we arrived in Honolulu where we might have a good time, but the fourth would be almost over by then. Naturally he replied, "But sir, today is only the third". Needless to say I had to spend some time in explaining the implications of crossing the date line when you either lose a day or gain an extra one, depending on the direction of travel.

All was not lost, however, as the Americans seemed to stretch the 4th just like the Scots stretch New Year, and things were still in full swing when we reached mainland America on the 5th, already having had a splendid night in Honolulu. We had another two days off, this time at the McLellan Air Force Base, near Sacramento, about 30 miles or so inland from San Francisco and it may well have been a case of sitting around the pool all day long except for the fact that the "Big A" had agreed to take on board two American officers for the trip home. They could not do enough for us and on day one took two car loads of our gang into down town San Francisco. We saw just about everything, literally, as it turned out. First it was a fast ride into the city centre via the Golden Gate bridge with a very good view of Alcatraz prison on its small island to port, and then a little refuelling in a bar on Fisherman's Wharf. After that it was to the "Top of the Mark" for a few more. Top of the mark, by the way, refers to a bar on the top of the Mark Twain hotel, one of the tallest buildings in the city, accessed by an outside of building elevator, which gave magnificent views, and is a must for any visitor to those parts. Our two guides then said that we must try riding the rails, which meant clinging on like grim death to the outside of tram cars which go up and down the very steep inclines which are a feature of the city. They also insisted on a few final beers in a British type pub where we "might well meet one or two of our own country folk". Yes, we did meet one or two, however what we had not expected was that it was one of the first such places to have a troop of

Go-Go dancers- "topless ladies" who seemed more interested in gaining the top spot on a pyramid type stage than anything else. San Francisco had more than lived up to my own expectations and I will always remember that super day out. Other places such as New York and Chicago, which I visited later, failed to impress and it was only a night in Georgia that came anywhere near meeting expectations.

I did miss a trip on our second day off when our two American friends laid on another day out, this time to Lake Tahoe, high up in the Sierra Nevada mountain range to the east. I would be flying the next leg the following day and opted out of that one and, by all accounts, it had been another marvellous day out, although of a vastly different nature. The scenery had to be seen to be believed was one opinion.

We had lived on base during our couple of days in California and although I was well used to Officers' clubs, as opposed to Mess life, during our frequent visits to Honolulu from Christmas Island when all domestic chores had been carried out by local people, this was the first time I had seen home grown American ladies manning the bars and cafeteria. It seemed, and confirmed later at other USAF clubs on mainland America, that employed civilian staff did not wear uniforms or even aprons when waiting on diners. In order to distinguish themselves from the personnel, the staff at McClennan wore straw hats, with a long floating ribbon that indicated their role. At another base I visited they wore white shirts with bow ties.

When we took off on day three the plan was to fly two legs; the first up to the RCAF base at Nanaimo and then on to Gander in Newfoundland. It was during the ground turnaround that one of our ground engineers reported a defect that would definitely need fixing before the next take off. This was to take about 10 long hours, but although we had use of a RCAF crew room no one offered their various messes. A lack of communication that did not go down too well. When we eventually got away it was just about daybreak so we all had a good view of the landscape below. The first few hours were somewhat dreary flying over the prairies, but later in more northern latitudes the vista changed dramatically with countless lakes to be seen. In fact, it appeared that there was more water than land in some parts.

Travellers will well know that in some parts of the world you can immediately feel at home the moment you arrive and so it was in my case at Gander and even more so on many future visits. There was a permanent RAF officer on hand to look after transitting flights and many envied the appointment except for the fact there was no flying during a two and a half year tour. One officer who filled that appointment during my time on No 53 Squadron was Sqdn Ldr Peter Crouch who I had first served with at RAF Swinderby and again in Singapore when he was on the Wing Staff flying the Argosy. In later years he was one of the founding members of the Aircrew Association (ACA), then Chairman and eventually an honorary life Vice-President. He could tell a good tale or two about his time at Gander and even now I have a good smile whenever I recall one of them.

Apparently he was called out at short notice from his quarters one morning when a Belfast, which had taken off from the Bahamas, en route to the Azores, was called upon by our HQ in England to divert to Gander for some reason or other. The crew had been on a standard UK-Belize return and when in the tropics, one crew member, when probably under the influence, had seen fit to buy a parrot. Also, the entire crew were dressed in tropical uniform (KD) when the diversion came. Peter recalled that it was still early spring at the time, with snow all around, except on the cleared runway, when the Belfast arrived. He was in his usual position up in one of the viewing galleries, with many other interested onlookers from various parts of the world, when the crew eventually disembarked in the freezing weather, dressed in tropical gear and with one carrying a caged parrot which was squawking its head off as they plodded their way through the snow drifts towards the terminal building, one person was heard to say in a strong American accent- "Gee, look at that lot. Talk about mad dogs and Englishmen in the midday sun, this sure takes some beating". Perhaps he had a point.

It was also at Gander that a ritual that had been going on for years, from well before Peter's time, came to his attention. It started when one of his predecessors had approached an incoming crew and said you are entitled to a dinner on the RAF at this time of day, but as you may well have already eaten on the flight the caterers, who also operate the bar, can translate the price of the dinner into pints of beer if you should so wish. By a strange coincidence, whenever a crew eventually reached one of the two hotels used by the RAF, it was only a matter of time before the manager appeared with the same offer. Drinking your way through the equivalent of the price of two dinners on the same night for free, and all on the house, or the RAF to be precise, was indeed a novelty.

It was again my turn to fly another leg, this time the Atlantic, and the last of our world tour. With tail winds and good weather, no cloud flying recorded, it was all over in 7 hours and 15 minutes and something of an anti-climax.

Before signing off with the OCU, a solo route trip was called for and it turned out to be a very leisurely one indeed. Day one was to RAF Cottesmore, for freight pick up and then Cyprus return, keeping the same aircraft throughout. My total flying time for the Belfast conversion finally stood at 96 hours, but with a round the world trainer plus a solo Cyprus return it just about equated to the 50 or 60 hours that we gave to Hastings crews on their courses at Thorney Island.

CHAPTER 6
Flying the Belfast on No 53 Squadron

My first trip on No 53 Squadron was certainly a non-event being a 15 minute ferry flight recovering XR368 from RAF Lyneham. It was urgently needed as the next day our CO Wing Commander, later Air Vice Marshal, Spottiswood was taking two of his new crews, and I was Captain of one of them, on yet another route trainer. This was to be a Hong Kong return, and yet again on a leg and leg about routine. It seems strange to look back as two of the co-pilots had already reached the rank of Sqdn Ldr. The CO took the third new crew on an Atlantic trip which included Iceland and Greenland, and how I wished I could have been on that instead of the all too familiar Far East run, as I was never to visit the two Atlantic islands that I had heard so much about from ferry and ex-Coastal Command crews of WWII. Within days of returning to the UK I managed two day returns to Gutersloh on freight only runs because although I had been awarded a "D" rec "C" category, which meant that I was up to passenger carrying proficiency in flying I still had to acquire a minimum number of flying hours on type before I could carry any. That piece of dogma was blown sky high on my very next trip which, in theory, was to be another 'Freight Only' return to Cyprus.

Having been on the Squadron for only five weeks I was informed after landing in Cyprus that we would not be returning to the UK the next day we would be starting a once a day shuttle to El Adem in Libya. This was because Colonel Gadafi, having already seen off the British and Americans from their respective bases near Tripoli, was now turning his attention to the only remaining British base of El Adem and decreed that only one flight a day would be allowed into or out of that base from then on. The Belfast, being able to carry more than twice the load of the Cyprus based Argosy aircraft was chosen to be so tasked. I did not think No 70 Squadron at Akrotiri were too impressed that it was to be a Belfast,

Short Brothers Belfast

but that first bit of friction with Libya did not last all that long, although the final blow up was to take place six months later in March 1970 when I was again involved.

We soon settled into a routine which called for a dawn take off for the two hour flight to El Adem and then a lounge around while the Movements staff carried out the loading before a late afternoon return and, after a few bevies in the transit bar, a crew coach to our hotel in downtown Limassol. One morning an old friend of mine, Sqdn Ldr Green, who I had known in the Hastings world was laying in wait for me in the Operations Block. It turned out that he was by then in the Intelligence world and wanted to know if we could help out with a little problem of theirs. They had received information that a Russian warship was anchored in Sollum Bay, just across the Libyan border with Egypt and would like confirmation or otherwise of that if possible. He asked if we could try and sight it, without actually infringing Egyptian airspace. He went on to say that no doubt it would depend on cloud cover and visibility but I was able to say it could probably be achieved regardless. The capabilities of weather radar were unknown to both of us in our Hastings days, but I had soon found out on the Belfast that by slanting down the scanner, coastlines showed up extremely well and, no doubt, large ships would. I had never used it for that purpose until later that day, and even without any deviation from our normal track we picked up a blip in the reported position, which was still there on our return leg. Sqdn Ldr Green was most grateful and asked for an update after each return trip thereafter.

Having arrived in Cyprus in the freight only configuration, that is to say the entire cargo hold was bereft of passenger seats, although a stub deck had been fitted above the cargo bay, just to the rear of the flight deck with 30 seats for the use of double and supernumerary crew members plus passengers. The stub deck with its lofty view from the rearward facing seats was more often than not referred to as "The Minstral's gallery" and how I wished I had used that term when I was later a witness at a court martial after a certain Germany day return sortie, but more of that later. We made a point of inviting the many passengers we carried on to the flight deck to get a better view of the outside world and for those on the return to Cyprus leg, undoubtedly their last sight of El Adem. On one occasion a brother and sister soon let it be known that they knew me quite well. Although they had lived next door to us in married quarters at Thorney Island I did not recognise them because they had been school children when last seen. They were the offspring of one of the best known characters in the transport world, Navigator Les Duval. Another reason for the lack of recognition was the son was now resplendent in Army, or it could have been Royal Marine, Officers uniform, his KD dress did not make it plain which. They had been visiting their parents and had been due to return direct to the UK from El Adem on a flight which had been cancelled at short notice when the troubles began. Luckily a Movements officer who I had by that time got to know fairly well was on duty on our arrival back at Akrotiri and I made a point of saying 'I hope our two Duval passengers manage to get a seat on the next VC10 flight to the UK'. He gave a quick wink and that was that. Up until that point female passengers had been forbidden from taking passage on Belfast aircraft due to the lack of toilet arrangements, but as the old saying goes "rules are for the guidance of wise men and the obedience of fools". We carried many more on the shuttle flights after someone had decided that on two hour flights toilet arrangements hardly entered the equation. Later, when the official word was printed on that subject it stated that "serving females may be carried in Belfast aircraft on short legs only", meaning, of course, short on distance/ airborne time. One Belfast Captain who was sitting at the bar at Brize Norton, having partaken of a few beers got a slap across the face after he had been approached by a WRAF officer who had asked if there was any chance of a flight on the trip he was due to take the next day. The slap came after he had replied "I had better see how long your legs are first".

At the start of the Belfast to El Adem shuttle the question of whether females could be carried or not had reared up. We were due to carry a lady passenger- the wife of a serviceman returning from a family bereavement in the UK- who should have been on a cancelled Argosy flight the previous day. At first she had been accepted as a passenger by the Movements staff and her belongings stowed aboard, but a last minute change of heart had led to her being off loaded, but not her belongings. So, two days later, after being stranded in Cyprus with only what she stood up in, she was escorted by two RAF PM nurses to our aircraft under obvious sedation. The senior nurse took me to one side and said "we are not certain what her problem is, so would you keep an eye on her? I could not help but say, "Her problem is probably due to the fact that some silly sod took her off our flight two days ago, but not her baggage. I got that frosty stare that only ladies in authority can give.

To end the ladies on Belfast flights saga, the rules were relaxed even further and it was declared that if an entire aircraft crew had occasion to be ferried by the Belfast fleet, for whatever reason, and contained some female members, then so be it. Well, it was bound to happen, and not long after that a VC10 crew with 4 stewardesses among their number were stranded in Bahrain and the next aircraft out of there for Cyprus was a Belfast. The Belfast Captain, Steve Stephens, well known for his boyish attitude to life, was quite delighted to have them on board. The rest of the VC10 crew, gentlemen to the Nth degree, insisted that their lady members should have the use of the bunks which were standard fit in a special compartment for double crewing. After they had retired and Steve had judged that they would be at the undressing stage, the fire alarm button was pressed. They vacated their sleeping area in great haste and in various forms of dress. The Air Loadmaster, who happened to be checking the security of the freight at that time, reported later that the Follies in Paris had nothing on that lot. It took some time to restore order and, predictably, a couple of hours later when passing Tehran, and the girls were now back in their bunks and fast asleep, an engine fire warning did flash on and Steve was not only forced to close it down, but also press the fire alarm bell yet again. The ladies, locked in their bunk compartment, refused to respond, no matter how hard the ALM pleaded with them to unlock the door and take up emergency stations. All he got was a load of "once bitten twice shy" and "tell that to the marines", etc. I don't think higher authority ever heard of this!

Our very last load out of El Adem before another Belfast took over from us consisted of a small army unit who had been detached to those parts with their own jeeps and trailers. It had taken two, or possibly three, C130 runs to take them out there but they all fitted nicely into our cargo hold, much to the delight of the senior officer in charge. After landing at Akrotiri we thought they would be unloaded and that would be that. However, the next morning after checking in at Ops we were informed that the load from El Adem was still aboard our aircraft XR363 and it was to be taken on to the UK. The freight was such that a re-fuelling stop at Luqa in Malta was now called for. This was no big deal, of course, but it meant a late night landing back at Brize, which led to slight alarm. After the start of the let-down to the west of London, the weather was almost perfect although we began to notice one or two mist patches in the valleys as we approached the Cotswolds, so I opted for radar vectors to the ILS for a final approach. All seemed to be going according to plan with the runway lights well in sight until suddenly we entered a fog bank at about 500' AGL. I thought I would continue down to the decision height and was just about to call for full power for an overshoot and a certain diversion when I felt the co-pilot snatch the controls, shouting "I've got the lights again". A quick look up from the instrument panel and I too saw them, so I resumed control and knew full well that although we would land a little deep, reverse thrust on the engines would stop us very quickly indeed. The Army were soon riding off into the sunset, or on this occasion a foggy night, and were obviously well pleased with the RAF, on this occasion at least.

Why I should remember that incident so well is that having mentioned that I thought Runway Visual Range (RVR) minima for landing should be introduced into the RAF at Thorney Island some years ago. A similar incident occured shortly after mine at Brize and this time round the Captain was the late Jerry Garforth, then on the OCU Training staff. The wheels clipped the boundary fence, just feet from the main public road between Brize Norton and Bampton villages. The drivers of private cars at the traffic lights must have had the nearest sighting to an aircraft in flight that anyone is ever likely to get or want. Another shortfall of 50' or so and it would have been into a ploughed field and a monumental disaster. One romantic story is that the Station Commander, Group Captain "Jock" Kennedy, later Air Marshal, awarded the aircraft captain "four faults' for taking away the top half of the fence. The true story is that quite by chance I was talking to Jerry in the Ops block soon after the incident when the CO came out of his office. Before Jerry could say a word he was being complemented on landing safely in such appalling conditions. When Jerry eventually started to explain what had actually happened I beat a hasty, diplomatic, retreat. I have always doubted the "four faults' bit.

It seemed strange at the time that with a shortage of flying, for the crews on strength, due to some of the ten aircraft being away on trials, or back at Shorts for modifications, that I was off on another Cyprus return within a week of returning from the El Adem shuttle. This called for a night stop at RAF Coningsby- a Station which I was to serve on later for four years, for overnight loading. I suppose everyone involved at Coningsby realised that time was on their side but, even so, it was all rather strange that only two people arrived on the scene after Air Traffic had told us to shut down on the dis-used runway, which was a long way from civilisation in domestic terms. It was only after the tug driver and the aircraft marshaller had pushed us around and were about to clear off, leaving us stranded on the wrong side of the active runway, that I thought it high time I stepped in. What I badly needed was a telephone to get some action as regards crew transport, so I thought I may as well kill two birds with one stone by commandeering the aircraft tug and its driver to take me and my luggage to the Officers' Mess and a link with the outside world. We did not pass the Station HQ on the way, thank goodness, but got quite a few double takes, not least of all by the Mess staff who I don't suppose had ever seen an officer arrive in such style before.

My very next trip after the Cyprus return was portentous. It was to take a number of jeeps, trailers and soldiers to Aldergrove airport in Northern Ireland. After seeing the start of the off loading I went over to the terminal for a coffee. On return I was utterly confused to see the same load back on board, or so I thought. When I approached a plummy voiced young Army subaltern and asked why we were taking back the same load we had just brought in he replied, "Good God, that's not the same load, they belong to us, not that other lot you brought over, can't you see our Regimental badge on the side of the jeeps, they are completely different to theirs". That bit of nonsense did not last long when the troubles really started. From then on troops arriving in the province for a tour of duty would drive whatever was available.

Two more interesting trips came my way before the year of 1969 was out. The first was a double crew meander around America that took in New York (JFK), both inbound and outbound, plus a day off there, and

Chicago, Los Angeles and Robins Air Force base in Georgia. One or two lasting impressions of the USA have remained with me over the years. The first was a trip to the top of the Empire State building which fully lived up to expectation, but my first sight of mounted police horses in the Big Apple beggared belief, compared with their British counterparts they all looked downtrodden, unkempt and weary. Chicago lived up to its name of the "Windy city" and that was about all. However, I did have an exchange of words with an American air stewardess who I happened to share a lift with. She started the brief conversation by asking if I was here for the convention and when I indicated that I was also flight crew she asked; "With which airline"? I was a little stunned after saying rather proudly, "The Royal Air Force" when she replied "The who?". Ah well, WWII was probably over before she was born, judging by her likely age. We all enjoyed Los Angeles, although it was not in the same league as 'Frisco'. We did not have time to see film studios, but our magnificent hotel, in which I had a large suite of rooms all to myself, was close to Sunset Boulevard. It was our crew's turn for the next leg, a long flog across the southern states to Georgia, which took 6:40 flying time, only one hour short of our normal Atlantic crossing, which gives some indication of the vastness of the USA. We had VHF contact throughout that day, being passed from one control centre to another and it was in the deep south, and well off the beaten track as regards international air travel, that one controller asked me to repeat virtually every call I made. A little exasperated, I asked if there was anything wrong with our radio to which he replied "No, it's just fine buddy, but we have some new girl assistants down here who have never heard an English voice on the radio before". Normal service was resumed in as near a BBC voice as I could muster. One crew member threw a spanner in the works by asking if it really was Robins AFB that we were due to land at because he had once landed at a Dobbins AFB not that far away. The Navigator, always the custodian of the transflight, made a rapid search of his Nav bag to confirm he had got it right and the panic was over. We all enjoyed our one night stand in that part of the States. It was in a glorious setting and all USAF members on base made us particularly welcome.

That area was to become very familiar to all Belfast crews later, as some C130 wings on the RAF Hercules fleet needed urgent repairs by the makers, not long after entering service, and the Belfast was the only RAF cargo aircraft that could cater for their size. Those flights operated between Georgia and Marshals of Cambridge, a firm heavily involved in major servicing of that type for the RAF. The story behind the damage caused to the metal wings is truly bizarre by any standards. It was related that some years before the C130 entered service with the RAF, the American Air Force had found that micro bugs in jet aviation fuel caused corrosion to the metal wings of the C130, but advised that they had come up with an additive that put paid to those bugs before they could do any damage. They strongly recommended that the RAF used it too, but for a cost of £1 per 400 gallons some civil servant vetoed the purchase on the grounds of cost.

The second interesting trip to conclude the year started with a passenger trip in a VC10 to Singapore to await the arrival of one of our Belfasts which we then took to Darwin for a night stop where an RAF Lightning fighter, damaged in an accident, was loaded on to our aircraft by the Lightning ground crew we had brought with us after which we returned it to their base at Tengah in Singapore. We then again became VC10 passengers on a flight back to the UK. A very tiring few days indeed.

For one reason or another we had not stayed on base at Darwin, having been billeted in the best hotel in town, which was an eye opener in itself. Two of us had made the mistake of entering the rear public bar of that hotel when the five o'clock swill was well under way. It was the nearest thing one will ever get to see as in Western cowboy films- swinging doors, a long bar with beer all over the place, and empty glasses being slid to the bar tender. I fully expected a Sheriff and two of his men to enter at any time, however I was to be disappointed on that one. One person we did meet was an Austrian born carpenter who insisted in taking us to every other bar in town in his pick up truck, a hair raising experience in itself, but why was a chap born in one of the most beautiful countries in the world (in my opinion) living in tropical Darwin. There must have been a story behind it all.

The start of 1970 was strange in that I was slotted, along with another crew, plus the Squadron Training Officer (who would be in overall command), for another round the world trainer, this time westward. The only difference to the itinerary of my previous eastward circumnavigation of the world was that a landing at Offutt Air Force base in central USA had been substituted for the Canadian airfield of Namao. I had never before experienced such a low temperature as we found at Offutt, nor seen so much snow and marvelled at how the American Air Force had managed to keep the runways clear in such conditions. The weather had certainly taken its toll on our Belfast during the night; to the extent that the crew Chief reported over ten defects. However, luckily, all fit to fly items. After take off we raised and lowered the undercarriage a few times to make sure nothing had frozen up, but we need not have worried unduly because there was a marked increase in temperature as we flew westwards and all faults gradually cleared themselves. My suspicion that the training officer in charge of us had not actually been on a Pacific route before, which invariably involved a landing in Hawaii, was duly confirmed when I stood on the flight deck with him as the other operating crew were approaching Hickam Air Base and he said "You'll be seeing Pearl Harbour soon, it's this side of the airfield". It was, in fact, to the west of the field but I let it go.

Other trips came thick and fast and I will cover some of the most interesting in the order in which they came up during the rest of my time on No 53 Squadron. My first flying venture into the Arctic circle was when a Bardufoss (Norway) day return trip came my way. From an aviation point of view it was interesting enough in that the surrounding mountains called not only for a high minimum descent height if still in cloud, but also some tampering with the ILS glide slope. I think the ground transmitter must have been on high ground beyond the airfield because after becoming visual on our approach we had to lose height rather quickly to manage a straight in approach to land. Although Bardufos was to become a regular run, only once did I night stop there and sample life in a super Norwegian hotel, which was virtually on the airfield itself. An added bonus came after I thought I might as well have a look at the TV in my room to see if I could make head or tail of Norwegian programmes. Being a football fanatic I really thought it was my lucky day when live coverage of the Wembley Cup final appeared on the screen; what more could one ask for in the Arctic circle. It was not on TV in the UK, by the way.

A day return to the Belfast's maker's home of Sydenham on the shores of Belfast Loch, and less than two miles from the city centre, was of more than passing interest in that we had plenty of ground time to look around the factory that had turned out so many famous aircraft from the very beginnings of aviation in the UK. Later, I gave a nostalgic look across the water to where the good ship Orbital had laid at anchor for a night in December 1943 during our voyage from Liverpool to Durban.

My very next trip was something of an historic landmark, although we did not know it at the time. It started off as a normal double crewing to El Adem and return to pick up their airfield radar and I would be Captain on the return leg. I suppose we should have felt that perhaps the trip was of some importance when we were told that our Station Commander, Group Captain, "Jock" Kennedy, would be coming along as Commander of the flight. The return shuttle went according to plan but it was during our ground time there that the local Air Movers told us that we would be the second last flight out of El Adem, and the last flight the next day would mark the end of RAF operated airfields in Africa. For RAF historians I will just mention that our take off was in the evening of 22nd March 1970. The very last RAF controlled departure occurred the next morning when an Argosy of No 70 Squadron returned to its base in Cyprus. The RAF ensign was lowered for the last time at El Adem on the 28th March when all remaining British forces in Libya departed by sea from Tobruk, beating Colonel Gadaffi's deadline of 31st March by just three days.

It was not often that a little local difficulty occurred after a successful flight, but there are bound to be exceptions of course. In this case I had been approached by the Catering Officer at El Adem to see if I could possibly take some of his worldly possessions back to Brize Norton as his next posting was to be our Station where he would be Officer in charge of the new transit hotel called "The Gateway". No problem I said, they will be delivered to your door. It was within seconds of having bundled his rather large number of suitcases into the foyer of The Gateway that I was confronted by an irate female civilian member of staff who yelled "you can't leave your luggage there", to which I replied, "They are not my mine actually". This did nothing for her anger as she then said "I don't care whose luggage it is, it can't stay there". That was it, having been out of bed for close on 24 hours, with 14 hours airborne time, I snapped back, "the luggage actually belongs to the Catering Officer who will be in charge of you and everything and everybody in this building two weeks from today, so I suggest you take good care of it and keep them safe, goodnight!"

It was just a matter of time before I was made the Squadron Flight Safety officer, having completed a course on the subject three times over in London. With all Belfasts ever built on the Squadron, it was to prove an interesting secondary duty with all tit bits of a technical nature passing my way. The actual occurrences mainly involved engine failures about which we could do little. However, an increasing number of undercarriage lowering failures began to crop up, which indicated that continued use might be to blame. They all involved electrical failures so, being an ex airframe fitter, I followed the cable routing through the aircraft with interest and eventually noted a bit of chaffing on the outer insulation of the electrical wire at the point that it passed through a weight reducing hole in an aluminium former. It was not worn completely through but it did indicate that undue tension was being placed on the wire when the undercarriage was being lowered and the remedy was to either re-route the wire or make them slightly longer. When the new CO of No 53 Squadron, Wing Commander Neil Nugent read my submission, he called me in and said "I always thought chaffing meant vexing". I explained all and we had a good laugh about it but I have often wondered if he was pulling my leg. One thing was for sure, he was the most dedicated RAF officer that I ever served under and I was particularly upset when he was retired prematurely under the 1976 defence cutbacks which particularly hit the transport force. I learnt later from a very senior Officer that it was purely a numbers game, so many from one rank and so many from another right down the line with personalities not counting for a great deal. In this case, the RAF had certainly missed out.

One item from the technical world really sent my mind into overdrive. It was an edict that one of the two igniters on the Tyne engine was to be removed. The old American maxim of "If it ain't broke, don't fix it" again came to the fore and after asking many engineers what was the theory behind it all I never received a rational explanation. I got plenty of "Rolls Royce must know what they are doing" and that was about all. Little did I foresee that I was the first victim of that bit of nonsense.

Every available crew was involved in 'Exercise Bersatu Padu' (Malay for Complete unity) in one way or another in April of 1970. It was the largest airlift exercise ever undertaken by Air Support Command and it appeared that its main aim was to reassure our Malaysian friends that in any emergency after the final British pull out, reinforcements in large numbers could be made in a very short time scale. No 53 Squadron used five Belfasts and made eight round trips to Singapore within a few days, using slip crews positioned in Cyprus, Bahrain, Gan and Singapore. My crews involvement was to fly the sectors UK-Cyprus Bahrain-Gan before returning as passengers in a VC10. Everything was going according to plan until our final leg to Gan when the load aboard our aircraft was such that a re-fuelling stop was called for on the island of Masirah. After that little chore had been completed we again boarded the aircraft and started engines, or tried to. A reconditioned engine recently out of Rolls Royce and now with only one igniter fitted refused all our best efforts to get it fired up. The problem was that the maximum temperature allowed was being reached before the jet turbine fully spooled up and we had to shut down and hold a council of war. I had heard of four engined piston aircraft, particularly the tricycle undercarriage variety, being taxied at high speed down long runways on three engines to produce the torque load that leads to wind milling in flight. That took a mighty load off the starter motor and smooth out any slipping clutch problems. In the case of our turbine I reasoned that the build up of pressure on the turbine might lead to a fire up before the high temperature was reached. It did the trick on that occasion and we duly taxied back down the runway and made a normal departure. The problem, and our cure, was reported to the next crew but that particular defect did not recur during the exercise. It is always pleasing for a transport crew to have a one off special trip, particularly if its just an away day. My very next trip after the rather hectic days of Bersatu Padu was a good example.

The idea was to pick up a specialist Air Loading Team at RAF Abingdon, and transport them to my old stamping ground of Thorney Island where they would spend the day testing the feasibility of loading and securing a Royal Marines hovercraft in our aircraft which was on trials in that area and then reverse the procedures about eight hours later. It was a highly successful exercise but I never did hear of it being used in anger. On No 53 Squadron, with double crewing or using slip crews down the route to the Far East, we spent more time away from the UK than in the Hastings/Beverley/Argosy days, but total flying hours were well down than previously in the days of one aircraft-one crew trips, flown mostly in daylight. It had its compensations, of course, and nobody objected to a few days off in Cyprus, for example, with so much on offer, particularly so because long range crews were always housed in civilian hotels in downtown Limassol, which was ideal for relaxing in. Another feature of landing in Cyprus was that on the RAF Station itself there was a 24 hour reception building for passengers and crews alike and it was something of a ritual to have a few beers there before proceeding to our allotted hotel. It was often noted that some VC10 crews, who had been pre-flight briefing at Brize at the same time as a Belfast crew often looked up in almost disbelief when the Belfast crew arrived whilst they were still on their second or third beer. It was just like the old A1 road stories of passing a lorry way back and seeing it trundle by during a coffee stop. We had to suffer a bit getting jibes about flying the "Short Belslow" and being asked if any of our crew were suffering from scurvy yet! The Belfast was, in fact, fitted with a Mach meter which often read in excess of .5 in the cruise.

Even Bahrain had its plus points, not least of all because transit crews and passengers were housed at Britannia House, which was off base and run for, and by, the RAF. Bahrain also boasted a 'Malcolm Club' plus another Officers' Mess which was mainly for the use of the Royal Navy and Army, whose inmates always made visiting aircrew most welcome. With drink always available in Brittannia House, things could get a little bit out of control on occasions, especially when a crew knew that they would not be flying in the next two or three days or so. For one reason or another at least two C130 crews had been delayed there for some days on one occasion when our crew pitched up just after midnight. The bar and lounge area was one of complete devastation; chairs and drinking glasses all over the place and the outer crusts of sandwiches littered the place, the bread in those parts being almost inedible to our tastes. Virtually every bench seat was occupied with what, at first sight, appeared to be prone dead bodies. Our arrival at RAF Muharraq had coincided with that of an RAF VC10 crew and we had all shared the same crew coach into town. We noted that the VC10 captain, a newly promoted Sqdn Ldr, under the recently introduced idiotic scheme which had made Sqdn Ldr the lowest rank for VC10 captains, was regarded as the guardian of standards down the route, taking to task any aircrew of a lesser rank than his own who did not wear the standard RAF Transport dress in the tropics, full sleeve KD shirts with tie, and full length trousers, amongst other things. After our entry into the bar area we thought it was just as well that he had probably gone straight to bed after checking in, but that was not the case. While we were still thinking that perhaps we had missed out on a jolly good party, he suddenly appeared on the scene and was almost speechless. Eventually he spotted one officer who had not quite passed out and barked at him "I'll need to know your name and squadron number because I will be reporting this disgraceful scene to your Commanding Officer when I get back to the UK", to which a voice from another Officer, who seemed to be completely out of this world, replied "I shouldn't bother if I were you, I am his Commanding Officer. Although all on No 53 Squadron had taken the sudden promotion of many VC10 Captains from Flt Lt to Sqdn Ldr in their stride, we had long thought that for most of the time they were just civilians in uniform, flying human cargo up and down the route on the Singapore run, which had previously been carried out by Eagle Aviation, and several other airlines over the years.

A lucky break came my way during the summer of 1970 when it was decided to bring in one or two Chipmunks to Brize to give air experience flights to Air Training Corps cadets during their annual camp. It was RAF Colerne all over again, with not many transport pilots qualified on that type, so I had four glorious weeks of non-stop flying in an aircraft which was second to none, in my book, for handling characteristics. Back at the coal face we had many UK and/or Germany to Decimomannu (Sardinia) flights in connection with the Nato air firing and bombing range which had been established there. Sardinia is part and parcel of Italy, but they had one very strange rule about their rights over that island. If military aircraft flew in from the UK or mainland Europe that was fine, but if it was from Cyprus then a customs clearance in Italy was required. It was just my luck to have to land at Brindisi on one such flight to find that not only was the crosswind just in limits but the turbulence on finals was almost unbelievable, one landing I could have well done without. The Customs Officers were not the slightest bit interested in our cargo but did ask to be shown around the flight deck which seemed to impress them greatly.

1971 got off to a good start with a major exercise in the Bahamas. Our crew was pre positioned at the USAF base at Lajes in the Azores to await the arrival of another Belfast which we would then take on to Nassau direct and, after a rest day, fly it back to Brize direct. The ground time in the Azores was to be 36 hours so we saw a great deal of the local area, and also became quite friendly with a Britannia slip crew on the same exercise. We took off about 30 minutes before the Brit crew who soon overtook us, and made quite a few sarcastic remarks over the radio such as we'll have another drink together in Nassau, if you ever make it there that is. It did take us over 12 hours in the event, but we all had a smirk on our faces during that time when we heard on the radio that the Brit was having to divert into Bermuda for fuel because of higher than forecast headwinds. We made a point of buying them a drink later after they eventually checked into the same hotel as ourselves. The drive from the airfield into town had been one of pure delight to those of us visiting Nassau for the first time, noting a number of small float planes on one or two small lakes in idyllic surroundings. It has been one of my unfulfilled ambitions to fly one of them ever since. Ironically, the only time I had to divert for fuel uplift was two days later after we had set off for the direct flight to Brize and, again, it was to Bermuda, this time because of lower than predicted tailwinds.

It was about that time that I had a real shock to the system when I was told that I would soon be called upon to attend a court martial as a witness. I became completely mystified when it was stated that it revolved around a day return to one of the RAF airfields in Germany just before the previous Christmas. I soon found out from a member of the Sgt's Mess, the 'Freemasons' of the Royal Air Force, that our crew chief on that flight, a flying ground engineer, had been charged with misappropriating a part from a car during our ground time in Germany which he had found impossible to buy in England for his own car. It was with something more than trepidation that I entered the courts marshal room and took the oath, not only because this was, for me, the first and thankfully last time that I was confronted with a Judge Advocate General, a civilian in wig and gown. Most of my answers to start with were 'yes, your honour' when being asked such mundane questions as, can you confirm that you were the captain of the flight to Germany on such and such a date, was the accused a member of your crew for the entire trip, etc. Among other things I confirmed that it was not one of my duties to check the cargo for unauthorised items or anything of that nature. I soon settled down and thought it was nearly over until the prosecuting lawyer got to his feet. It started with "What was the mood amongst the crew that day?" To which I could only reply "much the same as normal as far as I can remember". In a Rumpole type voice he said, "as far as you can remember indeed, but it was just before Christmas and perhaps you and your crew had a few drinks after landing in Germany?" I just could not believe it, but managed to splutter "my goodness no, there has to be eight hours between bottle and throttle". The judge then intervened to say, "For the benefit of the court would you kindly explain what this business of bottle and throttle is all about, is it something to do with drinking alcohol out of a bottle or what?" After I had explained that drinking any alcohol of any kind was forbidden from eight hours before planned takeoff time for any flight. He gravely observed "I think we all understand now". However, there was more to come when the prosecuting lawyer asked me, "did you notice anything out of the ordinary about the defendant when he boarded your aircraft for the flight back to the UK?" To which I replied, "I didn't actually see him board, but I do remember seeing him on the stub deck after takeoff and asking if everything was all right from a technical point of view?" This seemed all too much for the Judge Advocate General, who might well have had an excellent lunch, and he snapped, "poop deck, poop deck, surely you don't have a poop deck on an aircraft, isn't that all to do with sailing ships and Lord Nelson and all that?" I was really at a loss for words and trying to avoid his steady glare. As I turned my head sideways in embarrassment only to notice that I was looking straight into the eyes of a young WRAF officer who was the only female among five junior officers detailed to attend the proceedings as observers to gain experience. Although the four male officers all looked stoney faced, not understanding the judges intervention, she was having as much difficulty maintaining a straight face as myself. The dear lady had recently become engaged to a Sqn Ldr Ken Newman, one of our Belfast navigators, and was obviously aware of stub decks and minstrels galleries etc. Goodness only knows what might have been said, on reflection, if I had used the nickname Minstrels Gallery. "Orchestras on aeroplanes, thought they only had them on ocean liners," might have been a riposte.

All aircrew get a bit wound up when the time comes for their annual medical examination and I was no exception, my blood pressure had been remarked upon on what seemed to be alternating years. However, at Brize Norton each squadron now had its very own M.O. and ours, Flt. Lt. Gill, was known to be fairly strict, although he did believe in mixing with the boys in the bar whenever possible. On the professional side he thought that some of our double crewing, which were often immediately followed by long passenger flights home, made it imperative that crews really did get some sleep during those trips and invited all crew members on the squadron to ask him for mogadon tablets to induce that state. After a month or two he took me aside in the mess one day and said, "Jacko, you are only one of two captains on No 53 who have not asked to be put on mogadon tablets, are you sure you don't need them?" I had vaguely guessed what was coming and replied, "Thanks a lot, doc, but I have found my own cure for insomnia." He just gave me the nearest expression that any doctor ever gets to of, "I think I know what you mean".

By the early seventies the number of wartime pilots on front line squadrons was dwindling fast with most of those remaining being on instructional duties or elevated out of the rank range. For obvious reasons, those who had actually served in India, before their independence in 1947, were a very small proportion of those few and with hindsight I think it was just as well that I was, quite by chance, the captain of the Belfast that transported the first Sea King helicopter for the Indian Navy in Goa. As previously mentioned, the Indians had been heavily indoctrinated by the British civil service when we ruled the sub-continent, and protocol was taken to extremes for most of the time. It could be like walking on egg shells on occasions and when the air load master asked me how many manifests he should take I said, in perhaps a too off-hand manner, "better make it a couple of dozen". He said " You are joking aren't you, I thought about ten at the most would do it." I insisted on the twenty-four and, sure enough, on our arrival in Goa that was one short. Every department on the base seemed to need one for some reason or other. That was a minor point compared with what was to come because, whilst being thanked for the safe delivery of the Sea King by a three ring naval Officer, another three ringer appeared on the scene who, it transpired, was the chief customs officer from the port of Goa who made it very plain indeed that his team should deal with us and not the Indian Navy. A real ding-dong followed, I don't know whether it was when the customs officer was trying to back down a little that he announced that he could possibly treat us as visiting foreign seamen. The roof nearly did fall in at that, the naval officer went into orbit and raged "Visiting foreign seamen." twice over, and finished with "don't you realise that these chaps are from a Commonwealth country just like ours?" It was almost like Karachi all over again.

The hotel in downtown Goa left a lot to be desired and that was putting it mildly. Having arrived at daybreak and not due to depart until late the next night, flow control at Upavon had really cocked it up yet again. We had plenty of time on our hands which enabled us to have a good look around the town. Two memories remain with me, the first was the sight of a statue of Vasco-De-Garma laying prone and broken in two after having being toppled from its base in the grounds of a church. The second was noting that the beautiful beach on the waterfront had recently been used as a public toilet and later actually seeing it put to that use.

A bit more protocol reared up when a junior Indian Navy Officer appeared at our pre-flight briefing and happened to mention that although the base, except air traffic control, was now stood down, the Commander was working late in his office on some important business that evening and he would be glad to see us before departure if we had time to spare. It was as good as an order, of course. I took along my navigator, Sqn Ldr Thompson, for company and we were duly ushered in. He started off by saying he hoped we had enjoyed our stay and was the hotel up to standard? I assured him that everything was just fine and how glad I was to be back in India again after 25 years. He then said one of his Officers would be paying the hotel bill the next day to which I replied it had already been paid for out of our Impress and that was always the routine for the RAF. He then asked if there was any hotel limit placed on us and we both assured him that was never the case which seemed to be well received. He next wanted to know why were we continuing to Singapore that evening and not returning to the U.K. because the Indian Government was footing a return flight to Goa only, and he hoped they would not be charged extra for the extended flight. I really bent over backwards with that one, saying whatever sum civil servants in London had come up with would be the bottom line and their only interest would be in hearing that we had made a safe delivery. It was a very pleased Commander who bade us farewell. On the walk across the tarmac, Sqn Ldr Tompson said "I never thought the day would come, particularly about you Jacko, when I would say I think you have missed your vocation, you should have been in the diplomatic corps and not the RAF". It came as no real surprise to note that the crews on the next nine Sea King deliveries to Goa, to complete the order for ten, were all housed in a five star hotel, recently built to cater for the forthcoming tourist and hippy invasion, and no Customs interventions occurred again.

I was quite miffed that very dark night as we flew across southern India from coast to coast without being able to see the ground and take in the sights, particularly so because our track was almost identical for most of the time with the rail track on which I had travelled between Poona and Madras a quarter of a century before. It was in the middle of that night that we had some trouble in maintaining radio contact with the airway controllers using the frequencies provided by the planners back at base. Being in the Bangalore area my mind again went back to the war years when in Egypt I had been given the option of Spitfires or one of four other types and I recalled that all my friends who had gone for P47s (Thunderbolts) finished up in a place called Yelahanka near that city for a ground attack course. It did occur to me that even if such an airfield still existed its name might well have been changed, but what the hell, we had nothing to lose, so I asked the nav. to see if any reference to such a place was in the Far East en-route documents. I was more than surprised when he confirmed there was, and even more so when a very chirpy Indian voice answered our first call, after re-dialling their frequency. He laid on a first class service thereafter, until handing us over to Madras.

Dawn was breaking as we entered the Malacca Straights for the last hour of our flight. In fact, my log book records that of the twenty hours of flying time between Cyprus and Singapore, eighteen and a half hours had been in darkness. Some trip, and now we had to face the long flog back to the UK in the back of a VC10. On checking in at Changi Creek transit hotel, which had a notice board displaying all inbound and outbound transport flights, we did not at first pick up any mention of our arrival from Goa but eventually decided that we must have arrived from

Dabolim, a name not familiar to us, but later confirmed as the airfield name for Goa. This led to much confusion with many of our friends on the VC10 and Brittannia fleets asking where on earth was Dabolim? Educated guesses covered most of the countries in the Far East. It had been an interesting flight and I might just mention that navigator Sqdn Ldr Thompson went on to gain his PPL and also set up a small civilian flying club on Brize Norton airfield and, after leaving the service, took up an appointment with the CAA. It turned out during the flight that my co-pilot on that trip, Flt Lt Harper, had married the daughter of the family run "Old New Inn" in Burton-on-the-water, the hotel that Betty and I had stayed in during our 1949 honeymoon after Paris. It was nice to learn that the hotel was still with the family.

The very next trip was a dream ticket, a four day jaunt to Ottawa and return via Boscombe Down to recover one of their helicopters which had been in Canada for cold weather trials. The big bonus was that it was a one crew detail which meant flying on four consecutive days without any pre-positioning or passenger flying involved. Another plus was that in addition to two night stops in Gander, we also had one night in one of Ottawa's top hotels. The only drawback in Ottawa came on a well remembered Sunday. If anybody thought our drinking laws in those days were archaic then Canada would have been a real eye opener. Ladies were not allowed to use bars and their escorts had to transport drinks for them to adjacent lounge areas. That did not affect our all male crew, of course, but the shattering news was that being a Sunday we could not even buy alcoholic drinks of any kind, even after explaining that we were bona-fide residents of the hotel. However, all was not lost because a porter took us outside and said: "See that building over there, that's our Parliament and after passing that and crossing the bridge over the river, you'll be in Quebec where the bars are open all day and every day", enough said.

Our two stop overs in Newfoundland could not be bettered. It was such a peaceful setting with the locals always particularly friendly to visiting RAF crews. We all bought salmon at what seemed give away prices, which was duly stored in the Oxygen compartment up front of the Belfast, and always freezing cold. I was still in the habit, despite my experience in French New Caledonia, of getting up early in the mornings to have, hopefully, a lonesome breakfast, but it was not to be on our last morning before our Atlantic crossing. The restaurant would have been completely empty except that a massive round table in the centre of the room was already occupied by ten people. That would have been just fine by me except that after taking up a small table in a far corner of the room a male voice suddenly boomed out: "You look so lonely over there all by yourself, come on over and meet the family, we'll soon have another place set for you". Being in uniform I thought it would be letting the side down if I didn't comply, but certainly hoped that it would all be over before the rest of the crew arrived. You can probably guess the rest; they did arrive, almost en-masse, and apart from knowing smirks I took a fair bit of stick after take off with such remarks as "I always thought you liked to be all on your own at breakfast, Jacko".

That spring of 1971 also saw a visit to RAF Brize Norton by the Queen which took in an inspection of the Squadrons and also an official luncheon and this time it was the padre's assistant who took a bit of stick, however that charming young lady, Miss Pat Billington, did have the last laugh. On a number of dummy runs she stood in as the Queen and the lads around the bar, which she supported more for a chat than a drink, had pulled her leg. After the final dress rehearsal she had to take a few comments of: "Had another big lunch then Pat, you want to watch your figure you know" and "I suppose that was another waste of time Pat, I bet it went off perfectly and would have been fine on the day without another practice". Pat looked the chap straight in the eye and said, "No, it didn't. In fact when the steward served my side salad a creepy crawly came out from under the lettuce, so I don't think those rehearsals have been a complete waste of time, do you?" Pat was ideal for her post and when a very popular Air Loadmaster died of natural causes, she masterminded the funeral service and committal at the local crematorium with military precision and a great deal of diplomacy with the bereaved: a very rare talent.

The middle of summer 1971 was unusual in the diversity of the tasks that came my way, all well remembered for one reason or another. The first was hunting around the Brize area for rain bearing clouds, which might seem strange, but we did have on board a specially installed device, the brain child of Field Aviation, which pumped a certain type of fluid onto the windscreen to dissolve sticking rain droplets. It was our lucky day as we found several such clouds and the system worked extremely well, but that was the last I heard about it until recently when I fell into conversation with a chap who had actually worked on the system. The information was that it had worked quite well on most fixed wing aircraft but had been a failure on Helicopters, the type which would have benefited most from such a system, so the project was abandoned.

Later that month I was to airlift the heaviest single item that had ever been carried by the RAF up to that point. It was a 52,000 lbs stone crusher, and with another 10,000 lbs of back up equipment it was quite a load but, even then, well within the Belfast's capabilities. It was urgently required on the island of Masirah, off the north eastern tip of Oman and our pick up point was Shajah, one of the United Arab Emirates. The planners, quite rightly, had allowed 24 hours ground time for loading and unloading at the two respective locations. Shajah was normally off the beaten track for the strategic fleet and almost all night stops in the Gulf were at Bahrein. However, it was imperative in our case and full advantage was taken of the situation. We had arrived quite early in the morning at Shajah after a mainly night time flight direct from Cyprus and with the next take off not due for another 24 hours we took the obvious course of delaying sleep until that evening. We did not have long to ponder on what to do with ourselves for the rest of that day before an Air Movements Officer, a chap who I had first met in Singapore and who was now in charge of the difficult task of loading our aircraft, suddenly said, "If your crew would like a trip into Dubai, I can put a driver and transport at your disposal for the afternoon". It was music to my ears, at least, having come under its spell when passing through there as a flying boat passenger towards the end of WWII. This time I would have quite a few hours to browse around the shops and again enjoy the sight of Arabs plying their trade in the fabulous setting of Dubai Creek. Nothing disappointed, and it was a day to remember if ever there was one in the context of route flying.

The next morning I would not say I was exactly apprehensive, but two points did cross my mind. The first was that with one massive item of freight on board was it's position in just the right spot to ensure the centre of gravity was as shown on the weight and balance sheet? The second point was that if any mishap on landing occurred, could the aircraft restraining points stand up to any sudden deceleration of such a massive item. In the event that was the least of our worries because nearing the end of our short 1 hour 30 minute flight, Air Traffic at Masirah came up with the news that the wind speed there was now higher than previously forecast and across the runway. It was way outside our limits, but the helpful Air Traffickers then said they had a natural surface runway which was more or less into wind, and nearly as long as the main Tarmac runway. I had landed a Hastings on grass at Manston and used the hard packed red soil at Nairobi on a regular basis, and even the Dambusters airfield at Scampton, like most other pre-war stations, was a grass only field until mid WWII. When I called downwind and finals for the secondary runway, I received the predictable reply of "at pilot's discretion". In the event the landing was normal but I refrained from using the reverse thrust in case later I was called upon to explain why all four engines needed changing due to sand ingestion. Even on the normal runway I had never intended using reverse thrust, if at all possible, because of the load aboard. Before we had vacated the aircraft, the air movers were already going into action and unloaded the extra 10,000 lbs of fright in no time at all. Now, however, came the tricky bit; removing the stone crusher, which had taken so long to load, I decided to stay and watch the proceedings along with our loadmaster. Things were not going at all to plan and for every foot or so of movement towards the rear ramp, the movement had to be reversed because the beast of a load was edging sideways towards the side fuselage. This went on a number of times until, in desperation, the Movements Officer leapt into the operating cab and started up the stone crusher's engine. I had no doubt that he had never driven a self propelled vehicle of that size before, but it was too late to do anything about it. Both the loadmaster and myself doubted the wisdom of such tactics and also the concept of starting up such a massive engine on board an aircraft, but that discussion only took place after it was all over!

Upavon had again allowed for a 24 hour stop period to cater for the unloading, but on the island of Masirah there was no Dubai to resort to, in fact, there was nothing at all. I sent a signal to Upavon stating that our task was complete and we had plenty of crew duty time left so should we re-position to Bahrein. It seemed to be less than one hour later when the reply was received which stated that we should fly direct to Cyprus if possible, otherwise to Bahrein? The flight time to Cyprus was a full eight hours, however being a westward flight we had two extra hours of daylight and it seemed quite remarkable to look back on all we had achieved in the hours of daylight on that June day. A slip crew awaited our arrival at Akrotiri and soon XR367 was on her way back to the UK. It was over a few wind down beers that one of our crew suddenly said, "Do you realise that it was only early yesterday morning that we took off from here for Sharjah"? None of us did, but it was true. That was life on No 53 Squadron, certainly different to any other transport squadron in the RAF.

The only other very special load that I was ever to carry on No 53 Squadron was unknown to me until after its safe delivery to the RAF staging post of Gan in the middle of the Indian Ocean. I say safe delivery,

Fifty-Two Years in the Cockpit - Volume Two

which it was as far as myself and the rest of the crew were concerned, but not so for a very interested Flight Sergeant who was watching the unloading of the freight although it was nearly midnight, with more than a passing interest. He nearly went spare when one of the massive wooden boxes we had been carrying slipped off the side of the loading ramp with a shattering thud, causing substantial damage to the crate and, no doubt, whatever was inside it. Later that evening the Movements Officer called by the Transit Mess, as was his want, and enlightened us on the near hysterical behaviour of the F/Sgt concerned. When he started off by saying "It was all to do with satellites" we all looked a little bewildered, he did go on to say that the Skynet Communications satellite launched by the Americans from Cape Kennedy in late 1969 was to be used by the RAF, and that Gan would be involved. It turned out that the F/St was something of an expert on the installation and working of the system so he had been sent out on a twelve month tour on Gan to await the imminent arrival of the bits and pieces needed to make the system work- that was ten months before our arrival, so all was in vain. He would be tour ex and back in the UK before replacement items for his Skynet arrived, so his outbursts were understandable under the circumstances, having spent ten months with precious little to do.

Gan, like Bahrein, was one of those places where the unexpected often cropped up on the domestic side, with all crews being billeted in close proximity. Being a small island there was the added problem of looking after 150 or so passengers during each VC10's downtime and under the same roof as for transmitting and slip crews. There was, however, one bar set aside for aircrew only, which helped a lot during peak periods. On one occasion when the bar was packed with crews not due to fly again for some time, a lady, who was obviously not aircrew, pushed her way to the counter and demanded two double gins pronto. All around watched with interest as she downed one glass, and was about to do the same with another when two more ladies, who, although in civilian clothes, most of us recognised as RAF Casevac Nursing Sisters, arrived on the scene. They were just wonderful with the poor lady at the bar, who was obviously on her way back to England under their care, but had slipped her leash for a few moments. She was one of a few European housewives who found the life of having nothing to do all day long in the tropics too much to cope with.

On a lighter note, a tale about a VC10 crew on Gan has amused me over the years, even though it is a little lewd. It had better be noted, first of all, that most manual and menial tasks on the island were carried out by foreign labour and in that department there was two extremes; Pakistanis, who had been left over from the reconstruction of that base in the 1950s and carried out the heavy out of doors duty tasks, whilst the indoor jobs, such as serving on at table, fell to the local Maldivan males from the next island of Hittadu, which being connected to Gan by a coral built causeway, meant they could go home to their families each night and live the life they had always been used to. To say the Pakistanis were worldly wise would be an understatement, whereas the Maldivans, most of whom had never even left Addu Atoll in their lives, were simple souls who had been brought up to never tell a lie and that was the crux of what happened one evening at dinner. A Sqdn Ldr VC10 Captain who was well known for liking dignity and good form on all occasions managed, whenever possible, to round up his crew and have a few drinks with them before proceeding into the dining room en-masse. He was sitting at the head of the table on the night in question when he said to a young Maldivan steward "My compliments to the chef and tell him my steak is not quite up to standard tonight. A few minutes later the ever smiling young lad returned and said, "Chef, he says you can stick the steak where the monkey sticks it's nuts"! All conversation on the Captain's table came to an abrupt end, and we could not help but notice that the younger members of his crew were having great difficulty in containing their mirth. It was not all that often that visiting aircrew were invited into the permanent Officers' Mess, but on one such rare occasion I was approached by a lady who said "Weren't you flying Hastings on Christmas Island about ten years ago?" History was repeating itself as she had been one of only two WVS ladies on Christmas Island and was now serving on Gan.

The rest of 1971, except for the last month, was a little mundane, but I managed more AEF Chipmunk flying during the summer plus two distinct weeks away from flying aircraft altogether. Both were in an advisory operation, with the first being to RAF Gutersloh in Germany during a transport reinforcement paper exercise. That is to say, it was all pretend and I was on hand to say what might have been for the Belfast fleet as regards turn round times, probable fuel uplifts, etc. Before returning to the UK the Indian born Squadron Leader in charge of the supply squadron there took all concerned out to dinner in a nearby town at his own expense, a very nice touch, appreciated by all. The second week was in Malta, but this time it was for real, and the difference was startling, with Belfasts being delayed in the UK for technical reasons, flights taking longer than expected, unloading and loading not going according to plan, etc. However, it turned out to be a good practice for what was to happen the following January when the RAF was forced to pull out of Malta unexpectedly, albeit for only a short period, before the final withdrawal from that lovely island in 1979.

Sometimes short trips around the UK and western Europe, with a number of landings at various locations in one day, could be far more demanding than, say, an Atlantic crossing, and particularly so in the northern winter months. One of those came my way late in 1971 when what should have been one of the easier trips turned out to be anything but. It was a triangular flight with the first landing at RAF Kinloss on the Moray Firth in Scotland which, being on the eastern side of the Highlands had a fairly good weather factor for most of the time but that was not the case on that particular day. Shortly after crossing the Scottish border it was non-stop cloud flying until shortly before touchdown following a radar talk down. The low cloud base had certainly not been part of the Met briefing at Brize, so we had to have a rethink about our next leg, which was to pick up freight at Benbecula, a rocket range on North Uist, part of the Outer Hebrides. It boasted two navigational aids in Tacan and VOR, but no radar. A phone call to that outpost elicited the information that there was no rain, good visibility, a steady wind down the main runway, but pilots had reported a 1,000' cloud base with 8/8 cover. With no radar let-downs available the navigator and myself thought we would invent our own: The Tacan would give us an exact range, and by using the 300' of altitude per mile to run, plus 50' for any altimeter error, we could approach the airfield on a 3° glide slope and by dialling in the magnetic heading of the runway in use on our VOR, we might well be able to make a straight in approach to land. We noted on our maps the high ground to the south of the airfield and decided that it would be safe to descend to 1,000' before calling it a day if still in cloud. In the event we broke cloud just before that point and landed dead ahead. It had been better than a talk down with the navigator mentioning the height we should be at from time to time, instead of the constant yak one often received from sometimes over excited ground controllers. From the reception we got after disembarking we might as well have been Martians. The few locals present just stood there gawking at the size of our aircraft, the navigator and myself did likewise after looking at the high ground which had been on our port side during the approach. It looked far closer to the airfield than we thought when studying our maps at Kinloss, but probably wasn't.

After leaving the service, Al Newing - one of 53 Squadron's most popular Captains- started flying for a small Scottish airline, although he retrained his house near Brize. One night in our local pub he recalled "they are still talking about a monster aircraft that once landed at Benbecula, Jacko". The loading of our aircraft up there took far longer than expected and eventually we were driven to an Army Mess for a few hours. We thought we might have seen, or at least heard, a rocket blasting off or, failing that, had a chat with the missile operators, but it was not to be. In fact in that Mess we only saw one person, and that was a locally employed civilian manning the reception area. If anybody wanted to make a film about a ghost airfield Benbecula would be ideal.

The dear old Belfast did confirm one of my long held views which went back to my basic instructing days. The Central Flying School (CFS) pre- and post- WWII, preached day and night that power controlled the rate of descent of an aircraft and nose up or down, speed. I had never come to terms with that concept, particularly on finals to land when, if the view from the cockpit looked to be right, but the speed was high or low then why not use the throttle to control speed and keep the nose steady. On the Belfast, when carrying out automatic ILS approaches, the autopilot lifted or lowered the nose to maintain the glide slope and the auto throttle device increased or decreased power settings to maintain the speed figure, dialled in by the pilot. A direct opposite of CFS doctrine, but I understand from a friend who is still serving that CFS gradually came around to a change, but only after stiff opposition from the die-hards.

The Belfast OCU at Brize Norton had at least one diehard whose main claim to fame, which he loved to tell anybody who cared to listen, was that he had never actually served on any Squadron, always having become an instructor on type after various aircraft conversions. He really should have kept his mouth shut because it showed at times when he was route checking pilots who had been at the game for years. On one occasion, after I suffered one of my three engine failures during my tour at Brize, near Crete -en-route to Cyprus- I flew on to Akrotiri where the engine change would be a formality. A couple of days later, an inbound crew reported that one of the OCU instructors had opined that I should have diverted to an airfield in Crete, it being the nearest and the normal procedure. "Was it Flt Lt 'X'"? I asked, to which I got the terse reply "Of course, who else?" He was really stuck in a time warp. Although it was after my time on No 53 Squadron, RAF Boscombe Down did carry out a feasibility study into the concept of three engined ferries for Belfasts, but it was far too late for use by the RAF. The Belfast falling foul of the mid 70s defence review after only 10 years in service.

The December of 1971 had been more than hectic with a single crew operation to Texas and back followed by two Cyprus shuttles connected with the shut down of bases Bahrein and Sharjah. On the very last leg we actually brought back to the UK one of those COs. Needless to say, he got the full treatment. It is one thing for a Station Commander to close down an airfield in the UK or Western Europe, but quite another to switch off the lights before leaving the very last RAF Gulf station- an area that the service had operated in since the early 1920s.

If December had been hectic and diverse, the January of 1972 was to be just the same. In the second week of the new year I was called out at short notice to fly to Luqa in Malta with no particular reason given to start with. On boarding the aircraft I was a little surprised to note that the only item of freight aboard was a towing arm for some type of aircraft or other. At first, it reminded me of being part of a double crew operation to middle America, via RAF Waddington just to deliver a Vulcan towing tug and thinking that surely the USAF could have provided a similar vehicle. However, this time it was something completely different, which we did not appreciate until- once having taken off- we had to land again with a fairly serious technical defect. It was during the five hours that we were back at Brize that I received a phone call from a Wing Commander at Upavon to say we had to get our aircraft to Malta even if we had to push it there. He went on to say that No 203 Sqdn, based in Malta, was having to redeploy to Sigonella in Sicily at short notice for political reasons, and being in the middle of converting from Shackletons to Nimrods they had, at that time, only one towing arm suitable for Nimrods, and they would need another for Sigonella before the transfer could even begin. Eventually we arrived in Malta, well out of crew duty time and ready for bed. Sometime during that night another Belfast crew had been flown out from Brize and taken over our aircraft to start a Sigonella shuttle of 45 minute flights each way to transport ground crews and support freight to Sicily, which was to be No 203's home for the next three months. Our crew eventually joined in but not before a one day return to Cyprus to help deploy No 13 Squadron, operating Canberras, for the same political reasons.

It was in the early hours of a very dark night that after settling into the cruise at about 10,000' to the east of Malta that we were intercepted by a very fast moving aircraft that on one pass came across our nose far too close for comfort. After complaining rather bitterly to Malta control they became more agitated than ourselves, stating that there were no notified traffic in our area and could we identify the aircraft type. That was impossible at night, but RAF intelligence officers on Cyprus gave me a grilling after landing, propounding the possibility that the aircraft concerned could have been operating out of Libya, I never did hear the outcome.

Another incident, of an altogether different but no less surprising nature, took place after landing. This occurred shortly after dawn when, after vacating the aircraft, I heard the shouting of orders, stamping of feet and even a bugle call all coming from the rear of our aircraft. In total bewilderment I made haste to see what on earth was going on and arrived at the loading ramp just in time to see a Flt Lt with two escorts proudly marching off No 13 Squadrons colours. That flight was one of the very few on which I had never left my pilots seat to have a prowl around the freight bay to see exactly what our load was. The radio work had kept me fully occupied for most of the flight after our interception.

After a quick turn around it was back to Malta and a number of shuttle flights to Sicily. After returning to the UK I carried out two more Luqa returns before becoming involved in another long range effort to conclude the month, and that was something of an epic in itself.

It was a double crewing flight to Belize in British Honduras, following more ongoing tension between that country and the bordering country of Guatemala which had long held claim to that territory. The other Captain was the late Pete Breslin, who I got on particularly well with and also his lovely wife Bunty. He was a colourful character and an ex-Halton brat like myself. The plot was that I would fly the first leg to the Azores (that called for a landing at a place called Santa Maria instead of the usual USAF base of Larjes). Pete would then fly us to Bermuda and I would fly the final outbound leg to Belize, which would be my lot because after Pete had flown us back to Bermuda both our crews would be out of crew duty time, even after allowing for the extra duty hours allocated when double crewing. A day off in Bermuda would have suited us just fine but it turned out that another crew would be ready and waiting to fly us all back to Brize as passengers. We got off to a bad start when our aircraft was found to have a defect which would take a few hours to rectify. Being a Friday night our squadron building had shut down for the weekend and there was nothing for it but to retire to our respective messes for a bit of relaxation and a soft drink or two. On entering the bar, sitting on her perch, was the Padre's assistant: Pat Billington. She lost no time at all in querying my choice of a soft drink. I explained that but for a technical hitch I should have already been on my way to Central America. She commiserated and followed this up by the usual chat about this and that. We did eventually get away later that evening for a very pleasant 5 hours of completely uneventful flying. It was on the ground at Santa Maria that events took a bizarre twist.

I had wandered back to our aircraft for something while Pete and his navigator were busy with their pre-flight briefing and came across his flight engineer none too happy to say the least. During his walk around checks he had found an RAF NCO, out there on detachment for a major exercise, propped between two of the starboard bogey wheels of the undercarriage, obviously the worse for drink. His speech was reported as incoherent and he had refused the Flight Engineer's request to remove himself from the parking area. I rounded up members of the mobile Air Loading team that were travelling with us and issued the order that I had last heard made by the Station Commander at RAF Tengah, Singapore, in 1945; "Use whatever force you deem necessary". The sight I saw of the miscreant, was a body being frog marched towards the air terminal. 20 minutes later we were on our way to Bermuda for more fuel. The only point of interest on the final outbound leg was ensuring that we gave the island of Cuba a wide berth which meant tracking through the Florida Straits, quite close to the well known point of Key West.

At Belize we only left the parking area for about 30 minutes or so for a cup of tea with the RAF locals, and then it was time for Pete Breslin to start the return leg to Bermuda and more or less back on the original tasked timing. Nearing Bermuda, however, one of our four engines started playing up. Ian Waller and crew awaiting our arrival, so that they could fly us all back to the UK, were not pleased when the travelling ground engineer pronounced that an engine change was required. Our two crews booked into the same hotel that Ian Waller and his crew had returned to and we left it to him to negotiate with Upavon as to what would happen next. They soon replied that our two original crews were to return on another Belfast that was due into Bermuda the next morning and Ian was to await the engine change. It was not all that often that three complete Belfast crews found themselves in one hotel with no chance of flying likely in the foreseeable future. The inevitable happened with parties starting in various rooms using cheap local grog instead of paying the extortionate prices in the average hotel lounge bar on that island. Ian was holding a party in his own room and had quickly changed out of uniform into a dressing gown only, intending to take a shower before turning in for the night. Being the good captain that he was, he made a few journeys by lifts to rooms on various other floors to impart any news to members of his crew that came through about the impending engine change. Rumour control reported the next morning that when Ian stepped out of the lift at one level, unnoticed by himself, the front of his dressing gown had become disarranged and two elderly American ladies trying to board the lift had gone into swoon mode!

Being a passenger in a Belfast is no fun at the best of times, if no stub deck is fitted, and you are down in the cargo hold with no side windows it can get quite tiring even on short trips. The ten hours it took to fly from Bermuda to Brize on the Sunday was beyond the pale and a drink in the Mess before going home was certainly called for. After ordering my beer I noticed that Pat Billington was again sitting on her favourite stool at the end of the bar. However, I had to think hard when she said, "Back on the grog again Jacko, I suppose your trip was cancelled then"? When I said, "No, we got away all right and completed it", that was all too much for Pat. "Pull the other one, Jacko, been to Central America and back all in the last 48 hours" she said. I tell that little story because many Station personnel who worked Mondays to Fridays only and saw a Belfast, or a VC10, sitting in exactly the same position on Monday morning that it had occupied on the Friday afternoon, could never come to terms with the fact that it might well have been to Singapore and back over the weekend. This led to a suspicion that we did not do an awful lot of flying.

Although Betty and I had thoroughly enjoyed living on a married patch again, ominous signs of a housing price boom became apparent and when an RAF friend from Singapore days, who was leaving the service, offered us first option on his property in the delightful village of Bampton we jumped at it. It was only three miles from Brize and many RAF types had already settled there so we soon got into the swing of the local community. One feature of that village of about 1500 people was that it boasted ten public houses, though the Talbot was the RAF's favourite by far. It was used by all ranks, and that was literally true because one regular was an elderly widower who shuffled in most mornings for a couple of drinks. He was a New Zealander who I eventually found out to be none other than Air Chief Marshal Sir Roderick Carr; one of Bomber Harris's AOCs and later RAF C in C India, right up to the time of self government for the sub-continent. The landlord tipped me off that he did not care to talk to people about his life, so we all left him in peace with his memories.

Having to furnish a house from scratch is a problem for all first time buyers of course, but having left it entirely to my wife, Betty, I missed out on all the hard work- although she did have a little laugh after relating her haggling with the manager of an up market furniture store in Oxford, who had eventually said to her in a very upper crust voice "And how long has Madam been back from the East"?

Bampton, in those days, was a place that if you ever forgot to lock your door on nights out, you need not start worrying unduly because burglary was almost unknown and minor misdeeds kept under control by two full time Policewomen, with the odd patrol car to show the flag at times. Even in a perfect world though, little ripples appear from time to time and although Betty and I are both broad minded we got a real shock to the system when one dark night returning from the Talbot, we came upon the two WPCs having a snog between two parked cars! The unthinkable was happening in our idyllic village. What next crossed our minds?

One strange trip to the Middle East at one point of my tour got off to a funny old start in that I received a phone call from MOD (Air) telling me that I would be carrying one extra crew member from their department and that our crew were not to question him about his presence on the flight. He appeared spot on time at Flight Planning, but no introductions were necessary because he was one of my old mates from our Hastings days. With the leg out to Cyprus taking place during the night hours we had a full day off in Cyprus and even during our usual wander around Limassol our sixth crew member never mentioned what it was all about. The next day we took off for a flag stop at an airfield that was not normally used by the Belfast fleet. It was while taxiing into dispersal that our guest went into action; sketching this, that and the other. No sooner had the engines stopped than an American officer came bounding up the stairs on to the flight deck, which in itself was most unusual, and said to me "I see you are carrying an extra crew member, Captain?" I asked myself whether he was in the know from our Lords and Masters or from other sources, although I will never know, one thing I do remember vividly is that when climbing out of my seat I noticed the 6th crew members note book, with sketches, was lying fully open on the Navigators table, but a steady stare at it prompted the Nav to hastily place a map over it. The American officer did try and induce us into leaving the aircraft for a coffee but we thanked him profusely and explained that we had to be off ASAP and had enjoyed a drink courtesy of our Loadmaster just prior to landing.

Mentioning the Loadmaster reminds me how important they could be, both in general and on the Belfast in particular with the varied types of load that we invariably carried. All Captains had their preferences in that department and my favourites were NCOs Jim Duff, Jock Gilchrist and Arthur Kingdom. The last two were at the two ends of the age spectrum for aircrew, Jock being of WWII vintage with Arthur being about the youngest member of the Squadron. Both Betty and I well remember Jock when taken into the RAF Hospital at Wroughton, near Swindon, and visiting him one night with a bottle of Whisky well concealed in Betty's handbag. The next week, on another visit, when asking the Ward Sister if we could see Mr Gilchrist we got the rather stern reply of "Yes, you can, so long as you haven't another bottle of whisky for him. Things got a little bit out of control after your last visit". At a Squadron reunion in recent times, 25 years after I had left the Belfast fleet, Jock was in fine fettle and the once young Arthur was still a serving member of the RAF and not only commissioned but a Squadron Leader. He was also happily married to an ex-WRAF Air Loadmaster who we had all flown with us as passengers at some time or other on VC10s. Just as the British make jokes about the Irish so transport crews tended to make them about 'loadies'. One or two, alas, are based on true stories, but invariably revolve around just one or two members of that branch of the service. On No 53 Squadron we had one who tended to speak before he put his brain into gear. On one occasion he caught a member of crew eating an apple that had been raided from his pantry. The crew member miscreant got a right earful including, "You know, sir, they don't grow on trees".

One bonus about the catering side was that somebody had invented a code for the Air Loadmaster's so that aircrews could radio ahead to the next staging airfield for uplift of meals. It was a two letter system starting with AB and worked very well down the standard routes, particularly so when carrying a number of passenger who would not be off loading other than to stretch their legs. ALMs, like all other transport crew members, were subjected to scrutiny by route checkers on a regular basis and given a full debriefing afterwards. On one such occasion our well known ALM was taken to task because during the flight he had, during breaks in his normal tasks, just sat in his compartment. He was told that on such occasions he should try and take an interest in other crew members' duties. "On your next flight", suggested the route checker, "go and stand behind the Flight Engineer for half an hour or so and ask him a few questions- I bet you don't even know the difference between AC and DC, do you"? "Of course I do", snapped our ALM, "One is beef curry and the other is plum pudding. For one reason or other the ALM was posted to the Belfast Ground School and during one lecture he gave on winter survival he warned his students that when walking to safety in the Arctic, you had to be particularly careful because you might well fall in a cravat (sic) at any moment!

Only two more significant trips, from my point of view, came my way before my final Belfast flight. The first was another UK away day to move an unknown squadron's ground equipment from RAF Leuchars in Scotland to their new home at RAF Binbrook in Lincolnshire. On landing in Scotland we were directed to a parking area very close to the Squadron's hangar, possibly too close in the event. With a full team of air mobile movers with us on that trip we estimated that we would be up and away in an hour or so, which induced most of our crew to remain aboard in the relative warmth of the flight deck. At about the mid-point of the loading operation, a rather flustered Wing Commander came bounding up on to the flight deck and announced that he was OC No XI Squadron and had received a bomb scare warning from Ops and would it be possible to have our aircraft moved further away from his hangar. It did not seem a good idea to me with unsecured freight and loading still in full swing, but we eventually agreed to take a chance and remain, with bomb scares being ten a penny in those days. The Wing Commander did stay long enough to look around our cockpit so I took the chance of saying that I had once been a pilot on Legs Eleven which induced him to look me in the eye, obviously trying to assess my age, before saying "Way back in the Jolly old Venom days, I suppose?" After I replied "Spitfires, actually", he said, "Jolly good, jolly good" and was off like a jack rabbit. It was the last time I ever mentioned the 1940s to younger senior Officers who only wanted to talk about the times after they had joined the Service. Just as well that I hadn't got around to asking if No XI had had any luck in tracing their silver last seen in Japan, or about my initial arrival on No XI by way of my own aircraft with all my worldly possessions stowed in the gun bays, I doubt he would have believed that one.

I was coming towards three years on the Squadron and wondering if I might be in for another spell of instructing with the OCU when a vacancy arose, but the roof really fell in for me when I was informed that my next post would be on the flight simulator staff. The thought of being in an enclosed and dark building for all my working hours after 30 years on continuous flying appointments did not bear thinking bout. Luckily, a navigator friend of mine by the name of Bob Kennedy, and well known throughout the transport world, had recently left the Brittannia fleet at Brize to instruct radar bomb aimer and navigators at the Strike Command Bombing School (SCBS) at RAF Lindholme in Yorkshire, flying Mk 5 Hastings. Being a bachelor, he often returned for weekend visits and it was he who told me that Des Pankhurst, a New Zealander and Hastings QFI at Lindholme, was due to leave the Service shortly to return to his native Country and no one had been nominated to replace him at that time. If any urging was needed to encourage me to try and wangle that post, it was supplied by the added snippet that one Hastings pilot there was always the nominated pilot to demonstrate the world's-at that time- last flying Lancaster bomber. Would I ever be lucky enough to fly the Lanc myself if a posting north could be arranged immediately went through my mind. I put it to my immediate boss, Flight Commander Sqdn Ldr Tony Woodford, later Air Vice Marshal, who seemed particularly sympathetic to the idea. However, I was off on a West Indies return trip before hearing any more about it.

This flight was, in the event, to take far longer than scheduled due to yet another engine failure. We got off to a good start, not only flying to RAF Wyton to pick up support spares and ground crew for an impending detachment of No 543 Squadron Victor B/SR aircraft to Barbados, but also completing the first of three Atlantic legs to Lajes in the Azores for a night stop. The second leg to Bermuda for another night stop was also uneventful, although the planners had allowed us far too much time on the ground at Lajes which meant we did not arrive in Bermuda, the island we all wanted to see more of, until late evening. On the final leg down to Barbados the flight engineer became concerned about one of the engines which was running at a higher than normal temperature. Things did not get any worse until after landing at Seawell aerodrome where we had the most bumpy ride I was to ever experience on the Belfast, and far worse than the desert landing strip on Masirah. This was due to the surface being made of giant concrete squares, possibly of WWll vintage. It was the last straw for the suspect engine and no sooner had we turned off the runway then the flight engineer called for the engine to be shut down.

A great number of signals flew between Barbados and Upavon before we finally made it to our hotel, which was to become our second home for the next 14 days. The hotelier was a Canadian who really took us under his wing and drove us to any part of the island that took our fancy plus a daily trip to the airfield to check if any incoming signals had arrived for us. One well remembered signal called for us to try and find a suitable crane for the removal of our Kaput engine and to reply soonest. Even in Europe cranes that could reach the height of a Belfast wing were not all that common at the time, and finding one on a tropical island did not bode well. However, our Canadian hotelier said that the only possibility was the islands brewery and, sure enough it proved to be true. Our replacement engine eventually arrived and the brewery crane really came into its own for a few days. However, when it came time to leave that wonderful island the final task was to countersign hotel bills, and one was for the crane, billed at $10,000 (Caribbean Dollars) exactly and I seriously thought about ringing up and saying could they make it 10,100 or something like that, because accountants back in the U.K. might think it too much of a round figure, especially for a brewery and conclude that the RAF had been having too much of a good time during their two weeks free holiday.

We gained a lot of local knowledge from our Canadian hotelier and one bit of information was certainly going to cost him plenty. It was after he had noticed that some of us had taken to the local favourite of rum and coke that he said, "For the price you are paying for each of those drinks over my bar counter you could get a full bottle of rum at the store on the corner, and I will turn a blind eye so long as other guests are kept in the dark." Luckily, the other guests were little in number, the high season not having arrived. He told us that a couple of weeks later we would have been lucky to get into his hotel as hordes of his fellow countrymen would descend on the island having lived through yet another bleak Canadian winter and who wished to soak up the sun for a week or so. He also mentioned that about half of them would be young, unattached females who were also on the lookout for a bit of the "old bamboo". The bit about the old bamboo did not register with any of our team, but when he mentioned the young girls and the old bamboo a couple more times, one of us asked him to explain. He said "I thought you would have guessed, you must have heard that all west Indian males are supposed to be very well endowed, well some of the young lads out here who virtually live on the shore line are called beach boys and the girls call it having a bit of the old bamboo!" The mind boggled. He also negotiated a cheap cruise on a last century type of sailing ship going under the name of the 'Jolly Roger' which flew a skull and cross bones flag with a captain wearing an eye patch, but no wooden leg or parrot. The normal price would have been quite hefty and we soon found out why. All rum was free during our four hour voyage, with the crew actively encouraging all passengers aboard to drink to their hearts content. If only I had a cine camera with me, especially during the last half mile of that epic voyage back to the jetty with many drunks walking the plank and others jumping overboard from high up in the rigging, a rare day to remember.

On another away day, the landlord took us to see Nelson's old dock yard, about a mile from his hotel and virtually in the centre of Bridgetown, the islands capital. After that it was along the coast to the world famous Hotel of Sandy Lane, the second home of millionaires wintering in those parts. It was while taking in the sight of that hotel from its very spacious grounds that we eventually realized we were being stalked by a white European man who eventually caught up with us and respecfully inquired if we were actually guests of the hotel. Our Canadian friend immediately leapt in and said he was the owner of the Royal Caribb hotel and he was showing some of his own guests, a stranded RAF transport crew, Barbados' finest hotel. It was like opening a magic box, the gentlemen who had been stalking us for the last few minutes then announced that he was the house detective and if we followed him into the hotel all drinks would be on the firm for as long as we stayed, well played Trusthouse Forte!

One strange aspect of our enforced stay on the island was that we never had sight nor sound of the Victor crew, which was partly understandable because they were staying in another hotel some distance away from ours. However, the two different ground crews, after the arrival of the engine change team, obviously met on the aircraft parking area and I asked our team if they could find out how long the Victor aircraft would be staying before returning to the U.K. in case it would be worthwhile asking Upavon permission for them to stay put to save another Belfast recovery flight to the island to recover the Victor's support team and equipment that we had brought in. The answer I received from a call to Upavon, was that they would be staying as long as it took to complete a photographic survey of an area of northern South America. On one trip to the airfield when the Victor was not flying, I noted that it carried air scoops on the wings, which might have meant something or nothing. It had already been made public that prior to that time Victors had been on detachment to South America to scoop up air at high altitude after the French had exploded atomic bombs in the South Pacific. If that was their task this time, I concluded, it was as well to let things rest and just ask Upavon for a revised itinerary when the engine change was complete.

That particular trip to the airfield was on a Sunday and it was a pleasure to see hundreds of mostly female locals, all dressed in their best finery, proceeding en mass to various churches in villages we passed through and hearing their wonderful singing on our return. In a phone call to Upavon, I requested a non-stop flight to Brize if the wind conditions permitted. I got the usual reply of 'At Captain's discretion'. The flight in the event took all of 13 hours and 30 minutes, equalling No 53 Squadrons longest time in the air for a Belfast, but not breaking the longest distance record. After take-off and turning right onto heading I doubt if we ever changed course by more than 20 degrees, and certainly never saw any land until coasting in over Cornwall. We only had two options for diversion over the Atlantic for technical or extra fuel uplift and that was when passing to the right of Bermuda and to the left of the Azores. However, all went well until R/T contact was made with RAF St. Mawgan in Cornwall when a WRAF asked for the point of our last take-off and when we replied, "Barbados", she got a little snappy and said "Your last re-fuelling stop, not where you've been to" she not being able to visualize a non stop flight from a place not far off the South American coast to the U.K. by a propeller driven aircraft.

During my two-week absence, my posting to RAF Lindholme had come through and Wg Cdr Nugent, the gentleman that he was, had personally informed Betty about it. After checking in at the Squadron after a couple of days of stand-down, my flight commander, Sqn Ldr Tony Woodford, asked me about the trip. Later he said he had given someone at Upavon a right dressing down and told them they should try and get their act together after they had suggested that I had taken it upon myself to return to the U.K. instead of waiting out there for the Victor crew to complete whatever it was they were doing. It certainly pleased the late Sqn Ldr Bob Brighton that we were back because a week later he was given the task of returning all from Barbados. Like myself, he had always wanted to sample the delights of the jewel in the crown of the West Indies.

Time was now running out for me on the Belfast fleet but I did manage a double shuttle to Northern Ireland from RAF Wittering, which was a rather hectic day with six sectors involved. The final trip was, however, out to Cyprus, two full days off, and then return via Malta. Quite a jolly by No 53 Sqn standards and one I will remember. Thinking, erroneously, as it later turned out, that it would certainly be my last flight into that island while still in the RAF, I went a little overboard on the wind down drinks in the transit bar after landing at Akrotiri, albeit supported by the rest of the crew. When we finally left for our downtown hotel I offered thanks to the driver of our 32-seater coach for his forbearance over the long delayed departure to Limassol. He replied, that it had been no problem because they worked 12 hours on and 12 hours off for three days before a stand down and he had just finished 12 on when he first dropped us off, so he concluded that we must have been drinking for 12 hours or so. We were in no state to doubt his mathematics, but it sounded about right.

With it being my last route trip on the Belfast fleet I was in something of a reflective mood during our stay in Cyprus. On the plus side I concluded that the past three years had been the most fulfilling in my time in the RAF thus far, flying a wonderful aircraft, and on many occasions in a most productive role in that we often carried loads that no other aircraft in RAF service could cater for. One view, shared by everybody who had anything to do with the Belfast was that higher authority undervalued it and it was a case of crass stupidity when the entire fleet was disposed of after only 10 years in service. However, their potential had not been lost on civil operators and most of the five sold to them played vital roles in the Falklands war of 1982. Even in RAF service they had started to garner a penny or two for the government when chartered by various firms to hump jumbo-jet engines, 747 flight simulators, and rapier missiles, amongst other large items of freight, to many parts of the world. On another occasion, a Belfast captained by Tony Woodford was flown in support of Concorde's first Far Eastern trials.

The only problem I had to deal with in my early days on type was the lack of an air signaller amongst the crew, because for the previous ten years when flying the Hastings I had hardly made, or received for that matter, a radio call. That was because the signaller would make and receive all calls while the rest of the crew remained on intercom only. This was the norm even in the circuit when the captain would press his button and say something like "call downwind Runway 29 to land" and would receive a response via the Siggy of, for instance, "you are No3, call finals with three greens." Now on the Belfast at least one pilot, the captain or co-pilot, had to listen out for every minute of the trip on either VHF for short range work, or SSB (single side band) for long range communications. Like every other boring task there was usually lighter moments. In one case on a very dark night over Turkey, and listening out on airways VHF as required, although out of range of any ground station because the Turks, like the Spanish, had been slow off the mark in the introduction or forward relay stations, the air suddenly became alive when two Lufthansa pilots struck up an air to air conversation. Their jabbering went on and on until between one short break, I pressed the R/T button and called "Acthung Spitfire." The night immediately became deadly silent and in my minds eye I saw G & T's, or perhaps stewers of lager flying all over the place.

There was only one other occasion when I was rather naughty in that connection, and I relate this one because in this day and age it is difficult to recall that weather ships were still on station in the Atlantic until the early seventies. I had never actually called one myself because after selecting one of their VHF frequencies it seemed only a matter of minutes before someone else called them for the London Heathrow weather, which was not all that far away from Brize, if eastbound. If westbound it was New Yorks JFK, which was of interest, being near enough to our first American landing point when inbound to a southern states air base. Recording of the weather information passed, cut down on the workload of the weather ships operator and, no doubt, many other aircraft captains took the same view. I think, however, that on one particular crossing all aircraft pilots listening out must have taken an added interest when a call from the ship asked one Panam pilot if he could speak to their chief air stewardess. The dear lady soon came on the radio and the upshot was that the weather ship crew would soon be back in New York, and the bachelors among them intended running a raffle with the first prize being allowed the privilege of taking a stewardess out to dinner and could she provide a name and contact number of a willing volunteer among her young ladies? The senior girl seemed a little unsure about it all in her reply, so the weather ship operator added, "it would be a top hotel occasion and there would be no hanky-panky and she would be perfectly safe and treated like a lady to which I added "he's got to be joking." After a few more ribald remarks from other aircraft that had not checked in with their call-sign, the exasperated weather controller finally said "I guess we have some military up there today, give us a call on your return flight will you?

One last little story of life down the route concerning radio: It was about another colourful character that No 53 Sqd seemed to attract in the persona of "Rocky" Oliver. His American long-range radio, built by Collins, had played up a little over the Atlantic and he was certainly in for a shock after landing and shut down at a USA civil airport. He noticed a civilian walking across the Tarmac with what, at first sight, seemed to be a small briefcase. However, that gent eventually appeared on the flight deck and announced that he worked for Collins and he had followed the Belfast's radio calls across the Atlantic and noted that there was something not quite correct, but with the captains permission he could probably fix everything in no time at all, which he dully did via the tools in his briefcase. Could that have happened in those days in England – never? - or shall I today. If something unusual happens on a route trip, it is invariably followed by another incident. In Rocky's case it came after landing in New York at the end of the next leg when he took a short night stroll for a breather and was held up at gun point and told to hand over his cash. When Rocky replied that he did not have many Dollars on him, the Gunman replied, "So sorry, bud, I didn't realize you were English" and promptly disappeared into the darkness.

My last week on the Squadron was made unusual in that Sqn Ldr Johnson who had been my first transport command flight commander and was now based at Upavon in charge of all pilots postings in the Group, happened to be paying a station visit when we bumped into each other and his first words were "I'm terribly sorry about your posting mix up, we could certainly have changed it earlier if we had known you were not keen on the Flight Simulator. Very kind words, but what happened next was almost unbelievable.

I was taken to one side in the squadron coffee bar on three different occasions during my last week at Brize with virtually the same message which was to the effect that each captain would gladly have taken my place in the simulator, if only he had known about it, because their wives were getting fed up being left at home so often. Was it really true that all three wives had complained – very doubtful? The three pilots concerned were all on their first transport tour and not particularly keen on being away from home for days, and sometimes a couple of weeks, at a time. One point that could be made by any pilot flying Belfasts on No 53 squadron after late 1971, when the last one of the ten built finally arrived, was that they were among the very few RAF pilots who had actually flown every aircraft of one particular type, that had ever been built.

CHAPTER 7
Return to The Hastings

My move up to the Strike Command Bombing school at RAF Lindholme was to be short lived as it was already known that in four months time the entire unit would amalgamate with No 230 Vulcan Ocu at RAF Scampton. However, the task of training navigators for Phantom's and Vulcan's in the art of map reading and bombing by way of the wartime H2S radar would continue, but at a lower rate. The SCBS had already been reduced to just seven Hastings, five Mk 5's fitted with H2's and Mk 1's still in the normal transport configuration and used for pilot conversions, plus numerous other tasks. The Mk 5 Hastings was a conversion of the original Mk 1 in preference to the later, and more pleasant to fly Mk 2 because the Mk1's had generators on all four engines with the Mk2's on three only, it had seemed prudent to have the extra electrical power that was available to cater for the use of the H2S radar.

The only other aircraft based at RAF Lindholme was a sole "Beagle Basset" on detachment from the Northern Communications Squadron at RAF Topcliffe, for the use of No1 Group staff officers based at nearby Bawtry. However, with only one available a Hastings aircraft plus crew had always to be on stand-by whenever the AOC was due to make important trips. The situation continued even after our move to RAF Scampton and was often deployed, the Basset having a poor reliability record. One small plus for the AOC and his staff travelling by Hastings was that on call-out we took-off and landed at RAF Finningley to pick them up, which was even closer to their H.Q.'s at Bawtry, then Lindholme. The four months I was to spend at Lindholme proved to be most enjoyable and it soon became apparent that the Hastings was very often used for purposes other then training radar navigators. Some trips would not have passed scrutiny on an operational transport station because having an aircraft stuck in Germany, or some such place, for a whole weekend could not be justified especially when the object of the exercise was taking a station golf team out there. However, that type of trip was a rarity and many flights were very cost effective indeed, such as flying spare parts to a stranded Nimrod in Iceland or ferrying crews to makers airfields with Salmesbury and Bitteswell being regular runs.

One flight that had taken place before my arrival was undertaken by Flight Commander "Chalky" White who was tasked with flying to Goose Bay in Canada via Iceland and Greenland with the Red Arrows team leader aboard so that he could familiarize himself with that route in preparation for the Reds first visit to the new world. I had first met "Chalky" at Thorney Island when we both instructed on Hastings and heard of his exploits as a bomber captain flying Whitleys against targets in Germany and, on a second tour, various targets in North Africa and Italy, when based in the Middle East. He could also relate some good stories about his post war career, which include the Berlin airlift. Many did not believe one of his favourite tales, but he always insisted on its veracity. It concerned a very junior officer who was always in trouble to the extent that, predictably, he eventually finished up in front of his AOC at Group Headquarters, to be interviewed. The crew room was agog the next morning with everybody dying to know how the young scoundrel had got on. However, it was not long before he appeared, all smiles and on top of the world. When asked what the AOC had said to him he replied, "Oh, everything went off rather well, in fact he's made me his sexual advisor". With incredulity another officer asked, "What did he actually say to you?" "Oh", replied the young offender, "he shouted after me as I was leaving his office that in future if he ever needed my F****** advice he'd bloody well ask for it!" Be that as it may, one of the funniest stories during my time in the service was about "Chalky" himself. Although he never mentioned it, other members of his crew often did.

Shortly after his arrival at Lindholme he was off on a weekend trip to an RAF base in Germany along the usual route, which was joining airway "Blue One" near Hull, transferring to Dutch control halfway across the North Sea until near Dusseldorf when, for protocol reasons, it was necessary to talk to a German control there for a couple of minutes or so before contacting RAF Clutch Radar which then directed RAF transit traffic to their inbound destinations. Unluckily, Chalky's radio direction finder (ADF) went on the blink shortly before entering German airspace and he was wandering around the sky which seemed to antagonise the German controller to the extent that he eventually asked Chalky if he had ever been to Dusseldorf before, to which Chalky replied, rather too quickly, "Well not since 1942 actually." Above Chalky was Squadron Leader Burton, a charming full career officer with a Coastal Command background flying Shackletons. When the Hastings got involved in two major Naval exercises, we could not help but think that our boss had volunteered our services so that he could get back to doing what he liked best, maritime reconnaissance, even if it was only for a few short days. However, it did underline one significant point and that was that our H2's radar was ideal for such a purpose. Its 360 degree radius of scan was a definite plus compared with the front line Nimrods radar which had a limited scan spectrum left and right of dead ahead. Even our staff navigators became very impressed with the range that they picked up surface contacts. On the first exercise, I was given the Southern North Sea to patrol and it only seemed minutes after starting our first West to East run before our two operators down the back picked up numerous contacts and gave vectors for interception. Yes, it was the entire enemy force for that planned exercise that we had sighted and, according to later reports, we had certainly put a spoke in the wheels from the planner's point of view. They may well have regretted our involvement, but they did call upon us once more for a second go but this time way out in the Atlantic. However, "Boss" Burton was the first to come upon one of the biggest ships in the world at that time, the United States Aircraft Carrier JFK, and we on the Hastings fleet thought it was hilarious when it was revealed after the exercise was all over, that the JFK reported being shadowed by an "unidentifiable" aircraft!

RAF Lindholme was definitely something from the past in many respects, even in the ever so short history of the Royal Air Force. In its heyday of the Second World War, thousands of bomber crews had passed that way and now it was down to just eight aircraft and five crews. The lowest number of both that I ever came across on any one station in my time in the Service, yet the tradition of having separate messes for students and staff officers still went on as if nothing had changed. It was also probably the last station in the 1970's on which wartime aircrew still outnumbered the postwar entrants, although that was reversed dramatically after our move to Scampton. On the pilots side we had George Smith, a gentleman if ever there was one, plus Chalky white and myself from WWll, with navigators S/L "Jumbo" Cowan, a veteran of No101 squadron which had suffered the second highest percentage loss rate in bomber command as it operated a secret device over Germany coded ABC, or airborne cigars to the crews, plus Flt Lt. Ballentine, another bomber command survivor who hailed from New Zealand. One other staff navigator, Flt Lt. Bob Kennedy, deserves a special mention. He had joined the Royal Air Force in the late 1940's and prior to his posting to Lindholme had flown a tour on Sunderland flying boats in the Far East and survived a fatal accident followed by numerous tours in Transport Command flying Hastings and Britannias. He was certainly something of a legend in his own lifetime but, sadly, succumbed to the big "C" shortly after he left the Service.

We also had a very high percentage of flight engineers on strength with Derek Butcher, Bob Brown-John and Ian Gibson all having operated during that period. Bob had completed two bomber tours, one at RAF Waddington and his second at RAF Metheringham whilst Derek, operating out of what is now Humberside airport with 166 Sqd, once landed by parachute from a stricken Lancaster and twice escaped from his German captors, finally living in a Brussels café until that city was liberated. Another member of his crew who also survived was Donald Pleasance who became a famous actor.

Even the station commander, Group Captain Phillips was a rarity indeed for that position and time, having also served during WWll, which was by then, more than a quarter of a century in the past. He certainly liked to keep his ear to the ground and seemed to be well informed about every single flight that had taken place on any particular day.

Looking back on that happy band of warriors it now seems strange that although they all passed their stringent annual aircrew medical, three of them should make their final take-off for the runway in the skies in a very short time span with one from each of the three main aircrew categories. First to go was pilot George Smith when stationed at RAF Leeming, next was navigator "Bob" Kennedy and finally Flight Engineer Ian Gibson died not long after his wife's sudden death.

The group of staff radar navigators who passed on their expertise down at the back of the Hastings, all came from a very different generation of aircrew. They had all flown numerous tours on "V" Force bombers and despite the generation gap we got on particularly well with all of them. One of the most popular was Flt. Lt. "Robbie" Stewart who later became a household name during the Gulf War after becoming an Iraqi prisoner subsequent to the shooting down of his Tornado bomber by anti-aircraft fire.

The 'supposed' main task of training nav/rads was pleasant enough in its own right. It called for flying at 250' above ground level (AGL) for approximately four hours on one of two standard routes which, between them, covered most of the scenic areas of the U.K. The Northern route started at Barrow-in-Furness and then took in the Lake District, Solway Firth, across the Grampians then southwards crossing the Firth of Forth near Bass Rock. Then over the Cheviot hills and Eastern Pennines before returning to medium level south of Harrogate for a return to base. The southern route was less popular because of the long haul at medium level to the start point on the south coast. However, it then took in Dartmoor, Exmoor and all the Welsh Mountains before terminating over the Irish Sea near my home town of Southport. Two features on the northern route I was always on the lookout for was the progress on the building of HMS Invincible in the Barrow shipyard. From the keel laying to the launch by Her Majesty the Queen took about five years and almost coincided exactly with my five years of Hastings flying on that route. At times when looking down at her I felt as if I had seen every single rivet being put into place.

However, never during those five years did our primary task of radar training exceed in flying hours per month those flown on the one off trips already mentioned. Some of which will stick in my mind forever. Not least was the Radar Flight's departure from RAF Lindholme to RAF Scampton when, having only five crews for seven aircraft it was decided to fly a vic of five on day one, and pick up the other two the next day. Two of the captains were young pilots who had recently been upgraded from co-piloting and had never flown a four-engined aircraft in formation before. Under the circumstance, they performed remarkably well although I did see the plane on my side, next to the lead aircraft, overlap the leaders port wing for a few heart-stopping seconds. Our reception at RAF Scampton was excellent and we seemed to get on particularly well with the 'V' bomber boys which, unfortunately, led to two minor incidents which we could well have done without. Both occurred when I was drinking in the Mess bar with my big mate of those days, George Smith, a no-nonsense down-to-earth Yorkshire man with a sharp wit. The first incident was when the OC administration, the last aircrew officer I ever came across to hold that position, caught sight of us across the bar and after sauntering over with a fixed look at our Flight Lieutenant rank badges said "Wartime NCO pilots I take it". George, without even looking up from the bottom of his beer glass replied, "quite right sir, just like Ginger Lacey and Johnnie Johnson" – game, set and match. The second incident, to which even George didn't bother to reply, was when a young pilot, not long out of Cranwell told us "The sooner the Air Force get rid of the wartime dross the better". Scampton of all places – Dambusters, Guy Gibson, etc with 'Nigger's' Grave just a few hundred yards away. Both George and myself were in battledress with ample evidence below our pilots brevet, of wartime service. By something of a coincidence that all changed a few months later when the battledress was consigned to the dustbin of RAF history. That, in itself, led me to commit a faux pas because, at first, MOD Air decreed that flying badges and medal ribbons would not be worn on the pullover replacement, known to all as a 'woolliepully'. Flying badges did eventually return and just after that time I have often been quoted as saying to one young Vulcan pilot: "terribly sorry I've not had a chat with you before now, but I though you were a navigator". There was often a lot of banter at that time between pilots and navigators, sometimes along the lines "would you really let your daughter marry a navigator? My clanger was that I had meant to say "I would have loved to have had a chat with him about piloting Vulcans, with the possibility of a flight in one".

With the known move of the Hastings from Lindholme to Scampton I had not been allowed to put my name down on the married quarters waiting list at the former, but mine was allowed to go forward at the latter, which led to yet another incident. This was unusual in that I was asked to take over a quarter even before our official move. The 'marching in' as it was called meant a very early start from Lindholme. This involved dealing with a troupe of about six civilians. The barrack warden himself plus one to read the electrics, one for the gas and its boiler, barrack damages, inventory of furniture check, etc. However, with not a person in sight at the appointed hour, I was beginning to wonder what my next move should be on an unfamiliar Station when help arrived from a most unexpected source. Yvonne Brown, who I had first met in Singapore when she had arrived to take up an appointment with the Malcolm Club at Changi and later married "Bad News" Brown out there was now in a quarter at Scampton close to the one I was supposed to be taking over. She came out and asked if I needed a phone to see what was going on. The barrack warden was quite adamant, the time was to be 14:00 hrs, and so it was, but not before Yvonne had said "There'll be nothing doing in the Mess at this time of the day, Jacko, would you like me to take you to a pub in Welton, they open quite early?" That took care of the four hours delay nicely. From then on things went smoothly until the barrack warden and his entourage were departing down the front path when he suddenly stopped in his tracks, turned, and said "I'm sure you'll like this quarter,

Sir, second nearest to the mess and it's bar, just across the field from here". It was said with an ever-increasing smirk on his face, which was soon removed with a chin drop when I replied, "I'm teetotal actually." I went through the motions of closing the door but left it slightly ajar for a bit of earwiging. I soon heard him muttering, "Teetotal, I'm sure I smelt drink, funny business."

In addition to our normal radar training details the "one offs" really took off with the "V" Force and others soon realising that they now had a virtual aerial taxi service at their disposal. However, it was a very happy time and reading my old log-books of those days makes me wonder how we coped on some days without the stringent rules of Transport Command which laid down crew duty and rest times. One day in September 1973, I flew eight sectors, which were: Scampton, Honington, Leuchars, Stornoway, Aldergrove, Leuchars, Coningsby, Honington, Scampton. With loading and unloading at each airfield it must have been a long, long day. I flew over 80 hours that month with only 5 sorties, less than 20 hours devoted to our primary task of radar training. Not all trips are remembered for flying reasons and one had a sad ending. It was to pick up retired Air Vice-Marshal Blucke from RAF Coltishall and fly him into RAF Conningsby where his son was then the Station Commander. I thought he looked a little subdued as he boarded our Hastings, which turned to a look of pride when he found his son awaiting our disembarkation. However, his son was in his last few months in command and, probably, in line for further promotion but it was not to be. Group captain Blucke took-off in a Phantom a few weeks later in what proved to be his final flight, a low level sortie. In a one in a million chance, his aircraft collided with a crop spraying Pawwee aircraft near Bexwell, Norfolk. Even in peacetime, life can often be tragic in the RAF. Author Colin Cummings in a series of books records that the RAF lost 1,100 aircraft between 1959 and 1996 (Lost To Service), 1,400 with 750 deaths between 1954 and 1958 ("To Fly No More") and 1,800 between 1950 and 1953 (Last Take Off).

Overseas weekend trips were, of course, ever popular and I probably got more than my fair share. They took in Norway, Denmark, Germany, France, Belgium, Gibraltar, Malta and Cyprus. The two full days off on the Saturdays and Sundays would have been unthinkable in the real transport world and we certainly made the most of it. In Gibraltar, apart from going up to see the rock apes we could take a locally organized trip to Tangiers which not only included a return ferry but also a coach trip around the ancient city. One of the ferry captains was reputed to have filed an "Air miss" report on an RAF aircraft, which had nearly taken his main mast top off during its approach to Gibraltar in low cloud conditions. On one Gib trip a Vulcan navigator, Spike Reynolds, asked if we could possibly take his intended, a lovely nursing sister by the name of Gill from the RAF hospital at Nocton Hall, along for the ride. I said no problem, but she might like to bring along another nursing sister for company. The flight itself, not being allowed to over fly Spain because of the dispute over sovereignty of Gibraltar was the usual very boring Atlantic route. However, no sooner had we booked into the Officers' Mess, within yards of the Spanish frontier, than a steward rushed up and said the first officer of HMS Zulu wished to have a word with me. My mind went into overdrive as I made my way to reception – had we flown too close to the Spanish mainland on finals was one possibility. Another that sprung to mind was that for the first time on that route the two radar navigators down at the back had reported what appeared to them to be an unusual lock-on from a ground radar station, and obviously from Spain. Perhaps the Royal Navy had also picked up something odd too. I need not have worried because the first lieutenant, rather dryly, explained that his Captain, having seen our arrival, asked him to organize a visit to his ship by the Hastings crew. I thought I would let him off the hook by saying that although it was a wonderful idea, which we would have loved to accept, but for the fact that we had two nursing sisters with us who needed to be chaperoned on day one to show them the sights. His mood changed dramatically and he insisted that we bring them both along too and even when I said "I don't suppose for one minute that they have any slacks with them for going up and down gangways" failed to put him off. "Don't worry about that old boy we'll leave them in the Wardroom having a few pink gins with the young sub-lieutenants." It proved to be an excellent away from it all visit, and underlined the fact that the Royal Navy are second to none when it comes to entertaining. Spike and Gill married shortly before both left the RAF and what an occasion that was. The wedding was in Northumberland, her brother in Law was a captain on the old North Eastern Airlines" based at Woolsington. It was he who masterminded the occasion with the reception being held in the airport, and that turned out to be a never to be forgotten party if ever there was one.

    During our return to the mess after our RN visit I was delighted to see a Belfast parked on the strip and wondered who the crew might be. It turned out to be a route training flight under the supervision of Sqn Ldr Keith

O'Brian with a new to No 53 squadron crew under his wing. Keith and I had a lot to talk about of course, and he was particularly interested when I asked if No 53 Squadron had heard anything about its future? After a negative reply, I related that a few weeks before our Gib. trip, Betty and I had spent a weekend in London staying at the RAF Club and followed the usual routine of Betty unpacking while I had a few quick ones in the gents bar. As usual, there was a lot of talking shop going on, most of it trivia, but my ears pricked up when I heard one chap saying, "Remember that paper we had to write on our Staff College course about the future transport requirements after the planned pull out from east of Suez? Well, they are going to be almost exactly what we suggested, the Britannia's will soon be gone and then the Belfast." During WWll there used to be placards saying, "Beware, walls have ears." Another, "You never know who is listening." showing two little old ladies discussing the war with Hitler and Goering sitting behind them in full uniform. I never saw Keith again, but what I overheard in the RAF club came to pass and the RAF was to regret it, during the Falklands war especially.

The other nursing sister from Nocton Hall that Gill had brought along was called Barbara and also fairly well known to our Officer crew members at least, having recently become engaged to a Scampton Vulcan captain. They seemed to be a well-matched couple at the time but it was not to be, both going their separate ways before marriage. However, we did meet again under unusual circumstances. It was after I had taken over flying the BBMF Lancaster and, being billeted in one of the numerous Officers' Messes in Aldershot for the Farnborough air display week, that I received a phone call from young Barbara who, after going through the formalities, which included the fact that she had decided to give the RAF a miss and was now an Army Sister (QA) based in Aldershot, and asked if there was any chance at all of a Lancaster flight along with two other sisters. With only two ground crew aboard, and no rules in those days about passenger carrying during air displays, I gladly agreed. Why, one might well ask, was that particular trip of so long ago still well remembered? The display itself went off o.k. but in rather deteriorating weather with rain clouds in the distance. It was after calling for "undercarriage down" that it went pear shaped. A flicker of red lights but no greens for the fully locked down position. Luckily, the two main wheels could be seen quite clearly from the cockpit and they certainly seemed to be down, but one could never be sure. The rain had already arrived by the time one of the ground crew came on the intercom and admitted that the previous week the Lancaster had been up on jacks and the undercarriage contact breakers adjusted! That made up my mind and we landed soon afterwards and taxied in without the comforting sights of green lights. The Lanc was far from rainproof and the poor girl who had been in the bomb aimer's position looked like a drowned rat as we stood around awaiting transport. However, we all received profuse thanks nevertheless. The rest of that week went off in it's usual way with Plessey insisting on entertaining us in their chalet to a sumptuous lunch each day followed, after our display, by drinks. I did bring up the question of costs to the firm but that was dismissed as petty cash by their top man in charge who went on to say that it was a good talking point with his potential customers having a top RAF display team on hand. It turned out that the chief's dear wife had also been a nursing sister at Nocton Hall in her time, which might have been part of the story.

From a personal point of view, that particular Farnborough week had got off to a good start when at the first display briefing I noted that sitting next to each other in the front row were four pilots who I had helped to train during their pilots course. The first two were Duncan Simpson of Harrier fame, the next was the son of Sir Ben Lockspicer, who had already designed and built a small transport plane for use in Africa which he was due to display shortly. The other two, John Farley, another famous Hawker Sidley Harrier test pilot and Peter Ginger, who was Deputy Chief Test Pilot on Lightnings for English Electric at Wharton. Peter Ginger and John Farley, both my own students, had gained their wings on Vampires at RAF Swinderby in the late 1950's and Peter Ginger who I have already mentioned as having ejected from two Lightning jets, one RAF and the second at Wharton. After the briefing I was lucky enough to have a chat with Brian Trubshaw and mentioned that I had seen his first British built Concorde landing at Fairford. Another encounter that morning was meeting Rolly Beaumont and getting the low-down on the TSR2.

Trips in the Hastings also had moments to remember, both flying and otherwise. I managed three trips to Brussels, landing at the main international airport, although always parking in the military area across the two main parallel runways from the terminal. A four-engined piston Taildragger was definitely a rarity by the early 70's and we always received more than a passing interest from Belgium Air Force personnel. Their ground organisation could not have been better; fuel, power and transport spot on and the booking of accommodation first class. Invariably we found ourselves in four star hotels, never more than a few hundred yards from the Grand Plaza, the finest main square in Europe in my humble opinion. We soon found an excellent watering hole built and run on English pub lines next to the Belgium Stock Exchange which, itself, formed one segment of the square. Regrettably, when I took Betty who had heard so much about it to visit Brussels some years later it was no longer there – what a pity. It was in the middle of the first night in Brussels that I thought my number might be up when, having been awakened by noise, I saw the outline of flames and very bright lights trough my bedroom curtains and concluded that the hotel was ablaze. In a split second I was at the bedroom window and heaved a sigh of relief when I saw that it was a building just yards away across a side alley that was well and truly alight and not our hotel. Whilst walking to the square that evening we had noticed that the building in question contained a sales outlet for the Spanish airline Iberia and it later transpired that the fire was an act of arson by a militant group incensed by the Spanish for putting to death, by garroting, prisoners, of a capital offence. They say it always comes in threes and this long weekend in Brussels was no exception.

As briefly mentioned before, Derek Butcher, our flight engineer on this trip, had been shot down during WWII when his Lancaster, operating with No 166 squadron out of RAF Kirmington, now Humberside Airport, was shot down during a raid on Agenville. The aircraft crashed near St. Riquier (Somme), the two gunners had been killed and three others, including the late Donald Pleasence who featured in 200 films postwar, taken prisoner and the two other members of the seven-man crew classed as evaders. The Australian captain, F/O E.B. Tutty, was one and Derek the other. In Derek's case, he had been captured twice by the Germans and escaped twice, the second time after being told that if he tried to escape again he would be shot! Derek was taken under the wing of resistance workers and eventually finished up living above a café on the outskirts or Brussels until the Canadians arrived to liberate that city. The story did not end there, however, because after more then a few drinks on the Saturday night, Derek, who was small of stature with a dapper moustache, revealed that his carers, after providing him with a beret and other items of civilian clothing, often took him into the centre of the city for a few drinks, despite the fact that he did not speak the local lingo! He eventually said that he would like to take us all out to that café for old times sake and suggested we meet the next morning for a 9 am train. We had a full crew turn out on that cold and frosty morning on the almost deserted central station, and had already purchased our tickets when suddenly Derek said he couldn't face it. Like many others, the scars of Bomber Command operations over Europe during WWll would remain with him for the rest of his life. With 24-hour opening times the norm, there was nothing for it but to have a drink, after all, our next take-off was still 36 hours away.

These annual Brussels weekend trips were just another back door job, to convey retired top brass to a reunion for ex-NATO commanders and others who had been well up the ladder. With all on the trip being in mufti we had no idea who we were speaking to except for one exception. The exception was, unsurprisingly, ACM 'Gus' Walker known to all in the RAF of those days, as the 'One armed bandit'. One arm having been lost when he was CO of RAF Syerston trying to rescue the crew of a crashed Lancaster on that airfield during WWll. After our take off we got a weather update which suggested that the wind might well be outside our limits for our tail dragger at Northolt. I left my position to inform ACM Walker, who happened to be in one of the two seats nearest our cabin door, of our problem and the disruption it would cause if a diversion were necessary. The very military person sitting next to him, who, I later established to be a retired general, said "You must try your damnest to make it, old boy, my chauffeur is waiting for me at Northolt and it will be a blasted nuisance if we land somewhere else." Gus Walker didn't say a word but did give me a knowing look with a wry smile. One did not have to be a mind reader to receive his message, "A Captain's decision is final regardless of rank." With nightfall and the usual dropping off of wind strength we did manage to make a landing at Northolt and then head north for base.

We had two devices fitted in our Hastings which I had never come across before; Tacan, which not only gave distances from military airfields fitted with a compatible transmitter but also headings to steer to those airfields. Why oh why had Transport Command not fitted them? A strange old world indeed. The other device was "Sarbe" which was activated by distress calls on VHF 121.5 and UHF 243. Two needles on a cockpit gauge would come to life automatically on receipt of a distress transmission, and if they crossed left or right of a vertical line on the gauge, then turns could be made until the lines crossed exactly on the vertical line. Very simple but once again, why was it that second line Hastings were the only RAF aircraft that I ever flew which had the device fitted? I had often wondered since first contact with them how accurate they would be if we were ever to use them in anger. That was soon solved when someone mentioned that there was a ground device, made by the makers that one could practice on. With the co-operation of the senior air traffic control officer, (SATCO) an ex-bomber WWII flight engineer, the item was soon installed in the control tower for a few short days while we tried it out. It proved to be spot on. During each run we passed directly overhead the tower and would certainly have seen any dinghy, even in heavy sea swell conditions. One other Officer at Scampton on the electrical/instrument side of the engineering branch was something of an inventor and was for ever asking the Hastings Flight if he could use our H2S radar for special flights over the newly established Station of RAF Spadeadam, tucked away in the folds of the Pennines and, no doubt, sited there to prevent Russian trawlers picking up transmissions from that station which, it was rumoured, operated bits and pieces of radar from most parts of the world. We never did find out what he was up to, nor heard of any results, however that officer seemed happy enough with our efforts.

Probably it was something of a coincidence but a question by an MP in the House of Commons led to a great deal more flying for our dear old Hastings and that was all to do with Russian trawlers. The MP wanted to know why so many were now operating in the North Sea and on many occasions almost coming into contact with newly positioned oil rigs. The result was that several times a week we sent aircraft on patrols lasting between four and six hours, and we did indeed spot many such vessels. Officially, it was called "Exercise Heliotrope" and oil rig patrols suited us just fine. A hand held surveillance camera was always carried and, with the Hastings being unpressurised, we took out one of the fuselage passenger escape hatches above the left wing on sighting any suspect ships before banking steeply over them which resulted in some very impressive photographs indeed. On one occasion after spotting a Russian warship we took out the passenger door and from side on, at very low level, took a few shots. Numerous other types of photo calls soon followed which included shots of a Vulcan over an oil-rig, followed by it passing over Fylingdales and many shots of the BBMF aircraft with, probably, the best remembered being the BBMF Lancaster, named the city of Lincoln, circling Lincoln Cathedral.

With our two MK C1's being able to uplift up to 50 passengers, we often gave air training corps cadets air experience flights during their summer camps and that was not only at Scampton but many other locations too including, rather surprisingly, Ronaldsway in the I.O.M. I must admit that a few trips were on "the old boy network" and two of them come to mind. The first was a plaintive cry for help from a young Flt Lt at Marham, which decided that the Hastings flight should really try and help him out. His tale of woe was very convincing, he had tried everything for extra capacity for his air experience programme and it looked as if some of the young cadets would not even leave the ground, something they had been looking forward to all year. It so happened that I was to be the pilot to go to his rescue and it was just the type of trip that I thoroughly enjoyed. However, when we called downwind to land at RAF Marham, a rather exhausted sounding air traffic control officer called "You will be number five to land and are all of different types, so keep a good look-out." The Flt. Lt., who had struck oil, turned out to be "Rod Hawkins", a navigator whose next posting would take him to the Phantom simulator at RAF Coningsby and also become one of the part time Lancaster navigators. It was there that I found him to be not only a very likable person but also a workaholic and full of good ideas- an unusual combination.

Another "Old Boy" trip was to fly into Luton airport and give flights to cadets of 1066 Air Training Squadron, who had become attached to the Hastings flight for very obvious reasons. A bill for landing fees would have been a dead give away but the CO of 1066 said there would be no problem, he worked for Monarch Airlines based at Luton, enough said. However, that was a minor hiccup compared with what happened about two weeks after the trip. A telephone message from our link man at No.1 Group Headquarters stated that he had been asked to find out what on earth one of our Hastings was doing parked on the Luton apron two weeks previously. The Fl. Lt. was an excellent go between and said the request was from the Group Captain Ops who had seen our aircraft when boarding a plane for his annual bucket and spade trip to Spain. He went on to say the Groupy was a reasonable senior Officer who would probably accept any plausible excuse so I, without giving it some thought, said "Why don't you ask him if he's checked with Boscombe Down". Boscombe was the only other station still operating Hastings. About ten minutes later the Flt. Lt. was back on the phone and with a jocular voice said "the Group Captain says he never realized that Boscombe Hastings' also had a big bulge under the fuselage for H2S radar". No, they never had which, no doubt, the Group Captain knew full well. Perhaps the fact that we had been flying air cadets tilted the balance.

With the Royal Navy in 1969 taking over the "Nuclear Deterrent" via their inter-continental ballistic missiles launched from submarines, the outlook for the Vulcan Force was looking bleak which, in turn, meant our raison d'etre would, sooner or later, be brought into question. Initially, however, we had a slight increase in trade with the two seat Phantom gradually replacing the single seat Hunter in the fighter/bomber role which called for the navigators to be trained in the low level terrain following, and bombing art. A significant reduction in our fleet did, however, take place in December of 1973 when it was decided by higher authority that we should dispense with our two C1 Hastings, those without H2S fitted, which vastly reduced our passenger capability from 50 seats in the C1's down to about 20 in the Mk5's. Before losing the two Mk1c's, however, we did manage one more hefty passenger lift, which was deemed to have been highly productive.

It was decided that some of the civilian staff manning one of the few remaining maintenance units (MU's) in the RAF would benefit from a visit to one of their chief customers. In this case RAF Coningsby, flying Phantoms. The MU, now defunct, was located near Carlisle and without an airfield. A day return by coach would have been out of the question but by positioning one of our Mk1c's, at Carlisle's civil airport, WWll RAF Crosby-on-Eden, the night before the visit and lifting off early next morning they could have a full working day tour of Coningsby and be back home in the early evening. The flying side and visit went off particularly well, but that one night in the Mess at Carlisle was a little eerie to say the least. It was my first taste of life on a non flying Station and, without any aircrew and few equipment Officers, who mostly lived in married quarters, it was as dead as a dodo. However, things took-off when a Sqn Ldr and his wife arrived on the scene, a very popular couple that needed no introduction to any Transport Command crews of the late 1960's/1970's. He had managed the RAF's transit "Britannia Hotel" in Bahrain and had always chatted up visiting crews. Their life had certainly gone from one end of the social spectrum to the other. They seemed very happy to meet ex-customers, which was reciprocated.

TG 568 was flown into Bedford for practice rescue work and TG 536 to a museum at RAF Colerne, nr Bath. After that museum was disestablished, TG 536 went by road to the RAF fire-fighting school at RAF Catterick, that was not quite the end of the story. After leaving the RAF in 1983 and becoming the CFI at Sherburn-in-Element Flying Club in Yorkshire for a further 12 years of flying, I became increasingly involved with the recently formed Elvington Air Museum whose prime aim at that time was to reconstruct a Halifax Bomber. This type had been the main stay of the Bomber Command force in Yorkshire, equipping many Canadian and two French squadrons based in the country during WWll. A Large section of a Halifax rear-fuselage had been found being used as a chicken coup on the Isle of Lewis, which gave a flying start to the project. British aerospace at Brough gave invaluable support by way of their apprentice training scheme, giving their youngsters many and varied tasks in the programme. With Handley-Page, the makers of the Halifax and Hastings, having gone out of business, the chances of using their jigs and blueprints, even if they still existed, was no longer an option. However it was common practice during the war years, and for many after for that matter, for aircraft manufacturers to use jigs they had designed for one type of aircraft to be utilized in the making of a brand new type. Therefore the Halifax center section and wings were exactly the same as the Hastings. Another example was that of the Short Bros. Sunderland/ Stirling which led to the far from ideal Stirling undercarriage because for the high fuselage/wing connections and other examples abound. In the case of the Halifax project, it was known that the RAF's Fire School had moved on, yet again, from Catterick and had left their numerous aircraft types used for fire fighting practices on the grass airfield there. Luckily the wings and center section of the TG 536 remained intact and the RAF were only too willing to release them to help such a worthy cause. After a lot of hard work and help from many quarters, those wings and center section duly arrived at Elvington. Without the center section in particular, the idea of building a Halifax from scratch might well have hit the buffers. It is not often that miracles occur in aircraft restoration projects, but no sooner had the wings and centre-section of Hastings TG536 arrived at Elvington than a brand new set of wings were found at a scrap yard in Chichester, still in their original packing crates, probably from RAF Thorney Island when No 242 OCU started training C130 crews and not Hastings transports. Nevertheless, they would not have been of any use without the all-important centre-section.

With the reduction of our Hastings fleet from 7 to 5 aircraft and unit status to Flight from Squadron, it was decided, rather strangely in my opinion, that the post of Officer Commanding was no longer suitable for a full career General List Officer and a specialist aircrew Squadron Leader could fulfil the post instead. The upshot was that Sqn Ldr Burton went back to his dearly beloved Shackletons and, with promotion to Wing Commander, became OC No 8 squadron at RAF Kinloss. There was no problem filling his post, our own Chalky White, with his vast experience of multi-piston aircraft, took over and with my own promotion to Squadron Leader on January 1st of 1974, I became his deputy.

One plumb weekend trip would certainly have fallen into Chalky's lap but for the fact that he and his wife would be attending the event as VIP guests. It was to commemorate the 25th anniversary of the ending of the Berlin airlift, which Chalky had been heavily involved in, being held at the Berlin civil airport of Templehof; quite a change from RAF Gatow! The Germans certainly went overboard with their entertainment of all those lucky enough to be attending what turned out to be a magnificent occasion.

Two other blips that cast doubt on our continued existence reared up at about that time, the first was that we were called upon to make runs around our two main low level routes without students aboard, and purely for the video taping (VTR) of those flights in the expert hands of the radar tutors. No doubt that was the final nail in our coffin although it did not come about until the middle of 1977. The second blip was more immediate, and came about as a result of yet another Middle-East oil crisis, which resulted in a drastic shortage of petrol in many western countries. However, it was when I was manning the phone in Chalky's office one morning after he had gone flying that I received a phone call from a young engineering officer at RAF Binbrook, probably the first bomber Station in the RAF to go all jet at the time of the introduction of the Canberra, who said he had been trying to get rid of his Avgas stocks (Piston fuel) for some little time so that he could use the extra space for Avter (Jet fuel) would we like to help him out? You bet we would. The bush telegraph drums must have been beating later because we "Helped a few other stations out as well!"

Gill and Spike's wedding was only one of four aircrew marriages that Betty and I were privileged to attend during our time at Scampton. It was certainly not a case of four weddings and a funeral, in fact it was very, tragically, four weddings and two funerals, two bridegrooms being killed in Vulcan flying accidents and both overseas. One coincidence was that both brides were Roman Catholics and their husbands protestants. It was the first time that Betty and I had been in a Catholic church. The first wedding was between two serving officers, Flight Officer Pat Maguire, a Princess Mary's nursing sister, who I had first met during her tour in Singapore, and Squadron Leader Dave Beeden who had been a staff officer at our group headquarters at Bawtry before starting his tour with the Vulcan force on No 9 squadron at RAF Waddington. With

Pat stationed at the RAF Hospital at Nocton Hall, near Lincoln, their reception was held in the Officers' Mess there and the red carpet was really laid out. Tragically, the marriage was to be very short lived by RAF peacetime standards, which turned out to be in months and not years.

Dave was to lose his life when his Vulcan pilot having made a very heavy landing at the RAF base of Luqa in Malta had elected to go around again but leaking fuel from ruptured fuel tanks caused a fire which in turn led to the disintegration of the aircraft. Although the two pilots, the only ones with ejector seats, escaped, Dave and four others died in the ensuing crash. This was a re-run of a previous Vulcan accident at Heathrow airport when a round-the-world flight fell short of completion by a few hundred yards when again the two pilots ejected and the rest died. Luqa was certainly not one of my favourite landing runways, due to the colour of the wider than normal strip tending to merge with the rocky nature of the Island of Malta which often led to pilots, particularly those using it for the first time after long flights, misjudging the flare to land height. In Flt. Lt. Nigel Thomas's case he was one of two of a Vulcan display team which had been sent to the USA to perform at an open day at the Naval Air Station of Glenview. It was during a practice display after arrival that the Vulcan came to grief, this time the two pilots had no time to eject. However, one of the five man crew did arrive back in the U.K. fit and well and he was the then OC No 617 "Dambuster" Squadron at RAF Scampton, First navigator Wing Commander Stephenson – had not flown on the ill-fated sortie, which did not really call for a navigator to be aboard in any case. This last accident took place in August 1978, about a year after the demise of the Hastings and my own departure to take-over the Battle of Britain Memorial Flight at RAF Coningsby. However, I did manage to attend the memorial service in Scampton's village church and the wake in the Officers' Mess. One fact deeply appreciated by all was that the AOC of No 1 group, and later Marshal of the Royal Air Force Sir David Craig, attended both events. One officer at the wake mentioned that with No 9 Sqn having lost one in Malta it was just a matter of time before No 617 lost one too. The animosity between those two squadrons over which one actually sank the Terpitz in WWll still raged on and it was just as well that they did not share the same station, one being at Scampton and the other at Waddington, but still a little too close for comfort at times with the bulkhead of the German battleship still changing hands until recent times when a truce was called and the bulkhead placed in the RAF Museum at Hendon.

Fifty-Two Years in the Cockpit - Volume Two

Our final flight of a Hastings to the eastern Mediterranean was certainly not short on passengers, nor did it pass off without incident. The flight outbound plus a tour of Cyprus in a hired car over the long weekend was pure bliss, but from our scheduled return departure time onwards it was downhill all the way. When we were just about to start engines a voice came over the intercom saying one of our non-operating radar – navigators had not turned up and had probably failed to book an early call. There was nothing for it but to disembark and send someone to check his room. Whilst standing around in the windless early dawn, when one could probably hear a pin drop at 20 yards, we suddenly heard gunfire in the distance and opined that the British Army must also be up early too. It turned out to be nothing of the sort and the full story emerged after our landing for fuel in Malta a few hours later. However, before landing we had to take avoiding action on the Vulcan aircraft which, mistakenly, was positioning for the wrong main runway direction. It turned out that the Vulcan captain, the very likeable Mike Knight had been ordered at very short notice to divert to Malta during a direct flight from the U.K. to Cyprus and was not as well prepared for a landing there as he would normally have been if that had been his intended destination. During a general discussion in the Transit Mess, the duty Operations Officer arrived on the scene and declared that Archbishop Makarios, President of Cyprus, had been overthrown by a military uprising demanding Enosis, union with Greece that morning, and he would soon be arriving in Malta aboard a No 70 squadron Argosy, it had very nearly been our Hastings that would have carried him. That explained the gunfire but what took everybody by surprise was the upshot – the Turkish invasion of that Island five days later, which called for a massive RAF airlift of civilians to the U.K.

During my stays in Cyprus other events occurred that I recall, the first of which was more to do with sea matters and the Royal Navy than anything else. It all started when twenty or so people appeared through the Mess entrance doors in, not to put too finer point on it, a bedraggled state. They turned out to be members of the Israeli Armed Forces who had, at very short notice, been rounded up to form a search party for a submarine, which had failed to arrive in Haifa from the U.K. during its delivery voyage after purchase from the RN. However, all that was ever found of that submarine, and her 69 Israeli crew, was an emergency buoy, which later was washed up on a beach in Gaza. Historically, that submarine was first named HMS Totem but changed to Dakar by its new

221

owners. Of interest is that throughout her RN days it had carried the Totem pole of the Indian Cowichan tribe of Canada, whose chief had warned during the pole's handover to HMS Totem that if ever it sailed without the pole disaster would strike. Yes, this had been the first sailing without the pole! Over a quarter of a century later, the underwater robot that had discovered the Titanic, also located the Dakar, two miles below between Crete and Cyprus, but the reason for her loss remains unresolved. When I mentioned the state of the Israeli's uniforms I meant no disrespect, in fact it helped to underline one of my theories that spit and polish, the stamping of feet and the bellowing of orders did not necessarily go hand in glove with military efficiency. To date, the Israeli Armed Forces have never suffered a major defeat, albeit in their short history, and, in fact, have outfought much greater forces on two occasions since their independence.

The second event was the appearance of the easy to recognize Neil Williams plus his crew all of whom did not look at all happy with life. Neil, of course, had been one of the top aerobatic display pilots in his service days but was now a company test pilot with Handley Page, although still managing to continue his display work whenever time permitted. The reason for the downcast looks was that on landing at Akrotiri, after completing tropical trials in the Sudan, Neil had been informed that Handley Page had gone bust and he was on his own from then on. We had several long talks with him to try and help in whatever way we could, including the possibility of flying Neil and his crew back to the U.K. but Neil, being the chap that he was, decided to stay in Cyprus and await developments. Always on hand during those discussions was the chief flight test observer who just happened to be female and particularly good looking. It certainly came as no surprise when Neil later married the dear lady but later, very tragically, they were to die together when the Heinkel 111 Neil was ferrying from Spain to the U.K. crashed into high ground en-route.

Back in the U.K. our very varied flying life continued apace with new destinations cropping up at regular intervals. Trips to Macrianish or Stornaway being particularly popular with the latter giving non-Scottish crew members a real eye-opener when, on occasions, we spent a few nights in one of the main hotels there. I soon noticed in that part of the Scotland at least, it was not whisky and chasers but vodka and chasers, particularly when the fishing fleet arrived back home with, strangely, many of the sailors being of Russian origin. On one very memorable occasion the only two customers in our hotel bar one Saturday afternoon were myself and our flight engineer, Ian Gibson, who was more Scottish than you will ever see in the caricatures seen in such films as Whisky Galore.

The noise coming from an adjoining room was horrendous which, Ian opined, was probably a Scottish wedding festival, which would certainly not end after the fat lady had sung but only after the grand parade had taken place. The grand parade, Ian enlarged, was the marching around the ballroom in two's of all guests still capable of standing. No sooner had Ian given his explanation then a fearsome lady burst into the bar and demanded that we bring up the rear of the parade, which was just about to take place. We meekly surrendered and I've never felt so embarrassed in all my life, even Ian did not look his usual self. It was the final part of a longish day which had started with a call out to transfer urgent spares from Leuchars, in Fife to Stornoway on the Island of Lewis for a Phantom squadron which was on detachment there taking part in a rather important NATO exercise.

The weather had become marginal over the Scottish Highlands and on contact with Stornoway, which did not have radar in those days we were given a lower than predicted cloud base of 8/8 at 700'. However, for some reason of other, it was one of the very few airfields in the U.K. equipped with a Tacan Beacon actually sited on the station. It eventually gave us a distance to run with a heading to steer for the overhead so I decided there and then to make up my own let down procedure by flying to the overhead at the safety height for the area and then after turning outbound over the open sea to about the 15nm point before descending and turning inbound so as to be at 300' per mile to run plus 50' for altimeter error, eg at 10nm to run 3,050, at 5nm to run 1,550, etc. This was the norm for 3 degrees radar approaches and it worked out perfectly for us that day, breaking cloud with 2 miles to go and nicely lined up with the landing runway. It was just as well that we made the best of that Saturday because, rather late in the evening, two youngish lads left over from the wedding asked Ian and myself if we would like to join them in their usual trek up into the hills the next morning. We gently declined saying that after a stroll around their lovely harbour we would probably end up in the bar for a few more snifters. They did not exactly say "you'll be lucky, I say you'll be lucky" but we got the message that nobody, but nobody, could purchase alcohol on Sundays in the Outer Hebrides. For good measure they added that no Sunday papers were allowed on the island either but if we still cared to join them they had their own brewing still up in the hills. Another world indeed.

Those rules were all to do with the Scottish Presbyterian Church. A firm of city slickers, who had just built a brand new hotel on the outskirts of the town, soon found out to their cost just how powerful that church could be. Having read the small print of the local laws, they decided they could open their bars on a Sunday after all and did so. On the second Sunday a group of clergymen carrying placards and banners paraded outside but to no avail. However, the hotel owners eventually saw the light when such everyday items as bread, butter, meat, etc. suddenly became in very short supply from the island merchants. The cost of importing these items would have been prohibitive and the towel was duly thrown in. The ban on Sunday newspapers also had its repercussions to our very small Hastings world when one of our Captains was en-route to Stornoway on a direct flight from our Scampton base one Sunday morning when he was asked over the radio to divert to RAF Leuchars to pick up some papers for the Phantom detachment. Thinking 'papers' meant official mail, he obliged only to find that it was Sunday newspapers for the benefit of the Wing Commander who was detachment commander. The Captain admitted on return to base that he now knew how smugglers must feel.

I was at that time still managing to take free time off to give air experience flights to Air Training Cadets in Chipmunk aircraft and even gave a full week at other stations on occasions. It was during one of those sojourns, this time to RAF Abingdon, that I passed the 10,000 flying hours mark. I think Flight Commander Chalky White must have taken more than the usual passing glance at my log book when he had signed my last monthly summary and noticed how close I was to that event because a Wing Commander at Abingdon was forever checking the booking sheets and produced the station photographer for my landing off the exact 10,000th hour of flight. I don't know who was the more surprised, the ATC cadet or myself, but the snaps remain a happy reminder of the event and also of the aircraft I most enjoyed flying in my RAF days. It was during a cocktail party given by Wing Commander Pilkington, later AVM, the OC No 230 Vulcan OCU which the Hastings flight was part of, that he said "Would you mind stepping into the next room for a couple of minutes, Jacko?" I followed, wondering what social gaffe I might have committed, only to find that it was not a telling off, I think he realised full well that when he asked me if I was interested in taking over flying the Lancaster bomber, then with the Battle of Britain flight at RAF Coltishall, that it was akin to asking a small boy if he really wanted any sweets after taking him into a Toffee shop. That was the start of a very hectic period of flying covering the three years of 1975-77.

CHAPTER 8
The Cod War, the BBMF and the demise of the Hastings

The pilot I would be taking over from on the BBMF was my old mate Ken Sneller who I had served alongside when on my first transport tour with No 36 Sqdn. Ken had flown operationally in Coastal Command during WWII and continued in the Maritime world until the mid 50s, earning an AFC for coping with a double engine failure, both on the same side, when operating the last Lancasters in that Command. He was finishing his service career commanding the Wainfleet Bombing Range. Being a bachelor, he lived in the Mess at RAF Coningsby and was free to fly the Lancaster every weekend during the summer months without having a wife to explain his continuous absences to. Luckily, my wife Betty had long ago become used to my long detachments during the previous 15 years in the transport world. The Lancaster was limited to 55 hours flying per year to conserve engine and structural life, which severely restricted circuit bashing for new to type pilots. With having, albeit 25 years in the past, some experience of the Lancaster, Ken confined my re-conversion to normal display sorties. The very last trip with him could not have been more auspicious and although it took up more than two and a half hours of the 55 allowed for the season it was probably the most meaningful of that year's display season. It was a round robin to Dunkirk and back, leading a formation of three Spitfires and a Hurricane. The weather was brilliant and the display given by Ken could not have been bettered. It was, of course, the annual remembrance of the 1940 Dunkirk evacuation carried out by ships of all sizes from rowing boats upwards. On this occasion a special tribute was being paid to the Small Boats Association whose honorary Vice Admiral was their chief organiser; Raymond Baxter, the famous TV commentator. The RN guard ship later sent a signal of congratulations which was deeply appreciated by all on the flight. With a round trip of over 200 miles to Coltishall by road, it had been a long long day but the thought of flying the worlds last air worthy Lancaster put that into the perspective of no-consequence. Only on two occasions when arriving at Coltishall we found that the weather at the display venue was below limits and there was nothing for it but to take the long road a winding back into Lincolnshire did I question this perspective.

Another particularly emotive flight for Ken and myself was the positioning of the Lancaster at my old station of RAF Brize Norton for a No 5 Group survivors dinner night in the Officers' Mess. The event was hosted by the then Deputy C in C of Strike Command, Air Marshal Beetham, a very distinguished WWII Lancaster pilot who later became Marshal of the Royal Air Force. It was not only a splendid evening but somebody had the wit to position the Lancaster within a stones throw of the Mess, pointing straight at the front entrance and brilliantly illuminated. It certainly brought tears to quite a few eyes that night and I have never seen any aircraft displayed so well. I must explain that the Lancaster was on a runway perimeter track which passed closer to living accommodation than on any other RAF station that I ever came across. This was due to the extension of the main runway by the USAF during their occupation of the base post WWII. I very much doubt if that extension would have come about otherwise.

We stayed in the Mess one extra night, Sunday, so we could cater for a request to call in at RAF Benson, not normally open at weekends, on our return flight to our Coltishall base. This was to give Group Captain George Black, a dyed in the wool fighter pilot, a familiarisation flight in the Lancaster. It had been calculated that there would be one or two hours to spare before the Lancaster went into second line for its winter servicing after our return, so what better way to knock one off than let one of our lords and masters have a go at the controls of the most famous RAF bomber of all time? We arrived at Benson and Ken agreed that there was no point in my going along just for the ride, so I became an interested spectator, along with a growing number of others. We had expected the Group Captain to carry out the usual circuits and bumps to get the feel of the beast but no such thing. After initial take off the Lanc was climbed to about 3,000' overhead and then thrown around the skies more like a Spitfire than a heavy bomber. Ken was well known for taking things in his stride, but he did look somewhat subdued on leaving the aircraft after landing, and I was startled when, after bidding farewell to the Group Captain he turned to me and said, "Its all yours, Jacko, I'll be the co-pilot for the return to Coltishall". The reason for my bewilderment was that the flight would be Ken's second from last in the RAF as a pilot due to his impending semi-retirement from the service. After a planned fly past over the new gate guardian at RAF Scampton, Lancaster NX611, he would become a Reserve Officer, although still running the bombing range and also living in Mess at Coningsby. Luckily, the weather and aircraft serviceability did allow his last flight to take place. The flight back to base from Benson could not have been more uneventful. Having taken off on the north easterly runway we hardly changed course by more than 30° or so before making a straight in approach to Coltishall's similar runway. A fact I was able to relate by phone a few days later after receiving a phone call from an engineering Officer asking if I had been doing any practice displays and throwing the Lancaster around a bit on the flight from Benson. It was after explaining that we had hardly banked left or right on that sector that I asked him the reason for his interest. I was a little staggered at his reply on two counts. Firstly, it had never occurred to me that Lancaster PA474 had been fitted with a 'G' meter, and secondly, the high reading which had been found on it after our landing. With my mind going into overdrive, all I could think of saying was that technically I was not the Captain of the aircraft and perhaps they should approach Ken Sneller, whilst thinking about the impromptu display over Benson. Perhaps if they knew a very senior Officer had been the culprit the matter might be laid to rest, but it was not to be for the tech officer was well ahead of the game. He replied to me that they had failed to track Ken down at the bombing range, but knowing our reason for the Benson visit they had already approached Group Captain Black who had said "Why don't you have a word with the Squadron Leader who is taking over from Sneller? He was on board and might know something about it". I certainly did, but I suppose there is something in the old adage "All's fair in love and war". He was the same George Black whose two sons I had brought back from Germany to their school in Norfolk on one of my Belfast flights. Some years later, during a No XI Squadron reunion at RAF Leeming, I noted with interest that one was the Station Commander there. I wished the engineering Officer well with the winter servicing and said how much I was looking forward to the Air Test prior to the 1976 season. I should have known better, for he was back on the phone a few weeks later asking if I would be available to fly the Lanc again shortly. I said, "I thought it would have been in pieces by now"? To which he replied, "It is, but a staff officer from Strike Command has been on the phone saying Air Marshal Beetham wishes to fly it shortly. I told him it was dismantled but he later came back and said that the Air Marshal said, 'Well, put it back together again'". I must say the future chief of the RAF made a remarkable landing, just as if it had been yesterday and not all those years well in the past during his Bomber Command Ops with Nos 50 & 57 Squadrons. I think his appetite must have been wetted when he saw the Lanc outside the Mess at Brize.

1975 was to finish on a high note for the Hastings flight because a Vulcan navigational instructor had come up with the bright idea of running a bombing competition on the last working Friday before Christmas, with the results to be announced during the 'Thank God its Friday' Happy Hour. The concept was that the Hastings would take up nine navigator/bomb aimers with three from each of the three Vulcan squadrons based at Scampton and using the bomb/plot radar Station near RAF Coningsby, which could calculate, after the bomb release button had been pressed aloft, where the bombs would have landed in relation to the target. Our Hastings crews became very popular, almost as popular as after our frequent fish runs to Machrianish in Scotland. Our runs to that outpost of the RAF's empire, being an experimental station, had a more serious note of course, but it would have been unthinkable to return without an aircraft full of fish for the Officers' Mess and many others, despite the smell for days afterwards.

Our Hastings still retained two oversized doors, one per side, for the rapid exiting of paratroopers or cargo and they became particularly useful for air to air photography. A picture was taken of Lancaster PA474, recently named "City of Lincoln", whilst it circled the impressive Cathedral in that city, other bookings came thick and fast: two Buccaneers in formation out of RAF Honington over the North Sea, clips for a BBC film on the Spitfire, one of our Hastings formatting on a VC10 out of Brize, another of our Hastings patrolling the North Sea oil rigs, two four engined Avros in formation (Lancaster and Vulcan) over Lincoln and, finally, one which I was to be reminded of years later. This was to capture a Vulcan flying over an oil rig and later over the early warning station of Fyingdales, high up on the North Yorkshire Moors. The reminder came from the wife of Air Chief Marshal Sir John Willis, a delightful lady, who had been a neighbour and good friend of ours at Scampton, where her husband was a Sqdn Ldr Vulcan Captain. It was twenty years on during an official visit to the Lincolnshire Aviation Heritage Centre at East Kirkby, near Boston, that the dear lady said to me "I will always remember my first flight". Wondering just what to say, I could only muster "Was it exciting"? She replied, "It certainly was, it was in a Hastings flown low over the North Sea with the back door open and photographers trying to take a picture of a Vulcan passing over an oil rig. It was my husband who was flying the Vulcan. Don't you remember, you were the Hastings pilot?" It all came back to me like a flash.

The oil rig patrols, by the way, had been instigated because of the ever increasing number of Russian ships sailing far too close to the rigs for comfort. The idea was that our Hastings aircraft should fly from the most northern rig to the most southern, or vice versa, at low level and report any sightings with photos of same. The flights took 4 to 5 hours. Initially we made contact with quite a few but sightings became less frequent and eventually fizzled out completely. Had our Hastings made a difference? One will never know.

The February of 1976 was to see the Hastings reach yet another high in its longish life but in another world far removed from transporting troops and freight worldwide. The last, some people say lost, Cod war was in full swing to the extent that the Nimrod aircraft of No 18 Group, operating out of RAF Kinlosss, became stretched to the limits, which resulted in our H2S equipped aircraft being called upon to see if we could cope with the task of picking up Icelandic gunboats harassing our trawlers and their RN escorts. It was thus that we started weekly detachments to Kinloss and the results amazed everyone, with pick up distance as good as, if not better than, the Nimrod's, but with the added bonus of a 360° sweep against the forward looking radar on the Nimrod. Our Hastings' operated on alternate days when they would patrol off the eastern coast of Iceland up to their safe endurance limit of about 10 hours. One aspect of this task that truly amazed me was that all of our four Hastings were fitted with radio altimeters over one week end, which increased no end our low level safety margins when descending from the transit height of about 10,000' into the patrol area without knowing the sea level atmospheric pressure there. I'm not sure if the Nimrod had the capability of dropping supplies by parachute to the duty RN auxiliary depot ship which was always on hand, but we did. In addition to spare parts, we also dropped mail on every sortie. After contact with the ship, it would make a wide sweeping turn which, as is well known, leaves a large area of very flat water which we used for dropping our parachutes into during the run in for the drop, always making sure that the two man Gemini recovery boat had been launched from the mother ship and was on its way to the likely impact point. We always received profuse thanks over the radio for our efforts and, from trawlers, the offer of fish if we cared to drive over to Grimsby after their next docking.

On each sortie we always had to carry an extra crew member in the form of a Nimrod Captain who would offer help and advice on maritime matters. On my very first 10 hour sortie, which had been very uneventful, we had about 50 miles to run inbound to Kinloss when the Nimrod Captain said "we have a practice buoy in the Moray Firth for anti submarine work which we can usually pick up on our radar at 20 miles, but I suppose on your wartime gear it might be down to about 5 miles". It seemed only seconds later before one of our Nav/Rads came up with "Contact 42 miles dead ahead in position of the buoy". The intercom became strangely quiet from then on".

The day off between Heliotrope flights was most welcome, particularly when one of my ex FTS students, now in the maritime world, was also on a stand down and gave me and my co-pilot a conducted tour of that wonderful part of Scotland. We were not always so lucky as that, however, being called out on one so called day off to fly down to Honington and back via two other RAF stations which was even more tiring than a Heliotrope flight.

My final Cod war detail was very eventful indeed. The Royal Navy Officer who was part of the pre-flight briefing team announced that the RN ships on patrol off Iceland had lost track of the Icelandic gunboat Baldur, and any assistance in re-locating it should be given high priority on our flight. He went on to say that it might have taken shelter in one of the many Fjords on their eastern seaboard but we must on no account infringe their airspace. In the north of Scotland the number of daylight hours in February being very limited was overcome to a large extent by using two pre-dawn and two dusk hours for transmitting to and from the patrol area. On this particular flight we picked up a radar blip in a fjord on our very first northbound run and the Nav-Rads reported that no movement could be determined, so I decided it would be better if we continued our north bound flight so that if we ourselves had shown up on their radars, we might fox them into thinking that we had not spotted what later proved to be the Baldur. 30 minutes later, on our southbound run, the radar blip showed that she was now just exiting the fjord and a message to that effect was sent back to Scotland. Another incident took place shortly afterwards when a "Fokker Friendship" twin turbo-prop aircraft appeared from nowhere and not only formatted on our Hastings but also came up on our radio frequency. We answered their calls however, with a fair number of RN ships listening out, in a fairly circumspect manner. The Fokker kept alongside us for quite some time and it was only after descending and reducing speed rapidly for the usual air-drop that it peeled off. We had been told at one briefing that the only aircraft available to Iceland's military was a solitary Fokker Friendship, so perhaps my only claim to fame is that once upon a time an entire enemy Air Force formatted on me! One nice touch that rounded off the day was at the de-briefing from that flight, a signal from the Royal Navy at Rosyth had already been received and was readout. It stated, "This morning Hastings did good work in relocating and identifying Baldur. Thank you". Short but sweet, as is the Royal Navy style.

The very next day it was back to Scampton with the prospect of a day off but, once again, it was not to be. Awaiting me was the news that

The whole Battle of Britain Memorial Flight less the Hurricane D7A

the Lancaster was ready for Air Test at RAF Coltishall after it's winter inspection. With the weather set fair for the next few days it was judged to be better to get it over with as soon as possible so I found myself on the road to Norfolk by 7 o'clock the following morning. The commander of the Battle of Britain flight at that time, Sqdn Ldr Mick Raw, acted as co-pilot for the air test and, thankfully, everything was in full working order because it had been decreed that the historic flight would leave RAF Coltishall within the week for a new home at RAF Coningsby and, if available, the Lancaster would lead the mass formation. This duly took place on the 1st March 1976 and, after a farewell fly-past of Norwich and, of course, Coltishall, the formation set sail. It consisted of the Lancaster, one Hurricane and three Spitfires with one of our Hastings lurking alongside for the benefit of the press photographers. One Hurricane and one Spitfire had to be left behind because of technical problems.

The reason for the change of Station for the historic Flight remains obscure but what is known is that a group called "The Lincolnshire Lancaster Committee", including Mrs Hilda Buttery, Mr Stewart Stephenson and the future Mayor of Lincoln, Fred Allen, had been formed to try and persuade the MOD to return the Lancaster to its rightful home in 'Bomber County'. Eventually a reply by letter, signed by the Minister for Defence, Roy Mason, arrived indicating that the Lancaster would shortly be returning to Lincolnshire and instructions would be issued to the effect that whenever time permitted the Lancaster would over-fly the City of Lincoln during transit flights. The last part of that letter got us off to a bad start with RAF Coningsby in that after receiving our take off time from Coltishall, they guessed our arrival time, working on a speed of 180 knots, which was about right, as 12 noon. The Station Commander called a halt to all other flying from 11.30 until after we had landed. The only snag was we had already used up a fair amount of time carrying out requested fly pasts over Norwich, Marham, Cranwell and Digby before checking in with Coningsby and even then we continued northwards to circle Lincoln Cathedral a couple of times as called for in the MOD letter. The voice of the controller at Coningsby became a little strained when he asked just when did we intend to land? The balloon caption above my head visualised an irate Group Captain breathing down the neck of the controller, listening for the answer. Others that we had kept waiting in addition to the Station Commander Group Captain Allison included Fred Allen, by then the Mayor of Lincoln, Mrs Hilda Buttery, plus a host of media people who banged on about deadlines and other events that they night now be late for. My own schedule for that week was also tight with an oil rig patrol the very next day and a day return to Stornoway the day after that, taking our AOC, AVM Sir David Evans, on a tour of inspection. Sir David was a Canadian who immediately put all at their ease and it was a real pleasure to take him on any trip. After dropping the AOC off at RAF Finningley on the return journey news awaited me that the Lancaster was required the next day for the benefit of the makers of a French film called "Lieutenant Karl". Apparently they wanted shots of the Lancaster taking off and landing, but it turned into a bit of a to do.

The company had persuaded the RAF to alter the squadron code letter on one side of the fuselage from KM-B to KM-F. In WWII the KM stood for No 44 (Rhodesia) Squadron, the first squadron to operate Lancasters, and the B for the particular aircraft used by the late Sqdn Ldr

John Nettleton who had led the very first Lancaster daylight raid carried out against Augsburg on 17th April 1942. On that raid he also had under his command aircraft of No 97 Squadron. Sqdn Ldr Nettleton's aircraft was the only one from 44 Squadron to return and he was awarded a well deserved VC, but sadly- after taking over command of 44 Squadron the following year, he was to perish on a raid against Turin. One other addition that had taken place during the previous three days, and one which nobody could object to, was the painting of the cross of Lorraine, the logo of the Free French, on the upper front fuselage, just ahead of the cockpit. Before my arrival at Coningsby the film director, having noticed the Phantom aircraft using the main long runway, had already briefed his film crew on where to position their gear and was taken aback when I said the wind was outside the Lancaster's cross wind limit of 15 knots and we would have to ask if the short runway was still useable. The OC Ops readily agreed and after ascertaining its length, we made one take off and landing using a slightly lower than normal approach speed. Needless to say, the film crew asked for just one more run, which turned into three before they were satisfied.

Although March was not one of our display months, two more flights of interest cropped up before the end of the month in our new home. The first was an air test after the re-fitting of a mid-upper turret to PA474. The turret itself was found in Argentina, whose air force had flown Lancasters after WWII, and transported to the UK on board HMS Hampshire. The only problem was not the actual fitting of the turret, which had been in the country for some time, but the fairing, known as the deflector cam or taboo track, around it. This device was designed so that in the dead of night the mid-upper gunner could not shoot the fins and rudders off his own aircraft. Neither the RAF nor Avro could locate one, and it was only the perseverance and fund raising of the Lincolnshire Lancaster Appeal Committee that allowed one to be produced by Mariner Engineering Co. With the new fairing being a one off job and not by the original makers, BBMF's technical officer, quite rightly, called for an air test to include a fairly high speed dive. Everything went off all right and the Lancaster was certainly enhanced by its fitting.

The short runway landings for the film company stood me in good stead for the second flight which was to position the Lancaster, plus one of BBMF's Spitfires, at RAF Little Rissington, the then home of the RAF's Central Flying School (CFS), which was to be visited by their honorary Air Commandant, Queen Elizabeth the Queen Mother, prior

A newspaper photograph of HM Queen Elizabeth, the Queen Mother, inspecting the Lancaster

to CFS's relocation to RAF Cranwell. I well remembered that the main runway at Rissington, from which I had made my first jet flight from in a single seat Vampire and also my first Lancaster flying, now over 25 years in the past, was not even up to the usual 2,000 yards length, so on the day of the flight the wind direction and strength would be all important. My ill luck continued and cometh the day the wind was way out of limits for the main runway but straight down a secondary one which, I recalled, had a pronounced slope, luckily up into the wind on the day. Again knocking 5 knots off the recommended approach speed the Lancaster soon dropped her tail after a wheeler landing and all was well. In fact, we could have stopped in half the runway length and perhaps it would have been take off distance that might have been the problem if we had been due to leave later that day. The landing distance lent weight to one of my old hobby horses of whether the recommended threshold speed should always be 1.4 times the stalling speed? It was all very well in the Sopwith Camel days of WWI when the average stalling speed was around the 40 mph mark, making the threshold speed about 56 mph, but now in the jet age the figures could be up to 100 knots for stall and, therefore 140 knots for the flare: an ever increasing gap between stall and threshold speed. Could not the 1.4 equation have been reduced to 1.3 or even 1.2?

We had a wonderful night in the CFS Mess that evening, being made most welcome by the staff and students alike and meeting many friends of long ago. The next day, however, the day of the royal visit, could not have been more different. Our Lancaster and Spitfire were well to the fore for the inspection, however only aircrew on the strength of CFS would be on the parade or standing in front of A/C and all visiting aircrew were asked to keep a low profile in our respective messes. Even there we could not use the ante-room or dining hall and so it was that we, and even the crew of the royal helicopter, spent many hours in the billiard room on the assumption that the Queen Mum was unlikely to pop in, although it was rumoured that in her younger days she had played a game. Having a chat with members of the Royal Flight was interesting enough, but we were not too unhappy at their departure as we had been given permission to take off for base any time after they had lifted off with HM on board. That flight ended the BBMF's first month at RAF Coningsby, but what a month it had been! More was to follow, however, making it THE year as far as my time on the flight was concerned.

Yet another short runway landing was called for the very next month, although I was becoming used to them by then. This was at RAF Linton-on-Ouse who were hosting Candian bomber veterans of WWII who had used Linton, and virtually every other Bomber Command station in Yorkshire at the height of the bomber offensive. A funny twist to that particular landing was that I would be on finals for a longer period of time to make adjustments to speed and height. Unbeknown to us, of course, was that the Canadians were still in transit on board crew coaches from Harrogate railway station and we had flown quite low over the convoy. Safely on the ground, I lost count of the numerous congratulations I received for our overflight and queries as to how we had managed it. One big bonus from the Linton visit was that I was to meet Leo Hook, now the Chief Ground Instructor (CGI) there after a gap of just over thirty years when we had both been NCO pilots on No XI Squadron in Japan.

In the first week of May of 1976 I was to carry out the most unusual flight of my entire flying career. It was the first of two flights that the BBMF made to the Netherlands in 1976 and both highly significant. The first was a two day event at the invitation of the Dutch government to commemorate the 31st anniversary of the liberation of their country and Operation Manna when 550 Lancasters had dropped 6,684 tons of food over a 10 day period to a starving population. The plan of action was that on the evening of our arrival at the Dutch Air Force base of Gilze Rijen we would take off again so as to overfly the Dutch memorial to the crews of Bomber Command at sunset. This was situated at Dronten in the eastern polder of what was once the Zuider Zee. Sunset would be the climax of a massive memorial service there, being attended by many Dutch and British dignitaries. Luckily, the navigator for the trip was Sqdn Ldr Ray Leach who had not only been to Gilze Rijen with the Lancaster the previous year and made many friends, but was also an authority on British Army and Air Force matters of WWII. His knowledge was to prove invaluable during our visit. He was also a go-getter of the first order and the first thing I noticed when I went to stow my overnight kit aboard PA474 after arriving at Coningsby from Scampton on day one, was that a flare chute had been fitted since my last flight. Ray had really been busy, for it was his brain child to approach RAF Finningley who, it was known, were about to dispose of their Varsity aircraft, which had Lancaster type flare chutes fitted, and ask them for one. This was gladly given after which he contacted the Royal British Legion and requested 10,000 poppy petals so that we could drop them over the memorial service. Our arrival at Gilze Rijen was after given vectors by Ray to pass over Wg Cdr Guy Gibson and his navigator, Sqdn Ldr Warwick's graves at Steenbergen, where I gently rocked the wings in salute. With plenty of time in hand to fine tune details of our evening flight when timing would be all important, we called for help from a charming Dutchman by the name of Jac Thuring, in whose home Ray and I would be guests that night. He had been trained as a pilot by the RAF during WWII and now owned a Harvard aircraft which was, along with several others of the local flying club, hangared on the airfield. He, of course, knew the local area like the back of his hand and it was decided then and there that he should fly in the bomb aimer's position for the flight. It was also decided that Chief Technician, Dick Melton, the NCO in charge of our ground crew, would also fly on the sortie to operate the flare chute, and thus releasing the poppy petals when given the signal.

238

The Avro Lancaster

The visibility that evening was nothing to write home about but by following canals and looking out for church steeples as directed by the Nav and Jac we arrived over the ceremony spot on time after loitering over our last identification point for a little time. According to the spectators whom we later met, our approach from the west, with the setting sun as a backdrop, and the poorish visibility, lent a certain allure to the Lancaster's arrival. The dropping of the poppy petals came as a complete surprise to all on the ground, the only mishap being some of the petals dropped on a white fence that had recently been painted! When he was later offered compensation by a member of the Amsterdam RAFA Club, he would not hear of it, saying he could dine out on the story for years to come. Time was not on our side in the context of landing back at Gilze Rijen before darkness overtook us. Flying at night was strictly forbidden for all BBMF aircraft and at one point it looked as if we were getting ahead of the game until the main Dutch military radar station at Nieuw Milligen, which had been tracking us throughout, came up on our radio frequency to request an overfly. I think all our minds went into overdrive thinking how much extra time that would involve. However, Ray soon came to the rescue with the fact that a 10° change of heading would do the trick and add only seconds to the flight time. That overfly put the icing on the cake and made the Mess party that followed even more enjoyable. It was during that party that I really got to know our host- Jac Thurling. It turned out that in addition to himself, several other pilots at the aero club also owned Harvards and the highlight of their year was to mount a formation flypast of the RAFA rest home at Sussexdown.

I'm not sure if it was before or after our visit, but those same pilots and their Harvards took part in the epic film "A Bridge Too Far", heavily disguised as P47 Thunderbolts. I was a little surprised that no nit picker had pointed out that the RAF never used the P47 operationally in Europe, confining them to 13 Squadrons in the South/East Asia Command, where they gave valuable support to the 14th Army in Burma.

The next morning Jac took us on a mini tour of the area en-route to the airfield and to this very day I am still not sure if it was some kind of Dutch joke but after pointing out the prison in Breda he said, "You know there are only two German war criminals left in prison, both in Spandau"? After we had concurred he added, "It's three actually, we have one in there which we keep quiet about". Well, one never knows, does one?

The fact that this was the day that I would be leading a Spitfire and a Hurricane into an international airport, probably one of the busiest in the world, in a Lancaster with very primitive Nav aids was preying on my mind a little during the drive in, but the news that greeted us at Gilze Rijen stunned us all. It was to the effect that although our arrival time at Schipol airport was set in concrete, could we possibly take off earlier than planned and over fly as many of the major towns in Holland as possible en-route and, before landing, carry out a display over Dam Square in the centre of Amsterdam? Anticipating our approval, permission for the display had been sought and given. Could anybody imagine that taking place over Trafalgar Square? Never in a thousand years, although we did use that location as a turning point for an over fly of Horseguards Parade later that year- the first time in 30 years that a Lancaster had overflown central London.

Another shock for me, personally, was the added news that a Fokker Friendship of the Dutch Air Force would be manoeuvring around our formation throughout the flight for the benefit of photographers. I hoped that the pilot was just as capable as the one off Iceland barely three months before. The only lighter side to the Fokker news was recalling the old wartime story about the Flt Lt who got into a slight altercation with King George VI when he was receiving his DFC at Buckingham Palace. The King, well known for his stammer, managed to get out that it was for shooting down "Three Fok...Fok Wolfs", to which the Flt Lt replied, "Four, your Majesty". After another correction His Majesty concluded the conversation by blurting out "Well, you are only getting one Fok, Fok...medal", or words to that effect!

Ray Leach now really had a job on his hands to re-hash our planned flight but I soon noted that he was beginning to get fairly excited about our new route and a quick glance over his shoulder at his map revealed that we would be deviating from the straight lines between the major towns twice. It was his Army background coming to the fore again and, in addition to passing over Breda, Eindhoven, Venlo, Nijmegan, Arnhem, Utrecht, and Purmerend- which was our IP for the 8 mile run on to the 'Dam'- we would also be overflying Overloon with its memorial to commemorate one of the bitterest tank battles of WWII. In that museum we were to see a Spitfire and a Mitchell bomber, both in the Dutch Air Force markings of that war. The second slight deviation was to pass over the probable crash sight of two Typhoons of No 609 Squadron, shot down whilst attacking German motor transports heading towards Nijmegen Bridge. One of the Typhoon pilots was the elder brother of Mick Raw, who was flying the Spitfire in our formation. The other Typhoon pilot had been his best friend, Belgian born Sqdn Ldr Lallemant. It had been intended that Mick would break away and give a low pass over the area but as he reported after landing "The Fokker got in the way"! The clover leaf display over Amsterdam went according to plan although it lasted

Landing at Schipol airport

longer than planned, during which time we heard aircraft, both departing and arriving, being re-routed all over the place. Only one inbound pilot would have none of it when he requested to close in on the city centre saying in his best PanAm drawl that he wanted a better view of a sight that he was "Damn sure" he would never see again in his lifetime.

The reception after landing was quite fantastic with a band playing on the edge of our parking area plus hundreds of airfield workers having found some excuse or other to down tools for the afternoon. The RAFA Amsterdam Branch really laid it on for us that night for we found ourselves staying in the Amsterdam Hilton and later being entertained to a dinner in their Club where we each received a commemorative tankard and a branch tie. The pro-British feeling of the Dutch people was evident throughout our stay and deeply appreciated. We had taken a liking to low flying over major towns and cities and we covered quite a few more, including Rotterdam, on our return journey, before coasting out to the UK at Westkalle when normal service was resumed in that there was no more flying below 2,000' over built up areas.

I could have done with a day off after the past two, hectic, but most enjoyable days but I had been plotting my own special flight for May 7th of 1976 which was the day after our return. That day would mark the 30th anniversary of the very first flight of a Hastings aircraft, and it had been from RAF Wittering, not Radlett, where it had been constructed. I even managed to find out the exact time of take off via the Handley-Page archives and our aim was to carry out a touch and go landing at Wittering as near as possible to that time. The Hastings was almost certainly the first aircraft type to remain in front line service with the RAF for a 30 year period and I thought it might add something to the occasion if I went along as the co-pilot on the flight and let our youngest Captain, Flt Lt John Houlton, who not even born when the Hastings first took to the air, be Captain. I had, of course, to confer with the Senior Air Traffic Control Officer (SATCO) at Wittering to explain why we wanted one of our aircraft to carry out just one touch and go on his airfield at a certain time. The flight was readily agreed and everything went according to plan, including the exact timing. One thing we had not allowed for was that the SATCO had rounded up all his staff to sing "Happy Birthday to you" over the radio as we climbed away. It was real music in our ears and sounded better than any Welsh male voice choir. John Houlton is still flying with the RAF and recalls that particular trip with pleasure.

Less than a week later, I was involved in another anniversary and that was not only to mark No 53 Squadron's 60th year of service with the RFC and RAF but also the last year of it's existence when the Short Belfast, the finest British freight transport aircraft ever built, faded into history, as far as the RAF was concerned. Wing Commander Crawford Simpson was now the CO of No 53 and knew me well from my time on that squadron and was soon on the phone to me at Scampton with a request after it was decided to go ahead with a 60th anniversary celebration despite the fact that the Squadron's rundown had already begun. He was particularly interested in having one of our Hastings, a type that had played a prominent part in the Squadron's history in the 1950s, on static display for the occasion and wondered if I might manage to bring the Lancaster along also. The Hastings was no problem and again John Houlton would be the Captain. Having been born and bred in the Cotswolds, just north of Brize Norton, he was the obvious choice to return to his homeland, even if only for a couple of days. I eventually managed to land the Lancaster there too and give a mini display, despite the fact that the event was in the middle of one of the Biggin Hill display weekends. That was due entirely to the full co-operation of Jock Maitland, Biggin Hill's display organiser for many years, and one of the very few RAF fighter pilots to have flown operationally in the Korean war of the early fifties. The highlight of No 53 Squadron's weekend, however, was a flypast by a Concorde, flown by Chief Test Pilot Brian Trubshaw.

Two incidents of a non-flying nature occurred during the rest of 1976 which have remained with me over the years and might be considered funny if you have a certain sense of humour. The first was at Blackpool after we had positioned the Lancaster at Squires Gate airport for a fly past over a RAFA parade during their annual conference weekend. Having booked in to our hotel and finished flying for the day, we had retired to the hotel bar before getting changed into civvies. There we fell in with the one and only Ginger Lacey and also Johnnie Johnson. Our Co-Pilot, Jack Parker, one of only a handful of NCO pilots still flying in the RAF at that time, and myself eventually thought that it was about time that we got out of our flying suits and made our way towards the lift which was just about to depart upwards. It was fairly full but, not unusually in England, we pushed our way in and turned our faces towards the exit doors so as to avoid eye contact with those already aboard who might well be thinking that we had pushed our luck (pardon the pun) a little. No sooner had the lift doors closed than a gentleman's hand came over my shoulder and punched Jack in the back. I took a quick look to see who we had offended and, horror of horrors, it was the Chief of the Air Staff, later the Lord Cameron of Balhousie, who was in civilian clothes. However, he was all smiles and said "Hello Jack, long time no see, we must meet in the bar for a few drinks before dinner", at which point a red headed lady, further back in the lift, said, "No you won't, save yourself for the dinner". It turned out that she was the wife of the later Lord Cameron and had served in the WAAFs during the war, rising to the rank of Squadron Officer before marriage. Obviously I had been intrigued by the CAS's greeting to Jack and prised the story out of him that evening. It turned out that when the CAS had command of No 258 Squadron flying P47 Thunderbolt aircraft in Burma against the Japanese, Jack had been one of his NCO pilots and, after one operational sortie, the future CAS had thanked Jack for saving his life. Jack did not want to go into detail so I left it at that.

The other ground mishap occurred when I was put down by the Duke of Edinburgh, and joined the far from exclusive group who had suffered at his hands. It was not a particularly good day for the Lancaster crew in general on the day of the visit of HM the Queen and the Duke to RAF Coningsby on the 30th June. BBMF aircraft belonged to RAF Coningsby, but all of the Lancaster aircrew and some of the Spitfire and Hurricane pilots were employed on other stations. On the big day all that was required of the Lancaster crew was to be lined up in front of PA474, "The City of Lincoln" in a hangar and be introduced to the Royal party. Being from other stations, we would not be at the official luncheon or even pre-lunch drinks. That aspect did not worry us unduly because we thought that we could make other arrangements but even those fell apart at the seams in the event. We always used RAF crew transports to take us to RAF Coningsby and other stations for two very good reasons. Wives would be left stranded at base if we used our own cars and RAF vehicles almost invariably got the nod at the guardrooms, which saved all the hassle of booking any civilian car on to an RAF station. For somereason, on this occasion it was an RAF Waddington coach, with Ray Leach already aboard, that picked up Flight Engineer Derek Butcher and myself for that particular journey. We hit the buffers even before we had reached the guardroom when an RAF police corporal manning the main gate stated that no visiting vehicle, private or military, would be allowed onto the airfield until after the Royal visit was over. Even the fact that we were dressed in the distinctive black flying overalls of the BBMF held no sway. We eventually wound up in a grass field for parking, along with many other visiting cars and transporters. The half mile tramp to the display hangar took its toll on our previously highly polished flying boots, but we managed to repair the damage utilising blackboard dusters. The introductions of our crew to Her Majesty by OC Operations, Wg Cmdr Burrows, and BBMF Flight Commander Sqdn Ldr Mick Raw, went off particularly well and it was when I was introduced to the Duke of Edinburgh that the wheels fell off. After the introduction he definitely looked up towards the Lancaster cockpit and then said, "How many hours a year do you fly"? To which I replied, "We are only allowed 55 hours per year your Royal Higness". HRH's reply, with only half a smile on his face was "Only just over one hour per week, you are not exactly over employed, are you"? I started to open my mouth to mention my Hastings flying and working seven days a week in summer but immediately closed it again when I saw the Commander in Chief of our Strike Command, Air Chief Marshal Sir Nigel Maynard, giving me a steady stare from behind the Duke.

'Jacko' is introduced, along with his BBMF crew to HRH HM Queen (above), and (below) HRH The Duke of Edinburgh.

To digress, memories of that one and only brief sighting of our C in C came flooding back when in 1989 I read of his sad demise in the Daily Telegraph's obituary column. I will record one snippet from it; "However his twinkling blue eyes could steel up if he was displeased, and he was a stickler for doing things correctly, especially in ceremonial events". Yes, I well knew that part. There was a photograph of Sir Nigel talking to his father, who was a retired Air Vice Marshal at the time of the photograph, but no mention was made of his brother, Flt Lt Johnnie Maynard who had been killed in a Harvard aircraft during a Battle of Britain display at RAF St Athan in 1951, undoubtedly still using the flying helmet I had acquired for him when we were fellow pilots on No XI Squadron in Japan.

To return to the Royal visit, the fat lady had not yet sung by any means. With the Queen having led the way, she was left waiting under the nose of the Lancaster for the Duke to finish his review of our line when she was heard to say to her escort, "Are they all still in my Royal Air Force"? I must admit that co-pilot Jack Parker, Flight Engineer Derek Butcher and myself had all passed the 50 not out mark which left Navigator Ray Leach under it. They say ladies always have the last word but to be fair,

A typical display crew Jacko, Jack Parker, Peter Edge and Derrick Butcher. Both Peter and Derrick had been crew members of a 70 Sqn Hastings crash at El-Adem in October, 1961 when one crewmember and 16 passengers lost their lives

perhaps the Queen may have meant were we retired aircrew volunteers. The only bonus of our transport being parked in a field was that we soon made an escape from Coningsby over a fence without any fear of meeting the Royal Party head on again in another part of the camp. Driving north we stopped at the Blue Bell inn, one of the oldest inns in Lincolnshire, for a few wind down drinks, or so we thought. No sooner had we got halfway through our first beer than Ray said "We had better drink up and press on because the MT Officer wanted his coach back as soon as possible for an important job that afternoon and our driver might blow the gaff if we stay here much longer." A day to remember for many reasons.

Early July was to mark another milestone in my first year of captaining the "City of Lincoln" Lancaster. In those days each service took turns at being the premier display service for the Royal tournament at Earls Court and for 1976 it was to be the RAF's turn again. Somebody up the ladder had decided that a flypast by the Lancaster over the opening ceremony, which was to be a tri-service parade on Horse Guards, would make an appropriate start to the week, particularly if it was timed to coincide with the final general salute and march off. To achieve such timing would be difficult at the best of times but an added complication was that the PR boys wanted two helicopters to format on us for the last leg from the holding point at the Dagenham Ford works and then via St Pauls Cathedral and Trafalgar Square to Horse Guards. The two helicopters would be Pumas of No 33 Squadron based at RAF Odiham. These aircraft had a top speed of about 150 knots compared with our normal cruise of 180k, so to give some flexibility of trying to gain or lose time we had to select a speed of 125k for that sector which in itself called for a quarter flap setting. Several other factors had to be considered for such an important trip, not least of all was our limited and very basic radio fit of WWII vintage. This was overcome by the use of a lady Air Traffic Control Officer perched on top of the old Met Office in central London, the one time home of the Air Ministry, from where she would be in touch not only with us but also the parade ground and the London Air Traffic Control centre. During telecoms with her about the event it turned out that we had met during my transport days when she was Tarna Linton and later Tarna King. We did manage a Lancaster flight for her some time later when she was stationed at RAF Lyneham. The planners really had been busy and had arranged for Pete Edge, one of our two navigators for the big day, and myself, to have a flight in one of the Pumas down the Thames from Dagenham to central London to familiarise ourselves with landmarks. To complete

Fifty-Two Years in the Cockpit - Volume Two

that in one day would have been a tall order so I took one of our Hastings down to Odiham and we not only had a very useful helicopter flight but were called upon later to carry out a short local flight during which time the Puma pilots tried their hand at formatting on us at various photogenic angles. By the time we got back to base the planners had been at it again

Overflying Trafalgar Square

and, this too, was not a bad idea. Pete and myself were to report to the Intercontinental Hotel, about one hundred yards from the RAF Club, to meet the PRO people and some photographers to discuss the proposed flight. The idea was to be taken to the top most part of the hotel to survey the various possibilities of ground positions for cameras and discuss any help that we could give. Later we were well fed and watered and no one in management would hear of payment of any kind.

The day itself, July 11th, finally arrived and the Station Commander, Group Captain Allison- an ex-Brat like myself- would be the co-pilot and the extra navigator would be Ray Leach, armed with a stop watch. He would call for speed changes to arrive spot on time while Pete Edge would keep us on track. Other than that we would have four London press photographers aboard who MOD Air had insisted should attend the pre-flight briefing, although we would land them at RAF Northolt after the fly past. We would then take off again without even stopping engines because we had one more commitment before we could all sit

Fly past over London 1976

back and contemplate the day's events. After taking off from Coningsby we headed almost due south for our first turning point at RAF Wyton who we obviously had to contact before entering their airspace. It was a rather sleepy sounding WRAF controller who answered our call and asked for our destination. I had to think hard before answering that one, if I said Northolt she would have given us headings to steer for the north east corridor of the London zone which was the last thing we wanted, so I said "Buckingham Palace would you believe", to which she replied, "I believe" and that was the last we heard from her. The hold over Dagenham, formation join up and our rather stately progress up the River Thames went off far better than we could have ever hoped for. According to those on the ground, the RAF band had just struck up "Those magnificent men in their flying machines" as we appeared overhead. We obviously kept on straight ahead after the fly over to allow time for the two helicopters to disperse by which time we had overflown Buckingham Palace and noticed that there was no flag flying which, indicated nobody was at home. This allowed me to put Plan B into action, which called for a 180° turn to the right, which would allow both staff of the Intercontinental Hotel and members of the RAF Club, a close up view of the Lancaster. By that time we were also back to the normal power setting of +4 boost and 2400 rpm to produce the sound that people love to hear. The balcony at 128 Piccadilly, the RAF Club, was chock a block, one being our old friend Bob Kennedy and many memories of yesteryear came flooding back as we passed by. On our new heading, with the speed back up to 170 knots, it seemed no time at all before St Pauls came into view again, so we gave another run up the Mall and over Buckingham Palace. With the Duke's remarks to me still less than two weeks old, one of my balloon captions came to mind. It showed the Queen and HRH having lunch together and the Duke saying "I suppose he's just using up two more hours of his 55 "allowed". After disembarking the four press men at Northolt it was forever northwards to fulfil the commitment to a very small, in fact it no longer exists, flying club called Paul on the north bank of the Humber, just east of Hull. We must have still been 5 miles short of our target when we sighted the outline of, for those days, a massive aircraft. It turned out to be a Blackburn Beverley which made us wonder how on earth such a monster of an aircraft could operate out of a small grass airfield. The truth of the matter was that it would never fly again and had probably arrived by road. In later years it was moved to the Army museum in the town of Beverley and is still there to this day.

En route to Horseguards 1976

After our display over Paul, it was back to Coningsby to receive the news that the photographers, air and ground, were particularly pleased with their day's work. In the event, it was a photograph taken over Trafalgar Square when we were in a slight bank to port that really caught the public imagination and was published in five national newspapers the next morning. Quite recently I noticed a framed picture of same in the background when the Minister for Defence was interviewed on television in his office. Another regular reminder is that a painting of the Buckingham Palace overfly hangs above the downstairs bar in the RAF club. Hastings flying went on apace and although our radar training for Navigators was again beginning to fall away other tasks took an upturn with radar calibration at such places as the missile range on Benbecular and other places being well to the fore. We also kept the oil rig patrols going plus still being involved in the odd major exercise with the Royal Navy.

For the BBMF mid-June to mid-September called for display flying every weekend with regular bookings such as Biggin Hill, Duxford, Greenham Common, Bournemouth, Swansea, Cardiff, Coventry, Norwich, Humberside, Blackpool, Woodford, Prestwick, Teesside, Jersey, Old Warden and Mildenhall getting priority, which had a lot to do with geographical spread and the likely attendance figure. In addition, the bi-annual shows at Farnborough and Paris in alternating years were a must along with RAF Battle of Britain days and the Royal Navy display at Yeovilton. Even in my time of some years ago a few of those mentioned

'Jacko' in the distinctive black flight suit of the BBMF, in front of Lancaster PA474, the City of Lincoln.

Fifty-Two Years in the Cockpit - Volume Two

BBMF Hurricane (top), Lancaster (middle) and Spitfire (bottom) in formation

had started to fall by the wayside. In the case of Battle of Britain days it was the closure of RAF stations and shortage of manpower which was the reason whereas for those at civilian airports it was the very rapid increase in bucket and spade holidays that caused the problem with delays on inbound or outbound traffic no longer an option. In earlier days the odd arrival or departure could usually be fitted in with the display programme but no longer. In the context of showing the flag a slight diversion from planned track could pay dividends and I well remember looking down on 100,000 spectators at Silverstone after one such alteration. It did, however, slightly misfire on another flight when we over flew an England v Australia test match at Nottingham. The TV cameras showed us live all right, but the Australian commentator said "I don't know what those aircraft are, probably WWII types". Needless to say, I got a few leg pulls after landing along the lines of "What type did you say you flew, Jacko"?

We had our favourite display venues of course, and I think that Jersey must be top of that list. We were always greeted immediately after landing by Lord Sandhurst, a WWII Lancaster Navigator, who on one occasion did a double take when two females disembarked from our aircraft. One was Flt Lt Sue Harrison, an Ops officer at Coningsby who gave any of her spare time to help with the admin on the Flight and the second was

253

Coasting in to Jersey for their annual Battle of Britain day

a WRAF accounts clerk who hailed from Guernsey and was on her way home for a spot of leave. After the initial greetings we were always fussed over and pampered throughout our stay with the first night spent in the always welcoming RAFA club in St Helier and our final night in the Flying Club on the airfield. Both most enjoyable events when everybody could let their hair down. From a pure flying point of view, Jersey also topped the list because the flying display was not on the airfield itself but over the fabulous St Helier bay, which was ideal in shape and size and all one had to worry about was startled seagulls. On one departure from Jersey I thought history was about to repeat itself when, just as I was about to submit my flight plan, I heard an American voice from my rear say, "Excuse me bud", which instantly brought back memories of Karachi when I was trying to submit one there. However, this time it was so different, in that the ever so polite American gent explained that he was on a very tight schedule and would I mind if he jumped the queue. I

Fifty-Two Years in the Cockpit - Volume Two

Views from inside the Lancaster during flight and, over page) further interior views and a profile view of the BBMF trio in formation,

Fifty-Two Years in the Cockpit - Volume Two

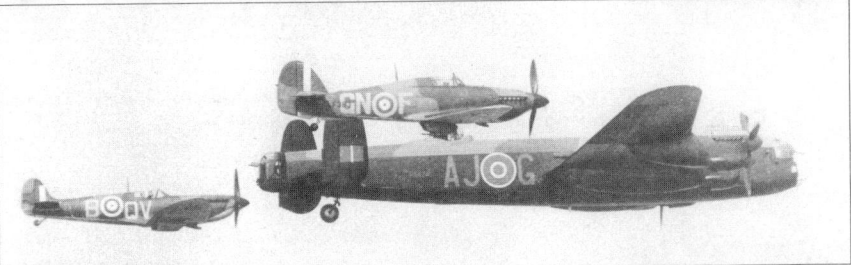

256

did not mind at all and when he said he was flying to New York, I tried to air my aviation knowledge by asking if he was off on the northern route via Iceland or the southern route via the Azores, to which he replied "Neither, it will be direct to New York". I could hardly believe my ears, particularly when he pointed to a very small executive jet on the parking area. Apparently it was tailor made to carry vast amounts of fuel and only two or three VIP passengers. One feature of departing Jersey was that it was the only civil airport in the entire UK to provide a face to face briefing with a Met officer and that was because it was part and parcel of the Jersey sea port department. Even to this day, each RAF airfield soldiers on with a Met Office costing about £40 million per annum when, in my opinion, teletext and TV could provide an equal service for next to nothing!

One regular visit on our days off in Jersey was accepting an invitation from retired Wing Commander Le Brocq, an ex-RAF pilot who then ran Jersey Aviation, an engineering firm which had been blacklisted as far as the UK military were concerned, by the Labour government of the day for overhauling and supplying spares for the South African Army's tanks. The tanks used a version of the Rolls Royce Merlin engine, hence the involvement of an aviation firm in their maintenance. The conversation during these visits invariably turned to the shortage of spares for Merlins and our host would gently ask one of our travelling technicians if we were feeling the effects yet. Strange but true, about two months after each visit a firm in Scotland, or one on the south coast of England, would ring our NCO I/C Groundcrew and say that they had some Merlin spare parts for sale and was he interested? Always the items that had a mention in Jersey of course, which made me wonder if trade embargoes are ever watertight.

One particular item that even our friends in Jersey could not resolve, and also with political implications, was the requirement to replace the ageing wooden propellors on our Hurricanes. After a thorough investigation it turned out that the only company in the world to be still making wooden props of the size required was the German firm of Hoffmans and even people of little imagination could surely invent the headlines there would have been if we had ordered any from them. The question often asked on our travels was, indeed, why did our fighters use wooden propellors and the Lancaster metal? The quick answer was that a wooden propellor would break up and not damage the engine, due to reductions of rpm from between 2,000 to 3,000 on a wheels up forced landing, when the blades made contact with Mother Earth. With fighters used for defensive work these landings would mostly be over friendly territory whereas for bombers it would be in about 80% of cases over enemy territory, or the sea. At one stage we did come across a spare four bladed wooden propellor which was not used on Hurricanes and only on later types of Spitfire, those from Mk 8 onwards. In desperation we fitted it to one of our Hurricanes and surprise, surprise that Hurricane actually flew a little faster than before and was quicker to react to power changes. However, the nit pickers had a field day, saying it just did not look right on a Hurricane. You cannot please all the people all of the time of course.

Another innovation was that soon after our arrival at Coningsby the ground crew, on their own initiative, decided to bring the bomb doors back into working order after goodness knows how many years. They specifically asked me if I would, during the required air test, open the bomb doors- initially above the airfield so that they could observe any adverse reaction. After a successful test I was a little bemused to notice that our marshallers and other ground crew looked a little sheepish when they asked how things had gone. Truth will out of course, and it appeared that all ground observers thought that the Lancaster had caught fire when the bomb doors first opened because years and years of dust had been dislodged by the slipstream on the initial opening, which gave the impression of black smoke. The ground crew had done an excellent job on the hydraulics but had failed to clean the inside of the bomb bay. Not to worry, it made an added attraction at air displays but it was a great pity that dummy bombs, made later, also suffered from the slipstream and were adjudged by our technical officer, Flt Lt Charles Ness, who came along on the first test flight positioned behind one of the two perspex bomb bay observation holes, to be far too unstable and likely to break away eventually from their racks. The observation holes, of course, were used in wartime to check that all bombs had actually dropped and, therefore, no nasty surprises awaited crews on landing back at base after a mission.

The summer weather of 1976 proved to be one of the best of the 20th century and combined with the 100% serviceability record of the Lancaster it was a marvellous first full year of Captaincy on the only aircraft of it's type still flying in the world at that time. Apart from the normal air days up and down the country a larger number of one offs than usual had been built into the events programme that year. With careful planning and a lot of road travel after leaving the Lanc at it's last display venue, or nearest suitable airfield, for a few days, we still managed to keep within the 55 hours flying time allowed for the year. One such case was the planned tribute to Air Chief Marshall Sir Arthur Harris and his American counterpart of WW2, General Ira C. Eaker, the Commander of the United States 8th Air Force at the time. Also present at the event would be the world famous General James Doolittle who had led the first bomber raid on Tokyo during the war. Oh what a trio and what a privilage to be taking part. The organisers had also managed to have the civilian operated B17 "Sally B" take part. The plan was for our Lancaster to position at Duxford and later take-off with the B17 leading and ourselves formatting 200 yards astern. I think our navigator was somewhat relieved that any error in timing would not be down to him! With the Farnborough air show the following week we landed at Northolt after the fly past and the total extra flying time could be measured in minutes rather than the 2 hours we would have clocked up if we had returned to our base at RAF Coningsby. When we eventually departed Northolt for Farnborough two days later we had been joined by our fighter boys. I noted that they had brought an extra Spitfire along so at the pre-flight briefing I stated that we would depart in the usual Vic formation up Northolt's north west exit lane before turning left for Farnborough after clearing the London zone. I told the extra Spitfire pilot he could fly line astern, or in the box in aviation parlance. Soon after take off, Northolt transferred us direct to Heathrow tower, which was most unusual, but all was revealed when their controller called and stated that we could forget about the exit lane and overfly his airfield so long as we remained below 500'. When I asked how low below 500' he replied "The lower the better". I took him at his word and really gave it some humpty, completely forgetting about the Spitfire in the box which would be flying about 50' lower than the rest of the formation to keep clear of our slipstreams. The box Spitfire pilot said after landing that he never thought he would ever get such a close up view of Heathrow controllers at work and from the cockpit of a Spitfire too! The Farnborough show went according to plan and then it was off to Jersey following a Battle of Britain display at our previous home of Coltishall.

Normally Jersey on a Battle of Britain day marked the end of the season for the BBMF but not so that year, for we had two more very important commitments to make. The first was back to the Dutch base of Gilze Rijen from where we would make an over fly of Guy Gibson's grave and that of his navigator, Flt Lt Bill Warwick, in the village of Steenburgen, not far from the site of the fatal crash of their Mosquito. The survivors of No 617 Dambuster squadron would be in attendance at the invitation of the local council. After take off we all had our fingers crossed that everything would go according to plan. In the event it nearly didn't. Map reading over Holland was even more difficult than over the Fens of East Anglia and that is saying something. We had assumed that we would have had the benefit of Jack Thurling's local knowledge to guide us but it was not to be because Jack would be leading a formation of Harvards over the event. Having strayed a little off the beaten track, assistance came from a most unlikely source. It was from a No 617 Squadron Vulcan aircraft, high up in the sky awaiting its turn for a fly past. The Nav/Rad could see all built up areas, rivers and coastlines and moving aircraft on his radar. Having noted that we might miss Steenburgen he gave us timely corrections of heading to re-gain track and all was well from then on, or nearly so anyway. What I had not bargained for was photographs of our fly past appearing in the British press which clearly showed our Lancaster to be somewhat lower than it should have been. A few questions from up the ladder did come my way but a bit of waffle about focal length of cameras and not having the local ground atmospheric pressure to hand for our altimeter setting soon quietened things down. After landing back at Gilze Rijen we were more than glad to welcome the No 617 veterans and let them have the freedom of the aircraft. In the evening we were all royally entertained by the local council, which turned into a night to remember. Among other guests, I was particularly pleased to see that an old friend from my Vampire days was a VIP guest: Group Captain Benjie Hives, being the RAF's Air Attaché to the Netherlands, he was the son of Lord Hives of Rolls-Royce fame.

    The second special flight did not take place until mid-October. It was to be over the RAF Museum at Hendon which is well inside the built up area of greater London. The event was the unveiling of a memorial plaque in honour of the designer of the Lancaster bomber, Roy Chadwick. VIPs attending would be Marshal of the Royal Air Force Sir Arthur Harris and Sir Barnes Wallis amongst many others. The outline plan sent to the BBMF called for the Lancaster to fly down to Northolt on October 18th and for the crew to be taken the next morning by road to Hendon to survey the surrounding area from the viewing site and then return to Northolt in plenty of time to start up and make the display spot on one o'clock. Although everybody on the ground at Hendon knew no better we

Bomber Harris and Margaret Dove, daughter of the late Roy Chadwick, designer of the Lancaster, watch an air display by Jacko over the RAF Museum, Hendon October 1976

had hit one or two snags. To start with, after landing at Northolt it seemed no time at all before we were exiting the camp gates towards a local hotel because blue asbestos had been found in the roofing of the Officers' Mess accommodation block. This, of course, made communications with Operations and Air Traffic Control not so easy as when living on base, but I had managed to make a call to the tower giving our take off time for the display which must have been misplaced or not properly recorded. During our ground visit to Hendon we had gladly accepted the invitation to be introduced to the two VIPs already mentioned plus two RAF VC holders- Bill Reid and Norman Jackson. This took up more time than planned and the road traffic on the way back to Northolt had more than doubled by that time. The upshot was that we had little time to spare but I did manage to make another call to the tower to ask if they could hold off any inbound or outbound traffic that might interfere with our departure time of 12.45. A rather cheery voice, which turned out to be that of an airman holding the fort said: "You'll have no trouble with that sir, we are closed until one o'clock for lunch". I could hardly believe my ears- an RAF station closed for lunch, it was unheard of since before WWII. It beggared belief that a station housing the Royal Flight and a transport communications squadron could shut down in the middle of the day. About ten minutes later I had joined the rest of the crew at the aircraft to break the news, when we spotted a jeep racing towards us from the tower with the driver giving the thumbs up. The penny had finally dropped. Pre-take off checks and taxiing out was carried out rather faster than normal and we just managed to make it on time. Although everybody on the ground at Hendon seemed well satisfied with our performance, one or two rang Northolt to complain about a low flying Lancaster over their roof tops, while others asked why the flight was not publicised in advance because they knew of many friends who would have loved to have seen it. Numerous photographs of the event arrived at the BBMF, the most moving being that of "Bomber" Harris shielding his eyes against the bright sunshine, looking up at one of his old aircraft and in good company with the two daughters of the late Roy Chadwick by his side. Another spin off from that particular flight was that an aunt of Bill Warwick, Guy Gibson's navigator, lived near Northolt and sent the BBMF a poem that she had composed after our display.

With it not only being my first full year of Captaining the BBMF's Lancaster, I had also taken over the Flight Commander post in charge of our Hastings unit when "Chalky" White retired in the April. That meant that during the display season I had been flying seven days a week which certainly added piquancy to the Duke of Edinburgh's remark about "not exactly being over employed".

1977 was to be another hectic year when quite a few more significant events took place which included a flight down the Derwent valley on the 34th anniversary of the Dams raid, the Queen's Golden Jubilee display at

Over the Derwent Water Dam on the 34th Anniversary of the 'Dams Raid' - 1977

RAF Finningley, BBMF Lancaster's first visit to Luxembourg, the Paris air show and finally the laying to rest of the RAF's last Hastings when I flew TG511 into RAF Cosford's Air Museum on August 16th.

The flight down the Derwent took some organising to say the least because among other things, the take off point would be RAF Odiham and not our own base. We had positioned there following a Biggin Hill display, after which our presence at Odiham was called for to honour ex-

RAF prisoners of war who were holding a reunion there. They proved to be the most receptive audience ever, most taking up their old crew positions to re-live various alarming events. Being the Hastings flight commander I had little difficulty in obtaining permission to have one of our aircraft fly alongside us not only on the Derwent run itself but also during dummy runs over Rutland Water when heading north, to at least obtain some aerial shots of the Lancaster, in case the Derwent valley weather proved to be unsuitable for formation flying safely. Also programmed for that day was the concept of a Vulcan aircraft joining our formation after leaving the Derwent area to over fly Lincoln Cathedral so that aerial photographs could be taken of two four engined Avros in unison over that historic building. If that was not enough we had to land at RAF Marham for a night stop to cater for a visit there of the Royal College of Defence Studies (RCDS) which our own AOC was attending. All in all a total flight time of 3 hours 30 minutes was recorded, which took care of a large chunk of our flying allocation for that year. Flt Lt Mick Mercer was the Hastings captain and his timing for Rutland Water was spot on with immaculate station keeping thereafter except when we both had to break away in some disorder during our first run down the Derwent valley when an RAF Jet-Provost was sighted heading straight towards us from the opposite direction. It confirmed my belief that NOTAMS (Air warnings in which our flight was recorded) are not always read. There was nothing for it but to re-form and try again.

One thing became very obvious, and that was that although a fair tail wind of about 20 knots had been forecast, down in the valley it was much stronger and probably up to 50 knots which made the descent to the Dam Busting height of 60' somewhat difficult to achieve in the short distance available. With the knowledge that most of the dams raid survivors were interested spectators, I was determined to get it right eventually, and it took quite a few more runs to do that. With such a wind at low level high turbulence was inevitable which really shook the aircraft to the extent that the upper escape hatch broke loose on the last run, which gave us more ventilation than we really needed for the next hour and half. Luckily, the hatch was identical to that of the Avro Lincoln bomber and Cosford Air Museum were delighted to lend us one for the rest of the season.

On board our aircraft we had carried three civilian guests; the presenter of the ITV childrens' programme "Magpie" and two of his cameramen and I well remember that when I was trying to book in at the reception desk in the Officers' Mess at Marham I was suddenly put on the back burner by the airman in charge when the TV presenter arrived on the scene to ask about his company's transport which was due to arrive from Odiham. The airman had obviously been an avid fan of Magpie for years.

The Royal Review at RAF Finningley to mark the Queen's Silver Jubilee, which took place at the end of July, had actually involved the BBMF since the middle of April when the first practise fly past took place. It called for a Vic formation of the Lancaster, Spitfire and Hurricane to take off from Coningsby and fly to the nominated holding point off Flamborough Head and then set course to pass the Royal saluting base at a specific time. My view was that the closer an aircraft was to the target, before commencing its final run in, the better to achieve accurate timings, especially for aircraft with a limited speed range and the Lancaster was certainly in that category. Also on my mind at the time was the extra distance and flying time involved in positioning at Flamborough in the first place. One practise only could have been catered for in our limited budget of flying hours per year but we were due to carry out runs on ten different days- eight practise, the day itself, followed by a public day. I took the bull by the horns and, after studying the route from Flamborough down to Finningley's main runway I soon noticed that it passed over the very prominent landmark of Goole, on the River Ouse, and decided to hold there on a four minute race track at right angles to the run in line so that we could break away at any given time depending on the wind speed. I had previously asked if we could use one of our Hastings instead of the Lancaster for practise runs and that was reluctantly agreed to. Our first practise seemed to have worked out perfectly well, including passing over a formation of Bulldogs led by a solitary Chipmunk at the mile to run point. I was probably feeling a little too smug when I and my co-pilot, Mick Mercer, took a Hastings to Finningley for a mass de-brief a day later. However our three ship formation holding over Goole, and not running in from Flamborough like the rest of the aircraft, had been clearly seen and noted by those in the tower watching the approach radar and fly past. Our antics got a special mention but the Group Captain in charge went on to say that we had better continue with our holding pattern as we had been within 5 seconds of our target time whilst a Nimrod had been about 50 seconds late. Most present found it difficult to take in when the Nimrod Captain stated that after realising that they had been late on target had, on returning to Scotland, checked the local BT on line time watch, and found that it was 30 seconds out. Do pigs ever fly?

Our ploy of using the Hastings instead of the Lancaster, to save flying hours on the latter, came to an abrupt end later when AVM Attlee, related to the first post-WWII Prime Minister, and a former Station Commander of RAF Brize Norton in my time there was now overseer of the event and stated that he wanted to see exactly what it would look like on the day itself and the Lancaster would lead the BBMF formation in future. He was spot on in a strange sort of way. We had probably been getting a little too low overflying the previously mentioned formation on finals in the Hastings without any undue worry to them, but the Lancaster was another matter because they had been blown all over the sky in the Lancaster's slipstream. This may seem rather strange, but if one looks at photographs of aircraft in flight, one will often see that some aircraft seem to be flying slightly nose up, or down, when in level flight. The Whitley, for instance, was nose down with an inclined upwash whilst the Lancaster wings and, therefore, engines had a down slope and airflow. We had no trouble with the Hastings slipstream because although, with its tail wheel configuration, it looked quite ugly on the ground, in flight it was quite majestic. The designers having got it exactly right with a straight fore and aft slipstream. The answer, of course, was to overfly the other formation at a higher level and hope to get down to fly past height in time which proved to be satisfactory in the event.

With reference to the up or down slope in aircraft, it was brought home to me on a jet age holiday when, I found walking forward up the isle of a Tri Star was definitely uphill. I don't know if it was the look on my face but a smiling air stewardess said to my wife: "Your husband needn't worry, flying is perfectly safe". For once Betty was lost for words!

On the big day at Finningley everything seemed to have gone according to plan and all concerned on the ground and in the air were well satisfied. The next day's papers, however, stole a bit of our thunder giving a deal of coverage with photographs of the Minister for Defence, Fred Mulley, sitting next to the Queen and appearing to be nodding off on Her Majesty's shoulder during the fly past. It had been a very hot day and not long since lunch after all! It made quite a change for me, being far removed from living under canvas for three weeks at RAF Odiham 25 years in the past for Her Majesty's coronation review. The icing on the cake was when all those taking part had sight of a message from HM the Queen which read: "Today's review at RAF Finningley to mark my Silver Jubilee was a splendid occasion. The colours parade was exceptionally smart and the spectacular flying display was executed with skill and precision. I was impressed by the indoor exhibition and I was glad to see the aircraft and meet the crews in the static display. I warmly congratulate all those who took part. Signed Elizabeth R".

Re-reading my log book for 1977 shows that between the start of rehearsals for Finningley and the actual event a lot had taken place, not least of all the final run down of the Hastings in RAF service. We had

Sqn Ldr Jackson and crew handing over TG503 and log-book to the Station CO Gatow (Gp Cptn Benson)

just 4 Mk 5s to dispose of and started with TG505 which we sent to RAF St Athen for use of the SAS at Hereford, then followed TG503 which I took to RAF Gatow, Berlin for gate guardian duties. It was not long after landing that we were informed that the Berliners wanted a special fly past of Western Berlin to remind them of the airlift days. I thought there might be political problems but the Station Commander, Group Captain Benson, produced a certificate, still in my possession, giving authority for the flight and signed by four national controllers: Soviet, French, American and British. Having noted that a former student of mine, Terry Keats, was stationed at Gatow flying their one and only aircraft- a Chipmunk-, I took him along as my co-pilot. When RAF Gatow closed down after the end of the Cold War, Hastings TG503 was given to the Germans and is now in the Berlin Allied Forces Museum. They have taken the H2S radar cupola off to make it look more in keeping with its airlift days.

The crew for delivery of TG503 had been, in addition to myself, our boss, Wg Cdr Crowder, OG NO 230 OCU. As Co-Captain Master Engineer Derek Butcher and Flt Lt Robbie Stewart, Radar Navigator After the demise of the Hastings Robbie became a Tornado Navigator on No 20 Squadron and on the 20th January 1991. His aircraft was shot down over Iraq by a Roland Missile. Although Robbie and his Captain Flt Lt David Waddington, ejected safely, they became prisoners of war. On leaving the service, Robbie, like many others decided that Lincolnshire was an ideal location for final retirement.

Nobody seemed to care which particular aircraft was to be disposed of next so I resolved to take TG517, one of my Cod War aircraft, to the nearby Winthorpe Air Museum, near Newark, and make the last ever flight of a Hastings, which was to be to the RAF Cosford Museum, in

The second from last landing of a Hastings Aircraft TG 517 at the Newark Air Museum (Winthorpe)

TG 511. I thought that TG511 should be last because No 511 Squadron had been in its day one of the foremost RAF transport squadrons. The delivery of TG511 to the rather cramped airfield at Cosford led to my only brush with RAF ground engineers. Being familiar with Cosford because of Chipmunk ATC flying there, I had concluded that I would sooner land on the easterly runway than the westerly one because of a rather steep railway embankment nearby and translating that into landing a four engined aircraft on its very last flight on a marginal length runway, I would sooner run into grass and a few shrubs rather than the embankment in the event of an overrun due to brake failure or whatever. Waiting for an easterly wind took about three weeks, but at one point an irate engineering officer rang to ask why I couldn't take it on board that he had about 10 servicing airmen awaiting postings after the last Hastings flight who had to sign our form 700 (the official record of technical servicing for each aircraft). My riposte, just before he slammed the phone down, was that he could post them tomorrow for all I cared because all flight engineers in the transport world were empowered to sign a F700 for all trades at any time and anywhere.

That very last Hastings flight was rather emotive for us all and due to the uncertainty of our take off time, awaiting a build up of the easterly wind, we had ordered our return motor transport for early the next morning. It was during the night stop that both messes at Cosford did us proud and it showed a little the next day too! Also crowded into that mid-summer was our very first visit to Luxembourg which was certainly something special. Taxying onto an international airport's arrival apron and seeing masses of people, barely under control, despite Police and their dogs, awaiting our arrival was out of this world. On the agenda was a night in the British embassy which could not have been bettered such was the greeting and informality, with everybody being put at their ease from the outset. Our accommodation was in a five star hotel, virtually on the airfield itself, used by many other visiting aircrew of many airlines. On night two one particular Luxair Captain, an Austrian by birth, seemed to take a particular interest in our crew and eventually asked if he could look over the Lancaster the next morning. This we gladly agreed to and still took place despite the fact that at some time during that evening a third party disclosed that the Austrian had been a Luftwaffe night fighter ace during WWII and had shot down a large number of RAF bombers.

One event which might well have been deemed the trip of the year, after the Royal Review, was the Paris Air Show at Le Bourget. The BBMF should have been there for a full week but the Lancaster got off to a very bad start. The day before our planned departure, RAF Coningsby was holding an open day with families well to the fore including my wife Betty, who had decided to take some cine-film of the air display. It was whilst looking through the view finder that she saw smoke and flames belching from our No 4 engine. We soon had the situation under control, ably assisted by my co-pilot who was making his very first flight in a Lancaster. Considering he was Group Captain Cabourne, Commanding RAF Binbrook and a dyed in the wool fighter pilot, it was quite commendable. After landing and recovering our composure, we assumed that the Paris trip might well be off but help, with that little bit of extra expertise, came from a most unexpected quarter. Among the spectators was a civilian who just happened to have changed many Merlin engines in his time during WWII. He volunteered to help out and stay in airman's accommodation until the job was complete. After our eventual arrival in Paris just one day late we learned from our Spitfire and Hurricane ground crew that we had missed a spectacle which I was rather thankful for. They related that soon after their own arrival in a Devon aircraft they had watched a USAF A10 Tank buster aircraft, starting a practice display with a series of loops and as it was getting lower and lower they kept assuming that surely he must finish them but it was not to be. He finally bottomed into the ground during his final pull out with fatal results.

Our old friends from the Farnborough Air Show, Plessey's, had an exhibition on site and made us just as welcome as ever. One person who made a beeline for us was Norman Tebbit MP, whose interest in aviation was well known, having been a pilot in an RAF Auxiliary Air Force Squadron flying Meteor jets. We all found him most interesting but, unfortunately, could not fit in a planned visit to the House of Commons that he had suggested.

An American national and his lady, who turned out to be well up the ladder at Racal electronics, took a particular interest in our aircraft, which resulted in an invite for them to board our Lancaster. Just before their departure they suggested that perhaps they could entertain us during the Farnborough show the following year. I replied that would be rather nice because my birthday fell during that week. I cannot remember actually giving the exact date but I did receive an invitation for September 5th during the following August. I was rather surprised to receive another communication, after I had declined that invite because the Lancaster had been grounded throughout 1978 due to corrosion problems, inviting Betty and I to dinner at the International Hotel in London, hosted by a member of the House of Lords. A birthday cake also appeared during that lovely evening. The Americans certainly have the nack when it comes to entertaining, far removed from our own rather stuffy protocol.

The day of our return from Paris was quite eventful in many ways. First of all, being an early riser, I had already ploughed through a copy of an English newspaper before a fleet of taxis arrived to take us out to the airfield, and had noted that the concept of several RAF stations having a nominated Royal Honorary Air Commodore had been introduced. RAF Coningsby was to have Princess Margaret. Quite by chance, Coningsby's Station Commander, Group Captain Bryant, who was one of the two fighter boys on the trip, was in our taxi and when I started on about the Royal appointment by saying "I expect you will already know, sir" I didn't expect the silence that my remarks were met with. It turned out that he didn't know about it at all.

We had quite a few ground crew aboard the Lancaster and one way of giving them a little comfort was to put two of them in the bomb aimer's position, which led to another little mishap. It was on the take off run and nearing lift off speed when the airspeed indicator suddenly wound down to zero. To go or not to go, that was the question. With the end of the runway looking uncomfortably close, I lifted off and with the undercarriage up and flaps in at the 300' mark, I called for the climbing power of 2600 rpm and +6" boost and climbed at a rate below the norm. I was quite happy with that situation, which was only disturbed when passing close to Stansted Airport who called for a low pass, which was given, also with a lower than normal rate of climb after passing the Tower. All that was left was the landing. This was to be my first, and last, landing of an aircraft without a working airspeed indicator. Although it was well known that during WWII pilots training on the Stearman in the USA, which was not fitted with an airspeed indicator, were taught to use power and aircraft attitude only. All pilots must have thought about the possibility of the Pitot cover, over the airspeed probe, being left on before take off at some time or other and, like myself, had probably concluded that in that situation if one could remain on the glide slope, be it by use of the runway threshold lights, instrument landing system (ILS) or radar talk down (GCA), and setting the average power for the 3° glide slope (300'/ mile) one would probably be within 10 knots of the correct approach speed. For very obvious reasons the Pitot cover being left on was more likely to occur at night and for WWII operations pilots did not have ILS nor GCA available and airfield lighting was at a minimum, which led to many disasters. However, it did occur in daylight too and one sad loss was Tony Benn's elder brother when operating out of RAF Tangmere in a Mosquito after a tour on Beaufighters in North Africa.

In the event, the height check before a wheeler landing, which was my normal type for the Lancaster and Hastings, seemed to be as usual so the airspeed must have been very near the norm. It turned out that the loss of the airspeed indicator was due to one of the ground crew reaching up and holding on to the airspeed pipe, which ran through the nose section, during the take off run. I was particularly lucky on that trip in having OC Ops, Wing Commander Burrows, flying as my co-pilot. His only mention of our problem during the transit flight from Paris was to ask if I would be declaring an emergency as we neared base to which I replied that I had once been on a station when one of my friends had met his end after taking advice from the many 'experts' who had assembled in the tower. Wg Cmdr Burrows had decided to stay on in the RAF despite having suffered severe leg wounds during a Javelin crash and full marks to him for that. He was a highly popular senior officer who would have been flying the BBMF's Spitfires and Hurricanes but for his Javelin accident.

It was during our wait for our transport back to Scampton that OC Ops asked if I would mind giving up one of my rest days to attend a de-brief of the Paris Air Show by the Station Commander. He was taken aback when I said I didn't have rest days and I would be airbourne in a Hastings for Stornoway in the Outer Hebrides by 0800 the next morning. When asked if perhaps somebody else could do that trip he seemed even more surprised when I said we were the only RAF flying unit with more aircraft than crews and every other Captain was fully booked.

Spending the night in Paris and the next in Stornoway was like chalk and cheese but it was the location and way of life in the remote Western Isles that I much preferred. The day was not quite over even then because no sooner had I settled back into our married quarter than the door bell rang. The caller turned out to be our boss, Wg Cmdr "Rickey" Crowder, with the news that I had been awarded one of the Jubilee medals. I have always regarded that as a unit award to the Hastings Flight rather than a personal one. That was borne out by two signals received shortly before the last Hastings flight ever. They read as follows:

From AOC in C to OC Hastings Flight 230 OCU

1. As the Hastings comes to the end of its days with 230 OCU I wish to place on record the excellent service which 1066 Sqdn has given, both to

Strike Command and to the Royal Air Force. You have not only fulfilled your primary task at all times, but on those many occasions you have been needed you have also augmented and supported the front line and carried out a multitude of other tasks in a most efficient and praiseworthy manner.

2. In spite of the vintage and maturity of the Hastings your splendid safety record and serviceability record is second to none and reflects commendably upon your aircrew and ground crew alike.

3. My thanks and best wishes to all who have fought the Battle of Hastings so well, be they Saxons or Normans. Matthew Chapter 25, verse 21. Signed David Evans.

For Hastings Flight 230 OCU from AOC

1. Please convey my thanks and best wishes to all the personnel of the Hastings flight on this the day that the Royal Air Forces's senior aeroplane finally passes into retirement.

2. The AOC in C has already complimented you on the professionalism of the flight, the way in which you have carried out both your primary role and the multiplicity of support tasks has done much to maintain the operational efficiency and morale of the Royal Air Force as a whole. I can only reiterate his view that your success is a reflection of the effort and enthusiasm of your entire unit. On this occasion you not only fought the battle, but, unlike the original home team, won. Good luck for the future to you all. Signed Philip Lagesen. AOC No 5 Group AVM

Just before Wg Cdr Crowder left our quarter he said: "By the way, Jacko, the CO's wife will be on your trip to Stornoway tomorrow and would be delighted if Betty could go along too". Betty's eyes positively lit up: she had heard so much about that far outpost of the UK from me over the past few years and had longed to visit it. In the event it far exceeded her expectations.

Not all of the action on the BBMF took place in the air flying our historic aircraft, and one or two events of some significance are well worth recording. One was the decision by the RAF Benevolent Fund to ask the renowned painter of African wildlife and RAF aircraft, David Shepherd, if he could manage to produce a painting depicting our Lancaster. It turned out that he was only too delighted to help such a worthy cause and although I was still stationed at RAF Scampton and only visited RAF Coningsby for weekend flying, I received full reports of David's efforts. He had spent quite a few days studying the Lanc from every conceivable angle and had spent some night hours aboard, in all of the crew positions, to soak up the ambience. He also took hundreds of photographs of PA474 and had written to numerous newspapers in East Anglia asking if anybody could loan WWII RAF vehicles to be included in his painting. The response had been amazing with offers of fuel tankers, oil bowsers, staff cars and bomb trollies. One offer was even from a Vicar in Norfolk! All added to the scene when "Winter of '43" was finished. More than once other artists asked me how David had managed to paint the water on the concrete that the Lancaster was depicted on so well. That was one question I could give an answer to. He had asked his RAF liaison officer, Sqn Ldr Pete Edge, if he could arrange for the station fire service to spray water over BBMF's dispersal area. The final product of the limited edition of "Winter of '43" was an immediate sell out and is a much sought after print to this day- particularly those signed by Bomber Harris and Barnes Wallis.

One situation that might have soured relations between David and the RAF came about when he requested a flight in our Lancaster and was turned down flat by high authority at MOD level. I thought that after he had raised £80,000 for the Benevolent Fund through his painting that it was the least the RAF could do for him so I threw caution to the wind and took him on a transit flight to an air display at Humberside Airport. David's name came to the fore again when a retired Air Marshal, running the RAF Benevolent Fund, rang the Flight and asked if I and other members of our crew were prepared to take part in a "This Is Your Life" programme. It was a request that could not be refused but nothing seemed to come of it at that time and nearly a full year later when I met David prowling the flight line at a Biggin Hill display I asked if somebody had blown the gaff on it. He seemed quite shocked and said surely they didn't really want to record a programme about him to which I replied: "I'm terribly sorry, I felt sure that your wife would have been in on the secret and let you know by now what had been proposed after it had fallen through.". He said that no doubt she did know but she was not the type to break a confidence. A year later and the programme was on again but BBMF was not to be involved that time.

One well known person that the MOD boys said we had to give a flight to was Max Hastings who was in the process of writing his book "Bomber Command". Max turned out to be six foot plus so on the day of his flight he spent most of the time in the gun turrets, rear, mid upper and the front/bomb aimers standing position- which suited him best of all. His book, "Bomber Command", did not please all veterans of WWII, but one at least did admit to thinking that to a certain extent he had probably got it right. Perhaps in the last few months of WWII Bomber Harris could have taken his foot off the accelerator and let Bomber Command become a deterrent, like the atom bomb later.

Alex Cowan, our Sqn Ldr Navigator on Hastings, phoned me after his retirement asking for a special favour which we did manage to squeeze in. It turned out that No 101 Squadron were holding a reunion at RAF Waddington and, unusually, his entire wartime crew would be there. Although on the day in question we should have been taking off on our second Luxembourg visit from Coningsby, we managed to alter the departure point to Waddington to give Alex and his crew a final flight in a Lancaster. One thing I had not bargained for on that day was that Air Marshal Griffiths was also there. He had been Station Commander at RAF Waddington at the time of Lancaster PA474's reincarnation in the mid sixties, and one of its Captains on initial test flights. I offered him the Captain's seat and certainly got more than I had bargained for. It was a good job that our wheels were fully up as we made several low, very low, passes over the main hangar and beyond the main party of bomber veterans.

25 years later, when attending a BBMF funeral, I got the full story about one of the most amazing incidents of its kind. Alex had, during our Hastings days together, mentioned on a couple of occasions that he had been involved in a mid air collision with another Lancaster during one of his Ops. Not having found any mention of it in Bill Chorley's books titled "Bomber Command losses of WWII" I asked Alex for more details. It transpired that after the collision on the night of 11/12 May 1944 during a raid on the rail yards at Hasselt, Lancaster JB 409 of No 626 Sqdn had lifted up and struck the underbelly of Alex's aircraft. With control restored it was decided to continue to the target and then return to their base of Ludford-Magna. No 626 Squadron's aircraft, after going into a near vertical dive eventually exploded and all the crew were lost. In Alex's case, the only injury was sustained back at base when their aircraft, due to damage, swung off the runway and a WAAF standing on

the control tower balcony fearing the Lancaster was about to crash into the tower leapt backwards and sprained an ankle! Bill Chorley told me that Alex's aircraft was only mentioned later in his book because it had been repaired and lost later after Alex and crew had left No 101 Squadron.

The 1977 season was drawing to a close when one extra display was called for and one which just had to be flown if at all possible. It was particularly special because it was a display for a No 617 Squadron reunion at RAF Scampton, their home at the time of the Dams raid of 1943, and most of the survivors of that raid would be present. With Lancaster PA474 "City of Lincoln" fitted with dual controls, as per heavy conversion unit aircraft, we usually had a qualified pilot up front instead of the flight engineer acting as the co-pilot for take off and landings which had been the norm for squadron operations during WWII. We had many volunteers to act in that capacity but on this occasion I decided that the newly arrived SATCO (Senior Air Traffic Control Officer) should be offered the chance to get airborne in a Lancaster again after a thirty odd year gap. I had first met Colin Megson, a New Zealander by birth, in the mid 1950s at RAF Shawbury. He had completed a full bomber tour with No 75 Squadron during WWII and had decided to return to the UK to rejoin the RAF like many others. Some, the holders of the DFC, were only allowed to re-enlist in non-commissioned ranks despite the fact that, since 1950, all newly trained pilots and navigators were automatically commissioned upon graduation from their wings course. What a crazy period that was in RAF history. On one occasion at least, one of those NCOs found himself serving under an officer who had been one of his NCOs during WWII when he himself had held commissioned rank the first time round. Although Colin was in the right hand seat for that special flight, I allowed him to take the controls for most of the trip.

Unbeknown to us it was not only the last flight of that season, but it was to be the last flight for any Lancaster for another 18 months. In later years it was rumoured that the Russians, who had repaired a badly damaged RAF Lancaster during WWII and used it for their own bombing operations but had managed to keep it flying until at least 1980. Perhaps somebody out there could confirm or refute that tale?!

CHAPTER 9
Hiatus

The defect found on BBMF's Lancaster was that corrosion of the metal skin on parts of the wings had been around many of the rivets. It turned out that the corrosion had been induced by the use of dissimilar metals between rivets and the metal sheeting during WWII. When told of the problem my mind immediately jumped back nearly forty years when, after starting my fitter airframes course at RAF Halton, one of the very first lessons was that the joining of dissimilar metals would cause corrosion. It had certainly taken its time. However, during WWII it had been established that any bomber was unlikely to survive the 100 hour flying mark and that might have had something to do with the situation. In fact, of the 7,000 Lancasters built only 2,000 survived the war. When it became known that the main planes would have to be completely re-skinned, and the only RAF unit capable of such a task was based at RAF Abingdon led to the question of should the Lancaster be flown down there or the Abingdon team travel to and fro from their station arriving midday Monday and departing Midday Fridays? I offered to fly PA474 down there but quite rightly it was decided to consult Avros, the builders of the type, and ask for their views. An Avro team of two men duly arrived and pronounced immediately that the aircraft should not be flown again under any circumstance until the extensive work required had been carried out. This led to the four day working week by the Abingdon engineers which, in turn, extended the grounding. The Avro team made frequent visits to offer advice and soon became known as the "long and the short of it" team. One was about 6' 7" tall and his partner 5' something or other. We shall never know, of course, but the WWII No 617 Squadron spectators at our last display flight of the season might have witnessed a spectacular end to one of their beloved aircraft. In the space of just two months I had gone from flying seven days a week; weekdays on Hastings at RAF Scampton and weekends the Lancaster with the BBMF at RAF Coningsby. Now it was just one Chipmunk aircraft at my disposal but I must say it was quite a year to remember for many reasons.

The BBMF had grown out of all proportion since our arrival from RAF Coltishall with the number of actual displays almost doubled. For the first year at our new location, the BBMF had only two small rooms to operate from; one for admin and planning and the other for technical personnel, but not even in the same hangar. We certainly went from the ridiculous to the sublime when No 41 Squadron was redeployed to RAF Coltishall and we took over their hangar and office block. At the time of my own arrival at Coningsby for full time work after the demise of the Hastings, my posting notice read "Phantom simulator instructor" as there was not, officially, a post of Officer Commanding Battle of Britain Memorial Flight; the work being carried out by the Squadron Leader Ops, who thus wore two hats. However, the time when one man could cover Ops and the running of the BBMF had long gone, but nobody had got around to making OC BBMF a nominated post. One upshot was that the simulator was one instructor short and when its OC complained bitterly about the situation to the Officer Commanding Operations Wing, Wing Commander Sawyer, he called me into his office for a chat. He said: "What would you say if you had to spend your last tour here at Coningsby instructing on the Phantom simulator"? I replied that the only reason I was now flying the Lancaster was because I had once said, during my time on Belfasts at Brize Norton, that I would sooner go back on Hastings when threatened with a simulator tour there with every working hour spent in a fully blacked out hangar. "And what would you say this time round"?, was his next question. In those days long service personnel were allowed to choose a last tour posting and with Betty now back in our first civilian bought house in the Cotswolds, near Brize Norton, which had been rented by a USAF couple for the last five years, I had no hesitation in saying I would apply for an Ops desk job at Brize Norton rather than try and instruct, on a simulator of an aircraft type that I had never even sat in, let alone flown. With the Wing Commander picking up his phone I thought it was about time I left his office, but when I started to retire he waved me down. When he spoke I noted that it was a Flight Lieutenant at Command HQ he asked for. The conversation was rather brief but he was grinning and winking at me at one stage when he said that if he had been in Sqdn Ldr Jackson's shoes he would also be applying for a last tour of his choice and that he certainly wouldn't call it blackmail. He also asked the Flt Lt where we would get a Lancaster pilot from now that the Hastings aircraft was no more and why did Command not increase the Phantom simulator instructor establishment by one and then it would be back to strength. It was shortly after that the post of OC BBMF was officially established.

The winter of 1977/78 was now upon us but the paper work plus numerous telephone calls about possible air displays abounded. Unusually for any military organisation our lords and masters were not at Group, or even Command Headquarters, but at the Ministry of Defence. We came under what was called "The Participation Committee" who had the final say in which air shows and fly pasts the BBMF would be tasked for the following year. On the air side of that committee there was a serving Group Captain, and one RAF Squadron Leader -who for most of my time was a WRAF officer by the name of Cynthia Fowler, who eventually became an Air Commodore, the highest rank attainable for a lady in the service- and the rest of the members were all civil servants with little or no experience of aviation. However, they were all dedicated, enthusiastic and very quick to take on board the technicalities of achieving the maximum number of displays within the constraints of flying hours allowed, locations of sites bidding in proximity to each other, flying times between each venue and, of course, likely attendance figures to gain highest publicity. Not an easy job by any means. Each autumn a mass meeting of reps from the various display units such as the BBMF, the Red Arrows, Vintage Pair, the Falcons, etc. took place in London when discussions and final decisions were made. This was an event looked forward to by all delegates. It involved a prompt start at 9 am which called for at least one night in London; at the RAF Club in my case. The meetings invariably finished by 12 noon and then it was off to the civil servants' favourite pub near Trafalgar Square when plenty of off the cuff talking took place. A civil servant's life could be quite interesting by all accounts, providing you could weedle your way into a preferred department and MOD seemed to suit most of them just fine. Before the final London meeting a small party, no more than three or four, carried out a grand tour of the base stations of the display teams -almost all in Lincolnshire. We at Coningsby enjoyed their company, particularly the after dinner sessions in the bar. By that time most had taken up the offer of a Chipmunk flight around the local area. It was during one evening session that one of their team dropped a real bombshell. It came from the only lady on the civil service team who was about 30, blonde and particularly good looking but, for some reason or other, still unmarried.

The dear lady started by saying that she just loved their annual mini tour of Lincolnshire because it was the home of Ruddles beer which always made her randy and she had found only one pub in London that sold it! What an advert that could have been for the firm! The stunned silence soon passed when one of our more vociferous officers leapt into the breech. Not exactly saying "Oh look up there everybody" but something like that.

With a long waiting list for married quarters I was to spend a full year living in Mess at RAF Coningsby before we came top of the list which meant a drive down to the Cotswolds each Friday night with a return journey on the Sunday evenings. However, with the Lancaster grounded it was no big deal, with Chipmunk flying invariably carried out between Mondays to Fridays.

Some good news awaited me on arrival home that winter at the start of the Christmas break of 1977/78. The first thing that Betty said on my arrival home was that Wg Cmdr Crowder, our boss at Scampton, had telephoned to say I had been awarded an Air Force Cross in the New Year's Honours List. Staggering news indeed.

After the start of the next display season, the weekends in the Cotswolds suddenly ceased when one of our Spitfires suffered a complete engine failure, followed by a spectacular force landing on the old Woodhall Spa airfield -once the home of the No 617 Squadron, just three miles north of our base. The Spitfire was completely untouched but there were two spin offs. Being a weekend there was no qualified Spitfire pilot available, except the Station Commander, to field the flood of phone calls asking about the incident. Most mentioned seeing the Spit doing an aerobatic display over a boarding school on the outskirts of Woodhall Spa when the engine failure occurred. The flight not being on our official display list, and authorised by the Ministry of Defence, was a little unfortunate to say the least and probably the reason why the pilot did not receive an award for the safe landing. The second impact was that the Station Commander thought that perhaps I should make myself available at weekends for the rest of the season, just in case something similar occurred. However, he also added that perhaps my wife would care to drive up to Coningsby each weekend and live in the Mess. When I returned to the Mess for lunch my batwoman proudly informed me that she had already placed an extra single bed in my room! At the request of the Station Commander no less!

My full time availability to fly BBMF's Chipmunk was put to good use throughout the eighteen months of the Lancaster's grounding and some are well remembered for a variety of reasons. One of those was the request by the Sqn Ldr Admin who asked to be taken to RAF Honington with a very early start. It turned out after our arrival there that he wanted to see at first hand what the impact of the building of hardened aircraft shelters was having on the running of that station, as the contractors would be moving up to Coningsby to build them on our airfield. All I could think of on the return flight was that if RAF front line aircraft now needed hardened aircraft shelters for defence against enemy air attacks, were the days of makeshift airfields as per the Western Desert and the Burma jungle strips now over forever? Even the number of airfields available in the UK and mainland Europe would be extremely limited by financial constraints if nothing else. Had air power finally peaked?

Many of my Chipmunk trips were to fly our Hurricane and Spitfire pilots to various airfields to position their aircraft at other stations when they had been left at their last display locations to save flying hours. Although all of our historic aircraft were strictly limited on flying hours per year, nobody seemed to give a damn about Chipmunk flying hours which was rather handy to say the least. Life became rather hectic after the start of the Air Training Corps Easter and Summer camp seasons which called for the import of a few extra aircraft and visiting pilots from many other stations who had readily given up some of their annual leave allowance to help out. It was about twenty years later when one Air Vice Marshal, later Air Marshal, said to me "I always remember one of the biggest bollockings I ever got was from a Sqdn Ldr for being twenty minutes late for one of his Chipmunk flights". All I could think of saying was, "Who on earth was that, sir?", to which he replied, with a grin on his face, "You Jacko". They do say that your past always catches up with you don't they!

One stroke of luck that year was the posting in to the simulator staff of Flt Lt Rod Hawkins, already mentioned for his efforts acquiring visiting aircraft to fly ATC cadets at RAF Marham. He was the most dynamic officer that I ever met and not only did he become number one navigator on the Lancaster when it eventually took to the skies again, he also put his heart and soul into helping me run the BBMF. His first effort was almost bizarre. It was after mentioning two items, one essential and one decorative that he went into action. The essential one was a badly needed planning board of large proportions so that we could record who was flying which aircraft and when, at named display locations. It might well have taken some time to obtain one through official ordering. I must have mentioned to Rod, at some time or other, that the board we had for the Hastings flight at RAF Scampton until its disbandment was ideal. I must also have told him that I had suggested to the OC Operations Wing at RAF Waddington that the official certificate recording the adoption of our Lancaster PA474 by the City of Lincoln, when it was based on his station, should now be passed on to the BBMF for display and not left hanging on a wall in his Ops centre. He replied, more or less, that would be over his dead body. It came as some surprise that Rod one day asked if I had anything special on for the following morning because he had persuaded the officer in charge of MT to lend him a crew coach and also agreed to Rod driving it himself. Most unusual to say the least. Being in RAF uniform and aboard a crew coach, we soon found ourselves being waved through the main gate at RAF Scampton and shortly after that in my old office on the station which we discovered was clearly not in use any longer. Needless to say, Rod had brought his tool kit with him and in a matter of minutes the programme board was loaded. Just a few quizzical looks from airmen seeing two officers carrying a large board but that was all. Rod's planning was excellent in that he delayed our arrival at RAF Waddington until the lunch hour break when all senior officers would have left the Ops block. He asked me to keep a lookout whilst he went into action to remove the citation framework from the wall. The only other person I saw approaching in the long corridor was an Ops officer, but I managed an interception, asking him one or two banal questions and then it was off back to Coningsby with our loot!

Rod had another of his good ideas which the first I knew about was when looking through my office window and seeing Rod and one of his friends erecting a flagpole on the front lawn of our hangar. My mind went into overdrive: Surely not Waddington again? Possibly Digby or even Cranwell, but that might have been too dodgy. Before the end of the day the RAF ensign plus a Sqdn Ldrs penant was flying from the pole. I was to learn later in life that some civil flying clubs were not averse to 'relieving' RAF stations of their windsocks if they had been positioned too near public roads!

One joint effort was entertaining two of the senior 'Works and Bricks' men to coffee breaks during most working mornings. When we had really got to know them I had arranged for Rod to casually mention how strange it was that our hangar was the only one at Coningsby not connected to its office block via a covered walkway, and how on earth had the previous tenants, No 41 Squadron, coped with having to walk out into the open air in all weathers just to get at their aircraft. Within days a team of builders arrived to construct one! On the very few visits I have made to the BBMF since retirement, I always have a smile on my face when I pass into that hangar via the walkway.

Perhaps Rod's greatest coup was having a bouncing bomb, recovered from the WWII practice range on his native Kent coastline, transported to Coningsby. It can now be seen in the grounds of the Petwood Hotel, Woodhall Spa. The Petwood was the Officers' Mess of No 617 Dambuster Squadron at one time.

It was a sad day when Rod was posted to Germany, with his delightful German wife, for his last RAF tour which lasted for well over 12 years or so. He had obviously not lost his knack of manipulation!

Other events during the eighteen months that the Lancaster was grounded include a visit to Switzerland to arrange for one of our Spitfires to give a display there, and one by sea to Jersey with support equipment normally carried in the Lancaster for that island's Battle of Britain week. My Swiss visit was by way of a Devon of No 207 Squadron based at RAF Northolt to assess the suitability of the grass airfield of Bex, pronounced 'Bay' by the locals. We landed both outbound and inbound at a French airfield near Dijon for re-fuelling. The Devon, with a very small prop to ground clearance was not allowed to use grass strips at Bex so we used the hard runway airfield of Lausanne in Switzerland for the overnight stay. The red carpet was laid out for our visit which included an evening with our hosts after inspecting the display airfield which was about 20 miles out of town. The airfield runway length of Bex was within Spitfire requirements and quite even for a grass strip although a little narrow, as one might expect in that mountainous country. The only recommendation I made, via an RAF Wing Commander on the embassy staff, was that a farmer's fence, which was quite close to one end of the runway, be removed prior to the display day, just in case of an overrun.

I had been back in the UK about 10 days when news came through that there had been an accident at the air show involving our Spitfire. It had been badly damaged, but our pilot, Peter Thorn, was perfectly all right. When the full story emerged it transpired that another display aircraft, a Harvard flown by a KLM Captain, had pulled out of a parked line of aircraft onto the runway to backtrack it for take off when Peter had already started his take off run. It is well known that forward vision from a Spitfire cockpit when the tail wheel is still on the ground is strictly limited and there was no way in the world Peter could have seen the Harvard dead ahead. Our Spitfire had already completed its display commitment without any problems and was on the return to the UK sortie when the accident occurred. It was later recovered by an RAF team and still flies with the BBMF to this day.

However, things rumbled on with one senior officer of post WWII vintage asking why had the Spitfire been allowed to use a grass strip and wouldn't it damage the undercarriage Oleo legs? I gently pointed out that all RAF airfields pre-WWII had been grass only, except for a few hundred yards at RAF Cranwell to assist three Wellesley aircraft to take off on a one stop flight to Australia and most fighter airfields in the UK remained so throughout WWII. I also mentioned that as a Halton trained Fitter Airframes until pilot training in 1943, it had been often stated that heavy landings or taxiing over rough ground was no bad thing for undercarriage Oleo legs because it lubricated a greater area of the leg than on tarmac. I was somewhat taken aback when the question of who had actually sanctioned the idea of allowing one of our Spitfires to take part in an air display in far off Switzerland in the first place was asked. That question arose from our Group HQ at Bentley Priory who did not seem to realise that we came under the direct command of the Participation committee at MOD (Air) for displays and that they were the only people that could have authorised it. When the question was again raised by Group I felt obliged to mention that during my two day recce of Bex, a retired Wing Commander had mentioned that he was a close friend of a serving Air Chief Marshal, both names withheld for obvious reasons, and he had brought up the subject with him. No more questions arose from then on. Its definitely who you know and not what you know.

Our Chipmunk certainly came into its own, for myself, after I had received the very sad news indeed that one of my very best friends, Flt Lt George Smith, had died suddenly whilst still serving at RAF Leeming. I had hoped to make an early morning take off for that station to attend his funeral, but a minor snag delayed the departure and it was only thanks to one of my ex- co-pilots, Ron Handfield, who was awaiting my arrival, that I managed to attend the service after a high speed car dash across the station. Another use of the Chipmunk was that during tactical evaluation exercises, "Taceval", when the station was under a supposed wartime situation and the British Army units made up an attacking force, my job was to patrol the major roads leading to the station at about 1,000' and report 'enemy' movements. What I had long thought was that in mainland Europe camouflage of motor transport could be a dead give away and Pickford vans would have been a better bet was proved to be correct. They also drove in convoy with their lights on, as they still do to this day! The only time I failed to pick them up was when they had travelled by night and hidden in a barn very close to the station. The farmer who had given them permission to use it also happened to be an honorary member of the Officers' Mess which did not do his popularity any good at all.

The use of our pick up truck for the Farnborough/ Jersey week worked rather well and although there was no Lancaster that year, the people of Jersey made us just as welcome as ever and a good time was had by all, particularly so in the RAFA club in the evenings. One lasting impression was the return overnight ferry when, nearing Southampton, I noticed the Captain prancing up and down his bridge with a telescope under his arm- all kind of thoughts went through my mind as one might well imagine.

1978 had been a most unusual year for myself; no Hastings, no Lancaster, but plenty of Chipmunk flying. An incident at the start of the year was almost bizarre in that now H R Highness Princess Margaret was our honorary Air Commodore her first official visit was in the planning stage and the admin. Officer tasked with the organisation had called a meeting of all flight commanders. When it came to the flying display part

Fifty-Two Years in the Cockpit - Volume Two

of the visit, he said "and no doubt you will be flying the Lancaster along with one of your Spitfires and Hurricanes, Jacko?" He was obviously taken aback when I replied "Most unlikely, the Lancaster is grounded and will probably remain so until next year". He must have been one of the few on the station who did not know. In the event, the visit was postponed due to the first bout of serious ill health for HRH and when it did eventually take place, one year on, the cross wind was way out of limits for our historic aircraft. However, Princess Margaret showed a great deal of interest in our vintage aircraft and spoke to all individuals present, aircrew and ground crew alike. I was reintroduced to the Princess at pre-lunch drinks which seemed to irritate one WRAF air control Officer who had watched BBMF's inspection from the tower and been in a group in the ante room that had been by-passed due to a shortage of time. She told me later that it was most unfair that I had spoken to HRH twice and she had not had the pleasure of even being introduced once! You cannot win them all.

It was not the last time that I was to fall foul of WRAF Officers. The next occasion was when Prince Andrew arrived by air with his pilot instructor, Sqn Ldr Harrison from RAF Leeming where HRH was on his wings course. Sqdn Ldr Harrison had been a flying instructor on Phantom aircraft at Coningsby prior to his latest posting and thought it a good idea to show the Prince around an operational station. The visit included a night stop when a jolly evening, by all accounts, was had by all in one officer's married quarter. The proposed take off back to Leeming the next morning had, however, to be delayed due to mist and fog in the Vale of York. With our ground crew having serviced and hangared the Bulldog training aircraft, it was only natural that HRH and his instructor had used our coffee bar to await the expected clearance in Yorkshire. When the small talk began to dry up a little, and with the weather in Lincolnshire being fine, I made my escape via a spot of local flying in our Chipmunk. Eventually the Bulldog did get away and after my landing I made for the Mess for a couple of sniffters. The jungle drums must have been really beating because a group of three WRAF officers pounced on me as I entered the bar and said they understood that the Duke had spent nearly all morning in our coffee bar and why on earth had I not sent for them to look after him? I normally try to put my mind into gear before opening my mouth but failed miserably on that occasion, blurting out something like "That would have worried me no end".

That was not to be the last meeting with royalty for the year because I

Prince Andrew taking interest in a Spitfire technical problem during his visit to RAF Coningsby

had already received official notification of the AFC award and asked to select a preferred investiture date out of a list of three. When the big day arrived my nerves began to jangle during the long wait among the ever dwindling throng in the reception hall. The Air Force Cross, or 'Avoids Flying Consistently' to some, turned out to be the lowest of the low in the pecking order of merit awards so I was the very last person to receive an honour on that particular day. According to my guests; my dear wife, Betty, and my brother, Harry. The BBMF did receive a special mention when Her Majesty asked what type of aircraft I flew after saying "The Avro Lancaster, your Majesty" she asked if I had been at the controls on her visit to RAF Finningley. After confirming that I had, she said what a marvellous day it had been, seeing our formation of a Spitfire, Hurricane and Lancaster being one of the highlights of her visit. As I marched off, my wicked sense of humour ran along the lines of 'if only the Minister for Defence, Fred Mully, had been awake to see it too. As previously mentioned, Fred Mully appeared to be nodding off on the Queen's shoulder during the fly past, which had been caught on camera by the press. After lunch in the RAF Club and bidding farewell to my brother and sister-in-law when leaving for their return to Southport, Betty and myself decided to get out of our clobber and relax in the "Flying Horse" bar of the club, but events took a most unexpected turn. It was when passing one of the entertainment rooms that Tony Iverson, now President of the Bomber Command Association, spotted us and shouted to all others in the room, after ascertaining the reason for my being in No. 1 uniform, to be quiet, before bellowing that Jacko had just been gonged at Buck House. A big cheer went up which really had made our day, the assembled being veterans of the No. 617 'Dambuster' Squadron Association which included many of the few survivors from the dams raid. What a day it had been.

Although making full use of BBMF's Chipmunk, not flying a four engined piston aircraft for nearly eighteen months posed the problem of which type I should

Sqn Ldr K R Jackson with Mrs B Jackson after having received the Air Force Cross from HM the Queen

gain experience on before taking the Lancaster to the skies again after such a long lay off. The first person to broach the subject was a staff officer at MOD (Air). I immediately suggested that he should contact Farnborough and ask if they could check me out on their Dakota. It was some days before he came back to say that Farnborough thought that flying the Avro Shackleton, being a four engined piston tail-dragger, would fit the bill better than a twin engined Dakota. In theory, yes, but in practice not a particularly good idea. To start with, the Shackleton had contro-rotating propellors which eliminated the swing on take off due to four props rotating in the same direction. Secondly, the centre line on that type was at a far lower angle to the ground than on the Lancaster which meant that the rudders became more effective far sooner than on the Lancaster whose rudders were partly shielded until lifting the tail which, in itself, induced a lot of swing, just like holding a spinning bicycle wheel and changing it from say, 45° to the vertical. However, arrangements had already been made and I duly set course by car for the two day journey with a night stop at RAF Turnhouse, to RAF Lossiemouth, on the Moray Firth, to report to No. 8 Squadron, the RAF's last Shackleton squadron, for five hours flying. The OC was Wg Cmdr Burton, who had been our last full career commander on Hastings, which made a good start and, surprise, surprise my instructor was to be Flt Lt John Elias who had been one of my students 30 years in the past at RAF Ternhill! After gaining his wings there, John's first tour had been on the RAF's last Halifax unit, carrying out Met flights from Gibraltar, and he had remained in the maritime world from then on. He will undoubtedly go down in RAF history as the pilot who had flown more hours on RAF aircraft than any other; over 17,500 in total, when he retired.

Avro Shackleton

I found the Shackleton a delight to fly, far more forgiving than the Lancaster in cross winds, and even more so than the Hastings which was the greatest leveller of them all for unwary pilots. John was the

Shackleton display pilot at that time so, after a couple of intro flights, we both went through our routines to fill in the required 5 hours and then it was forever southwards back to Coningsby to prepare for the first Lancaster flight in the world in the past 18 months. Ironically, after I had left the BBMF they acquired a Dakota when the Shackleton fleet went into retirement.

It was some three weeks later before Lancaster PA 474 was finally ready for her big day which went off without a hitch. However, our Station Commander, Group Captain Sprent, told us after landing that the AOC, AVM Latham, who had led the Treble One Squadron's very famous mass formation aerobatic team at many air displays in his time, had been on the phone, yet again, asking just when would our Lancaster take to the air. Group Captain Sprent went on to say that having heard our engines on start up, he had opened his office window and held out his phone before saying "You probably heard her on take-off, sir". To which the AOC replied, "I certainly did, kindly let me know when she is safely down". Before AVM Latham finally retired from the RAF he called for one last flight in one of our Hurricanes which led to a wee bit of chaos.

To start with, the usual Chipmunk check ride before anyone who was not in currency on type was a problem in that our only Chipmunk was away on major servicing. No end of phone calls eventually resulted in the loan of one from RAF Finningley. However, the wind on the day of the proposed flight was so high that no tail dragger should have taken off in such conditions. Sqdn Ldr Geoff Roberts, our fighter leader, who was to have checked out the AVM, understood that everything was cancelled. It being a Friday, I thought I would have a couple of halves in the Mess bar before calling it a day. I was just being served the second when the Station Commander tapped me on the shoulder and said, "I see you are just about to have your first drink, Jacko", stressing the word FIRST, "put it down, the wind has dropped somewhat and the AOC thinks he could at least fly the Chipmunk". And so it came to pass. Around and around we went doing circuits and bumps with myself thinking "when will the AOC have had enough"? It turned out that he must have been thinking the same because he called on the intercom "Isn't it about time we stopped, it will soon be too dark to fly the Hurricane"- which he did. The weather having abated sufficiently, although still a little marginal.

CHAPTER 10
OC BBMF and back on display

With the Lancaster fit again, 1979 was not only a full year but very gratifying to meet again so many people who had missed the Lancaster so much, with some saying they only attended shows that it was due to perform at. All our crew could not help but notice that some of the fans attended displays hundreds of miles apart just to see the "City of Lincoln" in flight.

The final flight of the year for the Lancaster. had been to Kemble for a major servicing which would take up all of the winter months and also the early spring. The air test, due to take place en-route from Kemble to Coningsby is well remembered for all the wrong reasons. Shortly after our arrival by road, the Flight Engineer reported that Kemble had taken it upon themselves to top up our fuel tanks to full- 2150 gallons- when we normally took on about 800/1000 for UK only trips which was always more than enough. It also meant a shorter take off distance than W.W.II operations and, more importantly, safety speed (the lowest speed that directional control can be maintained under the worst conditions- those being max. take off weight of 65,000 lbs and losing an outer engine) took longer to achieve. Another factor for such a vintage aircraft was that during displays, when the aircraft is thrown around a little, the lower the weight the less stress on the airframe structure. After the take off from Kemble, and having got the undercarriage up, the flight engineer suddenly shouted over the intercom for No. 1 engine to be shut down due to falling oil pressure on that engine. Being still below safety speed that would have spelt disaster. However, I did throttle back a little on No.1 which in turn reduced the minimum control speed but the build up to that figure was very slow. It seemed an eternity before we finally shut it down. With Kemble having the standard wartime 2,000' runway and a much larger one at Brize Norton being only a few minutes flying time away, I elected for the latter. Although that was my shortest flight ever in a Lancaster (10 minutes) it had seemed like ten times that figure. The phone lines from Kemble had already been red hot after declaring our diversion and a team was on its way to Brize by the time we disembarked. It did cross my mind that perhaps they knew something about that engine that we didn't. In the event, it was a gauge failure and within a couple of hours we were airborne again bound for base. All's well that ends well I suppose.

That year vetting of display pilots by a senior officer had been introduced and it was another week or so before one could be arranged which put the mockers on a couple of displays, but it had a far greater implication the following season. That following year the first display was to be in Germany at RAF Laarbruch. It was to be the very first time a Lancaster had been to that country in over 20 years. It raised a few diplomatic questions to the extent that both the RAF Public Relations department and also the participation committee both thought that they should send two reps each to note the reception from the local populous. They needn't have bothered- thousands turned out on our three day visit just to see a Lancaster in flight with no ill intent seemed to be the motivation. The trip was very nearly a non-starter at one stage due to a late start on the major winter servicing which was carried out at RAF Abingdon and not Kemble or base as was usual.

Abingdon twice put back the acceptance date for the start of the servicing but the first delay was a monumental plus mark and the result of a phone call from one of my ex-Vampire students of the mid 1950s. In those days we often had full courses of RAF doctors and also technical engineers who virtually all returned to their professional duties after gaining their wings. I can only recall two who managed a flying tour after 'wings', one doctor and one engineer. Tragically the doctor, by the surname of Fox-Linton was killed in a flying accident whilst the engineer, the then Flt Lt Wardell, had managed a Hastings tour. It was during a phone call from the latter that he told me that he was now at MOD (Air) and had a lot to do with telecommunications at which point I said he should come and have a flight in our Lancaster if he wanted to see what it was like in W.W.II as regards radio fits. I will always remember him saying "I can hardly believe it, what you really need is a TR175 which will cover all the frequencies you will ever need and not just VHF. If you would like one I will have it fitted". And so it was, within a couple of weeks and complete with a successful air test. Over the years a lack of modern radio had caused quite a few incidents, particularly with the London control zone.

The second delay in getting the Lancaster down to Abingdon had a slightly humorous side to it. Virtually the only time any of the four Station Commanders that I served under during my time on the BBMF had offered any advice on policy was when one had paid a visit to our office and heard one or two phone calls about air display submissions for the following year. He stated that "You had better tell any more callers to contact me personally in my office and I will deal with them". I doubt if he had been back at his desk for more than ten minutes before a Flt Lt called and said "Provided the Lancaster is serviceable, and weather permitting, the Chief of the Air Staff (Sir Michael Beetham) will be coming up to Coningsby next Tuesday to fly it". All I could think of saying was "It is fully serviceable" to which the reply was "Good", before the phone went dead. It took me some time to pull myself together before dialling the CO, still wondering how to explain the situation but even then it went badly wrong. I got no further than "A Flt Lt has been on the phone..." when the CO said "I trust you told him to contact me?" to which I had to reply "He didn't give me much of a chance, Sir, he was more or less telling me what would be taking place". "And what was that pray?" was the testy response. When I did eventually get a word in about the visit everything suddenly changed. The talk from then on was all about preparations for a unique occasion. In those days, a Chief of the Air Staff visiting a station was almost unheard of. However, Sir Michael Beetham's landing of the Lancaster could not have surpassed his one at RAF Coltishall, but it was just as good.

Another few days passed before we did eventually take-off for Abingdon and that was a trip to remember. Having failed to find a navigator who could be spared from his normal duties on a weekday for the flight and it being well known that civilian ferry pilots during W.W.II delivered Lancasters with just a pilot and flight engineer aboard, we decided to do likewise. Even the late master engineer Derek Butcher, who was a W.W.II Lancaster veteran said he found it a bit eerie flying with just two aboard. So did I and it brought back to mind a hilarious incident at the height of the Second World War. During an AOC's visit to one of his bomber stations, the Air Vice Marshal had just finished congratulating the Group Captain Station Commander on cancelling all flying for the day due to the appalling weather conditions when the unmistakable roar of four mighty Merlin engines was heard overhead. By the time the two senior officers reached the control tower the two man crew, or should it be one women and one man crew, were already booking in their delivered Lancaster. Some observers recalled that when the two officers saw that the Captain was a lady of about 5'6", to say that they were shocked would be a gross understatement.

The winter of 1980-81 dragged on a bit after our delivery flight to Abingdon, but with a five month gap before our Germany weekend we all felt quietly confident that the 'City of Lincoln' would be up and running long before then. Once again, it was not to be, and after the predicted finish time for the aircraft servicing of mid February had been and gone, our Engineering officer, Flt Lt Hordley, suggested that we take a Chipmunk flight down to Abingdon to check progress after being fobbed off with one excuse after another during many phone calls. It worked wonders having face to face talks about technical problems. However, we were down to one week only before we took off on an air test from Abingdon. In fact, we flew another three times that day. The second flight was a practice display for our crew, the third our vetting display watched by No 11 Group's Senior Air Staff Officer (SASO), Air Vice Marshal Collins, and a fourth short trip for the SASO himself. It had already been agreed that if all went well, the Lancaster would remain at Abingdon for the rest of the week before departing for Germany. That, in itself, would save about 1h 30m of the meagre 55 allowed per year by not returning to base before setting sail. With four civil servants, five ground crew and our normal crew of four aboard we duly took off for RAF Laarbruch for celebrations connected with No 15 Buccaneer Squadron.

The airfield there had not existed during W.W.II, being built for the RAF in the early 1950s by the Germans as part of their reparations programme and it certainly showed. The Officers' Mess being by far the best I ever came across. It was whilst awaiting our room allocations in the foyer of that mess that one of the biggest rows that I ever heard in my time in the service broke out. It was between the senior guest of honour- who had just arrived- a retired Air Vice Marshal, and the Officer organising the weekend events. It was mainly one sided with the AVM having had a bad day at the old Corral- A late take off from the UK by civil airliner, nobody or transport to meet him on landing at Dusseldorf etc. I doubt if the young Officer would have given as much as he took if the Air Vice Marshal had still been serving. It was like Wimbledon all over again and my wicked sense of humour nearly got the better of me when I thought of saying, "We could have given door to door service in our Lancaster, one more passenger would have got us away from the unlucky number of 13". It would probably have caused an atomic explosion if I had! It came as no surprise to find out later that the AVM was an ex-Trenchard brat of the mid 1930s! The air display on the Saturday was pure bliss from our point of view; no precise take off time nor time limitation on the display and, most unusually for the Lancaster, no Spitfire or Hurricane to fit in with which allowed us to throw the Lancaster around a bit more than the norm. There was an official reception in the Mess that Saturday night for No. 15 Squadron to which the Red Arrows, who had also arrived and given a display that afternoon, were invited but not our crew. That suited us just fine but did not please our Station Commander at Coningsby, Group Captain "Bill" Wratton (later Air Chief Marshal), when he found out about it quite by chance some time later. The living in members of the mess not on the strength of No 15 Squadron had to take an early meal that afternoon to clear the dining room for the reception and take to the bar immediately afterwards. Many of their girlfriends also drifted in, nearly all Dutch, with their frontier being less than two miles away. With our civil servants, this made for quite a mix, turning the evening into an humdinger by any standards. It was just as well that our return to the UK was not planned to be before noon the next day!

With our second scheduled display of the season being the next day at Staverton, near Gloucester, we would be pre-positioning at RAF Lyneham for a night stop. Our Navigator soon noted that our track to that station would take us to within a few miles of Abingdon so we gave them a low flypast to let them know that all was well with their handiwork. Which went down rather well, apparently. The following weekend was to Biggin Hill's Spring two day event so it was decided to leave the Lancaster at the secure base of RAF Lyneham for the next few days which, again, saved at least two more flying hours. After Biggin Hill we eventually headed north for Lincolnshire but even then it was not "home sweet home" because, being a bank holiday weekend, most RAF Stations were on stand down except for the RAF's master diversion airfields. RAF Waddington, just 15 miles from our base, was one of those, so we left our display aircraft there for a couple of days.

Unbeknown to myself, 1981 was to be my last season with the Battle of Britain Flight. It was all to do with my retirement date being on the horizon and it made sense to give my successor as much time with the Flight as possible before taking over the reins. That last season of 1981 was just as hectic as all the other six I spent on the flight.

One flight was very sad but proved that even the best laid plans could go awry. It revolved around one of the crew of the B17 Flying Fortress display aircraft who we had met and made friends with over the years losing his life during an air display at Biggin Hill when flying an American twin piston. His partner contacted me by phone and asked if his ashes could be dropped from our Lancaster. It was a request that I would never have refused. However, in those days, unlike today, ashes dropped from an aircraft had to be scattered at least five miles out to sea and with one of our future trips being from Chester to Norwich via Skegness, that was the obvious one to go for. After displays at Blackpool and Manchester we had left our Lancaster at Chester for a display due there a week later and, therefore had to travel back there by road the night before the event. I made arrangements with No 207 Squadron at RAF Northolt, to fly our station Padre with the ashes in one of their Devon aircraft from base to Chester to join our flight to Norwich, and also for our Chipmunk to pick up the Padre to return him home after our landing at Norwich where we would be based for the night. It crossed my mind that not many RAF Padres would have flown in three different aircraft types all in one day.

Having been informed that the ashes had arrived at Coningsby and were on the altar of the Station Church, I made my way down there to have a chat with the Padre to finalise details. Having found his office empty, and leaving the building I noticed a lady sweeping one of the exit paths. I should have known better but I started by saying, "I take it you are the cleaner, have you any idea when the Padre will be back?" I got the rather terse reply of "I'm the Padre's wife, actually". Could things have got any worse? Yes, they did. Having completed our air display and noted the arrival of the Devon we carried out a briefing with the Padre and Derek Butcher, our flight engineer. The ashes would be dropped via the flare chute located at the rear end of the aircraft by the Padre after I had called him on the intercom. Plan "B" was that if the intercom failed for any reason, Derek would make his way down to the back 10 minutes before the drop time and ask the Padre to keep an eye on him and commence the service when he gave a thumbs up from his front seat position. Not having received a reply from the Padre on the intercom after take off, we put plan B into action. We had experienced a very rough flight having to keep below the Manchester control area in ever increasing wind conditions. Every severe bump was followed by an expletive from one crew member or other on the assumption, of course, that the Padre was not hearing a single word. As soon as we had coasted

297

out over Skegness I called "Let's get it over with, giving the thumbs up to the engineer". Much to our astonishment, a voice suddenly boomed out "Ashes to Ashes, dust to dust, we commit our dear brother", at which point our Navigator's voice came on line with "What the bloody hell is going on Captain, say again". The other voice said "I say again, Ashes to Ashes, dust to dust, we commit our dear brother..." etc. It was well known that in the days before GPS (Ground Position Systems), which could give you your location to within 6 meters or so via satellite) the navigator was always hard at work with his maps and charts etc., immediately before take off and often not fully aware of other details and so it was that Jim Jackson, our navigator on that flight, had been caught on the wrong foot. After disembarkation at Norwich airport, Jim and myself made off to a fair distance to have a chat which included what the Padre had thought of all the language. When the Padre was en-route between the Lancaster and Chipmunk he made a detour to have a word with the two of us. Even to this day I don't know how we controlled ourselves when we saw his face was covered in black marks. Had there been a blow back up the flare chute? The truth came out when one of our ground crew let it be known that the Padre had not picked up the new headset we had provided for him, but one of the three or four used, mainly, by our ground crew when in flight as ear defenders and, not belonging to anyone in particular, rarely tested or cleaned. It also came to light that for hygiene reasons they would never put the oxygen masks right up to their faces before flicking the on/off switch to make calls on the intercom.

My very last display was soon approaching and, like most previous years, the Jersey Battle of Britain week in mid-September was just about the end of major displays for the year. That was far from uneventful for my signing off. On leaving dispersal in Jersey for the homeward journey the flight engineer noticed that when brakes were used the pneumatic pressure dropped far more than the norm and suggested a shut down. Unlike the Americans who, quite rightly, preferred hydraulic braking, almost all British aircraft of the late '30's until the mid 40's had pneumatic systems and it was not uncommon for an air bag to burn out with a high loss of pressure. However, the pressure would soon build to max if no braking was used. When two of the last four Hastings in service had the problem at RAF Benson on the same day, I carried out trials of shutting down all four engines at the same time on a secondary runway to see how far the aircraft would roll before coming to a halt. All others on board including myself were staggered at the short distance it took, probably due to the drag of winding down props not under power had a lot to do with it. With that in mind, I decided to take off and close down after landing at RAF Coningsby if needed. In the event we got back into dispersal with some air pressure to spare by using as little braking as possible.

A couple of short Lancaster trips with Scott Anderson, my successor, was enough to convince me that the "City of Lincoln" would be in safe hands for the next few years and concluded my flying time on the flight. The non-flying events over the time I was on the BBMF seem quite fantastic in retrospect. In addition to the royal visits of the Queen, Duke of Edinburgh, Princess Margaret and Prince Andrew, we did indeed have the privilege of meeting. King Hussein of Jordan at a Biggin Hill air display. Being a Cranwell trained pilot in his own right he took a great deal of interest in our historic aircraft despite being on a tight time schedule.

The second in line to be presented to King Hussein of Jordan was our Navigator Flt. Lt. Jack Thompson who, tragically, was killed during a practice air display at RAF Abingdon the day before the Battle of Britain Day which was then cancelled for that year

We also catered for two book launches from our premises. The first was Alex Henshaw's autobiography titled "Sigh for a Merlin". Alex was, of course, the famous Spitfire test pilot of W.W.II. Two of the guests on that occasion were the one and only Ginger Lacey and would you believe a gentlemen who had first flown aircraft in 1912. Captain

Marcus Marendaz who was also a famous car builder in the inter war years. During the event Alex let it be known that the reason for the title came about because we had once flown over the large caravan site that he had built in Skegness in V formation and he had given a deep sigh! His thoughts must have gone into overdrive. The other launch was the second in a series called "Action Stations" by Patrick Stephens of Cambridge. This covered the history of all RAF stations in the East Midlands. Once again a large and distinguished gathering was on hand and all seemed to enjoy being in the coffee bar of the BBMF. As usual, Betty was helping out behind the counter.

Off base, other events of note included invites to Sir Barnes Wallis' 90th birthday in 1977, the 40th anniversary of the Battle of Britain, with the Queen Mother being guest of honour and then Bomber Harris' 90th in 1982 which was held a few months after the actual date. Unbeknown to all, until the next morning, this had ended on a very sad note indeed. Douglas Barder, who had given a speech at the banquet had died on his way home or shortly afterwards. All three events had been held in the Guildhall. There were two further events, both in the RAF Club, and both at which I had been called upon to say a few words (a terrifying experience for anyone with no previous experience). The first was at the behest of Raymond Baxter, not only a famous commentator but also a very distinguished Spitfire pilot with many hours of operational flying in the Middle East behind him. However, the invitation from Raymond was in his capacity as the Hon. Vice Admiral of the Association of Dunkirk little ships. It was a great pleasure to meet the Captains and crews of those little ships that we had flown over almost annually off Dunkirk and learn at first hand about their efforts during the Dunkirk evacuation of 1940, a major turning point of W.W.II. One guest of particular note was Miss Celia Johnson the actress who was most affable and friendly to all, a most charming lady.

Unbeknown to Betty and myself a massive farewell party was in the planning stage for us by Station Commander Group Captain Wratton, later Air Chief Marshal Sir William Wratton C in C Strike Command and OC Ops Wing Wg Cdr Davis, later Air Vice Marshal Davis. It was to be held in the Petwood Hotel, the one time Officers' Mess of No. 617 Dambuster Squadron during W.W.II. It turned out to be a fantastic occasion and far exceeded anything a mere Sqn Ldr and his lady could ever have expected. The guests came from all aspects of the air display world both service and civilian. Among them was Mr Michael Fopp, now curator of the RAF museum Hendon who presented me with an excellent hand made model Lancaster which is now on semi-permanent loan to the "Lincolnshire Aviation Heritage Centre" at former RAF East Kirkby. Also present were Lindsey Walton- collector and pilot of vintage aircraft, most of which I was privileged to fly and display over the following two years-, Arthur Gibson- the famed aerial photographer who produced a magnificent framed picture of one of our departures from Jersey-, John Blake- the well known one armed air show commentator who had lost his arm in a W.W.II tank battle-, Spencer Flack- who later had the misfortune to land up in the RAF hospital at nearby Nocton Hall after his Hawker Tempest lost its engine near RAF Waddington. What a gathering, what a night.

CHAPTER 11
RAF finale

With the achievement of 40 years of continuous flying, without scratching the paint or ever having been a co-pilot, in my sights, I requested a last posting to RAF Newton flying Chipmunks on the Air Experience flight based there but it was not to be. It turned out to be flying Chipmunks all right, and only half the distance from my home in Woodhall Spa than RAF Newton was. The unit was the Flying Selection Squadron and was based at my old stamping ground of RAF Swinderby, although under the command of RAF Cranwell. It was a reincarnation of the PNB W.W.II scheme when all would be pilots received 12 hours tuition on Tiger Moths and were then graded for pilots, navigators or bomb aimer's courses. Many students regarded it as a supply and demand selection. In the long term, some who had gone solo in double quick time failed to reach wings standard and many slow starters went on to become distinguished pilots in the long term. During my previous instructional tours I came to the conclusion that about 50 hours of flying was the telling point. Not surprisingly, the unit did not last all that long. One snag about the posting was that I was sent back to the Central Flying School at RAF Leeming for a refresher course and what a change that turned out to be. At least half the staff wished they had other appointments, unheard of in my previous passages through CFS. Times change and it was by then 33 years since my first CFS course when all students went solo on eight types that included the DH Vampire, the first jet flight for most students, and without dual instruction because the trainer version had yet to be built, and 25 years in the past that I had my second CFS course when I flew another jet for the first time without dual instruction as the two seater had yet to be built. It was the Hawker Hunter in which I completed my first, and last, supersonic flight.

This last CFS course did involve three types of aircraft however this time round I was only allowed solo on the type I was current on- the Chipmunk. The other two; Bulldog and Jet Provost, had nothing to do with the course anyway but proved to be of interest. On the Bulldog, which had replaced the Chipmunk as the RAF's standard basic trainer, recovery from spin was causing some concern, particularly after a very experienced instructor and his pupil had been forced to abandon ship after failure to recover from one. A number of practice spins had then been carried out by CFS staff without any conclusion. Paddy Cullen, my instructor, who was due to carry out two flights of eight turn spins and recoveries took me along to practice them. It made a lot of sense having both seats occupied from a centre of gravity point of view. It was the first time I had carried out spin after spin after spin for a full hour or so but all recoveries seemed to be normal. Paddy once talked about his Spitfire days and, looking at his age, which was not compatible with RAF Spitfire squadron days, I said "I didn't know you had been on the BBMF"? To which he replied "Oh, it was with the Irish Air Force". The penny dropped and another of my old hobby horses surfaced. That was, if only we had been given dual instruction on that type during W.W.II with someone like Ginger Lacey in the back seat of a dual version, more enemy aircraft would have been shot down and less Spitfire accidents would have taken place. It was, of course, the Irish Air Force who, after W.W.II, had purchased Spitfires but had insisted on a number of them being dual control versions. The third type I flew in was the Jet Provost and confirmed my worst fears of being too easy to fly for U/T pilots. The trip itself was an away day for the then Flt Lt Bill Ramsay, now Wg Cmdr and CO of RAF Scampton and the Red Arrows. I had first met Bill during one of our voluntary Chipmunk detachments to help out with Air Cadet experience flights during the summer months. Later, he became a Vulcan pilot at Scampton during my Hastings days and we have remained friends ever since. The trip he took me on was to the Harrier base at RAF Wittering and he allowed me to do most of the return flying which included a number of circuits and bumps at RAF Dishforth, Leeming's relief landing ground. After selecting undercarriage down and flap settings plus percentage power settings at given points the aircraft virtually flew itself. Very satisfying and pleasant but far too easy for a training aircraft in my book. Having said that, teaching people to fly in today's aircraft is far easier than teaching them to drive a car safely.

My last tour in the RAF could have been very boring indeed but for one or two factors. With all our flying instructors living off base there

Bristol Bulldog

BAC Jet Provost

was never a TGIF (Thank God it's Friday) drinking in the mess for our gang, nor Saturday evenings and Sunday lunch time sessions either. However, we did get on particularly well with the many non-aircrew officers on the station who outnumbered aircrew, Swinderby being the RAF's recruit training centre at that time. A monumental bonus for me during summer weekends, however, was the fact that Lindsey Walton, who owned a small fleet of historic aircraft at Long Sutton, had contacted me and asked if I could help out by displaying some of his aircraft. Needless to say, I gladly accepted and flew his ME108, built in France in fact, the Stearman bi-plane trainer and the Cambodian gunship Nord 232. One event on each of the three types will always remain with me for various reasons. The first occurred when Lindsey tried to sell his Nord at an aircraft sale on the airfield of Stapleford, just off the north east tip of the London control zone. It was a grass strip and Lindsey warned me to be extra careful if a certain uphill runway was in use, because of the Nord's poor rate of climb, nobody bought the aircraft and yes, it was the uphill runway in use by the end of the day and after take off I seemed to be hugging the ground for a long, long time. That round trip was my last flight in the Nord, I was not too sorry about that.

The second aircraft, the ME108, used for Luftwaffe pilot training during W.W.II, was the only type I ever flew with an electrical controlled

Fratting with the enemy display ME 108 at RAF Swinderby 1983

variable pitch propellor. It was a delight to fly and I took it to many displays up and down the country. The swastika on each side of the fuselage seemed to attract a lot of interest, too much in fact on one occasion. RAF Swinderby had decided to mount an air show and the ME108 was to take part. It being my home station I was in normal working uniform when I flew the ME108 in the day before the show and somebody or other had taken a photograph of myself, with the swastika well to the fore, leaving the aircraft. The local press made hay, Jacko, having given up flying the Lancaster bomber now flies a German fighter, etc. That show was a particular disappointment for me personally as Peter Thorn had not only flown in a DH Dragon Rapide for the event, and knowing that was the type in which I had first become airborne back in the mid 1930s and had longed to pilot myself one day, Peter asked the owner if I could do so. Permission had been granted but just as we were about to walk out to the aircraft together his secretary rang and said "Sorry, the flight is off, we have just re-checked the insurance policy and your friend would not be covered". What a let down.

My very first flight in the Stearman open cockpit bi-plane was somewhat bizarre in one or two respects. Firstly, I was to give an aerobatic display without any dual instruction on type or even a practice aerobatic session. Secondly, it was at the pre-WWII RAF Station of Swanton-Morely and day to day flying no longer took place there. Its role at that time being an RAF engineering base, which had repercussions in an odd sort of way. After shut down, and being in civilian clothes, I was told that it would be quite all right to use the Officers' Mess which, along with other visiting pilots we duly did. From the very beginning all of us in civilian clothes were spoken to as if we had never been in an Officers' Mess before or even in the Royal Air Force. Nearing the end of 44 years of continuous service, I did not know whether to laugh or cry. In the afternoon, and only my second take off on type, I went into an aerobatic sequence of a few loops and climbing rolls during which the engine did not sound quite so sweet as during the flight down using a constant power setting. I cut the display time and headed back to Full Sutton to be met by the ground engineer who had seen me off in the morning. He stated that perhaps the aircraft should have had a shake down flight before the trip after all, it being the aircraft's first flight since winter servicing. It turned out that one plug had not been fully tightened down and was working itself loose.

Lindsey's grass strip was unique in that a power line ran across the runway and one had to make sure one was firmly on the ground after landing before passing beneath it and also make sure not to lift off before passing under it on take off.

In addition to the three aircraft at Full Sutton, I was also flying the then Wing Commander Allison, later Air Chief Marshal, Sir John's, Fairchild Argus. It was a high wing single engined aircraft and very easy to fly. It was also the type that myself and three other NCO pilots had been offered for use on our Spitfire OCU in the Canal Zone for a weekend in Cairo which we had opted out of just in case something untoward happened.

The first year back at Swinderby included another visit to Buck House, this time to collect an MBE for my six years on the BBMF. It was also

Receiving the Public Relations Award for 1981 from Marshal of the Royal Air Force Sir Michael Beetham at the RAF Club, Piccadilly

the year that the BBMF in its entirety was awarded an accolade that up to that time had been given to individuals only in recognition of their work in promoting the image of the RAF. The award was the C P Robertson memorial trophy which was sponsored by the "Air Public Relations Association" and usually presented by the current Chief of the Air Staff at an annual luncheon in the RAF club. Having left the BBMF some months in the past I felt quite honoured to be invited to the ceremony along with RAF Coningsby's Station Commander, the then Group Captain Wratten, BBMF's Engineering Officer, Charles Ness and Spitfire/Hurricane pilot Grant Taylor. The Chief of the Air Staff at that time was Marshal of the Royal Air Force Sir Michael Beetham. I had twice flown with Sir Michael in Lancaster PA474 "City of Lincoln", so no introduction was necessary. It was an event that went off particularly well and was enjoyed by all present.

When my turn came for a months rehabilitation course before leaving the service, or bricks and mortar to many, I was asked if I preferred

Catterick or Aldershot for the course to which I replied "Neither. Barry Tempest, the CFI at Leicester Aero Club has agreed to let me become one of his instructors for a month, if the RAF agrees". They agreed all right, but only if I used the nearest service accommodation to save money. That turned out to be the Army's veterinary establishment at Market Harborough. Quite interesting after one had become used to a lot of chat about dogs and horses with no mention of aircraft. In addition to the course, anyone leaving the service was entitled to 28 days paid leave and Barry asked if I could possibly help out during that period also. August was the busiest month of the year, when a lot of Air Training Corps cadets went to many flying clubs for about 12 hours of flying funded by the MOD. I gladly agreed but this time round it was to be in a farmer's wife's B and B, that worked out very well indeed; being close to the airfield. Those two months at Leicester Aero club gave me a real taste for private flying; no bone domes, oxygen masks, flying suits, boots or gloves on the mandatory list. In fact, one instructor even went flying in swimming trunks during that long hot summer! Barry Tempest, in addition to being one of the top aerobatic pilots of those times was also a born leader of men and highly respected by all who worked under him. He event brought to my attention that the Flight magazine had an advert requesting applications for a QFI post at Sherburn-in-Elmet Flying Club in Yorkshire and said he would put a good word in for me if required. That worked wonders and led to an extension of my flying career by another 12 years, up to the age of 72. In fact a week before leaving the Midlands Barry had received a phone call from Scott Anderson, my successor on the BBMF Lancaster, asking if I could be spared for a day and have a final flight in the Lancaster. Barry agreed and I visualised myself sitting in the WOP/AG's seat, or even the rear turret but, to my amazement, Scott told me to sit in the Captain's seat and from then on he never even touched the controls. Even if I say it myself, I made one of my better landings back at Coningsby after a flight which had taken in a circle of Lincoln Cathedral and a mini-display over my parent station of Swinderby, just 10 days before leaving the RAF some 44 years to the day after joining. My first flight in an RAF aircraft had been in a Miles Magister in 1939 at RAF Halton and now the last in an Avro Lancaster in 1983.

That last flight took on a rather funny twist a few days later. It all started when I took another day off from instructing at Leicester Aero Club to plod around Swinderby with my clearance chit. It had to start at Station HQ when I asked an airman, who had probably not long been out of basic training for the form, I saw him go through no end of documents deep in the admin. office. However, I was completely gobsmacked when he eventually came back to the counter to say "I cannot find any trace of you ever having been in the Air Force, Sir". He had no idea that all the pilot instructors based at Swinderby came under the RAF College at Cranwell, so after putting him right on that one I finally set off on my rounds. One of the first stops was the flying clothing section under the control of a WRAF corporal who, after binning one or two items such as gloves and vests etc. said, "I see you are wearing an aircrew watch, have you got a civvy watch with you?"? Having given a negative answer, she said "You will be lost without one, so I think we can forget about that item!" My last stop was somewhat different, it being the RAF guard room directly opposite SHQ. It was whilst exiting that establishment that a rather agitated Sergeant came running across the road shouting "The Station Commander saw you from his office window and wants to know if that is a clearance chit you are carrying, Sir". When I said it was, he went on to say "In that case he would like to see you in his office to say goodbye". The Station Commander at that time was Group Captain Davis who had been my flight commander when we had both served on No.53 Squadron at the same time flying Belfasts. He seemed a little miffed that he had not been informed of my impending departure but from then on it was a most affable interview although I found it extremely difficult to concentrate with my mind wandering back to the room next door when I had been an adjutant for two weeks in the 1950s, during my instructional tour on Vampires with quite a heavy loss rate for peacetime. In particular, the mid air collision of two Vampires resulting in five deaths, two of my friends and their Iraqi students plus a civilian lady on the ground. I was also recalling that it was due to a WRAF corporal assistant removing my name from a typed list, without actually being asked, that prolonged my flying career to 40 years out of the 44 I had served. The CO asked if I had seen the Lancaster display the previous week and I had replied, "Well, actually Sir, I was flying it". So ended my time in the Royal Air Force, having flown just over 12,000 hrs in 34 different types of aircraft, without scratching the paint and never a co-pilot. The flying had taken me to 64 different countries in 7 of the 8 continents of the world.

What of the RAF in peace and war, seen from the lowest rank, aircraft apprentice, to Squadron Leader? Well, we all know that hindsight is a wonderful thing, but some of the conceptions beggared belief, even before implementation. However, let us look on the bright side first of all and take note of the RAF's contributions to the winning of W.W.II. Obviously, the

Battle of Britain victory over the Germans was the most important of all the successes achieved by the RAF, making Hitler have a re-think about a possible sea invasion of the UK which led to him invading the USSR using about half his army in doing so. Also, many Luftwaffe squadrons were sent eastwards at the same time. Another high on the success list was the use of day fighters in the ground attack role which gave invaluable support to the 8th Army in North Africa and the 14th in Burma, in particular when many land victories came about after the RAF had taken care of enemy tanks and re-supply vehicles. The high point came after the Normandy landings when rocket firing Typhoon and Tempest aircraft came into their own in that role, having under performed when first brought into service. Armies always know how much land they have gained or lost and casualty numbers suffered but one pilot might have knocked out a tank or two at a critical stage of a battle but failed to return to be de-briefed due to enemy action. The Battle of the Atlantic, not often written about in RAF terms was, however, second only in importance to the Battle of Britain from an Allied point of view. Although the number of German U-boats sunk was about 50% by air and 50% by surface ships, the number of merchant ships saved from sinking was not, in all probability fifty fifty, with air power almost certainly saving the most by a large margin. This came about because U-boat captains, for the first three years of W.W.II, submerged at the mere sound of aircraft engines let alone seeing them. This not only cut their forward speed by half and any periscope sightings of convoys or lone ships to zero and, after re-surfacing, any ship that they may have been closing in on probably well over the horizon. That in turn led to Coastal Command aircraft remaining over patrol areas up to their max. fuel endurance limit even if they had already used up all their anti-submarine weaponry. However, at the start of W.W.II coastal command could only muster two long range squadrons, both equipped with Short Sunderland flying boats, with the rest of their squadrons flying Vickers Wellingtons and other medium range aircraft. The Canadian Air Force, operating from their Eastern seaboard also had limited range in aircraft which led to a large area of the mid-Atlantic, known to many as the black hole, being outside the range of land based aircraft, which led to a horrendous loss of Allied shipping in that area. Some relief came after the USA provided lend/lease Liberator aircraft. However, the Atlantic gap was finally closed when airfields in Iceland and the Portuguese Azores became available. Another dramatic turn of events came about when escort Aircraft Carriers came into being by the conversion of banana boats and other general purpose types., which proved to be the beginning of the end for U-boats. Another innovation on the allied side came into being just a little too late in the war to be fully effective. It was the combination of air to surface radar combined with Leigh Light, an airborne searchlight if you like. U-Boats, like the majority of rail trains these days, were propelled by diesel electric power. Because of the fumes generated, the recharging of batteries was carried out when the U-boat was on the surface during the night hours. Although the system worked, the Leigh light became an easy target for the U-Boat gunners to aim at. Above and beyond that, however, the Germans brought into service the snorkel, which allowed both the intake of fresh air, the discharge of fumes at periscope depth at any time of the day or night.

What of the perceived mistakes of W.W.II on the Allied and enemy side of the fence? Bomber Command, in my opinion, should not have been called upon to go hammer and tong for virtually the entire war. In the early days of the build up of four engined bombers to replace the far less effective twin engined types, would have taken place quicker if the number of raids had been reduced in number for six months or so. The Germans would still have had to build up their air defences in any case, which eventually employed over 500,000 personnel and about 60,000 88 mil anti-aircraft guns which, originally, had been intended as army support artillery. They could have made a huge difference on the Russian front. Also, the raids over Germany from the autumn of 1944 until VE day could not have made a great deal of difference to the outcome of W.W.II and many lives could have been saved. With hindsight, many people believe Coastal Command should have had equal priority with Bomber Command during the build up of the four engined aircraft force. The Battle of the Atlantic, which was very nearly lost in 1942 due to a shortage of long range aircraft might have been won much earlier than 1943. Reading the records of one of my old squadrons, No. 36, I could hardly believe that by the end of W.W.II they were still flying twin engined Wellingtons out of Iceland on anti-submarine patrols! In the Mediterranean theatre, politics appear to have ruled the roost. After the Germans had been evicted from North Africa and the Italian surrender of 1943, the Allies soon started re-routing convoys bound for the Far East through the Suez Canal again instead of the particularly long voyage via the Cape. That not only saved time, but also many ships and lives in the South Atlantic which had very limited air cover. With the Russians starting to beat back the Germans and the eventual success of the Normandy landings, meant that W.W.II could not be lost by the Allies and it was only a question of time before a German surrender. That might have happened far sooner than it did if the edict of unconditional surrender had not been imposed. That begs the question of why the Allies fought their way all the way up Italy. They had already taken Rome on the same day as the Normandy landings which many people thought was enough land gained, particularly so after the highly successful Allied landings in southern France in the August of 1944. In land battles, the attacking force will nearly always lose many more troops than the defenders so was it really necessary for the Allies to fight their way up the remainder of Italy, attacking one well defended line after another resulting in many casualties? They could have acted as a deterrent in that the Germans would have had to keep their forces in position just in case of an attack. Could it have been that the thought of Russian forces occupying not only all of the Balkans but the top half of Italy too that was unthinkable to the Allied politicians of those days? Another example, which was relatively late in the war, was the plan to try and recapture one of the Greek islands without full air cover. Six Royal Navy ships were sunk. What a waste of lives and resources.

 Hitler was prone to stupidity too, his biggest mistake was, of course, the invasion of Russia. It was almost a repeat of Napoleon Bonaparte's disastrous conflict with that country in 1812/13. One thing that Hitler did get right, however, was that after the successful German invasion of the island of Crete in the Mediterranean, where his paratroopers took a hammering, even against minimal defending forces, that they should never be used in the air drop role ever again, and act in ground infantry assaults in the future. One former Chief of the British Army pointed out a few years ago that in the many minor conflicts since the end of W.W.II UK paras had only once been dropped in anger and that was during the Suez campaign of 1956. Once paras have been dropped, and the location made obvious to an enemy, the chances of re-supplying them with food and ammo would be pretty remote. Perhaps their numbers should be vastly reduced and a UK special forces arm set up with an amalgamation of the Paras/SAS and Royal Marines?

CHAPTER 12
CFI, Sherburn in Elmet Flying Club

They say there is no life after death but my flying log book records that I made my last rehabilitation flight at the Leicester Aero Club two days before my 60th birthday, the official ending of my 44 year RAF career, and the next flight was the day after my 60th at Sherburn-in-Elmet Aero Club in Yorkshire. It was at that club that I was to continue flying for another 12 years, running up 7,000 hours on 38 new types of aircraft.

Sherburn became one of the highlight's of my career, along with my Spitfire and BBMF days. The CFI when I joined was John Harris who I had served with at RAF Scampton when he was on Vulcan bombers and I was running the last Hastings unit in the RAF. He had already served the Club for five years before my time there and made many improvements. His daughter not only gained her PPL but also became a fully qualified instructor and is now an airline pilot. John eventually decided to move to pastures new, firstly to a club in Scotland and finally Nottingham Aero Club. When I first joined the club, the fleet consisted of five Cessna 150/152s for pilot training and one four seat 172 for PPL touring. They were added to by one of the very first Slingsby T67M Firefly's, a low wing aircraft that could be used for both pilot training and aerobatics, which proved to be very popular indeed, the RAF bought a fleet later. Towards the end of the 1980s a new low winged aircraft trainer became available at a very reasonable price and Sherburn snapped up four PA28 Cadets. I think that it was about the time that high winged monoplanes began to pass into the history books with all pilots, when turning left or right, wanting to keep visual contact with their surroundings and not finding themselves only looking at the underside of one of their wings.

The instructional staff consisted of two elements. Firstly, the full time staff who came under the CFI who worked Tuesdays to Fridays plus alternating Saturdays/Sundays. The second group were the part timers under the excellent leadership of the highly popular Douggie Beaumont, whose team of dedicated instructors gave up one day of their weekend breaks from various occupations to help the Club. At that time Monday, the least popular day, was a non-instructional day but that did not last long following the closure of two other local flying clubs which not only required Mondays to be used but evening flying also from the Spring to Autumn. The original full time group I joined consisted of the CFI, John Harris and Jane Evans, the ex wife of one of the original "Red Arrows" pilots, plus one hour builder. Hour builders were normally young pilots who had just qualified as flying instructors but still needed more hours to reach the required number of 750 called for by the CAA before they could become commercial airline pilots. By RAF standards that was a load of tosh and it was, in fact, revoked by the CAA but that, in turn, led to quite a shortage of instructors at some clubs. At Sherburn, however, we were lucky enough to have two older ones who were in no hurry to leave. The first, Chris Patton, who was rather unique in that before becoming a pilot he had been Chief Purser on BA's Concorde fleet and was so well thought of by BA that they allowed him to take a coach load of Club members and staff down to London Airport for an onboard look over one of his former aircraft. A day to remember indeed. Chris was still soldiering on when I left the club in 1995 but eventually left to become an airline pilot in his beloved north east. The second, Chris Stringer, was in the theatrical world before becoming a pilot and now runs his own flying club at Humberside Airport. Both had given me, along with Jane Evans, tremendous support during my time as CFI 1985/1995.

Early during that period two decisions by the committee at their monthly meetings which I attended, had a profound effect on the Club and myself. The first was after it came to light that catering was running at a loss of £10,000 per annum and, according to the Chairman, Ray Holt, there was hardly enough cash in the bank to pay the next weeks wages. After a long discussion it was decided to put catering out to tender and in stepped Mrs Sue Warrel who remained with the club until recent times after giving nearly twenty years of service. It was also decided that the engineering section should also be put out to tender after it had failed to keep up with our ever increasing number of flying hours. The outcome was that the incoming chief engineer, Les Scattergood, was not a qualified pilot and, unlike his predecessor, could not carry out the required air test after a major servicing. The situation was resolved when I became a CAA test pilot after a thorough briefing by a retired RAF Wing

Commander Stinton, employed by the CAA. The upshot was that I could air test aircraft types that I had never flown before. That, of course, led to an ever increasing number of types flown with many members of other Clubs using Sherburn's facility. It did, however, lead to the only close call I had at the Club, almost on a par with the two I had on Spitfires, not responding to elevator control in a dive over Egypt and two colliding just in front of me over Singapore, plus twice on Vampires when recovery from a spin was very late.

On this occasion it was due to a technical problem. The aircraft was a high winged, twin piston and I had the chief engineer alongside me for the required air test. With Sherburn having shortish runways for twins 15° of flap was the norm for take off and it was after selecting them in at about 400' that a violent and almost uncontrollable swing to port occurred. I made the usual call on such occasions- "Suspect engine failure port side" to which Les replied "All power gauges reading normal" quickly followed by "The port flap is still out". It was decision time with a vengeance and I called for the flaps to be lowered back to 15° and was rather surprised when control returned to normal. We then decided to lower full flap and the port one went down in unison with the starboard one so I called it a day, or so I thought, and went round the circuit for a full stop landing. Twenty minutes later, and still pondering on what might have been, Les appeared on the scene and asked if we could give it another try. He did go on to say that after applying more lubricating oil to the moving rollers on the flap system all seemed to be back in working order. We duly took off again, but I made a point of not bringing in the flaps until about 3,000' when all went well thereafter. The only non-club aircraft that I air tested and had flown before was a Tiger Moth belonging to Austin and Ulla Mercer. Ulla was a lady from Finland who had once shown me a photo of herself in her schooldays holding a model of a Tiger Moth, a dream come true.

Many members gave me a chance to fly their private planes and three of them I will always remember. The first was a Pitts Special, a single seat open cockpit aerobatic bi-plane and I was seen off by two part owners, Richard Gee and Cas Smith. After engine start, Cas rushed over to add a Biggles touch to the occasion by wrapping his red scarf around my helmet. For my part I thought I would give them a mini aerobatic display over the airfield despite it being my first flight on type. I should have known better because, luckily, it was in a steep climb after a loop that the scarf unravelled and completely blocked my vision. With one hand on the control column it took quite a few seconds to remove the scarf when I was well up in the sky. Both Richard and Cas went on to be award winners in various aerobatic competitions. Although Richard is now an airline pilot it is recorded in a book by John Facer "Flying at Sherburn" that he took longer to gain his PPL than any previous student at the Club. The story behind that, however, is that his first lesson was at the age of twelve and the CAA did not allow anyone to go solo until they became seventeen. His course was duly completed within days of reaching that age.

My second well remembered flight was taking to the air in a home built aircraft which had taken six years to complete. It was owned by three times Chairman of the Club Ray Holt, who was a remarkable man in many ways. Ray thought up no end of improvements needed at the Club and, unusually in my experience, never dogmatic about his ideas and welcomed other people's views at all times. Like most other pilots, I had never taken to the skies in the first ever flight of an aircraft after its construction so I was just a little apprehensive. However the flight went off reasonably well apart from a slight left low wing condition which was soon rectified. The flight had been in our local training area which was under the control of RAF Finningley and when I was asked by the well known voice of one of the WRAF controllers what type of aircraft I was flying, I got a very cryptic reply of "I see" after calling that I was not sure and that the aircraft had never flown before. That lady's voice was often quoted about two incidents.

The first was when two of our pilots were flying in marginal weather and the controller was trying to establish their flight conditions. After a long altercation she asked in an exasperated voice if they were IMC (on instruments) or VMC (visual) and got the reply of "Nay lass, we are Jim and Fred on way to Blackpool for a day out". The second occasion resulted in a lot of ribald calls from other aircraft after the plane she was radar vectoring to overhead Finningley, and then on to Sherburn, made the call "I'm losing contact with you as you enter my dark area".

I was later asked to air test another home built aircraft that had taken even longer to build than Ray Holt's. My luck was in on that occasion because on the day it was due to take place the pilot/builder told me he would just like to give it a run to the runway and back before the flight. It was on the very first turn to the left that the entire undercarriage collapsed!

The third, and most nostalgic from my point of view, first solo on type, was in a Miles Magister, the first aircraft in RAF roundels that I had been given an air experience flight at RAF Halton on joining the service in 1939, 50 years in the past. The aircraft had been flown in from the old bomber airfield of Breighton, about 10 miles east of Sherburn. The Magister was, of course, dual controlled so I thought that the pilot who had flown it in would be coming along with me for the epic flight (from my point of view) especially as the wind was getting a little gusty, but he would have none of it saying Tony (Smith) who owned the aircraft had told him no dual tuition would be required with my background: very flattering to say the least. Tony, known to most as Taff, had also served in the RAF but on joining for pilot training the medics perceived a slight eye problem which precluded his training. However, he decided to stay on in the RAF Regiment. After leaving the service he set up an industrial firm which proved so prosperous that after becoming a civilian pilot he started out on one of his life's ambitions, which was to fly historic aircraft and own an airfield. That led to the forming of "The Real Aeroplane Club" at Breighton from which over the following years he flew both the Spitfire and Hurricane amongst many others. He also let me loose in his single seat CAP21 aerobatic aircraft which, although a delight to fly, I found difficult to come to terms with. It's landing speed for a light plane was over the 100 mark because the airspeed indicator was in Kms and not the normal mph. Taff also gave me a trip in his pride and joy, a Bucker Jungmann bi-plane, registered G-Taff in which he had already completed a truly fantastic journey. He had the aircraft dismantled and shipped out to Australia and then sent out Les Scattergood to re-assemble it so that he could fly it solo all the way back to the UK. He received a well remembered arrival party at Sherburn at the conclusion of his fantastic flight.

The Club was particularly lucky in having Digby Lamb as the landlord who invariably agreed to all the requests put to him by the committee for minor alterations to the premises or major ones such as the construction of an extra hangar, and the addition of a third runway. Digby was a born and bred local farmer who, like the Club's historian John Facer, had joined the RAF's cadet force and had made flights in RAF aircraft from Sherburn during W.W.II and could tell a story or two about those days. Digby had also become a pilot at the Club later.

It was on three occasions that I was asked if I could fly an aircraft not based at Sherburn, with two of the flights rather strange in some respects. The first was for me to ferry a Venom, surplus to the requirements of the

Swiss Air Force, back to the RAF Museum at Cosford. Although I had 1,000 hours on the similar Vampire I had never even flown the Venom. The time scale involved precluded me from a flight I would have loved to have undertaken. The second request was to fly one of the ten Short Belfasts from RAF Kemble to Hucknall after it had been purchased by Rolls Royce engineering, not for any further flying by the way, but to use the four Tyne engines for experimental work! It was by then over 13 years since I had flown the type and finding a flight engineer who had operated on them during their short ten year life with the RAF might well have proved very difficult. However, I remembered that one Belfast Captain who had remained at RAF Brize Norton after the disbandment of No. 53 Squadron in 1976, was Eddie Epps so I took the liberty of passing on his name to Rolls Royce. The third cry for help was from Lindsay Walton who had hoped that I could once again give aerobatic displays in his PT17 Stearman but the workload at the Club by that time precluded that, unfortunately.

Ray Holt's Waco Aircraft

One request I could accede to, because it was Sherburn based, was when Ray Holt bought a large American open cockpit bi-plane called the Wacco. He brought an American pilot over who showed me the ropes before I gave dual on type to Ray and a few of his friends. The big radial engine well forward of the cockpit reminded me of my Spitfire days and when I started doing descending curves onto finals the American pulled me up and said oblong circuits should be flown to give a longer time on finals and descending curves was for piston engined fighters only- I kept my mouth shut! One feature of the Wacco was that it had a tail wheel lock. Even the Lancaster bomber, unlike the Hastings aircraft, did not have such a lock. Perhaps if one had been fitted to the dear old Lancaster many accidents due to swings on take off and landings could have been averted.

The ground operational staff at the Club was virtually all female and no one could have wished for a better team than I inherited. First of all, we had Joanne Richardson, who had started helping out in the cafeteria when still at school, continued during her teacher training in Ripon, and even after becoming the deputy head teacher at a local school. She still works behind the Ops desk on one weekend day. One occasion that will never be forgotten by those on duty at the time was that after a phone call from her mother informing her that her father had died during a game of golf, she refused all suggestions that she should go home because she was the only member of staff on duty who knew how to work the newly installed computer for taking flying dues. It was late that evening before her sad departure.

The other two stalwarts, Sue Williams and Morag Hannah, in addition to their normal duties, worked wonders when making or receiving phone calls achieving far better results than the average male could ever have hoped for, particularly so when dealing with the odd noise complainant. However, we did have one incident after taking on board one young lady straight from school. She was a workaholic and always on the lookout for extra work. However on days when the weather prevented flying she often sat behind the Ops desk painting and polishing her finger nails. It was on one such day when we had four or five Yorkshire men looking through the windows near the desk opining on the chances of an improvement in the weather when Jenny suddenly boomed out, without even lifting her eyes, "have you anymore of those Bulls... letters to type, Jacko?" The old saying that one could have heard a pin drop was, on that occasion, very true indeed and I was too far from a window to shout out "look up everybody, I think the sun is breaking through". The story behind Jenny's outburst was that back in my BBMF days I had become used to writing short terse letters to higher authority and civil servants but possibly over embellishing some to civilians when they had asked for information, often about sad events that had occurred to close relatives in the past. That trait had obviously continued with me into civilian life.

It would be remiss of me not to mention one or two club members who had given excellent support on many occasions via their own expertise and/or the firms they ran, plus one philanthropist extraordinaire, Jack Robinson who had donated large sums for the building of a new hangar at both Sherburn and the Rufforth Aero Club near York. He was chief of the A1 motor transport haulage company who had been known on occasions to fly his own aircraft out to the Continent to check that his drivers were sticking to the schedule he had issued! Dick Howard, who owned a firm of road builders, on more than one occasion re-tarmaced parts of the club's taxi ways and parking area at a knockdown price. The late Stan Pickering who, although an insurance agent by profession, was by far the best DIY man I ever met, building a new Ops desk, installing false ceilings throughout the vast wooden structure of the Club and many other odd jobs in double quick time. Then there was Nev Binks, who later became a highly respected chairman of the Club, providing hundreds of stone paving slabs for an outdoor sitting area which became very popular during the summertime. Last, but not least, was Bryan Bonser, who not only took over the editorship of the Club magazine "Swordfish" but also had it printed by his own company. Many other club members gave up any spare time they had to help in any way possible and three in particular come to mind. John Shaw, Tony Cook and Fred Hemsley who must be one of the longest serving committee members of all time. Tony Cook actually gave up his lucrative motor business, not to spend more time with his family, but to help out at the Club. One quote, too often used in my opinion, is "close knit" but the bonding of many families when one member took up flying was quite remarkable with sons, daughters and even wives following suit on many occasions.

It was not all work and no play during my twelve years at Sherburn with one or two of my long held ambitions being achieved. The first was to take part in ferrying a York pleasure boat down the River Ouse to Goole for a major winter servicing which was by courtesy of a Club member, Steve Kirton, who was a full time helmsman at York. He let me take the wheel for quite a time and I soon learnt that, unlike driving a car, one must look to the rear when taking a bend on rivers to make sure the stern was kept clear of embankments and also that those embankments suddenly became higher when approaching villages and towns so that any flood water would be dumped on waste ground or farmland. One of our keenest private pilots was Gerald Egan, BR's Station Master at Leeds and Harrogate who loved to take members of his staff on joy rides. On hearing I had always wanted to be up front on a train he quickly arranged for Betty and myself to travel to Kings Cross and back to Leeds with Betty in a first class carriage and I with the drivers. The first thing I noticed was that, like aircraft, the higher one sat the less speed one seemed to be travelling at and with the drivers cab higher than I had believed, the speed seemed quite slow at times but it was still a trip of a lifetime for me. Our escort for the day had been a senior Drivers' Inspector and I was a little surprised when he said that the train was an advanced model of the 125 but it would never run at its top speed until the signalling system was updated because the stopping distance from warning signs to railway crossings, point change, etc. was not long enough. Gerald invited me, when completed, to open the Leeds to Manchester Airport Line, another memorable day for Betty and myself. Gerald arranged for us, with Douggie Beaumont and his wife Elaine, to be on board the first passenger train from Leeds into Manchester Airport.

One of our part time instructors was Phil Cooke who, being in the higher echelons of Yorkshire TV, often arranged visits to their Leeds studios plus one out of town location used for the filming of Emmerdale. I was allowed to pull a pint or two from behind the bar of "The Woolpack". I had a smile when our escort said we could drink as much as we liked because the brewery who supplied the beer, Theakstons, said they required all beer to be drunk within two weeks otherwise they might well get a bad reputation. I knew one of the Theakston brothers as he had served on one of my old squadrons, No XI. I am often reminded of our visit when watching Emmerdale and notice that a framed photo of the Red Arrows is still hanging on the wall of the Woolpack Bar.

Opening the new rail link between Leeds and Manchester Airport.

We at Sherburn sometimes catered for film makers and one, was "Circle of Deceit" which involved quite a bit of flying. The star of that film was Dennis Waterman who was an avid cricket follower, and with a test match being played at that time everybody knew where to find him when required, glued to the Club's TV set for relaxation.

At the end of flying for the day, we had a well patronised bar to retreat to with one little alcove, which became known to all as the rogues corner, at the Club with regulars who included Mick Milns, David Mellor, Eamonn Williams (now an airline pilot), Graham Gore-Browne and John Shaw, all well to the fore at weekends.

Two remarkable events in my life took place towards the end of my time at Sherburn. The first came about when Chairman Ray Holt discovered that I was nearing my 50 years of continuous flying point and asked a namesake of mine, Bill Jackson, to try and find out if the RAF could organise a fly past to mark the occasion. I still think it was something of a miracle but Bill managed to persuade the RAF to provide twenty two aircraft with all but one passing over the airfield in double quick time. A bit of luck was involved in that a Harrier squadron from RAF Wittering had been on detachment to RAF Linton-on-Ouse and gladly altered their return to base time to coincide with the planned event. The nine ship formation of Harriers was closely followed by another nine ship of Chipmunks, this time from the RAF's Navigation School at Finningley with their Station Commander in the lead aircraft who rang me later that day to wish me well. The last three aircraft were two Tucarnos from RAF Church-Fenton and a Tornado from RAF Coningsby. The BBMF tried to contribute by way of their Dakota but after becoming airborne it had to return to base due to an engine problem. That was

Ray and Pat Holt present a gift to Jacko

not the end of the day by any means because Ray Holt had arranged an evening party in one of the hangars which was quite fantastic, going on until the early hours of the next day. Prior to the party, Austin and Ulla Mercer had let me loose in their Tiger Moth which, after the guests had arrived, was followed by Tony Smith and Alan Horsefall performing an aerobatic display in their respective aircraft out of Breighten which was particularly well received by all. Later in the evening Ray, on behalf of the Club, presented me with a wonderful wood carving, complete with a likeness of myself taken from a photo of me in RAF uniform. On each side is carved a Spitfire and a Lancaster. It was carved by Ray Bell and ex-policeman living in Woodhall Spa. He was known to an ex-chairman of the Club, the Late Reg Walters, who with his wife Gillian retired to Woodhall Spa from Yorkshire.

For the previous few years I had been in contact with those helping to set up the Elvington Air Museum near York whose main object at the time was the restoration of a Halifax bomber, a type which had operated from that airfield during W.W.II. They got off to a good start when the main part of a Halifax fuselage was found on the Isle of Lewis in the Western Isles being used as a chicken coup. British Aerospace helped out when they set a group of apprentices at their Brough factory the task of constructing the rear end of the fuselage, which was well carried out. However, the vital part of all large aircraft of those days was the centre section, for attaching the wings to the main body. To build that part would require blueprints of it. However, as the makers, Handley Page, had gone bankrupt some time in the past, it seemed unlikely that any had been preserved and the full re-build could not be completed. It was then that I recalled that during the run down of the last Hastings unit, the "Strike Command Bombing School" at RAF Scampton, we had disposed of one aircraft when it was flown to a mini Museum being formed at RAF Colerne, but had later been taken by road to RAF Catterick for use by the RAF's fire fighting school based there. It was well known that any such aircraft did not suffer a great deal of damage during practice fire drills and perhaps the RAF would gladly part with the wings and centre section for such a worthy cause. This duly took place with the help of local transport contractors. One remarkable side to the story was that shortly after the arrival of the wings and the vital centre section at Elvington a scrapyard dealer in Chichester reported that he had a pair of Hastings wings in his yard which had never been used, and still in the makers crates. With RAF Thorney Island being the last training school for Hastings crews it was obvious that they had been dumped when that station closed down. The wings were used in the re-build, however those of Hastings TG536 are still laying outside of the main hangar at Elvington. As a reward for informing Elvington of the Catterick possibility, I was made a life member of the Museum, with Betty.

With advancing age, in my seventy second year and flying at the rate of nearly 600 hours per year, I decided that I would soon have to call it a day and the only question was when. Having joined and left the Royal Air Force on birthdays, September 5th 1939 and 1983, the temptation was to do likewise at Sherburn, but I eventually decided that April 1st, the date of the formation of the RAF in 1918 might be a better date, giving Betty and I our first full Summer together. Arrangements went ahead and a final party was held at Rogerthorpe Manor Hotel, near Pontefract, thought to be the ancestral home of Lord Haw Haw, a British traitor of W.W.II. The hotel was owned and managed by a close friend of mine, Charles Birdsall, a member of the "Hey Brothers" family, who, until finally settling down had the rather unique hobby of buying and selling public houses and hotels. Not only was he a full flying member at the Club, I also took him on a night rating course and a twin conversion after he had purchased an Aztec aircraft. He also gladly allowed other members to obtain their twin ratings on his aircraft.

My last landing at Sherburn, or so I thought at the time, was on the day of the farewell party and the student was one of the ladies behind the Ops desk, Morag Hanah, who had decided to take up flying herself. With the final landing being just after five o'clock and the party due at seven thirty with the hotel some 10 miles away, it was panic stations but we did manage to make it. The party itself turned out to be a magnificent occasion with John Stradling, Chairman of the Club, heading proceedings. It was quite a shock when he read out two congratulatory letters, one from Lord King of Warnatby who had been a club member and flown his own aircraft out of Sherburn just after W.W.II and later became chief of BA. The second was from Air Chief Marshal Sir John Allison, Commander in Chief of RAF Strike Command who had flown the Hurricanes and Spitfires during my time on the BBMF. When Sir John retired from the RAF he kindly invited myself and Paul Day, the longest serving Spitfire pilot on the BBMF, plus our wives, to his own dining out night at High Wycombe which we felt highly honoured to accept.

My own final party had not been fully completed because the fat lady had not sung and during the three days that Betty had allowed for a final clean up of the Club flat the bugle sounded. It turned out that my successor as CFI was not twin engined qualified, and a committee member, the late Barry Softley, had been out to Australia and gained a twin rating there. However the CAA said he must take a UK test before they endorsed his licence with that qualification. Charles Birdsall gladly loaned his Aztec aircraft and said would we like to fly down to East Kirkby Aviation Heritage Centre after the test was over? It was when we arrived at the check in desk at East Kirkby that all three of us got a wave through when Harold Panton, one of the two brothers who owned the centre, recognised me as being the BBMF Lancaster pilot of some years ago.

It was during that visit that Fred Panton, the elder brother, asked me if I would care to help out as one of their taxi-pilots on Lancaster "Just Jane" now that all four engines had been brought up to working order. What a lucky day that turned out to be. Ten years on, I am still making day and night runs and meeting some remarkable people with Marshal of the Royal Air Force Sir Michael Beetham, who had started his second tour of bomber operations out of East Kirkby, Lady Cheshire of Warsaw, widow of the late Leonard Cheshire VC and Richard Todd "The Dambusters" film star and ex-paratrooper who had dropped in anger over Normandy to name but a few.

From a parochial point of view that trip to East Kirkby had been a fitting end to actual flying and it was with a sense of pure nostalgia that I left Sherburn Aero Club, one of the three pinnacles of my 52 years of continuous flying. The other two being a Squadron Spitfire pilot and, of course, Captaining Lancaster bomber "City of Lincoln" on the BBMF. The only very sad day at Sherburn was seeing the start of the demolition of the last one of eight W.W.I hangars that had been used as an acceptance park for RFC aircraft. Other notable events occurred during W.W.II which included the moving in of two fighter squadrons, Nos 46 and 73 from RAF Church Fenton from the early days of W.W.II until May 1941 and No. 7 ferry pool of the Air Transport Auxiliary being established at Sherburn in November 1940. The largest unit of all to move into Sherburn, however, was the airborne forces experimental establishment who arrived from Ringway, now Manchester Airport, in June 1942. It had been at RAF Sealand that I, and half the station personnel, watched what was thought to be their first practice attack by parachute troopers on an airfield. However, the most important contribution to the winning of W.W.II was, undoubtedly, the making of the major parts and assembling them for Swordfish aircraft when virtually all of the 1700 built made their very first take off from Sherburn. One remaining building of the Blackburn factory still remains on site and is now used by Kwik Save as a depot.

In addition to Lord King, two other notables had strong connections with the Club. They were Neville Shute, author, of 'A Town Called Alice' fame, who flew from the Club and the other was the one and only Ginger Lacy who had been a flying instructor prior to W.W.II when flying had been moved to Yeadon, now Leeds/Bradford airport. In his book "Ginger Lacey Fighter Pilot" he attributes his B of B success to the fact that he had amassed several hundred flying hours to his credit whereas some pilots had not even reached the hundred mark. A tribute to Ginger can be seen in one corner of Sherburn Aero Club lounge.

CHAPTER 13
Afterlife

Many people think that on retirement from full employment they will have plenty of time on their hands to enjoy themselves pursuing favourite hobbies, games and visiting foreign parts, etc. However, it often turns out that they hardly have a moment to spare and I soon found myself in that category. In addition to family history research for myself and many others, I was involved in helping out, in addition to taxi runs, at the Panton brothers "Lincolnshire Aviation Heritage Centre". It being in my opinion the finest tribute ever to the 55,000 aircrew who paid the ultimate price out of the 132,000 trained for bomber operations (with another 15,000 becoming POWs and many more who had been so badly injured by enemy fire and aircraft crashes that they never flew again). The original concept by the Pantons was to build a memorial to their elder brother, Christopher, who had lost his life on the ill fated Nurnberg raid of 30/31st March 1944, whilst serving with No 433 RCAF Squadron. The loss of 94 aircraft on that operation, plus 11 crashes on return made it the most costly raid of W.W.II with 537 aircrew killed and 157 taken prisoner. The memorial started with the acquisition of a Lancaster Mk VII bomber from Lord Lillford in 1988 after it had been the gate guardian at RAF Scampton since the famous "S" for Sugar had been taken down to the RAF Museum at Hendon. After intensive restoration work it was not until 1995 that the Lancaster, by then named "Just Jane", was ready for taxi-runs which became very popular with old and young alike. Since then the centre has gone from strength to strength with the control tower now exactly as it was during W.W.II, a hangar extension to cater for an ever increasing number of exhibits of all kinds including parts of aircraft from crash sites, the cockpit of a Canberra bomber, and historic RAF motor vehicles including a "Queen Mary" to mention but a few.

My main contribution took place during the restoration of the station chapel when it was decided to place "Roll of honour" boards on the two main walls of the Chapel, listing all the 848 aircrew of No 57 and 630 squadrons who gave their lives operating out of East Kirkby between its opening in August 1943 and the end of W.W.II. It was also decided to place details of all known graves of the victims on the altar. The Commonwealth War Graves Commission provided most of the details but, as the name implies, it did not have records of non-Commonwealth citizens. Frequent visits to the Public Records Office, now re-named National Archives, at Kew, took place and Bill Chorley's volumes of Bomber Command losses of W.W.II proved particularly helpful. However, it was not all one way traffic and a few errors were found by cross references to various sources, and thanks received for pointing them out. David Stubley, leader of the Aircraft Recovery group, was an equal partner in the research which led to a splendid service to re-open the Chapel.

Another task that David and I have gladly undertaken over the years is answering requests for information, or pointing people in the right direction to obtain details of veterans service in the RAF during W.W.II. It is well known that those who did survive the horrors of bomber operations have been very reluctant to talk about those days, even to their sons and daughters which has led to many of them and their children seeking information. With a large number of reference books on hand at East Kirkby, many of the questions are answered on the spot.

In conclusion, I would like to mention that without dedicated help Lancaster "Just Jane" would not now be one of only three left in the world that can move under its own power. The Panton brothers employ three full time engineers, Ian Hickling, Roy Jarman and Mark Fletcher, all ex RAF, and on taxi days a happy band of volunteers help out with the marshalling of "Just Jane" and in many other ways depending on their vocation. They include Bill Parsons, Pat Ellis, Andy Coupland, Dave Willey and Kev Baker.

It is now 10 years since I completed my 52 years in the cockpit, and through helping out at East Kirkby and being a Retired Officer member of the Mess at RAF Church Fenton during my time at Sherburn Aero Club and also at RAF Coningsby Mess, I have kept in touch with the Royal Air Force, to whom I owe whatever I have achieved although that would not have been possible without the full support of my dear wife, Betty. I am also a member of the Air Crew Association South Lincs Branch, we meet every month in Boston with our wives and also the widows of comrades who have passed on.

EPILOGUE

It was after purchasing a house in Woodhall Spa during my time on the BBMF that Betty and myself agreed that the idyllic village would be the best location for our eventual retirement, being halfway between the magnificent City of Lincoln and the town of Boston. The village itself, built in Victorian times, retains a great deal of it's former glory and is the location of three top class hotels. The Golf Hotel, The Eagle, now renamed the Woodhall Spa Hotel, and of course the famous Petwood Hotel. During WWII the Petwood became the officers mess of No. 617 (Dambusters) Squadron and the hotel still has a great deal of memorabilia of that period. The village has two golf courses, one of which is rated in the top fifty in the world. Over the years Woodhall Spa has gradually expanded with many people making the great escape from overcrowded cities up and down the UK.

After completing my 52 years in the cockpit with a final flight at Sherburn-in-Elmet in 1995 and settling down to retirement in Woodhall Spa I have managed to keep in touch with aviation in general and to-days Royal Air Force in Particular. The latter after becoming an Honorary member of the Officers' Mess at RAF Coningsby, the firs home of the Euro fighter, the Typhoon. Social events are always top class and carried out with precision by a superb staff. I have the added bonus of meeting and chatting to todays young pilots, occasions I always look forward to.

The final flight

Fifty-Two Years in the Cockpit - Volume Two

One other highlight of our retirement is the monthly meeting of the Aircrew Association, which meets on the third Friday of the month at the Ruddy Duck Inn on the outskirts of Boston for lunch. Wives and widows of former members and several associate members invariably attend to make a happy event. Two separate groups always forming - Ladies and Gents!. Three of the longest serving members of the branch who are always present make a very interesting trio, each came from different categories of aircrew of the five who manned RAF WWII heavy bombers. First Syd Marshall, our newly elected Chairman of the branch, a flight engineer and now a volunteer guide at the BBMF's Visitor Centre at RAF Coningsby. Secondly we have navigator Bob Reid, our treasurer, who ensures we maintain a healthy bank balance. Lastly our hard working Secretary, Buck Buckly, former air gunner in the then Sqn. Ldr. Beetham's crew, now Marshall of the Royal Air Force Sir Michael Beetham, GCB, OBE, DFC, AFC. Although all three are reluctant, like many others, to talk about their wartime days, when we do manage to prize a story or two out of them it makes fascinating listening.

We also have two official events each year that we all look forward to, a buffet supper in June and a dinner at Christmas to which we always invite the current Station Commanders of Royal Air Force Coningsby and Cranwell. The President of the Aircrew Association, Air Marshall Sir Christopher Coville, KCB. BA. PCIBD. FRAeS. has for many years supported the South Lincs Branch. He has visited us at Boston annually for many years without fail and kept us in touch with the progress of the modern Air Force.

Jacko with Buck Buckley and George Bulman. Ex Bomber Command WWII Air Crew during a visit to East Kirkby Aviation Museum. Both members of the A.C.A.

Fifty-Two Years in the Cockpit - Volume Two

On the 5th. September 2003, my 80th birthday, we arranged to meet two friends, Mo and Colin Middleweek in the Officers Mess for a drink during happy hour. Colin had served as Senior Air Traffic Control Officer (SATCO) at Coningsby shortly after I left the BBMF. AS we entered the Mess the thought occurred to me that 64 years ago to the day on my 16th birthday I joined the RAF as a Halton Apprentice. The lovely Mo had just acquired a new digital camera and decided to take a photo of us at the bar, where else, to celebrate the occasion.

Betty and Jacko at the Coningsby Officers Mess. 5/9/03.

RECOMMENDED BOOKS

Recommended books that I have found of immense interest over the years concerning the RAF are as follows:

1. A Series about RAF losses post WWII written in the following order by Wing Commander Colin Cummings RAF (Ret'd) and published by Nimbus Publishing, Yelverton, Northants:
'Lost to Service' - 1959/1996
'To Fly No More' - 1954/1958
'Last Take Off' - 1950/1953
'Final Landing' - 1946/1949
'The Price of Peace' - VE Day/End of Dec. 1945

'The Price of Peace' records that the RAF, on average lost 10 aircraft per day with 1,000 casualties.

2. 'Bomber Command Losses of WWII' by Bill Chorley. They are written in year by year volumes and give full details of dates, locations and crew names. Published by Midland Counties.

3. 'Lancaster at Peace' by Sqn Ldr Ray Leach MA, MBE, RAF (ret'd) A full history of BBMF's Lancaster PA474 'City of Lincoln'. Ray Leach was at one time the Navigator of the aircraft. Published by Elpeeko Ltd Lincoln